Vicars Choral
at English Cathedrals

Cantate Domino

History, Architecture and Archaeology

edited by
Richard Hall and David Stocker

Oxbow Books

Published by
Oxbow Books, Park End Place, Oxford OX1 1HN

© Oxbow Books and the individual authors, 2005

ISBN 1 84217 153 4

A CIP record for this book is available from the British Library

This book is available direct from
Oxbow Books, Park End Place, Oxford OX1 1HN
(Phone: 01865-241249; Fax: 01865-794449)

and

The David Brown Company
PO Box 511, Oakville, CT 06779, USA
(Phone: 860-945-9329; Fax: 860-945-9468)

or from our website

www.oxbowbooks.com

Front cover: Vicars choral of Wells Cathedral. Lithograph of a mid 19th-century drawing by F T Dollman (1812–1900) (photo by Richard Neale, courtesy of Wells Chapter Archives)

*Back cover: The vicars close at Exeter looking north-west
from a painting by George Townsend, 1870–92*

Printed in Great Britain at
The Short Run Press
Exeter

Vicar[s] choral. '...the assistants or deputies of the canons or prebendaries of collegiate churches, ... especially, though not exclusively, in the duties of the choir or chancel ...' (*OED*, 3623)

List of Contents

List of Contributors

John Allan
Exeter Archaeology
Bradninch Place
Gandy Street
EXETER
Devon EX4 3LS
john.allan@exeter.gov.uk

Julia Barrow
School of History and History of Art
University of Nottingham
University Park
NOTTINGHAM NG7 2RD
Julia.barrow@nottingham.ac.uk

Philip Dixon
24 Crown Street
NEWARK
Nottinghamshire NG24 4UY

Barrie Dobson
15 St Olave's Road
YORK YO30 7AL
barrie.dobson@britishlibrary.net

Naomi Field
Lindsey Archaeological Services
25 West Parade
LINCOLN LN1 1NW

Richard Hall
York Archaeological Trust
Cromwell House
13 Ogleforth
YORK YO1 7FG
rhall@yorkarchaeology.co.uk

John Harper
Royal School of Church Music
Cleveland Lodge, Westhumble
DORKING
Surrey RH5 5BW
dg@rscm.com

Frances Neale
Mellifont Abbey Barn
Wookey
WELLS
Somerset BA5 1JZ

Sarah Rees Jones
Department of History
University of York
Heslington
YORK
Srrj1@york.ac.uk

Warwick Rodwell
The Old Vicarage, Stockhill Road
Downside
CHILCOMPTON
Somerset BA3 4JQ

Nicola Rogers
York Archaeological Trust
Cromwell House
13 Ogleforth
YORK YO1 7FG
nrogers@yorkarchaeology.co.uk

John Schofield
Museum of London
London Wall
LONDON EC2Y 5HN
info@museumoflondon.org.uk

Ron Shoesmith
5 Marsh Cottages
Wellington
HEREFORD HR4 3DU
ron.shoesmith@btinternet.com

David Stocker
English Heritage
23 Savile Row
LONDON WC1 1AB
david.stocker@english-heritage.org.uk

Tim Tatton Brown
Fisherton Mill House, Mill Road
SALISBURY
Wiltshire SP2 7RZ

Nigel Tringham
Victoria County History of Staffordshire
History Dept., University of Keele
KEELE
Staffordshire ST5 5BG
hia02@his.keele.ac.uk

Preface and Acknowledgements

Richard Hall

Staffing medieval cathedrals was always a problem. Some English cathedrals introduced monks, but about half of them (Chichester, Exeter, Hereford, Lichfield, Lincoln, St Paul's London, Salisbury, Wells and York) put themselves in the hands of secular priests (the canons or prebendaries). As cathedrals became increasingly complex 'prayer factories' between the 12th and the 16th centuries, however, the canons appointed vicars choral to perform liturgical functions in their stead. This book is a study of this group of medieval priests in England.

From the moment of their first appearance in the 12th century, there was concern about the vicars' morals and behaviour, and for more than 400 years cathedral deans struggled to impose discipline. Eventually all of the English cathedral vicars were subjected to quasi-monastic discipline and were lodged in carefully designed and regulated colleges, which were strategically located within the Close and formed a very distinctive group of buildings. Several of these important medieval building complexes have survived, most famously at Chichester, Hereford, Lincoln and Wells, but significant traces of all nine colleges are reported upon in this study. Some have been the subject of recent architectural survey work and several have also seen recent archaeological excavations, thus augmenting the documentary studies that earlier were the principal (and in some cases sole) means by which vicars choral colleges were investigated.

This volume brings together the wealth of architectural, archaeological and historical information relating to these major, but little known, medieval institutions. It reveals an extraordinary interdisciplinary resource that can be used to understand not just the working of individual colleges and cathedrals, but also the life and work of the middle and lower ranks of medieval clergy in England. Set out below the reader will find an opening section introducing the vicars choral as a distinctive group, explaining their role within the English and European church and exploring the central contribution they made towards medieval liturgy and music-making. The central section provides detailed studies of the history, architectural history and archaeology of each of the nine English colleges, whilst the final section represents in-depth study of the college of the vicars choral at York, known as The Bedern.

The York Bedern is now one of the most well known of the English colleges, thanks partly to studies by Canon Harrison, Sarah Rees Jones and Nigel Tringham, all using the enormous archive of documentation which survives in York Minster Library. But such archives do not survive only at York; one of the most important realisations made during the production of this volume has been that most of the English vicars' colleges have comparable collections of documents – a large majority of which have not yet been fully explored. At York, this wealth of documentation is made even more valuable through comparison of the vicars' written record with the results from a major programme of archaeological and architectural research, undertaken by York Archaeological Trust between 1974 and 1980. This programme, of which the final publications appeared in 2001, represents the largest exploration of any vicars' college, but during their production it became clear that major surveys and excavations had also been undertaken at most of the other English colleges during the final quarter of the 20th century. It was clear, then, that the results from all this work needed to shared and to be put before the public.

So it was that York Archaeological Trust organised a major conference, held in St William's College York on 22nd – 24th March 2002. As well as a number of delegates from York and the other 'secular' cathedrals, and many individuals with a wide ranging interest in the medieval church, the conference was well attended by academic specialists in medieval history, architecture and archaeology. This was not surprising, for it was the first time that the evidence from these various locations and disciplines had been brought together. In addition, the very purpose of vicars' colleges was underscored in a memorable paper by Professor Harper on the music of the vicars, with aural illustrations and examples.

Throughout the weekend constant comparisons were made between the various colleges, and everyone took away new understanding both of their 'own' college and of the buildings and lives of the vicars more generally. It was clear that the conference proceedings would make a very valuable book, bringing together, apparently for the first time ever, a great wealth of new information from these different disciplines and permitting the first properly rounded view of this remarkable group of churchmen and their buildings.

The conference itself was organised and managed by staff of York Archaeological Trust. The Yorkshire Architectural and York Archaeological Society (YAYAS) and the Friends of York Archaeological Trust kindly made subventions towards lecturers' travel expenses, and thanks are also owed to the Dean and Chapter of York Minster for helping with the venue, and to York Minster Archives for allowing the display of their material. All contributions to this volume were given as lectures at the conference, with the exception of Philip Dixon's discussion of the York episcopal minsters at Beverley, Ripon and Southwell; two of these great churches have now become cathedrals, it was pointed out, even if they were not of this rank during the middle ages.

John Allen owes a particular debt to Richard Parker of Exeter Archaeology, not only for his meticulously researched reconstruction drawings (Figs. 5.11 and 5.12) but also for discussion about the college. He also benefited from the work of Tony Collings, also of Exeter Archaeology, on the leases and lease plans relating to this part of Cathedral Close. His typescript was prepared by Ms Pam Boyce. Naomi Field's contribution is based on detailed archive reports prepared by Michael Clark and Colin Palmer-Brown, who directed the excavation of the garderobes. Cathy Groves kindly arranged for the Lincoln tree-ring samples to be taken. Nicola Rogers would like to acknowledge the work of Dr Patrick Ottaway in the preparation of her paper. He identified and discussed

all the ironwork. Dr. Rachel Tyson kindly provided detailed comments on the Bedern glass vessels, which have been incorporated into the text. Thanks are also due to Penelope Walton Rogers, who studied the textiles, and to Marjorie Hutchinson who studied the gold ring. In Warwick Rodwell's Lichfield paper, the section entitled 'Outline History' draws heavily on researches undertaken by the Staffordshire team of the *Victoria County History* (ed. Greenslade 1970; 1990). He would also like to acknowledge his debt to Dr Nigel Tringham and Mr Bob Meeson for constructive discussions over the course of many years. The latter also kindly read the draft of this paper and offered helpful suggestions. Dr. Rodwell's and Ms. Neale's contribution on Wells is indebted to the Chapter of Wells Cathedral, who gave permission to study and cite the archives relating to the vicars choral. They have also been very helpful in permitting access, over many years, to buildings in Vicars' Close. Dr Schofield would like to thank the Museum of London Archaeology Service for information on the excavation at Juxon House which informs Fig. 4/4. Derek Keene and Jo Wisdom are also thanked for their comments on his text. Ron Shoesmith has drawn on the various reports of survey work carried out by the City of Hereford Archaeology Unit between 1987 and 1991. He is grateful to Richard Morriss and to the British Archaeological Association for permission to make use of material published in Whitehead (ed.) 1995. Ron is also deeply indebted to Rosalind Caird, the archivist at Hereford Cathedral Library, for sharing her invaluable knowledge and helping with the Library holdings. David Stocker is grateful to Julian Richards, Frances Mee, Patrick Ottaway and to many other staff and friends of the York Archaeological Trust who made his study of the York college possible. John Schofield provided helpful comments about the stone hall and its bay window and Nigel Tringham and Paul Everson made useful comments on early drafts of this text. His Lincoln paper could not have been written without the published and unpublished survey drawings and notes made by Stanley Jones, and a great debt is owed to him for sharing his thoughts. He is also grateful to Philip Dixon, whose comments on the north range at an early stage were critical in helping towards the understanding put forward here. Paul Everson also read and commented on drafts of this text and Naomi Field kindly let him see her unpublished records and reports on the 1995 work in the south range. Book production was overseen expertly by Rita Matos to whom the authors owe a great debt of gratitude.

1

The English Vicars Choral:
An Introduction

Barrie Dobson

'It was this little world of its lesser clergy, numerically much larger – but much more neglected – than that of its resident canons, which made a western cathedral a beehive in which everyone had a well-defined role to fulfil' (Millet 1993, 140). As institutions deliberately established to be the spiritual and administrative power centres, as the episcopal seats or *cathedrae* of western Christendom, the 600 or so cathedrals dispersed erratically throughout Europe by the end of the 12th century were inevitably the busiest and most conspicuous corporate beehives in medieval society (Dobson 1986a, 230–1). They were also the communities where the fundamental tensions – both creative and destructive – within the ideals and practice of the Christian religion were most clearly exposed to view. By their very nature, the various and often contradictory purposes of the medieval cathedral forced their clergy into an endless struggle to reconcile the apparently irreconcileable. Nowhere else in medieval Christendom was it more essential to meet the rival claims of Martha and Mary, of royal administrative need and diocesan pastoral care, of this world and the next. Despite many opinions to the contrary and despite the many criticisms levied against medieval cathedral clergy from their own day to the present, they were in fact by no means completely unsuccessful in resolving many of their dilemmas. After all, and however severe the exploitation of their wealth by the papacy, by secular governments and by careerist clerks, the great majority of European cathedrals were able to sustain from generation to generation an exceptionally demanding, complex and expensive round of choral worship within architectural settings which continue to attract and astound more visitors than any other memorials of the European 'heritage'. Without the commitment, day by day, night by

night, of its *ministri inferiores* to the recitation of the hours and the singing of the divine office, the medieval cathedral would rapidly have lost its primary *raison d'être* and disintegrated beyond repair.

The achievements of the English cathedral clergy in particular are perhaps all the more impressive because – by another paradox – there were so comparatively few of them in the country as a whole. The foundation of new, and even the re-location of old, cathedrals in the English kingdom came to a complete halt in 1133 when Henry I elevated an obscure and struggling house of Augustinian canons into the *cathedra* of the Border Bishopric of Carlisle. For the next four centuries, until the early 1540s when Henry VIII licensed the creation of six new episcopal sees from the proceeds of the vast ecclesiastical spoliation of the preceding few years, there were only seventeen dioceses in England, of which two (Bath and Wells; Coventry and Lichfield) were served at various periods by not one but two cathedrals. It need hardly be said that a total complement of only nineteen cathedrals is an astonishingly small number when set against the 235 or more cathedrals of later medieval Italy, the 131 of *Gallia*, the 56 of the medieval German *Reich*, the 33 of Spain and Portugal, the 27 of the three Scandinavian kingdoms and even the twelve of Scotland and 34 (no less) of Ireland (Eubel 1913–23, II, 281–6; Dobson 1986a, 230–1). It is now well known that one of the main reasons for the exceptional wealth of most members of the medieval English episcopal bench was precisely because there were so few of them (Lander 1980, 120). The same argument can certainly be applied to English cathedrals too, with the important proviso that in this country a quite exceptionally large number of those cathedrals were served by monks rather than by secular canons.

By a familiar oddity of English church history, for which Archbishop Lanfranc was primarily responsible, of the nineteen cathedrals which dominated the idiosyncratic English ecclesiastical map during the four hundred years between 1133 and the Henrician Reformation, no less than nine were served and administered by Benedictine monks (Bath, Canterbury, Coventry, Durham, Ely, Norwich, Rochester, Winchester and Worcester) and one (Carlisle) by Augustinian canons (Knowles and Hadcock 1971, 447) (Fig. 1.1).

For the reader of this collection of essays it is even more important to be reminded that by contrast only nine English cathedrals were served by secular canons after the Norman conquest, namely Chichester, Exeter, Hereford, Lichfield, Lincoln, London (St Paul's), Salisbury, Wells and York (Figs. 1.1 and

1.2). It could perhaps be argued that the distribution of these and the monastic cathedrals reflects, in a highly distorted fashion, Pope Gregory I's original optimistic hope of 601 that once the English kingdoms had been fully converted to Christianity the first archbishops of *Londinium* and *Eboracum* would each establish twelve suffragan bishops on sites (*singula loca*) presumably to be chosen because they were remembered as prominent urban centres in *Britannia* (Colgrave and Mynors 1969, 104–7). That said, the foundation and development of the cathedral and minster churches of Anglo-Saxon England were highly subject to the vicissitudes of temporary political circumstances. More seriously, how they were actually staffed and organised is almost totally obscure until and indeed a little beyond 1066. It is not inconceivable that choral worship in some

Fig. 1.1. Map of Medieval English diocese (drawn by Lesley Collett, copyright YAT)

CATHEDRAL	Number of Canons *c.*1300	Chapter value in Val. Ecc.	Vicars' College value in Val. Ecc.	Earliest evidence for residential Vicars college	Date of Royal or episcopal incoporation
Chichester	30	£310 p.a.	Little	1396	1465
Exeter	25	£1,179 p.a.	£204 p.a.	1387	1405
Hereford	28	£426 p.a.	£88 p.a	by 1375	1396
Lichfield	32	£275 p.a.	£199 p.a.	by 1315	?
Lincoln	58	£575 p.a.	£358 p.a.	*c.* 1270	1441
London (St Paul's)	30 + 12	£725 p.a.	?	by 1273	1396
Salisbury	52	£601 p.a.	£272 p.a.	by 1409	1409
Wells	55	£729 p.a.	£100 p.a.	by 1348	1348
York	36	£747 p.a.	£255 p.a.	by 1248	1421

Fig. 1.2. Table comparing the staffing and values of the nine secular cathedrals in England. Several of the valuations and dates given are approximations

Anglo-Saxon cathedrals was conducted by junior clerks who anticipated the role of the later vicars choral. However, it seems unlikely that we will know for certain whether the senior members of the communities of clerks who supervised the cathedrals of pre-Norman England ever systematically employed quasi-permanent deputies to worship in the choir on their behalf.

Only during the generation immediately after the Norman conquest, by any standards the most formative period in the long history of the English cathedral, did a series of major reforming initiatives introduce new and complex organisational structures within which vicars choral were before long to play an increasingly central and formalised role. However popular in the eyes of Archbishop Lanfranc, the practice of entrusting the administration of a cathedral to a monastic community was always open to the objection that monks who were expected to withdraw from the world were ill suited to supervise the most frequented mother churches of

the English ecclesiastical scene. Soon after the conquest a group of energetic Norman prelates introduced from across the Channel favoured the radically alternative practice whereby the communal ownership of a cathedral's economic patrimony was largely replaced by the creation of individual prebends, whose names and revenues were derived from a specific group of estates or churches and assigned to each newly appointed canon in his own right. By 1089–91 this revolutionary transformation of the structure of the non-monastic English secular cathedral had already been achieved at Lincoln, Salisbury and York, to be gradually emulated at Exeter, Chichester, Hereford, Lichfield, London and Wells within the following generation (Edwards 1967, 1–22; Lepine 1995, 1–2). Henceforward the senior cathedral clergy no longer shared a common dormitory and refectory but lived in their own houses within the Close. By yet another paradox of the medieval secular cathedral, the abandonment of the common life on the part of the canons made it all the more probable – as we shall see – that their deputies, their vicars choral, should begin to follow a common life themselves.

Less surprisingly, the mouth-watering attractions of being able to enjoy lucrative canonries *in absentia*, and with no cure of souls attached, came to be appreciated almost as soon as prebends began to be created in the English secular cathedrals at various dates in the decades after the Norman conquest. From at least the age of Henry II and Thomas Becket onwards no English monarch or archbishop can have been in any doubt that the secular cathedrals of the realm were the single most important instrument for the diversion of surplus wealth from the grass (or rather grain) roots of the English parishes to support not only the most sophisticated features of the medieval church but also the careers of the men who actually ran the ramshackle twin engines of church and state. Such outright exploitation of ecclesiastical wealth in the interests of the notorious absentee 'possessioners' of the late medieval cathedral could readily lend itself to a Marxist critique, which in fact it never quite received when Marxist historical analysis was at its most commonplace (but see Hilton 1966, 223–4; Hilton 1973, 207–13). Moreover, before the vicars choral of English and European cathedrals are too readily dismissed as the *petits bourgeois* of the late medieval church, one must remember that few contemporaries ever seriously criticised cathedral canons for leaving their stalls to the care of their vicars while they placed their own administrative skills at the disposal of kings and bishops (Millet 1993, 283–90). Even the young John Wyclif, that most aggressive scourge of the worldly clerics of his day, never opposed such absenteeism in principle and felt seriously disgruntled himself when in 1375 Pope Gregory IX passed him over for a Lincoln prebend and canonry, admittedly in favour of 'an immature stripling from overseas who had no intention of residing in England' (McFarlane 1952, 67). Not of course that a secular cathedral could survive without at least a few resident canons to constitute its chapter. Dr David Lepine's recent authoritative analysis of the *Brotherhood of Canons Serving God* has revealed as never before that residence levels among those canons varied very considerably from cathedral to cathedral. At one extreme there were still fourteen or so canons in residence at Exeter Cathedral on the eve of the Reformation while at the other York Minster was exceptional in rarely having more than two or three residentiary canons in its Close and chapter throughout most of the 15th and early 16th century (Lepine 1995, 95–100, 199–222; Dobson 1979, 145–74; Edwards 1969, 70–83). In no cathedral however can the canons in residence ever have been anything but heavily outnumbered by their vicars.

Although, in Dr Julia Barrow's words, 'the main cause of the vicars' appearance on the scene is absenteeism on part of the canons', the exact point of time at which that appearance made itself felt in particular cathedrals is more or less impossible to establish with any accuracy (Barrow 1989, 90). The problems here are compounded by difficult issues of definition and linguistic usage. Vicars representing their canons at divine services in the choir were not usually designated 'vicars choral' as such until the early Tudor period (Cross 1984, 1, 6; *OED sub* 'vicar choral'). Moreover, as the word 'vicar' *tout court* was used so generally and widely in the medieval church, its meaning can often be ambiguous, especially perhaps in the 12th-century charters and episcopal *acta* which offer us the first recorded glimpses of individual vicars choral. Can one be absolutely certain, for example, that the Walter de Templo, Simon, Hamo, William de Buum' and Ralph de Langtoft who witnessed a charter of Roger de Mowbray in 1175–6 as *vicarii Sancti Petri* were in fact vicars choral as the term was later understood (ed. Greenway 1972, nos. 122–4)? One of the many virtues of Dr Barrow's influential account of the origins of 'Vicars Choral and Chaplains in Northern European Cathedrals' is that it places the vicars within the broader context of the many other priest chaplains in the service of a 12th-century cathedral (Barrow 1989, 87–93). The words 'vicar' and 'chaplain' were in fact often used interchangeably, as in the case of several members of the York Minster clergy who witnessed charters as both *capellani* and *vicarii* of the metropolitan church of St Peter (ed. Farrer 1914–16, I, nos. 159, 288). All in all, and despite later claims to the contrary made at St Paul's London and Exeter Cathedrals, it seems most likely that English vicars choral emerged less as a result of deliberate acts of capitular policy than as a gradual and somewhat haphazard development. There is no particular reason to believe that such a development occurred earlier at York Minster than in any other secular cathedral. However, the six York clerks (three of them described as priests) who were styled *vicarii* when listed after the precentor and canons as witnesses to a land transaction between 1138 and 1143 probably do deserve their reputation as the earliest recorded vicars choral in English history (ed. Clay 1957–8, I, 53; ed. Richards 2001, 381).

Even more significant for the future cohesion of the secular cathedral was the date at which the appointment of a vicar to deputise in choir ceased to be optional and became compulsory on all absentee canons. Although, once again, the evidence for this critical stage in the constitutional history of the English cathedral is usually defective or ambiguous, it seems clear enough that by the end of the 12th century nearly all secular cathedral chapters had begun to appreciate that 'the best way to cope with an emptying choir was to insist that the absentees pay for vicars to replace them' (Barrow 1989, 90). Such a development was undoubtedly encouraged by the most conscientious bishops of the period, like St Hugh of Lincoln, not least because by 1200 the ever increasing complexity of liturgical routines in a cathedral's choir and at its many altars necessitated a large and dependable pool of priestly personnel. Accordingly it was soon accepted in many secular cathedrals that the appointment of a vicar choral should be compulsory not only on absentee canons but on canons in residence as well. Thus in 1291 the dean and chapter of York formally ordained that 'each canon in the church ought to have a priest-vicar serving for his master in the church of York', a vicar who was to receive 40*s*. from the fruits of that canon's prebend every year (*YCS*, 27). As Dr Kathleen Edwards established in her classic study of half a century ago, 'the full number of vicars choral had been instituted in all English secular cathedrals except Hereford by the end of the thirteenth century' (Edwards 1967, 264). By that date there was accordingly a total of some 350 vicars choral serving the nine secular cathedrals, ranging from 58 and 55 at Lincoln and Wells to some 25 and 28 at Exeter and Hereford (Fig. 1.2).

Once the secular cathedrals had achieved their full complement of vicars choral, the stage was set for two other complementary developments which were to transform both their constitutional status and their way of life out of recognition. In the first place nearly all vicars managed to secure – with remarkably little opposition from the canons for whom they deputised in the choir – the right to security of tenure. To take only one example, it was firmly decreed at St Paul's in 1260 that a deceased canon's vicar should not be ejected from his stall even if the new canon wished to present another vicar to the chapter instead (ed. Sparrow Simpson 1873, 68; ed. Page 1909 I, 422). One may readily assume that such security of tenure, apparently often retained until a vicar's own death, did much to foster the *esprit de corps* and communal self assurance which were to make the vicars choral such potentially restive subjects of their deans and chapters. This strong sense of intense corporate identity naturally became even stronger when vicars choral everywhere began to acquire substantial amounts of income-generating property to be held and enjoyed by them in common. Thus the vicars of Lincoln Cathedral are known to have been receiving grants of land from the unusually early date of 1190; and only a few years later churches were being appropriated to the vicars of Exeter by Bishop Henry Marshal (Maddison 1878, 3; Orme 1981, 80–1). At York Minster too the vicars were receiving grants of

tenements or rent charges from at least the early 13th century. By 1250 vicars choral everywhere were already busily engaged in acquiring and consolidating substantial blocks of urban property, thereby needing to acquire a common seal of their own as well as an increasingly elaborate administrative system headed by a *succentor vicariorum* or warden. Like monastic houses, so colleges of vicars choral everywhere developed what might be called an obedientiary system, whereby many of their members were required in turn to hold office as bursars, chamberlains, keepers of the fabric and so on. The vicars' archive at York, probably the best preserved of any English cathedral, contains long sequences of the annual accounts presented by these officers (mostly dating from after the Black Death) as well as a remarkable collection of nearly 600 charters (e.g. YMA, VC 3/1/1; 6/1; 6/2; 6/4; 6/6). Now that the latter have been meticulously edited by Dr Nigel Tringham, they document the creation of a medieval urban estate with a wealth of detail unrivalled in any other English town (ed. Tringham 1993, xvii–xlvi). It is easy to forget that for many inhabitants of nine English cities the vicars choral must have been more familiar as landlords than as members of the cathedral choir. This wonderful archive provided important information for the archaeological studies of the York Bedern during the 1970s and it amply justifies the inclusion of a discrete section on the York vicars below (p. 147–200).

The piecemeal grants of property that constituted the vicars' urban estates were usually made in return for obit services and other prayers on behalf of the donors, themselves quite often canons of the cathedral. To take a not untypical case, in 1274 the warden of the vicars choral complained that they had been unlawfully ejected from a messuage in the city of York which had been bequeathed to them by John Maunsel, the late treasurer of the Minster, in order to celebrate his anniversary in the cathedral (*Cal Pat Roll* 1272–81, 67; YMA, VC/3/1/1, f. i). A very much larger capital investment was necessary to provide those vicars with the prospect of living a properly communal life in hall, chapel and chambers within a residential college. The considerable if battered remains of these building complexes, above and below the ground, naturally figure very prominently indeed within the later chapters of this volume. Those chapters, like the copious surviving documentary evidence for their history, also reveal that although a residential vicars' college gradually became a universal objective of all secular cathedrals that objective was attained at very different times in different cathedrals. Indeed whether vicars choral themselves positively wished to abandon their informal private lodgings in the city for the much more regulated life of an inmate of a religious college is a somewhat open question. However, it was obviously always in the interests of a dean and chapter to keep its vicars choral under vigilant supervision within a closed ecclesiastical precinct attached to the cathedral Close itself. For the 'reforming' bishops and other prelates of the 13th and 14th centuries it was also hoped – perhaps too optimistically – that residential colleges of vicars choral would improve the moral tone of both cathedral and city. Thus in the 1380s Bishop Thomas Brantingham of Exeter attributed the insolence, negligence and worldliness of the vicars there to the fact that they lived alone in chambers dispersed around the Close, dined in the houses of laymen and sometimes even occupied benefices outside the cathedral (ed. Hingeston-Randolph 1901–6, II, 675–6; Orme 1981, 85). The single most common explanation for creating colleges given by their founders themselves was that such enclosed accommodation would keep the vicars off the streets. To that extent the motives in play were not at all dissimilar to those which led English bishops and others to found academic colleges in Oxford and Cambridge during exactly the same period. Even when worship within the English cathedral was being transformed out of recognition in the 1540s, Edward VI's chantry commissioners were still asserting that vicars choral 'shuld be and contynue in the said college att comons, and bed, and NOT abrode in the cytie' (ed. Page 1894–5, I, 25).

It was in fact the vicars choral of York Minster who, three centuries earlier, became the first such body in the country to secure collegiate residential accommodation – as a result of a bequest by the otherwise obscure William of Laneham, a canon of York who died in the late 1240s. There are however good grounds for believing that this new vicars' college, very rapidly called the Bedern for reasons which still remain somewhat mysterious, was by no means the achievement of William of Laneham alone: it was rather the outcome of a concerted collaborative campaign by Archbishop Walter de Gray (1215–55) and the senior canons of the Minster (Aylmer and Cant 1977, 89–91; ed. Richards 2001, 385–8). However, large perpetual collegiate establishments were always extremely expensive and problematic to endow. Many years were to pass before the other secular cathedrals found benefactors generous enough to enable them to follow York's example. Thus the common hall at the disposal of the vicars of St Paul's Cathedral in 1273 is mentioned in terms which make it quite uncertain whether those vicars were yet in possession of much in the way of residential accommodation there (Edwards 1967, 276; chapt. 9 below). However, by 1270 Bishop Gravesend of Lincoln had sponsored a vicars' college on a site to the south of the cathedral (chapt.

8 below). For many years, however, only the senior priest vicars could be accommodated there; but in 1328 a new building was constructed nearby for the junior vicars (Owen 1994, 148). However, despite the inadequacy of the evidence, there can be little doubt that by the early 14th century a residential college of vicars choral had come to be regarded as an indispensable adjunct of all the secular cathedrals in the country. In 1315 the vicars of Lichfield acquired a common house of residence from Bishop Walter Langton (chapt. 7 below); and at Wells in 1348 Bishop Ralph of Shrewsbury (1329–63) inaugurated what is now the most picturesque and celebrated vicars' close in England by handing over 'a hall, kitchen and bakehouse, and all the other houses built or to be built there' together with an endowment of £10 per annum (Rodwell 1982, 212–26; Reid 1963, 120–9; Edwards 1967, 277 – chapt. 11 below). Towards the end of the 14th century, common halls and living accommodation are recorded for the vicars choral of the four remaining cathedrals in rapid succession – at Hereford by 1375, at Exeter by 1387, at Chichester by 1403 and at Salisbury (surprisingly late in the day) by 1409 (Peckham 1937, 132–3; Orme 1981, 85–6; Edwards 1967, 277–8 – chapt. 10 below). Needless to say, the creation of these buildings enormously enhanced the corporate self-confidence of the vicars choral just as it distanced them from the canon whose deputies they formally were.

After being brought together within the precinct of a college, the vicars had every inducement to go further still and aim to become an even more legally protected corporation than perhaps the cathedral chapter itself. The acquisition of a charter of incorporation under the royal great seal has sometimes been interpreted as the climax of the vicars' struggle for legal self-definition and at least some immunity from the interference of their canons. Certainly such incorporation, which first occurred at Wells in 1348, was soon much sought after by colleges of vicars choral everywhere. In 1421, for example, 'the habitation in York called le Bederne' was transformed by royal letters patent into a 'college' under the authority of a warden, elected by his fellow vicars and then presented to the dean and chapter for their approval (*Cal Pat Roll* 1416–22, 360–1). By 1467 only the vicars of St Paul's seem to have failed to secure incorporation of this sort. That said, virtually all the privileges normally conferred by a royal charter of incorporation (the authority to use a common seal; licence to hold lands and rents in common and in the beneficiary's own name; and the right to implead and be impleaded in royal law courts) had long been enjoyed by the vicars choral of all secular cathedrals. Dr Kathleen Edwards was certainly correct to argue that these 'royal charters represented little more than a legal confirmation of existing rights' (Edwards 1967, 285; Peckham 1939, 134). Admittedly it may be that royal incorporations of cathedral colleges of vicars choral helped to save them from annihilation at the Reformation; but otherwise, as in the analogous case of similar grants to medieval boroughs and guilds, their significance can be easily over-estimated. On the whole it seems that cathedral chapters usually supported the vicars in their requests for royal charters of incorporation; and the latter certainly failed to protect the *ministri inferiores* of a cathedral from constant regulation and indeed inquisition by their residentiary canons. In an age when ecclesiastical visitation was the most dreaded weapon of the church's authority over its subordinate institutions, perhaps no groups of clergy in England were visited more regularly and critically than the vicars choral of its cathedrals.

Indeed the visitation material surviving within the archives of the nine English secular cathedrals, especially from the late 14th century onwards, is so copious that it presents acute problems of interpretation. Could it be true of vicars choral, as the late K B McFarlane once famously declared about 15th-century English politics, that it is the very abundance of the sources which has given it a bad name? A bad name is what the vicars choral of the late middle ages certainly have. For the younger James Raine, chancellor of the 19th-century Minster, 'the cases of immorality with which every class was charged, especially the clergy in York minster' was so 'painful a subject to dwell upon that it can serve no good purpose to introduce it here' (ed. Raine 1859, 242). No doubt vicars choral were rather unfortunate to be so much more physically exposed to the critical scrutiny of their lords and neighbours than were monks and canons, even canons resident at their own cathedrals. Nevertheless the late Professor Hamilton Thompson, the most judicious and sympathetic of all 20th-century scholars of the institutions of the medieval English church, had no doubt that vicars choral were 'at no times easy to control, and were constantly in need of discipline' (Thompson 1925, 185). To judge from the mass of surviving evidence, serious absenteeism from the choir and negligence in the performance of their choral duties was more common than not among the vicars of every single secular cathedral. Such faults have most recently been brought to light at Hereford, previously perhaps the least studied of all English cathedrals (Barrett 2000, 446). But then much more serious and scandalous abuses among the communities of vicars choral are not at all hard to find; and there were occasions, admittedly few, when the whole community was in grave danger of abandoning its responsibilities altogether. At several times during the period when the clergy of Lincoln Ca-

thedral were at the mercy of their cantankerous Dean John Macworth (1415–51), absenteeism among the vicars sometimes reduced attendance in the choir to only six or eight, making it almost impossible to conduct services at all (Bowers 1994, 55–6).

Despite the notorious dangers of interpreting visitation *comperta*, *detecta* and *injunctiones* in too simple-minded a fashion, these documents undoubtedly give a more vivid impression of life in a college of vicars choral than any other source. Where else, for example, would one learn that when eating within their common hall in 1440, the vicars choral of Salisbury were expected to listen quietly to devotional readings and to talk, if talk at all, sparingly in Latin. In practice, however, that hall was often used for games of ball and at times became the scene of quarrelling and bloodshed – the latter all the more frequent because so many vicars regularly wore knives at their belts (Thompson 1925, 185–6). More representative of the allegations brought against vicars choral are the detailed *detecta* produced at a visitation of York Minster in 1403. As tends to be usual in such documents, most attention was paid to faults and misdemeanours in the performance of the vicars' liturgical duties. Twelve of the 36 York vicars were identified as regular absentees from the choir while those who were present in choir tended to be so engaged in gossip and telling stories (*fabulis et garrulacionibus*) that only six or eight voices could be heard singing the divine office.

As in other cathedrals, sins of omission tend to appear more frequently in visitation records than sins of commission. Nevertheless in 1403 several vicars were found to be in serious financial debt while another five were accused of fornication with local women, not to mention the exceptional case of Silvester Markham who haunted city taverns and other dishonourable places, wasting his goods by giving expensive dinners to his friends in the town (Purvis 1943, 38–9). Another visitation at York Minster six years later (in December 1409) helps to correct any possible imbalance of the evidence by preserving the individual vicars' own grievances or *detecta*. The latter naturally tend to focus less on issues like unruliness and violence than on the lack of adequate lighting inside the church, the scarcity of Bibles and other service books in the choir and the dishonest behaviour of the other cathedral clergy, notably the canons, chantry priests and young choristers (YMA, L2(3)a, f. 7r; ed. Raine 1859, 244).

Perhaps the first and most obvious moral to draw from such complaints at York (as elsewhere) is that, when under criticism, the vicars choral – like most members of most institutions at most times – tended to blame everyone but themselves. More surprisingly perhaps, disciplinary action on the part of the chapter seems to have had remarkably little effect.

On the evidence available, the sanctions and penalties at the disposal of deans and chapters (an enforced pilgrimage to St John of Beverley was not unusual at York) did very little indeed to ameliorate ill-discipline among the vicars. Like British prisons in the early 21st century, so colleges of vicars choral 600 years ago tended to be filled with second or third-time offenders. Most unnerving for modern preconceptions are the fairly large number of vicars who seem to have kept their mistresses within the private *camera* of their colleges, often apparently on a long-term basis. In December 1461 one York vicar choral, William Benysleve, had to confess to the dean of York Minster that a woman called Margaret Shilton had 'lately bore him one child, that she was in his chamber with him for a month before the birth and for a week after ....and he had not sent her away'. Under closer examination Benysleve turned out to be a serial fornicator who had to be fined 6*s.* 8*d.* every time he was caught bringing any woman into his chamber. Only in the case of an exceptionally recalcitrant vicar, like William Easington who in 1417 was faced with six separate charges of fornication with six different women, was the chapter at all likely to deprive him of his stall. Some of the women who frequented the colleges of vicars choral, like Elizabeth Whetelay alias Wheldrik who lived in Hornpot Lane and entered the room of one vicar choral in 1488 on the implausible grounds that she was bringing medicine to cure his unspecified sickness, were almost certainly local prostitutes (Purvis 1943, 21, 28–9, 31–2, 34–5). It is hardly surprising that the York dean and chapter tried to ensure that the main gate into the Bedern should be firmly locked at nine o'clock (the ninth *pulsacio*) in the winter and at 10 o'clock in the summer. In 1396 the warden and vicars were even prepared to incur the considerable expense of constructing an overhead bridge or walk way which would enable the vicars choral to pass across Goodramgate (*ultra Goderomgate*) from the Bedern gate to the still surviving gateway into the Minster Close without the dangers of illicit encounters and affrays, especially at night (*Cal Pat Roll* 1391–96, 712; Purvis 1943, 39).

Perhaps it is by no means as certain as it once was that the inmates of the colleges of vicars choral deserve our condemnation for harbouring what may often have amounted to consolatory rather than squalid little nests of quasi-conjugal relationships. To judge from the comparative leniency with which these sexual misdemeanours were treated by cathedral chapters, it is unlikely that contemporaries were especially appalled by such behaviour. More alarming were the violent outbursts of street-fighting, now and then positively provoked by the tendency of turbulent vicars to prowl around their cathedrals,

sometimes dressed as laymen and with knives and daggers hanging between their legs (ed. Raine 1859, 243–3). When Hamilton Thompson encountered the evidence for physical aggression on the part of vicars choral eighty years ago, he was at pains to stress that the rise of little 'spiritual republics' within the huge late medieval cathedral complex inevitably led to conflicts between rival jurisdictions which became of obsessive interest to the participants and were waged with remarkable obstinacy and even violence (1947, 98–9). Instances of such bitter jurisdictional contests between the colleges of vicars and the senior cathedral clergy, often centring on financial issues, are indeed not at all hard to find and could even find their way to the papal *curia* (for a York case in 1399, see YMA, P1(1), iii and Harrison 1952, 177–93). However, it is important to remember that late medieval English towns were endemically violent and often murderous: vicars choral were not at all the only section of the urban population which 'visited taverns overmuch, ran about the city under the shade of night and sang improper songs' (Raine 1926, 55).

One of the other factors which may have tempted at least the younger vicars out of their colleges and into the streets of the cathedral city is that many of them probably had a considerable amount of time on their hands. According to Nicholas Orme's calculations of a few years ago, the vicars of Exeter Cathedral were only required to be in the choir for six hours or so a day, rising to eight hours on major feasts (1986, 63–71). Such figures probably apply, at least in theory, to other secular cathedrals, within all of which the labours of choral worship must have been by no means insupportable, even if often monotonous to a degree. However, most vicars were also heavily involved in saying masses at altars dispersed throughout the cathedral, some of them actually becoming pluralists by combining the role of vicar with that of a chantry priest. As many, possibly the majority, of vicars choral spent the whole of their clerical careers in the service of one cathedral (a term of 30 or 40 years was not uncommon at 14th-century Lichfield, for example), that cathedral must have seemed their home. Moreover, and however defective the evidence, it seems clear that a very great proportion of the vicars were recruited from the cathedral city. Such is certainly the impression left by occasional references in civic records and, above all, by the wills and testaments of vicars choral when these begin to survive in quantity towards the close of the 15th century (Jenkins 1956, 103; Orme 1980, xvii; Cross 1984, 1, 8–9, 29–31, 46–7). The fact that most vicars were apparently local boys, often trained in the cathedral's choir school, may indeed help to explain their occasional partiality for gang warfare and female companionship. The fact is that many vicars choral were by no means as secluded from the disruptive influences of their families, their male contemporaries and women friends as the founders of their colleges must have hoped. Perhaps the extreme example of such family solidarity is the case of one York vicar choral who in 1398 took the trouble and expense of securing a papal dispensation for having – at the age of seven – chopped off a joint of his baby sister's finger with an axe (Lawrence 1965, 228).

It is perhaps even more important to emphasize that vicars choral had little hope of career advancement. On that important issue nearly all the authorities seem to be unanimous. In a typically aristocratic northern French or German cathedral chapter, like Laon or Strasbourg, for example, it would have been inconceivable for any member of the lesser cathedral clergy to become a canon; and in a recent paper Hélène Millet has shown that such internal promotion was also more or less unknown in the cathedrals of the French Midi (1993, 138–40). If such continental analogies seem less than helpful (though it could be argued that the study of cathedrals and their clergy lends itself exceptionally well to a comparative European approach), it is worth adding that the scholar who must know the members of the cathedral chapters of medieval England better than they knew themselves has recently come to the same judgement; 'As the members of the chapter looked down the ladder, at the minor clergy below them, the vicars and cantarists known as the *ministri inferiores*, they could be sure that virtually none would clamber up to join them' (Greenway 2001b, 9). Of all nine English secular cathedrals, only at Exeter has much evidence yet been found of vicars choral playing an influential role outside the cathedral choir and college. Between 1380 and 1548 at least 73 vicars choral left the choir of Exeter Cathedral to make at least some impact outside the Close by serving as parish priests. Such figures seem quite exceptional by the standards of other cathedrals; but then (with the notable exception of Nicholas Orme's *The Minor Clergy of Exeter Cathedral*) the prosopography of the medieval vicars choral can hardly be said to have begun (1980, *passim*; Orme 1981b, 280). A detailed collation of all the biographical information about individual vicars choral preserved in their own archives as well as in probate registers, ordination lists and other sections of episcopal registers should gradually throw much light on the careers and life patterns of vicars choral who hardly deserve to remain totally obscure forever.

Meanwhile the provisional impression left by the wills of the last generations of vicars is less that of the riotous young delinquents of the visitation records than of somewhat careworn middle-aged or elderly men, intensely loyal to the history and traditions of their own cathedrals and colleges. Admittedly in the closing decades of the middle ages many vicars choral of English cathedrals had much to be careworn about. Economically dependent, as they all were, on urban rents, they were naturally more vulnerable than most landlords when those rents continued to contract for well over a century after the first onslaught of the Black Death in 1348–9. Financial disaster could sometimes be averted or postponed, either by good management or by a generous bishop, as at Exeter. However in most cathedrals these economic stringencies gradually became impossible to conceal. At York by 1509 only twenty or so of the full complement of 36 vicars could be supported from the common funds of the Bedern, 'th'occasion whereof is by reason of decaye of lands and revenues of the cytie of York, beyng sore in ruyne and decaye' (Orme 1981a, 89–90; Dobson 1977a, 93). It is hardly surprising that when the final crisis came in the 1540s and the new Protestant ideology deprived vicars choral of much of their purpose, the latter responded with a whimper rather than a bang. Although a handful of clerical vicars choral, now usually outnumbered by lay singing men, survived the Reformation and lingered on until the *Cathedral Measures Acts* of the 1930s, once the convocations of Canterbury and York had licensed clerical marriage in 1549 the corporate life of the cathedral vicars choral was doomed everywhere. On 27th June 1574 the long tradition of communal dining in the Bedern Hall came to an end. Less than a century later the city of York was petitioning the Commonwealth Parliament to create a University of the North in the area because 'the Bedern has a large hall for readers, and convenient lodgyng for the students as well as divers fair houses (of late of the deans and prebends) which may remain unto some pious uses' (ed. Richards 2001, 385; Drake 1736, 239). Two centuries later still the Bedern was notorious for very impious uses indeed, as the most notorious haunt of prostitutes (33 in 1843 according to the Chief Constable) in early Victorian York (Finnegan 1979, 48–51).

Autres temps, autres moeurs. But there are more serious reasons than the vanity of human wishes why the history and archaeology of the vicars choral of the medieval cathedrals deserve to be re-visited in this collection of essays. Admittedly the tranquil routines of regular communal devotion are inevitably almost impossible for posterity either to recapture or to analyse, perhaps more impossible indeed than any other human activity of the past. No doubt this is the main reason why the study of the English vicars choral has fallen victim to yet another paradox – the dramatic contrast between the enormous amount of scholarly attention paid to the cathedral as a building and the more or less complete

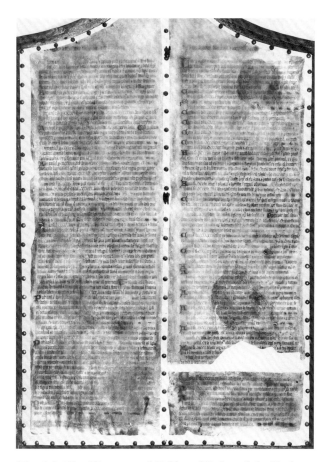

Fig. 1.3. The History and Tables of Rules of the York college of vicars choral. These remarkable boards were apparently hung in Bedern Hall at York throughout the later Middle Ages, as a reminder to the vicars of the aspirations of their college (photo and copyright, York Minster Library)

and administrative structures that the vicars choral, as the necessarily resident deputies of their canons, came to form the most coherent community of all. These were the men who more than any other group within the cathedral clergy (and certainly more than the largely absentee canons) 'consorted together' – consorted together most assiduously, most fractiously, most closely and, in the last resort, probably with the greatest sense of common purpose (Dobson 1986b, 181–200). Their loyalty towards their fellow vicars can perhaps be most readily appreciated – if often somewhat between the lines – from testamentary bequests which range from money to repair the fabric of their hall and chapel to books for the use of their surviving brethren. At least some vicars choral also wrote as well as read. The very last *Chronica Archiepiscoporum Eboracensium* ever produced, completed during the archiepiscopate of Thomas Wolsey (1514–30), seems to have been compiled by one or more vicars choral. The several internal references to the York vicars within the text make that hypothesis likely, not least the revelation that it was four vicars choral who carried the decapitated corpse of Archbishop Richard Scrope into the east end of the Minster choir on the day after his summary execution in Clementhorpe on 8th June 1405. This slender and somewhat jejune chronicle seems to have been addressed primarily to the pilgrim or visitor to the cathedral. As the York vicars also seem to have been responsible for the highly unusual two historical narratives fixed to wooden boards or 'tables' which still survive within the Minster (Fig. 1.3), it seems that the duty of maintaining some form of historical tradition within the mother church of the northern province had also fallen to the inhabitants of the Bedern (Purvis 1967, 741–8; Dobson 1991, 216–18). If the vicars choral of York and elsewhere acted as some of the first ever visitors' guides to the history and glories of their cathedrals, then for that reason too they deserve to be remembered with gratitude and affection by the authors and readers of this volume.

neglect, until very recently, of the men who actually worshipped within that building. But then admirers of the English cathedral can hardly be in any doubt that 'a great church is like a small universe: it is capable of absorbing any amount of study' (Morris 1979, 56). And it was within those complex religious

2

The Origins of Vicars Choral to *c.*1300

Julia Barrow

We are most aware of the vicars choral of medieval cathedrals as compact bodies of clerics, clearly demarcated from, and occupying a decisively lower position than, the leading clergy of the cathedral, the canons. We are used to vicars choral being bound by written regulations and housed in distinctive buildings, such as the close of the vicars choral at Wells (chapt. 11 below), or the cloister of vicars choral at Hereford (chapt. 6 below). Colleges of cathedral vicars form the main subject of this volume; however, long before the colleges were created, vicars existed, and the origins of vicars choral were by no means straightforward. They emerge into the daylight in the 12th century in a variety of guises, under a variety of terminology, and carrying out a variety of duties. This paper will look for the reasons for their emergence in cathedral and collegiate churches across north-western Europe, chiefly in France, the Empire and England, in the 12th and earlier 13th centuries, breaking off at about the point that one of the oldest corporations of vicars, that at York Minster, was established (Tringham 1993, 42–6, 160 nos. 72–3, 76, 284). This is a topic which I looked at many years ago (Barrow 1989), but coming back to it has allowed me to set the issue in a somewhat broader context and to draw on a rather larger collection of evidence. The materials chiefly used as evidence here are charters: this will lead to some differences of approach from the line taken by Kathleen Edwards in *The English Secular Cathedrals in the Middle Ages* (1967), which relied essentially on cathedral statutes, but not to essential divergences of opinion.

The origins of vicars choral are not clear-cut. For one thing, they are often hard to distinguish from chaplains; in some churches they can also be hard to distinguish from canons. There is also a good case for comparing their lives, careers and status with those of the numerous laymen who assisted in the running of cathedral services, for example as bell-ringers, and even, sometimes, as bouncers. For all of these reasons I am going to deal quite generally with minor cathedral clergy in this paper – chaplains, minor canons, vicars, undifferentiated clerks and sacristans, and I shall also refer to the canons whom they were supposed to serve and to the lay servants of the cathedral as well.

There are four principal aspects of minor clergy on which I wish to focus: these are the dating of their origins, the purposes for which they were felt to be necessary (and, bound up with this, the duties which they were expected to perform), the financial arrangements which were made to support them and the prosopography of the minor clergy – their family backgrounds and careers. Evidence for the last, before the middle of the 13th century, is extremely flimsy, but it is nevertheless useful to make this attempt. Underlying all these four aspects is a bigger topic: the development of worship within 12th- and 13th-century cathedrals and the implications this had for recruitment and deployment of clerical personnel, and for their ordination to the various grades

It will never be possible to provide an exact date for the emergence of minor clergy in cathedrals, but we might perhaps take the year 1103 in Angers Cathedral (Maine et Loire) as our starting point. The Loire valley was the home of many new cultural developments in the late 11th century and these had a number of consequences for the careers and activities of clergy. The most famous is the sudden freeing up of the educational system, exemplified by the career of Abelard, who, as a young clerk, was able to move from church school to church school along the Loire, rather than being encouraged to stay in one church as a permanent member of that community from his schooldays onwards (Clanchy 1997, 55, 68). The effect, in short, was to cause a separation between the training of the clergy and their eventual employment. Discrepancies between the numbers of clergy available and the number of posts they might fill were evidently no longer regarded as problematic. In a period when the number of parish churches and collegiate churches was increasing quite swiftly, this was perfectly understandable. At any rate, although we have no figures for the numbers of pupils at any of the schools in question, it is likely that the numbers of clergy overall were rising. Another obvious feature of the 11th century – and not just in the Loire valley – was the tendency to build ever larger churches. Even though quite small sounds might be skilfully projected throughout these large new spaces, it was clearly regarded as an advantage to have sizeable numbers of clergy participating in services, if only for the sake of appearances.

1103 was a significant year for Angers because it was in this year that Dean Aubri endowed chaplaincies to say anniversary services for two deceased bishops (Urseau 1908, 184–5, no. 100) and at the same time Bishop Renaud confirmed an arrangement set up by an earlier bishop, Geoffrey, ordering the clergy of the collegiate church of St Maurille in Angers, to assist the canons of the cathedral on the feast of its patronal saint, St Maurice (*ibid.*, 198–201, no. 115). Both phenomena, the foundation of endowed chaplaincies, and the use of staff from minor collegiate churches, are relevant to our topic. The latter was the traditional way of keeping up numbers, at least on occasions that really mattered, such as a major feast day. Since the number of canons at Angers Cathedral had been raised from 30 to 40 in 1096 (*ibid.*, 207–8, no.122) the total number of clergy attending on the feast day of St Maurice must have been impressive. For all cathedral cities where there were collegiate churches in addition to the cathedral, above all where these were subordinate to the bishop who would thus be able to enforce their subjection to the cathedral, this was an easy way of increasing numbers in choir. Most French and German cathedrals could rely on such arrangements because of the large number of collegiate churches in many cities. In some cases these churches had Roman origins, but in other cases, especially in towns east of the Rhine, they were episcopal foundations of the 10th and 11th centuries. In the 12th and 13th centuries, communities of the Alter Dom in Münster (Erhard 1847–51, II, 84, no. 307), Notre-Dame in Liège (Bormans and Schoolmeesters 1893–1933, I, 121–3, 135–8, nos. 76, 85), St-Lazare in Autun (de Charmasse 1865, 117–18) and St-Pierre-le-Puellier in Bourges (A-D Cher, 8G23) were all linked very closely to the local cathedrals, while the church of St Ansgar in Bremen was founded in 1187 specifically to provide extra manpower for Bremen Cathedral (Ehmck and von Bippen, 1873–1902, I, 73–80, 131–3, nos. 66–8, 111). It was not possible for English cathedrals to create similar links because there were few urban collegiate churches in towns with cathedrals, and those which did exist, as for example St Martin-le-Grand in London, were often under royal, not episcopal control, so cathedrals could make no claims on them.

While the reliance by a cathedral on the communities serving collegiate churches was a traditional response to a manpower crisis, the foundation of posts to provide for minor clergy in Angers in 1103 was an innovation. Minor clergy then begin to emerge, or at least to be visible, elsewhere in the kingdom of France and in Flanders in the 12th century: in Flanders at Tournai in 1112 (Pycke 1986, 179), at the collegiate church of St-Omer from 1123 (where a papal privilege referred to vicars as well as canons and schoolboys in choir – Duchet and Giry 1881, 8–11, no. 11), and at Térouane in 1134 (where an endowment of two prebends for priests to perform continuous residence and to say masses of the Virgin and for the dead is recorded – Duchet and Giry 1881, 13–14, no. 15). Endowments for minor clergy appear at Laon in 1131 (A-D Aisne, G1850, f. 113v), the collegiate church of Lille in 1143 (Hautcoeur 1894, I, 32–3, no. 24), at Le Mans between 1136 and 1144 (Lottin 1869, 133, no. 224) and Amiens in 1148 (Roux 1897–1914, I, 37–8, no. 28). It is in the 1130s-40s that the earliest reference can be found to minor clergy at York Minster, with vicars occurring in witness lists (Clay 1957–8, I, 52–3, no. 3 of *c.*1138 x 1143). The earliest reference to a vicar choral at Salisbury is in a statement made between 1142 and the 1170s by Robert, prior of Breamore, to Bishop Jocelin of Salisbury about how Thurstan, Abbot of Sherborne (1122–*c.*1142), had become a prebendary at Salisbury and had made Robert his vicar (Edwards 1967, 263, citing Macray 1891, 16–17). Unnamed vicars and 'other clerks', distinguished from canons, occur at Salisbury by about 1160 (Kemp 1999, 93–4, no. 124 dated 1155 x 1161). Thirteen clerks of the choir at Exeter Cathedral helped to witness a settlement between the chapter and the nuns of Polslo on 1st March 1159 (Edwards 1967, 261, citing Poole 1907, 49). 'Other priests and clerks' follow the canons in a witness list of 1162 from St Paul's Cathedral, London, and must be minor cathedral clergy (Gibbs 1939, 172, no. 217), while in the same year clerks of the choir occur in another St Paul's charter (Historical Manuscripts Commission 1883, Appendix I, 12). Vicars at Hereford are referred to in a charter issued between 1174 and 1183 (Barrow 1993, 102, no. 149); Lincoln Cathedral had vicars at least from the episcopate of St Hugh (1186–1200), who gave the dean and chapter licence to compel all non-resident canons to appoint them (Foster 1931, 260–1, no. 300). Wells had vicars by the end of the 12th century, at which time Bishop Savaric of Bath established prebends for the abbeys of Bec (1199), Muchelney (1201) and Athelney (1200 x 1205) within the chapter, on condition that the abbots (who could not be resident) should provide vicars to replace them (Ramsey 1995, 148–9, 180–1, 188–9, nos. 196, 240, 249). Savaric also provided for two priests to say daily masses for deceased bishops, who were to receive the same payments as the vicars of Wells (Ramsey 1995, 191–2, no. 253). Within the Empire, earliest appearances of minor clergy tend to be in the early 13th century, but the collegiate church of St Jan, Utrecht, had them from 1163 (Muller and Bouman 1920, I, 393–4, no. 440), St Thomas at Strasbourg from 1182 (Wiegand 1879, 99–100, no. 119) and Magdeburg Cathedral from 1185 (Israël and Möllenberg 1937, 530–1, no. 403).

The purposes for which minor clergy were established were very varied, and my attempt to date origins has not distinguished between the different roles they were expected to perform. The theory that the employment of minor clergy was chiefly the result of absenteeism on the part of canons was justly questioned, or at any rate carefully nuanced, by Kathleen Edwards (1967, 256–8, 264–6) who showed that the roles performed by minor clergy did not wholly overlap with those of the canons they were theoretically replacing. Some late 12th- and early 13th-century sources refer to the negligence of cathedral canons, and some refer to the reluctance of canons to seek ordination as priests, but they may only be telling part of the story. Some absenteeism had long been built into the system; service by cathedral canons at royal courts went back a long way (Fleckenstein 1966, 127–9). Admittedly, job opportunities for secular clerics soared in the 12th century with the burgeoning administration of kings and bishops and the development of higher education and professional law, but at the same time several cathedral chapters, notably Salisbury, Lincoln, York and Wells, increased very markedly in size. Several French chapters, notably Chartres, were markedly bigger even than these. So, although absenteeism should not be excluded as a motive for the employment of vicars and chaplains, it should not be seen as the only one. Provision of sufficient numbers to fill larger architectural spaces is another motive deserving consideration, whilst another less obvious one was probably patronage – canons might wish to provide for poor relatives or other protégés for whom a fast-track career in the higher clergy was out of the question. We will see some clearly documented examples of patronage operating when we look at the endowment of some of these posts.

From the earliest appearance of minor clergy in cathedrals the terminology used to describe them is extremely varied, and this can help us to understand the functions which they were required to perform, although the evidence has to be used with care as a single individual might be expected to perform several tasks. In the context of cathedral organisation the term *capellanus*, widespread across Europe, tended to refer to someone serving an altar, usually one of the minor altars in the cathedral, but this did not necessarily preclude service in choir. The term *vicarius*, meaning 'stand-in', was favoured by the papacy, for example in a bull of Calixtus II for St-Omer of 4 October 1123 (Duchet and Giry 1881, 8–11, no. 11) and was the most popular term in England. It was frequently used from the earliest emergence of cathedral vicars, at York Minster in the 1130s, contemporary with the earliest frequent use of the term 'vicar' in England to mean the stand-in for a parson (Barrow 1992, 65–6). In France the term *vicarius* was used rather less in an ecclesiastical context, even though the earliest ecclesiastical occurrences of the term go back in French-speaking areas to the turn of the 10th and 11th centuries (Niermeyer *et al.* 2002, II, 1420), probably because since Carolingian times *vicarius* had been the normal term for the count's deputy in secular jurisdiction, the *viguier*, and so in cathedrals *clericus chori* was often the preferred term. In north-eastern France and the Empire stress was often laid on priestly office and thus references often are to priests or to priest-canons, though the inferiority of the latter to the other canons was usually indicated by their smaller revenues, as we shall see.

The duties performed by minor clergy were extremely diverse. In part they reflect the dignitaries' and canons' normal responsibilities, but in addition a wide range of new duties was added as the range of church services became more complex in the 12th and 13th centuries. Canons and dignitaries, if resident, were usually supposed to take their turn saying mass at the high altar. Each canon would do this for a week at a time; hence the term 'hebdomadary canon' for the one whose turn it was for this duty. In addition they were supposed to attend the hours (the daily sequence of services of prayers and psalms) in choir and, if possible, anniversary prayers and masses where these had been endowed, for which they would receive a share of a distribution of money and sometimes food and drink. Besides this, each dignitary had responsibility for some important aspect of worship – for example the cantor or precentor was in charge of chant whilst the treasurer had the task of supplying the elements for communion and wax for lighting and also had charge of communion vessels and relics. Not surprisingly all dignitaries found it necessary sooner or later to have subordinates who could deputise for them in their absence, and, although it was often possible at the wealthier cathedrals to create fully endowed subordinate dignities within the chapter (for example at Chartres – Amiet 1922, 2; or, on a smaller scale, at Wells – Greenway 2001, 20–5), some cathedrals compromised by employing minor clergy in these posts. At Hereford all the deputies of the various dignitaries were minor clergy (Bradshaw and Wordsworth 1892–7, II, 62–3, 69, 71). However, the extent to which churches expected minor clergy to replace their superiors varied. At Liège in 1203, for example, canons' vicars were expected to serve sacerdotal weeks (Bormans and Schoolmeesters 1893–1935, I, 133, no. 84) and at Trier in 1222 a vicar was allotted a place in choir and was allowed to chant at the high altar like a canon (Beyer, Eltester and Goerz 1860–74, III, 158). More often, however, there were restrictions – they might be expected to say daily mass of the Virgin, as at the Alter Dom in Münster in 1181 (Erhard 1847–51, II, 157–8, no. 417), or daily mass at a particular altar, like the priest serving the altar of St Paul 'between the two towers' at Münster Cathedral in 1225 (Wilmans 1859–68, 115, no. 212). At Hereford no vicars could celebrate at the high altar except the dean's own vicar (Bradshaw and Wordsworth 1892–7, II, 73). Minor clergy were regarded as a supplement to the existing forces, not principally as a substitute for them.

Best documented are the numerous chaplains who served altars endowed in the 12th and 13th centuries. Their principal *raison d'être* would be to celebrate mass at a minor altar in the cathedral, and often also to say anniversary services for the founder or to say daily mass for the souls of the founder and of all faithful departed. However it was very often written into the prescriptions for chaplains that they should also serve in choir. At Tournai Cathedral, from the foundation of the first chaplaincy in 1173, the 'chaplains of the high forms' (that is the chaplains entitled to sit in the highest row of the stalls) had to say the hours as well as masses (Pycke 1986, 188); at St Thomas in Strasbourg in 1182 the clerk established in a chapel also had to serve in choir (Wiegand 1879, 99–100, no. 119), and so too did a priest appointed to say daily mass for the dead in 1225 (*ibid.*, 160–1, no. 198); at Laon *c.*1173 chaplains also had to sing hours in choir (A-D Aisne, G1850, f. 121); at Troyes in 1182 the four priest-canons serving the altar of the Virgin had to serve in choir (Lalore 1880, 46–9, no. 36); at Münster Cathedral in 1225 the priest vicar assisting the *custos* (i.e. the treasurer), had to celebrate at an altar and also serve in choir (Wilmans 1859–68, 115, no. 212); at Würzburg in 1188 a priest had to serve in choir (*Monumenta Boica* 1864, no.141); at Lincoln the chaplains serving the Faldingworth chantries *c.*1220 had to serve in choir

also (Foster 1933, 105–6, no. 393); at York in 1272 the chaplains serving the altar of St John the Evangelist also had to serve as vicars (Clay 1957–8, II, 122, no. 80). Thus the duties of chaplains often overlapped with those of vicars. Since permanently endowed posts for vicars are much less commonly recorded than those for chaplains, we have less information about their job descriptions, but at Wells in 1242 their main activity was saying the canonical hours (*HMC Cal 1*, 60). Similarly at Hereford on 3 June 1269 Bishop John le Breton refined existing arrangements made for six vicars choral in 1237 by Bishop Ralph of Maidstone by emphasising that the vicars had to serve continuously at the hours and that they had to make sure that they knew the antiphoner and the psalter within a year of their appointment (Capes 1908, 74–5, 123–4). The behaviour of minor clergy in choir was very carefully regulated. At Le Mans in 1206/7 the priests of the choir were told that they could sit in the upper choir stalls but only to read the lesson or chant the office, and they had to vacate these positions if canons turned up and found that there were no seats left (Lottin 1869, 132, no. 222). Clothing was also regulated: William the Lion, King of Scotland, gave 6 marks from the burgh *ferme* of Rutherglen in 1201 or 1202 to maintain a deacon and a subdeacon in Glasgow Cathedral who were to be decently dressed in surplices and black copes 'like the other vicars' (Barrow 1971, 403–4, no. 426). This was a standard form of attire for clergy. It can be found elsewhere, for example at Salisbury in the early 13th century (Jones 1883–4, I, 35), whilst in the *Statutes* issued by Bishop Richard de Carew for St Davids Cathedral in 1259, black copes were to be worn only in winter and canons and vicars were expected to dress alike in choir, save that the former, but not the latter, should wear amices (Barrow 1998, 150, no. 131).

In addition to celebrating mass at minor altars and chanting the hours, minor clergy might also be called on to perform a whole range of other duties. Some of them carried out parochial duties where these were attached to an altar in a cathedral, as at the altar of the crucifix in Le Mans Cathedral (Lottin 1869, 5–6, 22–3, nos. 8, 44). At Salisbury in the early 13th century the vicars were expected to help in fund-raising for the new cathedral building (Jones 1883–4, II, 11, 21); at the Alter Dom in Münster a priest serving an altar and singing in choir also had to play the organ (Erhard 1847–51, II, 157–8 no. 417 of 1181); at Würzburg the post established for a priest in 1188 involved not only singing in choir but also helping to move relics and to vest an altar (*Monumenta Boica* 1864, no. 141). Here we can see possible overlaps between minor clergy and the bottom tier of cathedral servants, the laity who performed tasks such as bell-ringing. Bishop Godefrid of Utrecht increased the income of the bell-ringer at Deventer 1176 to make sure that he would not have to serve the altar in torn clothes (Muller and Bouman 1920, 436, no. 489); Archbishop William of Sens established four *matricularii* to ring bells 1176 (Quantin 1854–60, II, 285–6 no. 267); Archbishop Michael of Sens laid down duties of the four *matricularii* more explicitly in 1198 – they had to keep watch in the vaults under the treasury, and they had to make beds in the church for the priests acting as sacrists, and pull off their boots, as well as folding vestments, decorating the church, and providing kindling for the thurible (*ibid.* 493–5, no. 484).

Funding for the positions occupied by minor clergy came from very diverse sources. Sometimes canons had to pay for their own deputies. All canons had to do so at Salisbury (Edwards 1967, 263). Non-residentiary canons had to do so at Lincoln (Foster 1931, 260–1, no. 300) by the end of the 12th century, and likewise at Lille in 1205 absentee canons had to pay dues to help pay for vicars (Hautcoeur 1894, 79–80, no. 75). Such arrangements, however, were often *ad hoc*, and much more information survives about the endowment of chaplaincies and perpetual vicarages. This could be achieved in a variety of ways. In the western areas of the Empire one method was to divide an existing canon's prebend into two and to give the two resulting half-prebends to priests who would be required to be resident (Hautcoeur 1894, 51–2, no. 44 of 1189). At Paderborn in the 1230 prebends for schoolboy canons were turned over to pay for priest vicars (Wilmans 1874–94, 123–4, no. 185 of 1230). In 1196 Henry VI of Germany divided his honorary prebends at the cathedrals of Liège and Utrecht to pay for two priests in each church (Bormans and Schoolmeesters 1893–1933, I, 118, no. 73; Muller and Bouman 1920, 471, no. 530). Similarly in 1215 the prebend held by the Bishop of Liège in his cathedral was divided in half to pay for priests (Bormans and Schoolmeesters 1893–1933, I, 179, no. 116). Bishops might also make other sources of income available for priests: Archbishop Dietrich of Trier endowed a vicarage in Trier Cathedral with a parish church (Beyer, Eltester and Goerz 1860–74, III, 158, no. 183); Bishop Otto of Würzburg supplied an income from the episcopal mint in 1220 to pay for a priest to attend in choir (*Monumenta Boica* 1864, 205–6 no. 198). Some English cathedrals persuaded abbeys to create prebends for their abbots to hold as honorary canons while supplying vicars in their absences. Salisbury set up this type of arrangement with Sherborne Abbey in about 1122 (Greenway 1991, xxxii; Kemp 1999, 103–4, no. 134), and this was followed by similar schemes linking Hereford to Cormeilles in 1195 and Lire between 1216 and 1219 (Barrow 1993, 136–8, 236–7, nos. 188, 305). Chichester was linked to Grestain in this way between 1198 and 1204 (Mayr-Harting 1964, 154–5, no. 97), Wells to Bec in 1199, to Muchelney in 1201 and to Athelney between 1201 and 1205 (Ramsey 1995, 148–9, 180–1, 188–9, nos. 196, 240, 249) and Salisbury to Bec in 1208, St-Wandrille between 1194 and 1207 and Montebourg in 1213 (Kemp 1999, 153–5, 198, 171–3, nos. 193, 236, 214; Greenway 1991, xxxi–xxxii).

Individual charitable donations were responsible for most of the chaplaincies founded, and the people most active in this area were cathedral canons, especially from the late 12th century onwards. At Tournai, canons began to do this in the early 12th century and were responsible for endowing many of the cathedral vicarages (Pycke 1986, 179–86). On the death of a cleric, property which he had held from a church was supposed to go back to that church and it was normal for cathedrals to encourage canons to set up anniversary distributions for themselves, either as a post obit grant or as a deathbed bequest. In the Empire particularly, where rules about the inheritance of clerical property were complicated by endless arguments between the relatives of deceased canons and the churches to which they had belonged over the destination of the property of the deceased, churches made more of an effort than did those in other parts of Europe to insist that canons should make grants to fund their anniversaries. These grants usually consisted of property bought by the canon in his lifetime which would not be claimed as patrimony by his kin. Among the possible objects of charity that anniversary grants could fund were side altars, and in the Empire from the 1180s onwards we find canons endowing chaplaincies to serve these, as at Magdeburg in 1185 or at Münster in 1196 (Israël and Möllenberg 1937, 530–1, no. 403; Erhard 1847–51, II, 236, no. 539). Blithard, cantor of Laon Cathedral, had made a similar endowment in 1131 with a claustral house and also a vineyard (A-D Aisne, G1850, f. 113v). A natural further development, of course, was the endowment of chaplaincies or perpetual vicarages to provide daily masses for the benefactor's soul, often attached to particular minor altars, and a whole sequence of such grants can be pieced together at Hereford from *c*.1220 onwards (Barrow 2002, xxix–xxx). Sooner or later, chaplains themselves started to establish their own chantries, as at Le Mans in 1239/40 (Lottin 1869, 145, no. 243). Equally unsurprisingly, founders of chapels wished the first chaplain to hold office to be one of their relatives – a canon of St Castor in Koblenz in 1212 set one up apparently for his son (Beyer, Eltester and Goerz 1860–74, III, 2–3, no. 2), while a canon of Laon in 1185 tried to set up a chaplaincy for his nephew, who proved unable to make up his mind whether he wanted to be a cleric or a monk and was thus unsuitable (A-D Aisne, G1850, f. 193v, 197).

The final point I wish to look at is the prosopography of the minor clergy. Admittedly we have much less information on them than we possess for canons; there are fewer mentions of them in witness lists, and when they do occur they are less likely than members of the higher clergy to bear by-names, thus making conclusions about their social and geographical backgrounds far harder to draw. However, for York there are numerous references to minor clergy in witness lists from the middle of the 12th century onwards, and many of those give nicknames or places of origin. Where the York vicars bear identifiable English place-names as by-names these are invariably local to Yorkshire, sometimes local to York itself: Beverley, Bugthorpe, Healaugh, Bootham and Goodramgate (Clay 1957–8, I, 75, no. 29; I, 76, no. 30; I, 83 no. 37; II, 106–7, nos. 61–2; II, 111, 113, nos. 68, 71), Such names differentiate the vicars from the canons of York Minster, whose toponyms suggest a much wider range of geographical origins. Some of the York chaplains distinguished themselves by the names of the altars which they served, and some of the vicars by the names of the canons whom they served. None of the minor York clergy in the 12th century appears to be related to a canon, but even so one of them bore the surname Ros (*ibid.*, I, 83, no. 37) and must have been a distant connection of that aristocratic family. For Hereford, where quite a few vicars and chaplains were recorded in the cathedral obit book (which contains names mostly of the 12th century and the first 70 years or so of the 13th), the picture is slightly different, since some of the chaplains and clerks (John of Hay, Simon de Clifford, Robert Foliot and William Foliot) bear the same surnames as canons (Barrow 2002, 53, 68, 72, 81–2, 95–6, 125, 130, 145, 149). Moreover one of them, Ralph de Kaukeberge, was the beneficiary of a chaplaincy established by his kinsman, Canon Roger de Kaukeberge (*ibid.*,

118). It is also possible that John of Hay may have benefited from the perpetual vicarages set up in the cathedral by the canons William of Hay II and Master Philip of Hay (*ibid.*, 124, 141). The frequent references in the Hereford obit book are also useful in recording the grade of ordination which the deceased had reached by his death, which allows us to form some idea of the ratio of priests to lower grades: out of nearly 30 people who can be clearly identified as minor cathedral clergy, eighteen were termed priest or chaplain and thus likely to be priest, while eight were in lower grades and another two are described as doorkeeper and clerk of the organs and were perhaps also in lower grades. The priesthood clearly mattered to minor clergy in the 12th and 13th centuries; it made obtaining a position at a cathedral much easier.

To conclude, the emergence of minor clergy, including vicars choral, was in part, but only in part, an attempt to make up for absences by canons. More often it marked an increase in the types of activity within major churches, as the number of private masses rose. It can also be seen as an aspect of the growing professionalisation of the 12th century, which drew the higher clergy increasingly into careers in administration and law. The lower clergy, too, had skills to offer, in their case singing and the ability to celebrate mass (see chapter 3 below). The endowment of positions for minor clergy reflects growing economic opportunities for those (chiefly canons) who established them, and, in addition, offered an opportunity for patronage, though usually ties between the patron and protégé ceased after the death of the first holder of a chaplaincy. More commonly, as at York, a 12th-century cathedral opened up the possibility of a job for life for local men of modest means but possessed of a good singing voice.

3

The Vicar Choral in Choir

John Harper

Vicars choral sustained the extensive pattern of daily worship in the choirs of the great secular cathedrals. As *vicarii* they were technically substitutes, undertaking this work on behalf of the statutory canons of the cathedral, most of whom were not resident. In practice, they formed a particular stratum of professional clergy, expert in complex worship; a stratum which, by the late middle ages, had expanded to include chaplains and chantry priests, not only in cathedrals but in other collegiate foundations and a significant number of larger parish churches. The evidence for their work in church is piecemeal. Only the bare framework of the music and ceremony of medieval worship can be observed in the choir and presbytery of the nine medieval secular cathedrals in England, often much altered by periods of Reformation, restoration and liturgical re-ordering. Most of the ethos and repertory of the medieval liturgy was displaced by the *Book of Common Prayer* and the *Royal Injunctions for Cathedrals*. Many of the books that contained details of the ceremonial that the vicars choral enacted and the music that they sung have been lost. This chapter, based on a paper given in York on the eve of Palm Sunday, provides an introduction to the musical duties and skills of the medieval vicars choral. It does not pretend to be specialist or comprehensive, but aims to give a flavour of their skills and their work in the secular cathedral churches. The evidence for this is scattered in statutes, chapter acts, injunctions, and visitation articles, but above all in the remaining liturgical books and music manuscripts.

Palm Sunday – music and ceremony

Palm Sunday marks the beginning of Holy Week, one of the most busy and complex periods in the liturgical life of the medieval cathedral. It includes some of the most ancient forms of service of the western church – the solemn liturgy of Good Friday, and the Vigil of Easter. In the middle ages, the pattern of services was so dense that, on the Saturday of Holy Week, the Easter Vigil had to begin in mid afternoon, ending with a shortened form of Vespers. On the morning of Palm Sunday, the cathedral community would have assembled for a great procession. This ceremony went far beyond the normal extent and complexity of a normal Sunday procession before High Mass. It was mimetic. In some cathedrals, such as Hereford, it began at another church in the city, and proceeded to enter the cathedral as Christ entered Jerusalem. And just as the early church gathered and sang on their way to the station church, so the medieval cathedral clergy sang the processional antiphons, responds and hymn on their way to High Mass on Palm Sunday.

At Salisbury the procession began and ended in the cathedral. The *Sarum Processional* indicates the level of ceremonial on such an occasion. There were two processions: one representing the crowd, the other representing Jesus and the disciples. The first procession was led by a lay verger. There was a boy bearing holy water, two taperers carrying candles, a thurifer with the incense, an acolyte bearing a plain cross (i.e. without a figure of Christ), a vicar serving as subdeacon, a vicar serving as deacon, and the officiant – probably a senior residentiary canon on Palm Sunday. If the bishop was present then he followed the officiant. They were followed by the remainder of the choir, in seniority order. The second procession consisted of seven clerics. One led the procession bearing a silver cross, two carried banners, then two clerks of the second form (see below, p.00) bore a feretory, a casket with relics and on this day a pyx with the consecrated bread – the host representing Christ. Another clerk preceded the casket with a lantern – the light of the world – and yet another held a canopy over the feretory. The processions proceeded separately around the outside of the cathedral to a series of stations. Symbolically the main procession (the crowd) met the smaller one (representing Jesus and his disciples). The two processions came together and proceeded through the cloister to the west end of the cathedral, up through the nave and into the choir for the solemn celebration of High Mass, with the singing of the Passion (ed. Rastall 1980 – a facsimile of the printed *Processional*, including illustrations; the ceremonies are described and the full musical text is printed in ed. Sandon 1996). Three general points can be elucidated from this description of the Palm Sunday procession at Salisbury. Ceremony, the visual, was as large a part of the great liturgies as text and music; it is simply less immediately evident to us, and less easy to reconstruct. The vicar choral needed to be skilled and knowledgeable in ceremonial as much as in music: the two processions required no less than fifteen persons from the foundation to undertake specific ceremonial duties. The choral body in processions and at High Mass had to provide for both musical and ceremonial functions – a substantial demand on the available manpower.

However, music and ceremonial were not always entirely dependent on the numbers of clerics. A manuscript processional of York Use from the modest parish church of Methley in Yorkshire is a reminder that comparable ceremonies with chant were carried out in places where there were as few as three priests, assisted by a parish clerk and boys and men from the parish (Oxford, Bodleian Library, Ms., E Museo 126 (3612)). Even in the secular cathedrals, those present in choir included more than the vicars choral.

The gathered body

In the liturgical beehive of the secular cathedral, the vicars choral were the drones. They sustained the music and the ceremonial of the services in choir from the early hours of the morning until the evening, a constant round amounting to at least 70 services each week. On top of the main services in the choir there were additional observances to Our Lady, to the saints, and to the dead. Some of the additional services were recited corporately in choir, some were said privately in choir, others took place at other altars and in other chapels in the cathedral. Some were delegated to chantry priests or other groups; but the lion's share of the work fell on the vicars choral, overseen by one of their seniors or by

a small group of minor canons. A contemporary summary of duties is found in Bishop Nicholas Heath's second set of injunctions for Rochester Cathedral (1543), at the time of its refoundation as a secular cathedral after the dissolution of the Benedictine monastery (eds. Frere and Kennedy 1910, 95–98). There is an excellent account of medieval practice at Lincoln (Bowers 1994/1999); a general musical account is provided by Harrison (1958, 1980), and a constitutional account by Edwards (1967).

Unlike monastic choirs with their two rows of stalls, the secular cathedrals included three ranks on each side of the choir. Those assembled in the cathedral choir on a holy day *c.*1500 numbered many more than the vicars choral. Walking into the choir of a medieval secular cathedral today, one may still observe the three rows of stalls on each side, intended for juniors, secondaries and seniors. The three rows are a reminder that the vicars were assisted by children and by young adults in minor orders. At the front, on the first 'form' on each side, may have been between six and twelve boy choristers, together with a variable number of juniors (including some former choristers); in the middle row were the clerks of the second form, including subdeacon or deacon vicars choral; and at the back were the senior clerks of the third form, all vicars choral and normally priests, generally seated in carved stalls alongside those of the canons (Bradshaw and Wordsworth 1897, 72, 79). On Sundays and feast days they were joined by the chantry chaplains, and members of the select Lady Chapel choir, some of whom may have been laymen. At Hereford or Chichester, for instance, while there may have been up to 27 vicars choral (and around twenty is a more likely number allowing for infirmity and vacancies), the total number in choir may have been as many as 50. At larger foundations, like Salisbury, St Paul's and York, the number in choir may have exceeded 80 (cf. Knowles and Hancock 1971, 411–46).

There was a progression of seniority from chorister to senior canon, exemplified in the allocation of the readers of the nine lessons at Matins. (This pattern is still echoed in the modern adaptation of festal Matins as the *Festival of Nine Lessons and Carols* where, in the form broadcast on Christmas Eve from King's College, Cambridge, the first lesson is read by a chorister, the last by the provost). Yet the vicars formed the core of the larger body gathered for worship. Many a vicar must have started life as a chorister, proceeding during his teens through the minor orders of porter, lector, exorcist and acolyte, and then in his early twenties to the major orders of subdeacon, deacon and priest; he must have progressed from song school to grammar school, and then in some cases to university, to employment in another institution, or to a post as a chantry chaplain. The cathedral undertook the training of its clergy alongside the conduct of its principal work – the two functions were integral. The use of the word 'form' to describe both academic and liturgical progression is indicative of this.

At Hereford, in the early 16th century, five of sixteen named choristers proceeded from chorister to subdeacon or deacon, and two juniors proceeded from minor orders to priest vicar. What is apparent is the bar that normally existed between vicar and canon. At Hereford there is only one example of this progression. William Chell, B.Mus., who had been in the foundation since 1518 and was succentor by 1526, gained a prebend in 1533, while remaining succentor, and finally became precentor in 1554. This was probably an emergency measure following the deprivation of the married precentor. The cathedral needed someone senior and well-established who knew all the old ways of the Latin rite, which had been in abeyance for the previous five years (Harper 2000).

Some of the skills and knowledge required of a vicar choral were taught to the choristers – singing, knowledge of the chant, and simple techniques of improvising polyphony around the plainsong (Flynn 1995). From at least the 15th century selected choristers were also being taught to play the organ. Choristers had specific, if limited, musical and ceremonial roles in the liturgy, allowing them to become familiar with the customs and patterns of worship. However, they attended all the services only on holy days (Sundays and greater feasts); on other days their duties were limited to allow time for learning. They will, nevertheless, have become familiar with the festal psalms, hymns and antiphons, the repertory of festal mass chants, and with the ceremonies in which they took a part. They knew how to chant a lesson and the special melodies of the final versicle, *Benedicamus Domino*, allocated specifically to boys. They also knew well the services they attended on a daily basis, especially the votive Mass, Office and Antiphons of the Blessed Virgin Mary, and, in the earlier 16th century, the Jesus Mass.

The three basic tests for admission as a vicar choral were competence in singing, competence in reading, and good character. A cathedral chorister was sufficiently grounded to be ready to progress from the song school to the grammar school, to ordination in minor and then major clerical orders, and thus to the second form in choir and to admission as a vicar choral – either directly or via a chantry chaplaincy.

Services

The Ordinal, Customary and the rubrics of Missal, Antiphonal, Gradual and Processional for Holy Week provide a level of ceremonial detail that is often unsurpassed during the rest of the year. This detail needed to be recorded precisely because it was so different from the forms of worship offered throughout the remainder of the year. Yet even with this level of detail it is often hard to be sure of exact practice. For instance, just how many candles were lit at the beginning of the Easter Vigil is not at all clear, let alone where they were positioned. The normative patterns of day-to-day services are even more tantalising, for there was often no need to write down what was done customarily every day. The daily round of services came in three blocks. Matins followed by Lauds began at midnight in winter, or just before dawn in summer. Next, from around 6am to 11am, there was a steady sequence of services: Morrow Mass, chantry Masses, Prime, Lady Mass, Chapter and Chapter Mass, Terce and High Mass, Sext and None. Then, starting at around 3pm, there was Vespers, the Antiphon to the Blessed Virgin Mary and Compline. Most services had additional observances attached to them: after Matins, for instance, would come Matins of the Blessed Virgin Mary, Matins of the Dead, and Matins of All Saints (Harper 1991). On Sundays and feast days, when everyone was expected to attend in choir, the services were more complex and longer. Matins consisted of three nocturns, each with a group of psalms, three readings and three responds. That service would take well over an hour. Also on Sundays and feast days High Mass was preceded by a procession, and there were often processions on these days at Vespers as well. On ordinary workdays, Matins was shorter. Although it is possible to discern an underlying pattern of daily worship, this supported a web of complexities in both music and ceremonial, and the vicars choral needed to be fully alert to the procedures and the detail. There were variants in the music according to the day. The same texts might be sung to a different melody according to the rank of the day and the season of the Christian year. Everything was regulated, and what was not codified followed local custom.

Duties were tabled weekly, by rank and by rota. In fulfilling his allotted tasks, each vicar, junior or chorister needed to know exactly what he was doing, where in the cathedral it needed to be done, and how it related to what else was going on in the liturgy at that time. Before every mass the correct vessels had to be in place, all the vestments set out, and the appropriate books placed at the correct lecterns. Everything was regulated and had its own ritual. Often no one person had a complete text of the whole service. Separate books included items sung by celebrant, choir rulers, soloists, and readers. It would be misleading to suggest that even a single cathedral maintained the same practice between the 13th and the 16th century. Not only were there local variants, but customs and repertory changed over time. New feasts were added, not least the feasts of the Trinity and of Corpus Christi, and new embellishments of text and music were introduced, including tropes, sequences, and polyphony.

The Chant

Plainchant formed the core of what was heard in a liturgical celebration, and the extensive repertory of the Latin chant was, by and large, consistent throughout the period. At the end of the probationary year (in some cases two years) a vicar choral was expected to know by heart the great body of Latin chant. That was a substantial requirement. They needed to extend their knowledge of the psalm texts from a repertory of about 50 that they would probably have known well as a chorister to the full 150. They needed to fill out their knowledge of around 130 hymns (most of which would be familiar if they had been a chorister). Most taxing was the knowledge of the repertory for the night office of Matins. This was by far the most substantial part of the total repertory of the eight daily office services.

The extent of the surviving chanted repertory is very considerable. The repertory for office services in the Uses of Salisbury, Hereford and York each includes over 1800 antiphons and over 850 greater responds. The *Salisbury Gradual* includes about 1200 proper chants – introits, graduals, alleluias, tracts, offertories, and communions. To these have to be added the sequences and the chants of the ordinary of the mass. The *Salisbury Processional* includes around 450 chants, some of which duplicate items in the office and mass. Broadly speaking this represents a typical repertory of some 5000 items of choral chant. The vicar choral needed to be familiar with all these chants, and to sing many of them from memory (Hiley 1993; Harper 2000, 397). At Salisbury there was a fail-safe process for ensuring that the right chant was sung at the right moment. The precentor gave the pitch by singing the opening of the chant. The beginners or rulers, singing from a book, then started the chant, and it was continued by the whole choir (Frere 1898).

There were layers of complexity to the chant: (a) simple repeated patterns, based on singing on a single note; (b) melodies where mostly there was one syllable to one note; and (c) elaborate melodies where most syllables were sung to a series of notes – melisma. The greater part of the liturgy was sung on one note, with modest decoration to indicate breaks in the verse, or punctuation in a prayer or reading. The psalms, canticles, readings, dialogues and prayers were all intoned on a single note punctuated by simple formulae. Examples of the formulæ of the Preface in the mass can be seen in Fig. 3.1. Each psalm or canticle was preceded by an antiphon, a text particular to the season or the day. Those for Magnificat and Benedictus are more elaborate; those for the psalms are generally simple. Among the most elaborate of the chants are the responds at Matins and the graduals at the mass – chants that require assurance and considerable vocal skill. Although parts of the chant are allocated to a solo group of more experienced singers, the sections sung by all in choir are also demanding.

The musical demands should not be underestimated – either in terms of complexity or quantity. On a day like Palm Sunday the choral body would sing around 50 psalms and canticles, with 46 special antiphons, nine greater responsories (each about three minutes of elaborate chant), eighteen processional chants, nine mass chants, and one or more antiphons of the Blessed Virgin Mary. Even if we disregard the large number of regular versicles and responses and comparable small items, it amounts to over 150 items in a single day, of which more than half are unique to Palm Sunday and will not therefore have been sung for a year.

Polyphony and Organs

Not everything was sung in unadorned chant. From at least the 10th century the church in Britain made use of sung polyphony and of organs. The best early evidence comes from English Benedictine monasteries, notably Winchester, but there is no reason to suppose that they were unique. Some of the surviving repertory overlaps with that of the cathedral of Notre Dame in Paris, where secular priests had responsibility for the conduct of music and liturgy (Wright 1989). Most of the early written-down polyphony was intended for skilled solo singers, rather than the whole choral body. Often this polyphony consists of embellishment of solo sections of the chant, but by the later middle ages it was quite normal for every member of the choral body to have basic skills in improvised polyphony (Caldwell 1992, 6–31). As part of their training in the song school, choristers were not only taught to sing the chant but also to sing a second melody line four notes above the chant (known as 'sighting' a 'discant'). They also learnt to improvise a freer third voice below the chant, making three-part polyphony. It seems to have been an assumption that vicars choral would be competent in this simple polyphony. At York in 1507, rule twenty-four of the vicars' statute and minute book goes further. There

Fig. 3.1. A page from an illuminated missal of the 15th century from York Minster (YMA, Ms. Add. 30) (photo and copyright, York Minster Library)

is an expectation that, in addition to improvised polyphony, a vicar should also learn to sing composed polyphony (pricksong): 'If he has a tenor voice, he will learn how to sing pricksong and faburden … If his voice be not tenor, he will learn how to sing, besides pricksong and faburden, discant.' (Harrison 1952, 63).

By the early 16th century the organ was used regularly in the office, especially at the hymn, and in the Lady Mass, especially at the offertory. Where there were few singers, it gave them respite by allowing them to sing alternate verses, while the organ played the other verses. In larger churches it served as embellishment. The earliest written-down examples of British organ music for the Latin liturgy date from the first half of the 16th century (Harrison 1963, 202–18; Harper 1999, 91–7). The organ was initially a ceremonial instrument. Indeed, there is evidence to suggest that it was first used as an outdoor rather than an indoor instrument. Rather like the bells, the organ sounded out to greet important visitors on their arrival. Most often it is

recorded that, on the arrival of a prince or prelate, he was met by the dean with the canons and choir, and *Te deum* was sung solemnly with the organ. When Richard III came to York in 1483, the ceremony is described very precisely: the dean and the canons proceeded to their stall, with the other ministers, when Amen was finished on the organ. There followed *Te deum,* begun by the officiating prelate and finished by the choir and organ (Harrison 1952, 112; ed. Raine 1859, 210–12). If the York vicars really were skilled in pricksong, perhaps the *Te deum* might have sounded something akin to a combination of surviving organ polyphony by John Redford and choral polyphony by John Taverner, both written around 1525–30 (Caldwell 1966, 10–17; ed. Benham 1984, 53–74).

Special cases

We know that vicars choral demonstrated a wide range of skills in conducting the ceremony of the liturgy, and in singing a large repertory of chant within it. We know that it was normal for them to be able to improvise simple polyphony, and that some of them could play the organ. Furthermore, the records of York suggest that by the early 16th century they were expected to be able to sing more elaborate, written-out polyphony. Certain individual vicars choral had additional special skills. For instance, John Hichons or Higgins of Hereford was also an organ builder. His career at Hereford was turbulent and probably the dean and chapter put up with his behaviour only because they wanted him to finish some new organs. He was admitted in 1525, the year in which money was also spent on a new organ in the choir. In 1529 he was suspended and then readmitted. In March 1531 he was forced to resign, but continued to be paid while he repaired an organ. In September 1532 he was dismissed by the *custos* of the college, but in October this was amended to suspension on full pay while he completed an organ. In July 1533 he was readmitted on condition that he finished work on two organs – one in choir, and one over the sacristan's room. Finally, in 1534, he was deprived on grounds of contumacy (Harper 2000, 389–90).

Less colourful, and also less certain, is the career of the composer Richard Davy. A Richard Davy was a student in Magdalen College, Oxford, in about 1483. In the financial years 1490–1 and 1491–2 a Richard Davy received a stipend as instructor of the choristers at Magdalen. We know that this was the gifted composer whose work appears in the *Eton Choir Book*, copied around 1500, for it records that he wrote a piece at Magdalen in a single day. He was evidently ordained, for the college made a payment to an Oxford bookbinder in 1495 for binding a book of masses and songs by Dom Ricardus Dave. A Richard Davy was ordained subdeacon and deacon in the diocese of Exeter, presented by Launceston Priory, in March and April 1491. And Dom Ricardus Dave was a priest at Ashburton Parish Church on the edge of Dartmoor in 1492 and 1493. Here he and another priest were paid for correcting the books at a time of particular musical activity in the church. Richard Davy was vicar choral of Exeter from Michaelmas 1494, a post he vacated before 1509. And Richard Davy became vicar of the Devon parish of Broadhembury in 1507 (Orme 1978, 395–410; Orme 1980; Hanham 1970). These Davys may be the same man. It may be that he was educated at Launceston Priory and sent to Oxford (there are later connections between Launceston and Magdalen College School), and that he returned to Devon, first as an assisting priest in Ashburton, a parish in the gift of the dean and chapter of Exeter Cathedral, then as a vicar choral at the cathedral, ending his days in a comfortable incumbency ten miles north of Exeter. It may be, therefore, that the boys and selected vicars choral in Exeter made use of Richard Davy's setting of the Passion to be sung at High Mass on Palm Sunday around 1500. (For an alternative suggestion, that there may be a connection with Richard Davy, clerk of Fotheringay College from 1512 until his death in 1538, see Skinner 2001, 83; for a modern edition of Davy's Passion see ed. Harrison 1973, 112–34).

Lay skills and the musical eclipse of the vicar choral

Notwithstanding the skills of men like Davy, in the second half of the 15th century there was a significant change in the musical expectations of cathedrals. At Hereford, it was Giles the clerk who was paid as keeper of the organs between in 1307 and 1318. But, from the early 16th century, the post of organist was held by a layman, often in conjunction with the post of verger (Harper 2000, 390–1). At Lincoln, where a vicar choral had undertaken the duties of playing the organ since at least 1310, this was handed over to a layman, William Horwood, in 1461. Horwood spent much of the next twenty years as master of the choristers (Bowers 1994, 58–9). Whereas this had been a supervisory role in the past, it now became a specialist role for a musician. The boy choristers, whose primary duties had been ceremonial, now became trained singers able to sing polyphony at the

Lady Mass, or in the daily Marian antiphon ceremony (Bowers 1994;1999). Polyphony at the Lady Mass had become normative in the 1430s at Lincoln, when four of the most musical vicars undertook the singing. But in due course it was common for the Lady Chapel choir to include lay singers, with boys working under a lay master of the choristers. Roger Bowers suggests that the reduction in numbers of vicars choral at Lincoln in the later 15th century and the rise in their stipends implies a raising of standards. It also signals the increased competition for musical clergy from the new colleges and from larger parish churches, often eager to enhance divine worship with polyphonic music.

The influx of lay organists, choir trainers and singers marks the rise of a new breed of professional church musician. The principal duties of these lay musicians were in the Lady Chapel, but on Sundays and feast days they came with the boys to share in the liturgy in the great choir. A description of this practice at the newly established secular foundation at Rochester Cathedral in 1543 survives (eds. Frere and Kennedy 1910, 95–8). In many cathedrals, monastic and secular, it was the Lady Chapel choir that formed the nucleus of the cathedral choir after the institutional and economic changes of the Tudor Reformation. The adult Lady Chapel singers became the new lay vicars and lay clerks who survive in cathedral foundations today. After the Reformation, with loss of income from chantries and the suppression of colleges, priests singing in polyphonic choirs became a minority. One notable exception was John Gostling, the famous bass singer in the Chapel Royal for whom Henry Purcell wrote especially wide-ranging solo parts in the 1680s. Gostling was also a minor canon of St Paul's and of Canterbury. The last ordained vicar choral was the late Rev. Philip Barrett, who resigned his post at Hereford in 1986 (p. 60 below).

Because our modern starting point tends to be the polyphonic cathedral choir, there has been a tendency for scholars to emphasise those institutions and choral groups that promoted polyphony in the later middle ages, and which made greater use of lay musicians. The study of the music and liturgy of the medieval cathedral choir has been relatively neglected by comparison with the polyphonic choirs of colleges, household chapels, Lady Chapels, even parish churches. Perhaps it is time for musicologists to do more to seek out the voice of the medieval vicar choral.

4

The Vicars' Hall
and Close at Chichester Cathedral

Tim Tatton-Brown

Soon after they were finally dissolved, on 4 May 1935, W D Peckham wrote an excellent history of the vicars choral of Chichester Cathedral (1937, 126–159). In this article Peckham said that he hoped to write a later paper dealing with the buildings which the vicars inhabited. Alas, this was never done, though a useful article on the houses had already been published by Ian Hannah (1914, 92–109) before the demise of the vicars, and this was used by Godfrey and Bloe (1935, 157–8) in the relevant *Victoria County History* volume for Sussex. My initial work on the Vicars' Close was done some twelve years ago (Tatton-Brown 1991), but since then I have been able to undertake further work on the houses of the east range of the Vicars' Close during major restoration works. This has been greatly facilitated by the Close architect, Richard Meynell.

By the early 14th century Chichester Cathedral had 30 prebends as well as its four dignitaries. Two of the dignitaries (the dean and precentor) had prebends attached to them (Peckham 1937, 137), so that in the choir there were officially 32 stalls for the dean and canons, as well as a similar number for vicars. Fine canopied choir stalls of *c*.1320 still survive in the cathedral, though they were very heavily rebuilt in the later 19th century (Tracy 1986, 147–51). Alas, the sub-stalls for the vicars had already been removed, and replaced by box pews, in the 18th century.

The medieval Close at Chichester was a small and compact area to the south and west of the cathedral in the south-west quadrant of the walled city (Fig. 4.1). By the later middle ages only the bishop and the four dignitaries had large residences, with the chancellor's and treasurer's houses flanking the bishop on the south-west side of the cathedral, and the large deanery complex to the south of Canon

Lane. East of this were two plots, later called 'the Residentiary' and 'the Chantry', which housed the resident canon and the precentor respectively. North of Canon Lane and east of the treasurer's house were two other canons' houses which, at the end of the middle ages, were divided up for chantry priests' houses (Tatton-Brown 1994). It is evident therefore that, even in the early 14th century, very few of the canons had residences in the Close.

Where or how the vicars lived before the end of the 14th century is not known, though it is certain that the majority could not have lived in the canons' houses. They were perhaps just dotted around in various small lodgings in the Close and possibly in the town. As at other secular cathedrals, it was decided that what was needed was a separate 'Close within the Close' to house (and no doubt control) this unruly group of about thirty young men. The initiative was taken by Bishop Richard Medford or Mitford (1389–95), who as the king's secretary was also a close personal friend of Richard II (Saul 1997, 125). In 1394 the royal *Close Rolls* record that Robert Blundell, chaplain, son of Robert Blundell, citizen of Chichester, conveyed to the king the tenement called the 'Gildenhalle between the cathedral churchyard on the north and a tenement, late of Robert Sexteyn, on the south'. The conveyance was witnessed by William Neel, mayor, the two reeves, and others (ed. Salzmann 1935, 92). Then on 10th August 1394 the king granted the premises to Bishop Richard Medford 'for the use of the vicars of the cathedral church'.

Remarkably, the very fine vaulted undercroft of this late 12th-century guildhall building still survives, beneath the eastern part of the later vicars' hall, and it was this building that must have been used by the vicars for the next three years (1394–7).

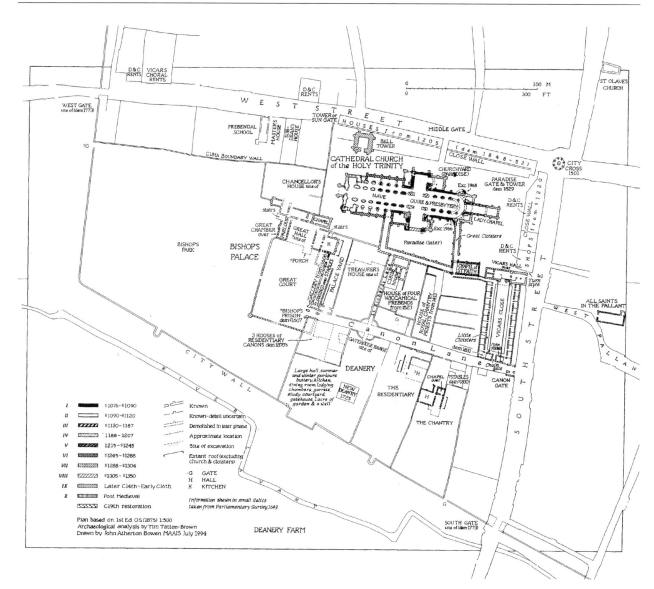

Fig. 4.1. Vicars choral of Chichester Cathedral. Plan of Cathedral Close, showing location of the college of vicars choral west of South Street (drawn by J A Bowen for Tim Tatton Brown, copyright J A Bowen)

Bishop Medford moved on to Salisbury in 1395, and as bishop of Salisbury (1395–1407) he probably started to create the vicars' hall and close there. Under Bishop Rede (1396–1415), a Dominican friar, work was put in hand to rebuild the old guildhall building, and to create a proper vicars' close. In Bishop Rede's register (one of very few episcopal registers to survive at Chichester), we read that on Tuesday 6 March 1397 the consecration ceremony for the foundation of a common 'mansion' for the vicars choral took place (ed. Deedes 1910, 435–7):

'The vicars being present, the Dean set forth in his own name and that of his brethren … how … to the honour of the holy and undivided Trinity, of Blessed Mary, St Richard, and All Saints, and for the common good of the Church of Chichester and the Vicars in the same, present and future, they were disposed and prepared to newly construct and build a certain common mansion within the close of the Church of Chichester, within which mansion

the Vicars of the church in the future times would be able to lead in common a good life, the grace of the Holy Spirit inspiring them, and with the counsel and aid of the noble Lord Richard, Earl of Arundell, who contributed many goods to the construction of the said mansion and promised to confer more in the future, also relying on the alms of others. But that a work of such magnitude might be begun and might better be brought to its desired end … the dean asked of the Vicars assembled … whether it was their will in the Lord to consent to this work and to the construction of the mansion aforesaid, and whether when the mansion had been built, prepared and fitted up … they would be willing, as it was fitting, to live together in it. When these questions were put, the Vicars then present saying, as though with one voice, 'Thanks be to God' expressly returned their common consent to all. And after this, on the same day the first stone of the foundation of the same work was laid … the aforesaid Dean placed the first stone in the first eastern angle of the foundation … in the honour of the Holy Trinity, having been first sprinkled with blessed water … William de Petteworth, canon, placed the second stone … John Paxton, Canon, laid the third stone … Robert Poplowe, Canon, the first mover of this work laid the fourth stone … '

Unfortunately, Richard Fitzalan, Earl of Arundel was arrested by Richard II only a few months after this, and then summarily executed on 21st September 1397. (His brother, the newly elected Archbishop of Canterbury, was deprived and exiled four days later). So only the Earl's initial gifts for the new mansion would have been received. Nevertheless, work on the new vicars' hall must have progressed quickly over the next few years, and once again it is remarkable that much of this building still survives, incorporating the earlier guildhall undercroft at its east end (Steer 1958). By the time of Bishop Rede's visitation of 1402–3 the hall was probably in use and the vicars' houses were perhaps being constructed (Peckham 1937, 133).

The new vicars' hall building was started by extending the old building about 65ft. (19.8m) westwards with a pair of long barrel vaults at the west end. These vaults are still intact and were probably made to support the stone floor for the kitchen (Fig. 4.2). In the centre of the new building, the principal floor tie-beams for the hall itself were supported down the middle by a great east–west longitudinal beam on sampson posts. The completely new first floor building, which extended over the old 12th-century guildhall undercroft, was externally almost 100ft. long and 26ft. wide (30.5m x 7.9m). The hall, about 53ft. (16.1m) long, was posi-tioned in the centre of this building; a timber-framed partition on its east side separated it from the great chamber (or vicars' parlour). At the west end of the hall, another timber-framed partition separated it from what was probably the kitchen, with a fireplace in the west wall. Over the eastern part of the hall much of the original crown-post roof (with wind braces) still survives. Set into the wall on the north side of the hall is a fine stone lavabo (wash-basin) supported by a carved figure with a cowled head. Above it is an ogeed arch with a rich finial (a window was unfortunately later made behind this), and directly opposite the lavabo is the principal doorway into the hall. This fine moulded doorway faces outwards onto a small landing, which originally had covered stairs descending from it to the east and west. As we shall see, these now blocked-up stairs lead down to the covered walks where the vicars' individual houses were situated. In 1583 the vicars had to dine and sup in hall on only one day a month, and not long after this that requirement too had ceased (Peckham 1937, 136). With the demise of the vicars' use of the common hall, this way of entering the hall went out of use. One side of the landing area outside the original entrance was turned into the storage area for the vicars' muni-ments and plate (Steer 1958, 6). From 1720 the hall was leased out, and a new entrance to it was made from the north. This entrance, from the churchyard, is still in use today.

The upper end of the hall is raised by one step, as this end is above the western part of the late 12th-century vaulted undercroft. This was, no doubt, used as the dais for the high table, and on its south side is a small projecting space, with two openings (door and window), which is usually identified as the pulpit. The 1534 statutes of the vicars, given by Bishop Robert Sherburne, specify that the:

> *'vicars at their meals do in turn (as is the custom), the Principal and Seneschal being excepted, read the Bible or some other lesson, at the Principal's apportionment; and that, while the Bible is being read, they altogether keep silence; that the aforesaid Vicars and Commoners, and each of them, conduct themselves in a seemly manner at the table, use on no account frivolous chatterings, unseemly story-tellings, deriding laughter and noisy talking ...' (Steer 1958, 6).*

There is, however, no evidence that the reading was done from a pulpit, and this space may have dis-played a precious item such as a statue, relics or the book of statutes, for it is apparent that the window originally held an iron grill, and that there are iron hooks for a (no doubt lockable) door. Alternatively, this space could have been used for both display and the pulpit, though no obvious lectern can be seen.

The hall also still contains several original two-light trefoiled and ogee-headed windows (rebated

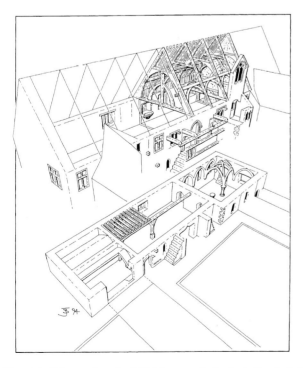

Fig. 4.2. Vicars choral of Chichester Cathedral. Exploded isometric view of the vicars' hall from the south-west (drawn by J A Bowen for Tim Tatton Brown, copyright J A Bowen)

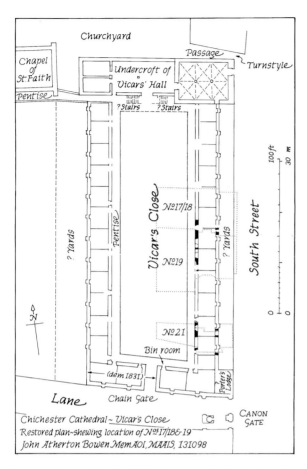

Fig. 4.3. Vicars choral of Chichester Cathedral. Plan of the vicars' close (drawn by J A Bowen for Tim Tatton Brown, copyright J A Bowen)

for shutters) with external square hood-moulds, and in its heyday, in the 15th century, it must have been full of life. Outside the north side of the hall (and along the south side of the churchyard) was a narrow passageway, which ran from the cloister (see below) on the west to South Street on the east. Just before it enters South Street there is a small postern gate (called the 'Turnstyle' in the 18th century), and above this there was originally a small chamber of unknown use, which connected directly with the vicars' parlour. The blocked-up doorway into it is still visible. There is also part of a window jamb of what may have been a squint, suggesting that this room could have been a small oratory (Hannah 1914, 104).

As we have seen, the vicars' hall was probably finished by 1403, and it is very likely that the construction of the vicars' houses, around the courtyard to the south of the hall, started immediately. This self-contained area had a gateway in the middle of its southern side; this was called the Chain Gate and led to Canon Lane (Figs. 4.3 and 4.4). Just to the south-east of this was the Canon Gate, the principal entrance into the Close itself (Fig. 4.1). Unfortunately the Chain Gate, and the neighbouring range to the west, was demolished in 1831, though there are several earlier views of the range (and the gateway) before demolition (Tatton-Brown 1994, 244, 247).

The vicars' houses were investigated by the present writer in 1990–1, and it was found that, particularly in the roofs, it was possible to work out

Fig. 4.4. Vicars choral of Chichester Cathedral. The south façade of the vicars' college looking towards Canon Gate, showing the vicars' gatehouse known as the Chain Gate. View from the west prior to demolition in 1831 (source, painting in Chichester Cathedral Library)

Chichester Cathedral~Vicar's House c1450, a restored view
(Nº 21 South Street from the North-West)
John Atherton Bowen MemAOI, MAAIS, 230198

Fig. 4.5. Vicars choral of Chichester Cathedral. Reconstructed isometric view of an original vicar's house (drawn by J A Bowen for Tim Tatton Brown, copyright J A Bowen)

the original arrangement of bays within the buildings (Tatton-Brown 1991). There are two ranges of houses on either side which probably each contained twelve almost identical dwellings, with each vicar having a living chamber below and a sleeping chamber above (Fig. 4.5). At the southern end were perhaps four more, slightly larger, dwellings, making 28 houses in all. This fits very closely with the known number of vicars at the beginning of the 15th century; in 1397 there were 28; in 1402–3, 27; in 1409, 25–6; in 1415, 30. From the mid 15th century, however, the numbers of vicars began to drop rapidly. There were only sixteen vicars in 1478 and by the early 16th century the average numbers were between twelve and fourteen (Peckham 1937, 138–9).

Each range had masonry outer walls, but individual houses were separated from each other by a timber-framed partition, which incorporated the tie-beam and braced crown-post (for the roof above) at the top (Fig. 4.5). Remains of various single- and two-light trefoil-headed windows, and of ground-

floor doorways, can still be seen in the main walls fronting onto the central courtyard. In the back walls a few slight external pilaster projections can be seen, which mark the sites of the internal fireplaces, and one base of a medieval stone chimney-stack (with broach-stops at the base of an octagonal flue) was also found (Tatton-Brown 1991, 15). Each house must have had a small internal stair, but no traces of these have yet been found, or of the garderobes that may have been on the backs of the houses. In 1998, work on restoring three houses in the east range of the Vicars' Close uncovered several more features, allowing the houses and their roofs to be understood more closely (Fig. 4.3). In No.19 South Street a fine early 16th-century wall-painting was found, which ran across two of the first floor rooms. This, therefore, confirms that the two houses had been joined together by this time. Unfortunately the east range of the vicars' close was 'turned round' in 1825, and given new frontages and shops in South Street. This meant that new 'back'yards were made in the central courtyard, and that all the houses were now entered from South Street. Much of the old back walls of these houses, with their fireplaces, were cut away at this time.

After the Reformation the numbers of vicars dropped from ten down to four or five, and in 1596 the number was fixed at four (Peckham 1937, 139–40). The houses in the east range were leased out, and those in the west range were then given to the four remaining vicars, who were each able to have three adjoining bays of the original houses. By this time the vicars were also married men, and in the 17th and 18th centuries various extensions were built onto the back of the west range, and the gardens were greatly extended to the west.

Not far to the west of the newly rebuilt vicars' hall was the 13th-century chapel of St Faith, the origin of which is obscure (Godfrey and Bloe 1935, 153). Mass was celebrated here by one of the canons, Master John Paxton, at the start of the ceremony on 6 March 1397 for the laying of the new foundation stones of the vicars' hall, described above. The chapel then seems to have become the chapel for the Vicars' Close, though at times in the 15th century it was used as a temporary store (Hannah 1914, 94). After the Reformation its shell was turned into a private house, in which state it remains to this day, with its backyard open to the air in what was originally the eastern, sanctuary part of the chapel.

In Bishop Rede's register (Deedes 1910) it is also recorded that Master John Paxton, the canon involved with the founding of the new vicars' hall, was accused in 1403 of making a common path from his lodging through the chapel 'against the ordnance of the founder of the said chapel and the great loss and alienation of the goods and things of the

Fig. 4.6. Vicars choral of Chichester Cathedral. West range of vicars' close looking towards the vicars' hall (photo and copyright, D Stocker)

[cathedral] church deposited in the same chapel for safe custody'. Paxton responded that the residentiary canons inhabiting his lodging (perhaps the 13th-century house, just west of St Faith's chapel, that became the house for the royal chantry priests in 1413) had always had the right of going through the chapel to the cathedral. He was also charged with taking timber that had been deposited in the chapel for the work of the cathedral.

If one looks at the remains of St Faith's chapel today, it is very clear that the southern part of the cathedral's east cloister walk has been cut through the extreme western end of the chapel, and it is almost certainly the building of the east cloister walk that is referred to in this dispute of 1403. An examination of the three cloister walks at Chichester shows that they are just a series of covered ways, and that they were built in stages, starting with the east cloister (Tatton-Brown 1994, 243). It seems likely that when the east cloister walk was built the other walks had not been conceived; and that this east cloister walk was built so that both the canons living in the later 'Royal Chantry' and the vicars in their new vicars' close could have covered access directly to the cathedral choir. (There is a similar arrangement of covered walks to the vicars' cloister at

Hereford Cathedral). At the south end of the east cloister walk a doorway opens to a narrow passageway called the 'Dark Cloister'. This was originally covered by a pentise roof, but is now open to the air again. It ran along the south side of St Faith's chapel, and along the side of the kitchen of the vicars' hall to the extreme north-west corner of the vicars' close. There must also have been simple lean-to-roofs, which abutted the walls of the vicars' houses at the projecting string-course below the first floor windows (Fig. 4.5), which formed another cloister in the Vicars' Close. Unfortunately these covered walks around the vicars' central courtyard, which was called the 'Little Cloister', were demolished in the mid 18th century.

The post-medieval history of the Chichester vicars choral has been well-told by W.D. Peckham (1937). As we have seen, there were from 1596 to 1929 only four vicars, who all lived in the west range of the Vicars' Close, in larger houses (Fig. 4.6). The number was reduced to three in 1929, two in 1934, and then the Corporation of Vicars was dissolved on 4 May, 1935. As Peckham says 'the effect of the permission to marry was as disastrous to the corporate life as it was good for individual morals'.

5

The College of the Vicars Choral at Exeter

John Allan

Introduction

Of the college of the vicars choral built by Bishop Thomas Brantingham at Exeter between 1383 and 1387 there stands today only a single remnant: the forlorn ruin of the hall, hemmed in by ugly post-war shops, in South Street[1]. This hall had survived intact until the Exeter Blitz of 1942, when its interior was burnt and parts of its fabric subsequently demolished by the City Council to create a picturesque ruin. The other elements of the college – two rows of lodgings extending eastward towards the cathedral, a gatehouse with adjacent rooms closing the eastern end and an outer gatehouse beyond – had been demolished by stages between 1850 and 1893[2]. The loss of most of the fabric, of course, restricts what can be said about the college buildings. Nevertheless, Exeter offers much to the student of vicars choral and their buildings, in part because the college preserved its own rich archives, both medieval and post-medieval (catalogued in Erskine 1962), but also because the large body of plans and drawings which accumulated before its buildings were demolished allows one to reconstruct much of its form and something of its development.

The history of the vicars at Exeter has been the subject of two major papers; the first by the Rev. J F Chanter, the cathedral treasurer (1933), looking at the entire history of the college, medieval and post-medieval, as well as its buildings and treasures, the second by Prof. Nicholas Orme (1981). The latter presented an authoritative modern history of the vicars in the middle ages as part of his series of studies of Exeter's medieval cathedral and its clergy, which also included his full listing of all the vicars and other members of the cathedral's minor clergy between 1300 and 1548 (Orme 1980)[3]. The study of the college

buildings in fact extends back to the generation before Chanter – to the work of Ethel Lega-Weekes, whose remarkable book *Some Studies in the Topography of the Cathedral Close, Exeter,* published in 1915, deserves to be more widely recognised as a pioneering exercise in the study of the topography of a medieval English town. Other aspects of the lives of the vicars await fuller study. The rich potential of the vicars' very detailed medieval tithe accounts to throw light on the economic history of Devon has only very recently been demonstrated (Fox 2001, 107–15, using especially the Woodbury accounts). The post-medieval history of the vicars has not had the attention one might have expected its impressive archive to attract. Here the most substantial contribution has been Ian Payne's account of the college in the century between the Reformation and the Civil War (Payne 1983), but there remains much scope for work on the social history of the densely packed properties in the area of the college, based on the fine series of leases in the college archive and the complimentary dean and chapter and city records.

The present account naturally draws on these earlier papers, but its purpose is different, offering a summary of what can be said about the college buildings, which have received no consideration since Chanter's paper of 1933. Although Chanter himself remembered the buildings as they stood in the late 19th century, and published the plan of 1850, much more can be said on this subject. He did not, for example, use the voluminous collection of unpublished plans of individual dean and chapter properties in the Close, many of which have remained unsorted until the last few years. These allow the bounds of the college to be established and also record some important details about its buildings where they abutted dean and chapter property. Chanter also published some of the most telling of the large number of topographical drawings and paintings, scattered among various collections in the city and beyond, showing parts of the college. Others, however, were probably inaccessible in his day, and have been used here, as have some hitherto-unpublished early photographs. The York conference has also served as an occasion to complete an architectural record of the remains of the hall. Unfortunately archaeological excavation has contributed hardly any information to the picture: the area of the major excavations in Cathedral Close in 1971–6 (Bidwell 1979; Henderson & Bidwell 1982) included the north-eastern corner of the site, but here nearly all remains of the college had been obliterated by the massive foundations and aisle basement of the enlarged Victorian church of St Mary Major[4]. Keyhole excavations in the college hall in 1999 (Dyer 2000) likewise encountered only modern disturbances.

The college foundation and its progress to the early 16th century

The earliest contemporary reference to minor clergy who may be equated with vicars choral at Exeter is in a document of 1159–60 witnessed by thirteen 'clerks of the choir' (Edwards 1967, 261; Orme 1981, 80). Exeter is, however, one of the two cathedrals where the possibility has been entertained that there were vicars even before the Norman conquest. The origin of the claim lies in the assertion of Bishop Bronescombe and the chapter in a statute of 1268 that, from the foundation of the church (i.e. from 1050), there had been twenty-four canons and twenty-four vicars. Kathleen Edwards' discussion of this claim in a national context showed that it is unlikely to be true (Edwards 1967, 259–61) but it remains at least an interesting reflection of the Exeter clergy's perception of the vicars as a long-established group within their ranks by the 1260s. In fact they first emerge as a distinct body in the years around 1200, when Bishop Marshall (1194–1206) donated the revenues of the important local church of Woodbury for their common use (Orme 1981, 81). Throughout the 13th and early 14th centuries numbers seem to have been maintained at twenty-four, each attached an individual canon; it seems likely that those attached to the households of canons who were resident in the Close normally lived in their houses, although others, presumably vicars of non-resident canons, commonly rented separate lodgings in the Close (*ibid.*, 83; Lega-Weekes 1915, 58). Here it is worth drawing attention to a distinctive aspect of the funding of the canons at Exeter. A considerable proportion of the dean and chapter income was paid from a common fund, and only to canons in residence, so the incentives to canons

to become resident were much stronger than in other secular cathedrals and the proportion of resident canons was evidently much higher here than elsewhere (Edwards 1967, 73–4; Fig. 1.2). The pattern whereby the vicar lived in a canon's house and ate at his table was therefore likely to have been especially strong here.

The impetus for founding the college came from Bishop Brantingham; he also paid for the building and secured a royal licence to endow it (Orme 1981, 85–7). His motivation, recorded in his Register (Hingeston-Randolph 1901–6, II, 675–6), was dissatisfaction with their conduct, regarding the vicars as insolent, given up to pleasure and negligent of their duties. There is often scope for casting doubt on accusations of this sort, but if confirmation of his claim were needed, it can be found in the contemporary series of Mayors' Court Rolls, which are an especially rich source of information about late 14th-century Exeter. Professor Maryanne Kowaleski's study of these rolls indicates that its junior clergy were among the most troublesome and violent sectors of Exeter's population (*pers comm*). Brantingham believed that a major cause of such evils was their dispersal and lack of supervision; he spelled out his intention to reform them by founding the college. Some vicars at least seem to have shown initial enthusiasm for the project (perhaps those who had rented lodgings in the Close and who may, therefore, have benefited financially?) but upon completion of the college in 1387 they proved unwilling to move in. Only the threat of excommunication finally persuaded them to do so, well over a year after the college was finished (Orme 1981, 85–7).

In her study of English secular cathedrals Kathleen Edwards (1967, 282–3) characterised the late 15th and early 16th centuries as a time when vicars choral experienced decreasing incomes, declining numbers, eroded privileges and relaxation in the rules for their common life. It is therefore interesting that there is substantial evidence that the opposite was the case at Exeter, where there are many signs that the vicars shared in the flourishing state of church life on the eve of the Reformation. The dramatic upturn in the local economy after *c.*1470, first identified by Eleanor Carus-Wilson (1963), was no doubt an underlying factor here. The endowments of Bishop Oldham (1504–1519) raised the college income to a total estimated in the *Valor Ecclesiasticus* in 1535 as £204 – an improvement of perhaps twenty per cent in their income since the late 15th century (Orme 1981, 89). The figure almost matched the £208 of the considerably larger number of vicars choral at Wells (nominally 50 compared to the twenty-four at Exeter: Hill 1998, 290). The numbers of vicars were also maintained at a high level. They had fallen as low as about sixteen in the

1420s, but had been restored to twenty in the 1430s; numbers were maintained at this level throughout the early 16th century. There are signs that the communal life of the vicars was strengthened rather than eroded at this time. Nicholas Orme (1981, 87–8) showed that, from the foundation of the college, bishops had periodically attempted to enforce the practice of eating in common, but the older customs of eating out of hall, whether at the tables of the canons or by purchase from townspeople, continued through the 15th century. Shortly after Bishop Oldham's appointment to Exeter in 1504, however, plans were drawn up for the establishment of regular common meals, and these became established at least by 1510 (*ibid.*). Again, there were developments in the provision of services as new daily masses were added to the long-established

ones. No doubt, however, these signs of vigour had their limitations; Orme (*ibid.*, 90) noted that, whilst they had a library, there was no evidence that the vicars ever engaged in scholarship, evangelism or pastoral work of any significance.

The site

The site chosen for the college, a plot to the west of the cathedral backing onto South Street (Fig. 5.1), was very restricted, squashed between the cathedral cemetery and parish church of St Mary Major to the north and the Deanery to the south, an area measuring *c.*58 x 25–35m (*c.*192 x 84–115 feet)[5]. The northern boundary, formed in part by the side of St Mary Major church, extended in an irregular curving line to South Street[6]. It is likely to represent part of the

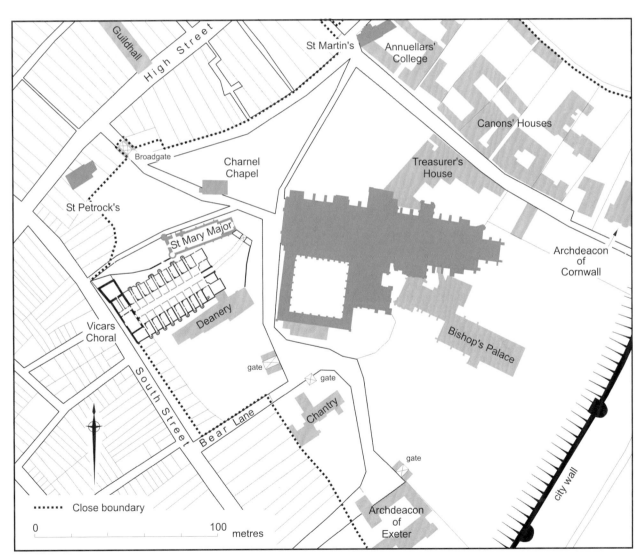

Fig. 5.1. Vicars choral of Exeter Cathedral. The plan of the Close c.1530. Where known, the late medieval ground plans and tenement boundaries of properties in the Close are shown; otherwise the earliest known plans are used. Property divisions outside the Close are taken from the OS 1:500 plan of Exeter of 1876 (drawing Tony Ives, copyright Exeter Archaeology)

boundary of an ancient enclosure. By contrast the boundary with the Deanery was precisely straight, and is likely to represent the subdivision of an older enclosure upon the establishment of the Deanery in 1225. At the centre of the plot lay Kalendarhay, a street which may have formed a component of the late Saxon town plan, being one of a sequence of parallel streets on this side of South Street. The street name – the *haga* or enclosure of the Kalendar brethren – refers to the fraternity of townspeople and clergy who occupied the site prior to the foundation of the college in the 1380s. Nicholas Orme has examined the history of the fraternity (1977). They had certainly come into existence by the reign of Henry I and may have originated in pre-Norman times. Not much is known of the character of their buildings; although they included a hall it is doubtful whether there were also lodgings. If there had been, however, it is possible that the general layout of the vicars' college reflected at least in part the disposition of their earlier buildings.

The college buildings

The layout of the college is known from four 19th-century plans: that by Coldridge (1819), the dean and chapter lease plan, drawn by Cornish (1850), the Ordnance Survey 1:500 (1876) and a plan of Messrs Drew (1884)[7]. These are progressively more detailed, so the best-recorded buildings are those which stood longest (Figs. 5.2 a-c and 5.8). Within the newly defined plot, attention was evidently given to achieving a symmetrical layout within the irregular site: the main buildings were laid out from a centreline parallel to the boundary with the Deanery, running from the centre of the inner gatehouse to the centre of the hall. According to an entry of 1388 in Bishop Brantingham's Register, the primary college buildings, built with all possible dispatch and satisfactorily constructed during the year just elapsed, comprised hall, chambers, kitchen and all other buildings necessary for the communal life (Lega-Weekes 1915, 48). Quite what the other buildings may have included might be indicated by later pre-Reformation sources, which mention the common exchequer or chequer chamber, the library, the lime-house, larder and pantry, a cook's chamber and the gate (*ibid.*, 50; Orme 1981, 87–8).

Even though the building programme can have lasted no more than four years (1383–7), there are signs that progress was piecemeal. The lodgings on the north side can never have been completely uniform; Ashworth's careful painting (Fig. 5.3) shows variations in the widths of doorways and the forms of the relieving arches over windows which were presumably primary features. Chanter (1933, 7) noted that the walls of the lodgings on the south

side were thicker than those on the north, a point evident in the lease plan of 1850 (Fig. 5.2b), which also records some irregularities in the planning of the northern range – notably between Nos. 6 and 7.

The master mason is not recorded, but there is a strong candidate. In 1377 Robert Lesyngham was engaged by the dean and chapter to design and supervise the construction of the cathedral's new cloisters (Harvey 1987, 181; Bishop and Prideaux 1922, 8–9, 91). He continued to supervise the project until 1394 and was very highly paid. He designed the new head of the great east window of 1389–90 and the north porch of the west front[8] and was also engaged in 1387 to repair houses in the cathedral Close (Harvey 1987, 181; *idem* 1978). The cathedral fabric rolls for the years 1376–87 do not survive, however, and his movements in the early 1380s, when the college was planned, are unknown. Even so, it would have been surprising if any other master was given this important commission. That said, no close match has been found among the few surviving architectural details in the college hall to Lesyngham's documented works, and the hall tracery contrasts with the Perpendicular windows of Lesyngham's work in the cathedral and the cloisters of what is now Gloucester Cathedral.

The hall

The hall was of three bays (Figs. 5.4, 5.5 and 5.6), the walls largely of veined volcanic stone of the Exeter volcanic series, the external faces of neat coursed ashlar, the internal faces of roughly coursed rubble, formerly plastered. Beer stone was employed for the mouldings of the windows and most of the surviving doorway; the latter also used Triassic sandstone and Salcombe stone. Its external dimensions are 13.69 x 8.10m and internal dimensions 12.18 x 6.13m. The bay divisions are marked on the east side by projecting buttresses, predominantly of vesicular volcanic trap, a stone which lends itself more readily to dressing than the veined variety. One corresponding buttress projecting into South Street was recorded prior to its removal in 1830, and others can be presumed (Fig. 5.4). The hall was lit by three windows (perhaps originally four – see below), each with a pair of lights with a transom and a quatrefoil in its head, the openings with cusped rere-arches, unusual in a south-west English context. At the north end the conventional arrangement of a central doorway leading to a passage and a detached kitchen beyond can be seen in the lease plan of 1850 (Fig. 5.2b). The battered jamb of the flanking doorway to the east still survives (Fig. 5.4) whilst part of the corresponding doorway to the west is visible in a pencil drawing of *c*.1830, which looks along the screens passage of the hall (WCSL B/Exeter D/6952). Oddly, the hall roof,

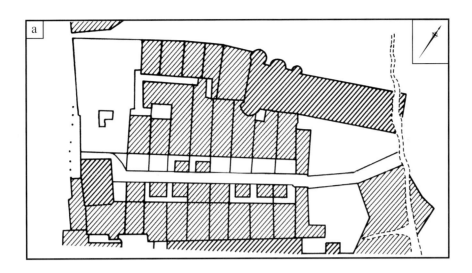

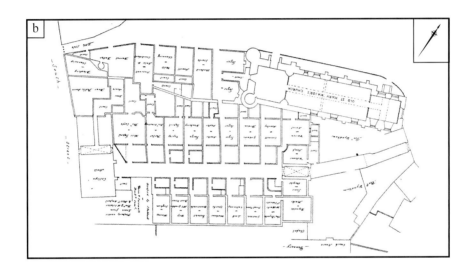

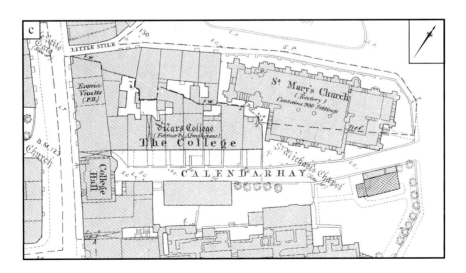

Figs. 5.2a, b and c. Vicars choral of Exeter Cathedral. Plans of the college: (a) Re-drawn from Coldridge's Ms. map of 1819. (b) The Cornish plan of 1850, re-drawn by Harbottle Reed and published in Chanter (1933, Pl XVII). (c) The Ordnance Survey 1: 500 map of 1876. Common scale 1: 750. (drawing Tony Ives, copyright Exeter Archaeology)

Fig. 5.3. Edward Ashworth's painting of the northern lodgings. The lower end of the hall is to the extreme left, abutted by the house of the custos of the college. The view was painted shortly after the rebuilding of the Larder House in 1870–1. (photo and copyright, Devon and Exeter Institution)

under which the Exeter Diocesan Architectural Society met for a century (1841–1940), seems to have escaped any form of record, save the brief comments of Lega-Weekes (1915, 55) that it 'was arch-braced' and Chanter (1933, 8) that it was of 'a usual fourteenth-century type'. One detail of its construction is evident from the trenches in its walls that mark the positions of its timbers: the roof was raised when the walls had reached the height of 4.30m. The top lift of walling was built around the feet of the principals and carried up to the upper faces of the common rafters; sloping trenches in the surviving wall tops mark their former positions. In his study of a later medieval example of this practice at Bowhill, Exeter, Stuart Blaylock has used the term 'beam-filling' (forthcoming).

Observing the apparently functionless gable over the end bay of the hall on the South Street frontage and the signs that the window of late 14th-century style below it had been rebuilt, David Stocker (2001, 597) suggested that the dais might originally have been lit by a projecting oriel comparable to those recognised at York, Chichester and Wells. Unfortunately, however, a different sequence of events accounts for these features. The gable, which accommodated a window, was one of a series inserted into the range in the late 16th century following the building of the city yarn market in South Street, whose construction necessitated the blocking of the medieval window lower in the wall. Following the removal of the yarn market in the 19th century the medieval window was unblocked and restored in 1901 (Chanter 1933, 38); this must have entailed the reconstruction of its head.

Other rooms in the South Street range

A large room abutted the southern end of the hall. Examination of its one surviving wall – the one shared with the hall (Fig. 5.4) – shows that it must have been a tall room of the same height as the hall, and that there was no communication between the two in the manner of the chambers in equivalent positions known at Chichester (above Fig 4.2) and proposed at Hereford (Fig. 6.3). A large splayed window opening in its south wall was recorded in a plan of *c*.1830 (Fig. 5.4 offers the best fit we could achieve). The room's function is not firmly known, but this was clearly not a lodging. Of the communal rooms whose site is unknown the most likely candidate is, perhaps, the library. The service range extended up South Street from the hall. Prior to its demolition in 1870–1 it consisted of two principal rooms: the Larder House, which abutted the hall, and the college kitchen, separated from the Larder House by a small courtyard. A revealing pair of photographs taken when the range was undergoing demolition (Figs. 5.7a and b) and several early 19th-century drawings provide information about these structures. Both displayed the narrow courses of ashlar still visible in the hall, and the technique of 'beam-filling' seen there, so may be presumed to belong to the same phase of building in the 1380s. The internal arrangements of the Larder House included buttery and pantry, below which were cellars, recorded in some leases of the late 17th and 18th centuries, with a room in the loft space. The kitchen was separated from the Larder House by a small yard, subsequently infilled. The photographs

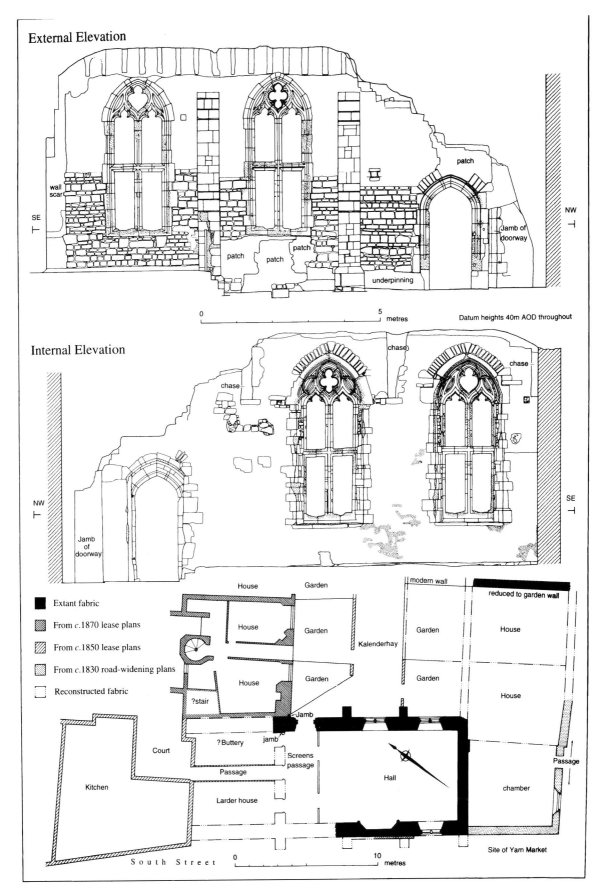

Fig. 5.4. Vicars choral of Exeter Cathedral. Elevations of the standing east wall of the hall, with a composite plan of the hall range and adjacent lodgings (drawing and copyright, Exeter Archaeology)

Fig. 5.5. Vicars choral of Exeter Cathedral. The South Street frontage of the hall in 1933. Some evidence of the long series of changes to its fabric may be detected in the photograph: the insertion of a fireplace stack in 1507–8; the addition of a weathering for the roof of the city yarn market of 1538 or its rebuilding in 1571; late 16th-century gables and windows; the insertion of the left doorway, probably in the late 17th century; the removal of projecting buttresses and stack in 1830–3; underpinning following the lowering of South Street, probably in the same years; insertion of the doorway to the right before 1876 and restoration of the medieval window in 1902 (source, Chanter 1933)

The rows of lodgings

The Exeter vicars' lodgings conformed to the type usual in colleges of vicars choral from the mid 14th century, consisting of regularly planned parallel terraces of individual houses, each with a separate front door, a ground-floor hall and first-floor chamber (e.g. Rees Jones 2001, 391–5). The choice is of some interest, since the alternative form of lodging – the 'staircase and chamber' type – was familiar in Devon. This had been used in the early 14th century at Okehampton Castle (Higham *et al.* 1982, 62–5) and was employed on a grand scale at Dartington Hall, built immediately after the college *c.*1388–1400 (Emery 1970, 203–58). There were eight lodgings on each side of the vicars' close in the early 19th century, but by that time the house nearest the hall on each side had been created by amalgamating two earlier lodgings, so there were originally eighteen in the rows. One cannot quite exclude the possibility that there were additional lodgings for vicars elsewhere in the college: two in the inner gatehouse range (see below), or perhaps one outside the quadrangle beside the small courtyard to the north known as 'the Throng'. Support for the likelihood that only eighteen were planned can be found in the bequest of £12 7s. by William Gervys in 1401, which was to add eighteen chimneys (Orme 1981, 88). This has been taken as evidence that the lodgings were at first unheated, but the example of Bishop Bekynton's reconstruction of the chimneys at Wells (p. 134–5 below) illustrates the fact that such expenditure could have entailed the building of new chimneys on existing stacks. Whether eighteen, twenty or even twenty-one lodgings were provided, however, it seems clear enough that the full complement of twenty-four vicars could never have been accommodated individually. At Exeter this could be taken to show that it was presumed that numbers would never return to their pre-Black Death

taken during its demolition show the kitchen's very substantial roof structure of two bays, with arch-braced principal trusses, each bay with a single tier of wind braces. Little is known of its internal arrangements; Chick (1918, 4) records that the 'original ogee arch of the fireplace' was found *c.*1871. This must have been in the north gable wall; its stack may be that visible in the plan of 1884 (Fig. 5.8). To its north lay the college oven, which was leased separately in the 17th and 18th centuries (EC D & C/VC/3437, 21711, 3402, 3414). Its form is known only from 19th-century plans (Fig. 5.2).

Fig. 5.6. Vicars choral of Exeter Cathedral. The interior of the hall looking south, showing early 16th-century panelling and fireplace (source, The Borough Pocket Guide to Exeter *c.1910)*

a   *b*

Figs. 5.7a and b. Vicars choral of Exeter Cathedral. Photographs showing the service range in the course of demolition in 1870. (a) The South Street frontage. The college kitchen with brick stack to the left, the 'Larder House' to the right and a later roof infilling between them. (b) The rear of the college kitchen, with the lean-to roof of the brewhouse in the foreground. The workman stands on the lower gable wall of the kitchen (photos and copyright, Isca Collection, courtesy Mr Peter Thomas)

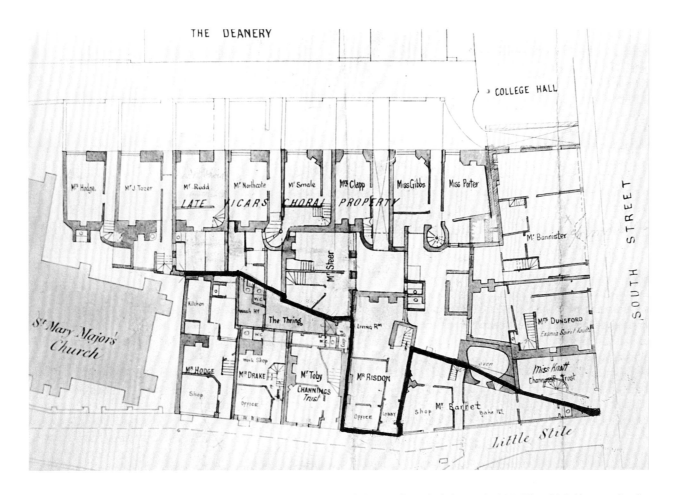

Fig. 5.8. Vicars choral of Exeter Cathedral. The Drew plan of the northern lodgings of 1884. The thick line marks the northern boundary of the college; north is at the foot of the page. (photo and copyright Westcountry Studies Library)

levels, but the same problem arises elsewhere in earlier contexts. Despite the restrictions of the site, the lodgings were not meanly built. Chanter (1933, 7) gives their external dimensions (presumably on the north side) as 14 x 23 feet (*c.* 4.25 x 7m) excluding the projecting stair; the average internal dimensions of all the lodgings were *c.* 4 x 6.5m. They were in fact quite generous by national standards, being only marginally smaller than those at Wells and larger than those at Lichfield and Chichester, as well as some more prestigious establishments, such as St George's, Windsor (Pantin 1959, 258). Their gardens, on the other hand, were tiny.

The Drew plan of 1884 (Fig. 5.8) and Ashworth's view of the frontage of the north range (Fig. 5.3) record much of the arrangements of the lodgings in the late 19th century, and allow suggestions to be made about their medieval layout. The front door-way was set at the edge of each property, giving access to a through passage which led to a staircase (three or four newel stairs survived in 1884), pro-jecting from the rear wall. A screen along the passage separated it from the only ground-floor room, which was lit by a two- or three-light window in the front wall. Little is known of arrangements on the first floor; the single-light windows of lodgings 6 and 8 were probably original features (Fig. 5.3, right side; No. 8 is shown in the drawing by James Crocker of 1885 – Crocker 1886, pl. XXXI). Presumably there was formerly a second symetrically placed window in each case, since the survivors were placed at the corners of the rooms. The rows seem not to have had garderobes (see below).

Two minor fragments of the lodgings survived the demolitions. First, embedded in the outer face of the hall is the jamb of the front doorway of the first of the lodgings on the north side. It confirms the impression of Ashworth's painting that these doorways were of volcanic trap, contrasting with the Beer stone dress-ings of the hall. Second, a length of party wall – that between lodgings 16 and 17 on the south side – still stands, although reduced in height to *c.* 1.7m and underpinned by later fabric. It marked the boundary of the demolitions of 1850, and later came to enclose the Deanery garden. Built of veined volcanic rubble comparable to the inner faces of the hall, it shows that the divisions between the lodgings, at least on the south side, were of stone, not timber-framed, as at some other colleges, such as Chichester (p. 27 above).

The inner gatehouse and associated rooms

At the east end of the lodgings was a range of rooms at whose centre was a gatehouse of three storeys with a vaulted entrance of three bays (Figs. 5.9 and 5.10). The room above served in the late 19th century as the Record Room or Muniment Room (Lega-Weekes 1915, 57; Chick 1918, 4; Chanter 1933, 6). It seems likely that this was its original purpose; the possibility that it was at first a chapel can be excluded, since the college did not have one (Orme 1981, 88; *idem* 1991, 166–8). The Common Exchequer or Chequer Cham-ber, in which the common chest was held (*idem* 1981, 87), was certainly also on the first floor of this range in the late 16th century, and presumably before the Reformation. Its position would have allowed tenants to come and pay their rents without needing to gain access to the rest of the college. A similar layout has been noted at Wells, where the Muniment Room and Exchequer Room adjoined in the equivalent range (p. 128–31 below) and the operation of its Exchequer has recently been explored in detail by Hill (1998, 289). On the ground floor of this range the rooms occupying the corners of the quadrangle were larger than lodgings, and were presumably for communal use. Chanter noted that one had formerly been the vicars' common room and he suggested that one may have been the medieval library (1933, 7). A lease of 1582 simply describes two of these ground floor rooms as 'Low Rooms'. All were let as lodgings after the end of the 16th century[9]. Finally, outside the quadrangle lay the vicars' common garden, later sometimes grandly called the Great Garden, originally apparently unenclosed.

Late medieval changes

Nicholas Orme noted documentary records of vari-ous improvements to the college during the 15th century. The eighteen chimneys of 1401 have been noted above. In 1470 the college garden was en-closed with a wall at a cost of £20, followed by the installation of a water supply by 1497 (Orme 1981, 88). Examination of the college plan indicates that the enclosed gardens in front of each lodging must also have been secondary features – a point evident at the junction of the hall with the garden of lodging 1, where access from the centre of the quadrangle to the screens passage of the hall was provided by reducing the garden to an awkward triangle (Fig. 5.8). Since the doorways to the gardens took the form of two-centred arches of moulded stone, it seems very probable that the enclosing walls were of late medieval date. The date of the little rectangular buildings placed in most gardens is more uncertain. These served, at least from the early 17th century, as privies but they may have been late medieval additions. According to a document of 1636, none of the lodgings on the south side and few on the north side had garderobes; night soil was emptied daily from barrels or bins in the front gardens (Chanter 1933, 24).

There were also changes to the internal arrange-

Fig. 5.9. Vicars choral of Exeter Cathedral. View looking eastward towards the gatehouse in May 1850, immediately before the first demolitions (photo and copyright, Westcountry Studies Library: Drawings, Medium B/EX.)

Fig. 5.10. Vicars choral of Exeter Cathedral. The Inner Gatehouse, viewed from within the college after the demolitions of 1850 and 1866, and before its removal in 1872. (photo, courtesy of Dr Sadru Bhanji)

ments of the hall. There is no evidence of a primary fireplace and it presumably had an open hearth. A richly carved new fireplace, whose stack was clearly an insertion (Fig. 5.5), was added on the South Street frontage. Whether the space it occupied had formerly been plain wall or had held a window is unknown; the latter possibility is shown in Fig. 5.11. The fireplace lintel bore the arms of those bishops who were especially associated with the vicars, from Marshall (1194–1206) to Oldham (1504–1519). A published photograph of 1933 shows either the date 1507 or 1508 on one of its capitals (Lega-Weekes 1933, plate opposite 359)[10]. This was one of a series of grand late medieval armorial fireplaces which were dramatic features of the architecture of Exeter's Close and which neatly expressed the relative status of the houses in which they were installed. The most imposing, and the earliest datable, was that provided by Bishop Courtenay in the Bishop's Palace in 1478–87, followed by two in the Chantry and three in the Deanery, of which two bore the initials of Vesey (Dean 1509–19, Bishop 1519–1551); remnants of a further highly carved fireplace have also been recorded in recent years at the Archdeaconry of Exeter.

A second addition to the hall, traditionally associated with John Ryse (Treasurer 1518–1531) was the provision of wall panelling of quite remarkable richness: three registers of tall linenfold, above which rose a further superbly carved register of arcading and foliage panels, surmounted by a band of Renaissance roundels and grotesques; the latter were perhaps of slightly later date. When complete this woodwork transformed the hall into what was arguably the most sumptuously appointed of any vicars' college in England, amply reflecting the favoured financial position of the Exeter college.

The outer gatehouse was probably also built by Bishop Oldham, following the enclosure of the garden behind it in 1470. Although its most obvious details were of the late 17th and 18th centuries, prior to demolition it retained above the entrance arch Oldham's arms, and those of England between two mutilated niches (Hamilton Rogers 1877, 407–8; Chanter 1933, 6 and plate 2)[11]. Like the nearby gatehouse to the Deanery, also probably an early 16th-century structure, its substantial later remodelling may reflect damage during the Civil War.

Post-Reformation changes

The loss of revenues in the years 1547–57, and the consequent sharp reduction in the college's affluence (Payne 1983, 102–5), may be presumed to underlie the structural changes to the South Street range. In 1576, 'for the increase of their poor living .... [the vicars] .... set out to make a shop of some void rooms' in this range; their actions brought a violent con-

frontation with their secular neighbours, who resented this commercial enterprise (*ibid.*). The rooms in question were probably in the Larder House, which was leased later that year (EC D & C/VC/ 21711), following the lease of the college oven in 1575 (*ibid.*). At some stage in the late 16th or 17th centuries a series of five gables and windows was inserted into the Larder House and hall, and into the room south of the hall. These are shown in several early 19th-century views; Figs. 5.11 and 5.12 have been compiled from their combined evidence. The changes included the creation of a first-floor room in the space above the screens passage, a development which was commonplace in the 16th century in the vernacular tradition of South-West England. Since the top registers of the early 16th-century panelling in the hall did not extend across the screens, an extra register of arcaded panelling, cruder than the earlier work, was added to raise it to the height of that on the other walls.

When one compares the changes to the lodgings at Exeter with those at other colleges, notably Wells, Chichester and Hereford, it seems that the character of late medieval and post-Reformation changes here was different from that in other colleges. At Exeter most lodgings had added attic rooms, with some new fenestration, and there were a few new fireplaces set diagonally in ground-floor rooms, but the practice of knocking together two adjacent lodgings to form a more spacious house was uncommon. In 1850, fourteen of the eighteen houses still retained, essentially, their medieval ground plan, as well as many apparently primary doorways and windows.

The pattern in the reduction in the vicars' numbers, both before and after the Reformation, must have been one factor in this contrast. At Exeter the nominal twenty-four of the later middle ages were reduced in 1547 to twenty (the existing customary number long before this), then to ten lay vicars and an elite group of priest-vicars (notionally six but in fact only four) after 1563 (Orme 1981, 90–1; Payne 1983, 102–3, 113). Numbers subsequently reduced to four priest-vicars and eight lay-vicars; they stayed at that level until the dissolution of the college in 1933. So after 1563 there must regularly have been six or more vacant lodgings in the college, and four or more after the amalgamations of the pairs of lodgings beside the hall. Each vicar, however, retained the right to occupy or sub-let a lodging, so there was always a very fragmented pattern of occupancy. The earliest surviving leases of lodgings in the rows date to the 1580s and several survive from the 1590s: the practice of leasing lodgings was common thereafter[12]. Following the sale of the college in the Commonwealth, when the hall served as a wool hall, no attempt at any form of community life was made after the Restoration, apart from the

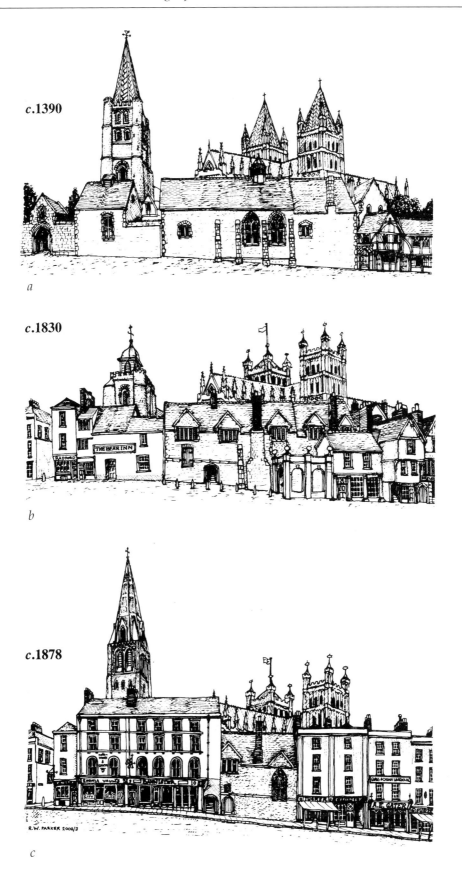

*c.*1390

a

*c.*1830

b

*c.*1878

c

Figs. 5.11 a, b and c. Vicars choral of Exeter Cathedral. Reconstructions of the South Street frontage, (b) in 1830 and (c) in 1878, based on contemporary drawings and photographs. (a) shows a suggestion of the same c.1390; the form of Little Style (left) is conjectural (drawing Richard Parker, copyright Exeter Archaeology)

Fig. 5.12. Vicars choral of Exeter Cathedral. Richard Parker's reconstruction of the college c.1580. In the foreground is South Street; the yarn market abuts the hall range. Surrounding the quadrangle of the college are 'The Throng' (centre left), St Mary Major church (upper left), the college garden and Audit House (upper) and the Deanery (right) (drawing Richard Parker, copyright Exeter Archaeology)

annual Christmas feast, paid for by the dean and chapter. After 1660 even the college kitchen was let continuously, later becoming the Bear Inn. Very few priest vicars occupied their houses, and only some of the lay vicars did so. Some moved to the cloisters; two built for themselves new chambers over gates elsewhere in the Close. By the mid 19th century only a single lodging was actually occupied by a vicar. The census of 1851 records no fewer than 32 separate households in the college. Many were let to scholars and single women, including several dressmakers and a washerwoman (1850 lease plan; White's *Directory of Devon* of 1850; 1851 census returns). By that time the college was regarded as unsanitary and sinking into decay.

Conclusion

In the form and development of the college buildings at Exeter there are of course many similarities to the other vicars' colleges, especially those of modest size. It is however the differences which seem particularly interesting and unexpected. The absence of a college at Exeter before 1380s might be seen simply as old-fashioned (Orme 1981, 85) but it may equally reflect the strength of the tradition of resident canons at Exeter, whereby its vicars lived settled lives in their households. The maintenance of the numbers of vicars at a fairly consistent level throughout the period from the 1380s until the Reformation and beyond at Exeter was also unusual. Accommodation for a complement of vicars fairly close to the number of lodgings in the college was still needed after 1547, and this may explain why the pattern of amalgamations which had begun elsewhere before the Reformation did not obtain here. By the mid 19th century such close-packed tiny homes were seen as suitable only for the poor and they fell into decay. Had amalgamations taken place, the lodgings would perhaps have been less vulnerable. Ironically, the very success of the late medieval college proved eventually to be an element in its demise.

Notes

1. Royal licence was granted to the dean and chapter in 1383 to acquire lands etc. to the use of the vicars for building a house for their residence (EC D & C/VC/5370/14). It was claimed in 1383 that building work had already begun (Orme 1981, 86); work was certainly in progress in April 1387. By September of that year Brantingham ordered the vicars to move into their lodgings (*ibid.*). Brantingham's Register records the college foundation date as 4 November 1388 (*ibid*; Lega-Weekes 1915, 48). The college was formally incorporated by royal charter in 1401 (Chanter 1933, 2, 9–10).

2. The sequence of demolitions was as follows: The five houses at the centre of the row, which backed onto the Deanery, were demolished in 1850 (EC D & C/VC/ 5359). Two adjacent lodgings to the east followed in 1856 (EC D & C Act 2.4.1856). Two in the north-west corner were demolished in 1866 to allow the extension of St Mary Major church (Chanter 1933, 36), followed by the gatehouse in 1872 (Lega-Weekes 1915, 57) and the last lodgings in 1893 (Chanter 1933, 38).

3. A further useful recent contribution to the study of the medieval vicars has been Ben Collingwood's thesis presenting the *Solutiones Ministrorum* of the years 1468–1500, which list in order of seniority the vicars choral and secondaries on the cathedral payroll, from which the careers of some of the vicars can be reconstructed (Collingwood 2001).

4. The sole exception was a length of the foundation of the gatehouse range, exposed in the excavation of 1976 (site archive).

5. For a useful general discussion of the layout in the context of contemporary colleges and secular buildings see Emery 1970, 131–3.

6. The boundary on the north side has been plotted from the following lease plans of dean and chapter properties dated between 1769 and 1856: EC D7/636/4a; P5/2/2; 6004/3/39a; 34/75528; P/5/3. So constricted was the site that the dean initially opposed the proposed college as it would be injurious to the Deanery; he consented only if the new buildings did not obstruct the hall, or the lights of his chapel (Lega-Weekes 1915, 46). In the event, however, the lodgings were only *c.* 10–12m from the dean's hall, and their construction probably accounts for the blocking of four 14th-century windows in its north side (*ibid.*, 77).

7. The original of this plan is not known to survive, but it was photographed by Weaver Baker in the 1930s; a photographic print made by him is preserved in West-Country Studies Library.

8. The porch is undocumented but can be attributed with some confidence to Lesyngham, since the mouldings are matched in the Gloucester Cathedral cloisters. I am grateful to Dr R Morris for confirmation of this point.

9. The lease EC D & C/VC/2/122669, dated 1799, records the conversion in the mid 18th century of the rooms between the gate and the Deanery; they became lodging rooms, a parlour, kitchen, pantry and cellar. A series of leases survives for the Low Rooms with chamber and two cock-lofts above (EC D & C/VC/ 5328 to 3466). They describe them as lying 'between the common garden on the east and the chamber adjoining the Chequer on the north'.

10. The fireplace and its heraldry are more fully described and discussed elsewhere (Chanter 1933, 8; Lega-Weekes 1915; 53–4; *idem* 1933; Orme 1981, 89). The date has been wrongly published as 1505 and 1518.

11. The first lease of 'the north part of the outer great gate of their habitation in Kallendar-hay' with 'chambers, enterclosures and rooms' is dated 1623 (EC D & C/ VC/3410). A lease of 1661 (EC D & C/VC/3425) mentions a new chamber.

12. Ian Payne (1983, 118) had some reservations about the claim of Chanter (1933, 24) that this was really the case in the early 17th century. The evidence of the leases of properties in Kalendarhay, however, shows that Chanter was right.

6

'A Brave and Ancient Priviledg'd Place'. The Hereford Vicars Choral College

Ron Shoesmith

Introduction – the early cathedral

The foundation of the Hereford diocese, although not necessarily the cathedral or the city, is usually considered to date from AD 676 when Sexwulf, the Mercian bishop at Lichfield, granted a church and land to Putta. However, the earliest documentary evidence for a cathedral at Hereford is in AD 803 when Wulfheard described himself as *Herefordensis Ecclesiae Episcopus* (Colgrave and Mynors 1969; Hillaby 1976, 44). Archaeological work has not produced any evidence for the original foundation of the cathedral but it has demonstrated the existence of a monastic establishment – later called St Guthlac's – in the Castle Green area, with burials dating from the 7th to the 11th centuries (Shoesmith 1980, 8–55).

The late 8th and early 9th centuries were an important period of growth for the city of Hereford. Either Offa, during his long reign as king of Mercia (757–96), or possibly one of the minor kings who followed him, was responsible for the expansion of Hereford. It grew from a minor religious centre, with a few scattered houses, to a planned royal town enclosed by a gradually evolving series of defences, the earliest of which was constructed about the middle of the 9th century. This plan still survives in the grid pattern of streets leading northwards from the line of King Street and Castle Street on each side of the present cathedral Close. The initial construction of a defensive line around the city in the mid 9th century, with gates at the northern end of Broad Street and western end of King Street, fossilised this plan and restricted the area in which the Anglo-Saxon cathedral precinct could expand. The growth of the Norman new town to the north of the Anglo-Saxon defences, the building of the castle to the east of the cathedral grounds, and the eventual construction of a bridge across the river, led to many of the streets in the Anglo-Saxon town diminishing in importance, and to the eventual closure of the central section of the original east–west road north of the cathedral (Shoesmith 1982, 70–95; 1992, 8–34).

The site of the pre-Norman cathedral is unknown, but has been assumed to be underneath or to the south of the present building. Referring to the Anglo-Saxon cathedral, John Duncumb (1804, 523–4) wrote:

> *'Its position is uncertain, but about 1650 Silas Taylor found, 'beyond the lines of the present building, and particularly towards the east, near the cloisters of the college, such stupendous foundations, such capitals and pedestals, such well-wrought bases for arches, and such rare engravings, and mouldings of friezes' as left little doubt in his mind that they were the foundations of the cathedral destroyed by Algar and Griffin'.*

The position as described could well apply to the eastern side of the chapter house yard (Fig. 6.1).

The cathedral built by Bishop Athelstan between 1030 and 1040 must have suffered in 1055 when the city was attacked by Gruffydd ap Llewelyn and, according to the Welsh chronicles, 'leaving nothing in the town but blood and ashes, and the walls rased to the ground'. The new cathedral was apparently stripped of its valuables, and may have been damaged, but it was not totally destroyed, for when Bishop Aethelstan died a year later he was buried 'in the church which he had built from the foundation' (ed. Jones 1952, 14–15; 1955, 25; *ASC*, 184–7; Thorpe 1848–9, i, 213–15).

The effect of the Norman conquest on Hereford may have been greater than that on many other towns. To protect his vulnerable western border, King William gave William FitzOsbern, Earl of Hereford, supreme powers in the border area from Chepstow in the south to Ludlow in the north. FitzOsbern saw Hereford as the heart of his defensive system of border castles and was doubtless

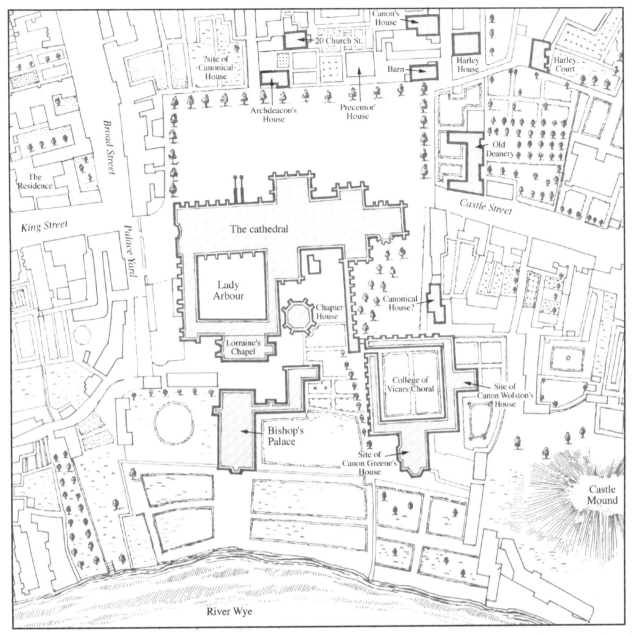

Fig. 6.1. Vicars choral of Hereford Cathedral. Schematic plan of the precinct, showing the location of the vicars choral college and several of the canons' houses (drawing Brian Byron)

responsible for the castle built to the east of the cathedral which totally surrounded St Guthlac's monastic site. He was also responsible for the magnificent market place – in effect a new town – laid out to the north of the Anglo-Saxon defences (Whitehead 1982, 17; Shoesmith 1992, 15–20).

The Norman cathedral was probably founded by Bishop Reinhelm (1107–15). It was laid out adjoining the main east–west road of the Anglo-Saxon city, with the road leading down to the ford across the Wye close to its western end. Immediately to the south was the double chapel of St. Katherine and St. Mary Magdelene, built by Bishop Losinga (1079–95), of which one wall survives. Between the chapel and

the river were the grounds of the Bishop's Palace, the present palace having its origins in the great hall built by Bishop William de Vere in the late 12th century (Bannister 1924, 27–31).

Because of these buildings and the early 12th-century date for the Norman cathedral, there would seem to be little possibility of Aethelstan's cathedral being directly to the south of the present cathedral. The location suggested by Silas Taylor, close to the College, is therefore a strong possibility, with the alternative of the present cathedral being partly on the site of the earlier building.

Hereford was among a group of nine so-called secular cathedrals in the country and was administered by prebendary canons. After the Norman cathedral had been laid out, the scene was set for the houses where the canons were required to live to be arranged in a grand semi-circle around the new cathedral. Some of these sites can still be identified as they still include recognisable canonical houses (Fig. 6.1). The earliest is the so-called 'cathedral barn', at the north-eastern corner of the present Close, which includes part of a 13th-century aisled hall, whilst slightly further to the east is the late 14th-century ground-floor hall at Harley Court. North of the present Close is the late 14th-century first-floor hall at No.20 Church Street and the hall of No.3 St. John Street. Slightly more modern buildings, such as Harley House and the Old Deanery, are obvious sites for other canonical houses. Some of these canonical houses were apparently of considerable status – on 4th April 1466 Bishop Stanbury was transacting business 'in the great hall of the residence of Master John Greene, Canon' (ed. Bannister 1918b, 182; Shoesmith 2000).

It would seem that the open space around the cathedral may have been smaller at the beginning of the 13th century than it is at present, but the whole precinct, including the canonical houses and their grounds, was considerably larger than it is now. The precise boundaries are uncertain and there is no conclusive evidence to indicate if it was separately walled or defended.

The early vicars choral

It was during the late 11th and 12th centuries that the cathedral services and chants became more elaborate and complex, with some parts of the liturgy being sung (chapter 3 above). This sometimes created a problem, for the canons were not necessarily chosen for their singing ability (Knowles 1963, 539–59). In most parts of the country it was the practice for each canon to nominate and partly support his own singing vicar, but in Hereford it was somewhat different, for most of the vicars choral were appointed by the dean and chapter and paid from special endowment funds. The abbots of Lyre and Cormeilles, who held cathedral prebends, were expected to appoint four perpetual vicars, together with the dean, who had to appoint one. In addition there were four vicars attached to four different altars in the church. In 1237 Bishop Maidstone (1234–9) obtained the tithes of Diddlebury church to support six more vicars attached directly to the church and chosen by the dean and chapter (Edwards 1949, 261–3).

It was almost a century later, in 1330, that the tithes of Lugwardine and its dependent chapels were appropriated to provide the funds for a further ten vicars, again appointed by the dean and chapter (*ibid*, 263–4). In 1384 the revenues of the church at

Westbury were appropriated, but this created a problem as the vicars were not allowed to own property because they were not a corporation. In 1395 Richard II regularized the situation by incorporating the vicars choral as a college with the form and title of *collegium vicariorum in choro ecclesiae Herefordensis*. There were then 27 vicars, one of whom was elected as *custos*. They had a common seal and were able to acquire and hold property (ed. Bannister 1918a, 82–4; ed. Capes 1908, 253–5).

Their foundation charter indicates that the vicars already had a communal residence – a building some 120m to the east of the cathedral on the south side of Castle Street, parts of which still survive within the present No.29 (Bannister 1924, 165). Set back from the street, and now incorporated into a complex of later buildings, are the substantial remains of a ground-floor hall. Despite being fairly small in area, the hall was sufficiently tall for both first and attic floors to have been inserted at a later date. The walls were of coursed, dressed sandstone and at the north end the blocked matching doorways of the screens passage still survive. They have two-centred heads; a wave-moulded external chamfer survives partly intact in the western doorway. On each side of the hall are the remains of two very tall primary windows with two-centred heads, probably once of two lights. Later buildings and the insertion of new openings have obscured any other significant masonry detail (Morriss and Shoesmith 1995, 157–9).

The roof, now a feature in the attic room, is of nine quite narrow bays, and was clearly once open to the apex. Rows of peg-holes at the ends of the collars probably indicate the former presence of arch-braces, so it is likely that there were no tie beams. Above each of the collars a pair of cusped raking struts rise to the principals (Fig. 6.2). The trusses support two tiers of moulded purlins and a ridge-piece. The lower purlins and the ridge are supported by wind-braces. These are paired and

Fig. 6.2. Vicars choral of Hereford Cathedral. Part of the roof of No.29 Castle Street (photo Ken Hoverd, copyright City of Hereford Archaeology Unit)

triple-cusped, and the solid spandrels create decorative arches. The central cusps have pierced spandrels and are tipped by ornately carved fleurons. There were just two common rafters to each bay, square-sectioned and of thick scantling. There is no trace of smoke-blackening in the roof and no obvious position for a smoke-louvre, both of which would be expected had there been an open hearth. However, the southern portion of the roof has been radically rebuilt so an open hearth cannot be ruled out, especially as there is no obvious sign of a side stack.

There has not been any dendrochronological dating of this building, but all the available evidence indicates a constructional date in the second half of the 14th century. In the absence of accurate dating it is impossible to establish whether the hall was built specifically for the vicars choral, but it was presumably used as their communal hall. The layout of the rest of this early complex has not been established, but the hall's position relative to Castle Street may indicate that there was a range of buildings along the street frontage. There is now a 17th-century wing to the south-west of the hall and an 18th-century range towards the street.

Purpose-built college accommodation

It was almost 80 years after their incorporation that the vicars complained to Bishop John Stanbury (1453–74) that their dwelling was 'so distant from the church that through fear of evil-doers and the inclemency of the weather, many of them cannot go to the church at midnight to celebrate divine service'. The bishop must have viewed this seriously for on 18th October 1472 he obtained a licence from the king to provide them with a site for a new building. The licence indicates that the new site was to the east of the bishop's garden and that it included the grounds and canonical house of the late Canon John Greene and a vacant plot which had contained the house of the late Canon Reginald Wolston (ed. Bannister 1918b, 83).

The bishops had claimed and exercised control of the canonical houses from early times and this allowed Bishop Stanbury to assist the vicars, whom he evidently favoured. Canon Wolston apparently died some time after 1411 and it has been suggested that his house had burnt down and the plot left vacant for some time (Marshall 1938, 20–9). Canon Greene died shortly before 31st March 1472 and his house appears to have been in good condition and of some importance. It seems likely that it would have been appropriated by the vicars for their own use, probably as their refectory or common room. Assuming that it was re-used, then its position would have been one of the determining factors in the siting and design of the new College. It is suggested that Canon Greene's

house occupied a prime site on the gravel terrace overlooking the river and as such would have been in a similar situation to the 12th-century Bishop's Palace, a little further upstream. Accepting this, it is most likely that Canon Greene's house was the building that was replaced by the present college hall in the latter part of the 17th century (Fig. 6.3).

A vertical construction break at the north end of the present hall's east wall may well indicate that the south range of the new college cloisters was built against an existing structure, and later references would seem to demonstrate the retention of Canon Greene's hall together with a solar or service wing. Thus in 1590 the organist John Bull was given the use of 'ye great upper chamber behind ye College Hall' (*Hereford Acts*, 1590) and two years later John Farrant was given 'ye lower chamber behind ye hall next unto the saffron garden for his use to teach and instruct ye choristers' (*Hereford Acts*, 1592). As the present hall dates mainly from the second half of the 17th century, these descriptions must apply to an earlier building on the site. They imply that there was a range, at least two storeys high, to the south of the college hall and probably attached to it. This may well have been a similar structure to that attached to the Bishop's Palace, which has been identified as a three-storey subsidiary chamber block over a semi-basement built into the edge of the River Wye terrace (Blair 1987, 59–67).

The site provided by Bishop Stanbury for the new college covered about two acres, but almost half of it is at a lower level and would have been susceptible to flooding from the Wye. The southern extremity of the present college hall is, to all intents and purposes, the practicable southerly limit for building. To the east of the site, and separated from it by little more than a track, was the high moated mound on which the great tower of Hereford castle stood (Fig. 6.1). Some repairs, including the re-roofing of the tower, had been carried out in the early 15th century, but when Leland visited the city 100 years later he noted that although

> 'the hole castle tendithe toward ruine ... the dungeon [great tower] of the castle is highe and very stronge, havynge the utter waull or warde 10 towres forma semicirculari, *and one great towre in the inner warde*' (ed. Smith 1964, ii, 64–5).

It was underneath the shadow of this great tower that the new college was built.

To the north was part of the cathedral Close and at least one canonical house would have been positioned between the college site and the western end of Castle Street. To the west there was, and still is, the Bishop's Palace garden; the stone wall that forms the boundary to the garden runs at an angle to all the buildings in the area and is evidently ancient. The design of the neighbouring part of the college is such that it can be assumed that this wall, or its predecessor on the same

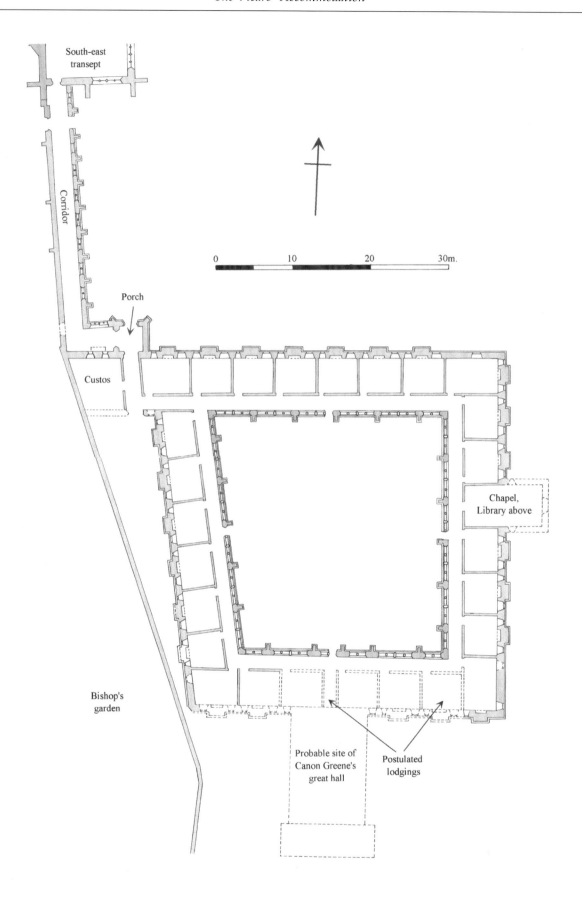

Fig. 6.3. Vicars choral of Hereford Cathedral. Postulated plan of the original claustral layout of the college (drawing and copyright City of Hereford Archaeological Unit)

alignment, pre-dates the construction of the college buildings.

The main residential accommodation for the college had therefore to be built within an irregularly-shaped space and had to provide chambers for the 27 vicars together with a chapel and library. The design was a typical claustral plan similar to that in many monastic establishments. Detailed surveys carried out by the City of Hereford Archaeology Unit (now Archaeological Investigations Ltd.) during restoration work in several parts of the cloisters have provided additional information about the original design and the constructional phases (Shoesmith and Hook 1987; Shoesmith 1988; Morriss 1989; Stone 1991; Morriss 1991a, b, c and d).

It has already been suggested that the cloister was built immediately to the north of the hall of Canon Greene's house, and it would seem that the asymmetry of the western range was caused by the position of the house and the limitations enforced by the existing boundaries. It would have been practicable to have built the western range at right angles to the

remainder of the complex, but this would have excluded from the main cloister the two lodgings at the western end of the north range. There may have been a late change in the design during the construction works, perhaps when it was decided that a chapel and library should replace one lodging on the eastern side. This would have meant that an additional lodging had to be included within the northern range, thus extending its length. Even then, one lodging, assumed to be that of the *custos*, was outside the cloister and adjacent to the entry (Morriss and Shoesmith 1995, 162–3).

This theory is based on the assumption that the four ranges were constructed in separate building phases, for which there is some evidence (Fig. 6.4). At the north-eastern corner a timber framework continues the line of the west wall of the east range throughout the width of the north range. A second frame, immediately to the west, is actually the end supporting frame of the north range. It would thus seem that the east range pre-dates the north one and that the timber framework was designed to act as an

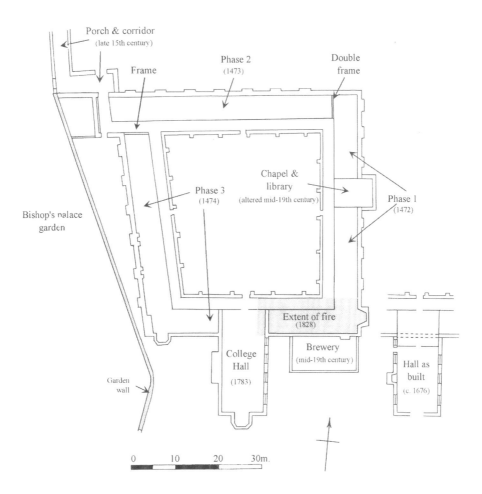

Fig. 6.4. Vicars choral of Hereford Cathedral. Outline plan showing postulated building phases of the college (drawing and copyright, City of Hereford Archaeology Unit)

external wall until the north range was added. A similar feature at the western end of the north range suggests that the western range was later than the north range. However, the evidence from the south-western corner suggests that the southern and western ranges were built at the same time. Unfortunately a fire in 1828 destroyed most of the timber features in the south-eastern corner. The whole building was probably completed in three years starting in 1472 (Bannister 1918a, 83). The eastern range (and possibly the eastern part of the southern range) was apparently built in the first season, the northern range in the second, and the project was completed in the third year. The main walls of the college are of the local Old Red Sandstone, with the external elevations, including the chimney stacks and a plinth, all of ashlar and the claustral sides of partially dressed and coursed rubblestone.

Each lodging consisted of a ground-floor chamber and a two-bay first-floor hall open to the roof. However, attic floors have since been inserted in many parts of the building, the earliest probably dating to the 16th century. The lower chamber was smaller than the one above because the cloister walk is incorporated into the ground floor and space was needed to accommodate the stairs. The cloister walk is separated from the lodgings by a close-studded timber-framed wall with an ovolo-moulded wall plate, and from the courtyard by an open stone arcade with gates at the mid points (Morriss and Shoesmith 1995, 163–4).

Although the original staircases do not survive, the window pattern indicates that in each lodging they were placed directly opposite the door leading from the claustral walk. Many of the original four-centred doorways leading off the cloister have been blocked, but their positions have been apparent since relatively modern plaster was removed from the close-studding in the 1930s (Marshall 1938, 24).

All the lodgings had fireplaces on each floor. Where room permitted they were served by external stacks – all now rebuilt above the eaves level. The fireplaces had four-centred heads with either hollow-chamfered or wave-moulded and stopped decoration; many still survive and several have been opened up recently. In each lodging the ground-floor room had windows only on the external face, usually on each side of the fireplace. On the first floor, both external stone walls had two windows, but while those on the courtyard side were of equal size, the external windows, which again flanked the fireplace, were of two sizes – a narrow light illuminating the presumed stairs, and a wider one which lit the hall. The main windows were of two four-centred lights with hollow-chamfered jambs in a square head. Many of the window-openings have been altered in recent times.

The partition walls between individual lodgings

usually consisted of wide-panelled timber frames carrying a closed roof truss; many still have the original wattle-and-daub infill. Most of these timber frames still survive, although doorways have been inserted where lodgings have been amalgamated (Fig. 6.5).

In each lodging the roof was divided into two bays by an arch-braced truss. A trefoil pattern was created in these trusses by the cusping of the upper portions of the principals and the tops of the collars. The principals sprang from chamfered and moulded timber corbels, with plain or tilting shields, set a little below the wall plates. The roof structure consisted of two tiers of chamfered and stopped purlins braced by cusped, chamfered wind-braces. Most of the purlins survive, but many of the wind-braces have been removed. In most lodgings the thrust of the intermediate truss was taken by the chimney-stack on the outer wall and a slightly offset stepped buttress on the inner, courtyard elevation. Originally the roof had overhanging eaves and was probably covered in stone tiles, but now a parapet runs around most of the building and the roof is covered in slate.

The claustral arcading is very simple, with shallow, almost straight, four-centred openings mostly in pairs below wider two-centred arches of the same pattern (Fig. 6.6). Many of the outer orders of these openings are technically two-centred – having angled, rather than rounded, junctions between jamb and head. Jambs and mullions are all moulded. The arches in the north range are different from those of the other sides, the outer heads being triangular and their arches being made of several pieces of stone. Above each arch is a rough, two-centred relieving arch. All the other arcade arches are constructed of moulded voussoirs and, except for the two northern-most arches in the east range, do not have relieving arches. Originally there may have been more elaborate tracery within the openings; a drawing published in 1685 (Fig. 6.7) shows each opening divided into two by a mullion and each narrow light with a trefoiled head below the main arch of the opening, but there is no surviving evidence for this rather unusual tracery (ed. Winnington 1867, cciv). At each corner of the cloister walk, on the angle of the arcading, a tall recessed panel with trefoiled heads, above which is a carved human head, is set in the masonry. Opposite, in the angle-posts of the close-studding, are the badly mutilated remains of decorative carvings.

The eastern range contained six standard lodgings, but may have been originally designed for seven, the central one being converted into a chapel and library during construction. This central unit occupied the width of a typical lodging, but included an eastwards projection (Marshall 1938, 25–6). The roof of the east range continued over the main part of the unit with

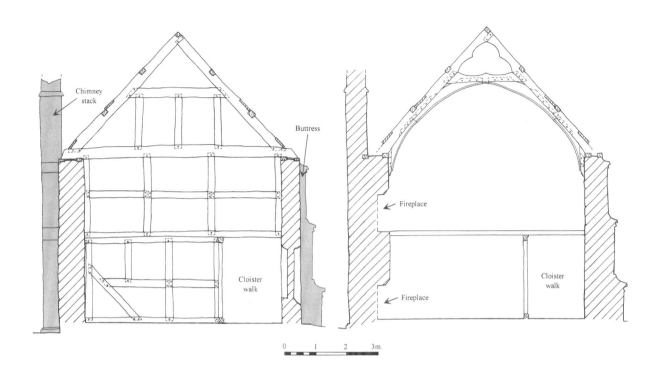

Fig. 6.5. Vicars choral of Hereford Cathedral. A frame between two lodgings (left) and an intermediate truss (right) (drawing and copyright, City of Hereford Archaeology Unit)

Fig. 6.6. Vicars choral of Hereford Cathedral. The east side of the cloister walk, looking north (photo Ken Hoverd, copyright City of Hereford Archaeology Unit)

Fig. 6.7. Vicars choral of Hereford Cathedral. View of college in 1685, by Dingley

a typical intermediate truss, arch-braced and tre-foiled. The eastern principal rafter of this truss was supported on a wall-plate which spanned the opening in the masonry for the eastwards extension. The north and south internal frames are of standard design down to tie-beam level, but below this they are close-studded. The close-studding is based on independent girding beams and it is possible that the timberwork could have been inserted into an open frame by reducing the thickness of the principal girding beam.

Traditionally, this part of the building contained the chapel on the ground floor with the college library above. This area was substantially rebuilt between 1835 and 1842 and now bears little resemblance to the original layout. As a result little is known about the design of the chapel, but chamfers in the surviving masonry indicate window openings in the north and south walls. The library, which is first mentioned in 1582, apparently had an oriel window in the east wall with a number of lights containing early 16th-century painted glass (ed. Winnington 1867, cc-ccii; Duncumb 1804, 588; Morgan and Morgan 1970, 24). The courtyard windows at this level, now part of a passage, are similar to those in other lodgings. The chapel would have had a direct access from the cloister walk, but access to the first-floor library was through a doorway in the north frame from the adjacent lodging. This may been the quarters for the librarian, giving him control over access to the library.

The northern range originally contained seven standard lodgings with the entrance passage on the west and a slightly larger lodging, assumed to be for the *custos*, to the west of the entrance passage. Although this lodging has been partly demolished and has lost its floors and roof, the general design is still apparent. The north wall, which included the fireplaces, also contained a doorway and windows, now blocked. The west wall was adjacent to the Bishop's Palace garden wall and thus at an angle to the remainder of the range. The east wall, which adjoins the entrance passage, is of close timbering and includes a blocked original doorway.

When the north range was built, a timber frame was constructed within a full-height gap in the masonry of its southern wall where the west range was planned to join. This frame still survives on the south side of the entrance passageway where the ground-floor section is close-studded. When the western range was added, a skeletal frame was constructed next to this infill frame in a similar fashion to that at the junction of the eastern and northern ranges. This frame was thus parallel to the northern range and at a slight angle to the skewed western range. The intermediate truss to the south was deliberately built askew in an attempt to compensate, and further frames to the south gradually pick up a right-angled alignment to the range.

The western range contained six lodgings. The northernmost one is the only lodging with an original cellar; it is stone-lined and there are traces of a stone stair, probably a vice, in the north-western corner, lit by two cellar lights from the cloister walk. The southern part of this western range is very close to the Bishop's Palace garden wall and, to allow access around the south-western corner of the college, the chimneys had to be modified. The ground-floor fireplaces and flues of the two south-ernmost lodgings are contained in the thickened width of the external wall, and the stacks are then corbelled out at first-floor level. The southernmost lodging has a skewed wall, but there is no obvious constructional break at this point as occurred at the north-eastern and north-western corners, and it is assumed that the west and south ranges were built more or less simultaneously. Three primary trusses which survive, although much altered, at the east end of the south range, indicate that it was built to join on to the south end of the east range.

The southern range has undergone more changes than the others and its eastern part was badly damaged by a fire in 1828. It is assumed that it was originally designed to contain a row of seven lodgings, with Canon Greene's hall to the south. These lodgings are unlikely to have been of the standard design because the position of the hall, and its presumed central access from the cloister walk, would have affected both window and fireplace positions. Elsewhere in the college the buttresses were designed to take the thrust of the roof trusses, but this was not so in the south range where their positions were clearly aesthetic. The assumed lodgings in the centre of the range were eventually removed to allow for a northern extension to the late 17th–century college hall.

The entrance to the college is at its north-west corner, between a standard lodging and the remains of the assumed *custos*' house. The entrance archway is four-centred in a square head with sprigs and shields in the spandrels and three defaced shields. The timber door is original with cinquefoil-headed panels and contains a small central wicket door with trefoil-headed panels (Fig. 6.8). From this point the college was connected to the cathedral by a cloister or corridor which passed to the north of the pre-sumed *custos*' house and then turned northwards to link with the south-east transept. It was built towards the end of the 15th century; a little later a two-storey porch replaced the south-eastern bay of the corridor and the adjoining bay was rebuilt (Marshall 1918, 71–81).

The main corridor is of ten bays and is 33m long. The bays are separated externally by buttresses which were replaced in 1862 and, apart from the southernmost, each bay contains windows of three

Fig. 6.8. Vicars choral of Hereford Cathedral. The entrance porch (photo Ken Hoverd, copyright City of Hereford Archaeology Unit)

The two-storey entrance porch, which, together with the adjoining bay, was added in the early 16th century, has an outer two-centred archway of two moulded orders, the inner springing from moulded capitals above grouped shafts (Fig. 6.10). There is a similar archway in the west wall leading into the corridor. The porch contains an elaborate fan vault. The one original window in the east face, now blocked, was of two trefoiled ogee lights in a square head. The north face has suffered badly from erosion and only remnants of the original ornamentation survive. The first-floor window, which replaced a niche for a statue, is of early 18th-century date (Rawlinson 1717). The porch was restored about 1862 as part of the general repairs to the college. It would seem that the *custos* and vicars were somewhat uncertain about the extent of work that was necessary, with an estimate from a Mr. Chick for 'base of College porch to be restored' at a cost of £14 14s. However, much more work was undertaken and at their meeting in September 1862 the *custos* and vicars authorised the steward 'to pay to Mr. Thompson of Peterborough the sum of £158 5s. 0d., the amount of his bill for repairs to the College porch and cloisters'.

four-centred lights in a square head; the mullions were replaced in 1862 (*ibid.*). The window in the penultimate bay to the north has been replaced by a modern doorway; a facing doorway leads into the chapter-house yard. At the southern end of the corridor a doorway, which replaced an earlier window, leads into the Bishop's Palace garden. The corridor has a king-post roof made of timbers of large scantling (Fig. 6.9). The cambered tie-beams support the king posts with curved braces to the ridge. The single purlins and rafters are all heavily moulded and the tie-beams and principal rafters are carved on both faces. The mythical, religious and heraldic subjects are often paired and represent various temptations and sports. Figures include an ox reading from a book held by two hands; a full length nude female figure with hood and comb; the head and neck of a wolf with a formidable array of teeth and an upturned female posterior in front of it; a stag being hunted by a dog; a very fat pig feeding on acorns; a head with flowing hair and the upper part of a nude female body; various fish swimming in water including a large one swallowing a smaller one. The timbers are also adorned with conventional foliage and tracery (Marshall 1918, 73–9; RCHME 1931, 118–19).

Fig. 6.9. Vicars choral of Hereford Cathedral. The roof of the corridor from the college to the south-east transept (photo Ken Hoverd, copyright City of Hereford Archaeology Unit)

Fig. 6.10. Vicars choral of Hereford Cathedral. The entrance to the college (photo Ken Hoverd, copyright City of Hereford Archaeology Unit)

During the work the columns that flank the archway were renewed using a banded, conglomerate sandstone. Even so, sufficient material survives to attempt a hypothetical reconstruction of the original (Fig. 6.11).

The small effigy of St John the Baptist, which is now in the cathedral, was apparently the one which stood in the niche. Rawlinson, writing in 1717, states that 'an Image [of St John the Baptist] stood lately over the entrance [to the college] but now removed to make a Light to one of the Vicars' Lodgings'. Jones writing in 1867 mentions:

> 'a small effigy of St. John the Baptist, dug up in 1840 at the demolition of St. Nicholas' Church [at the junction of Bridge Street and King Street] ... is believed originally to have stood at the gateway of the Vicars College, and was probably concealed at the siege of the city in 1645. The head having been destroyed by the workmen, has been replaced by a new one, coloured somewhat different to the rest of the figure'.

At a lower level two other niches for statues flanked the entrance arch.

Reformation and Restoration

When their new building was completed in 1475, the vicars appear to have entered into a period of relative stability, although several references suggest that their remuneration was meagre (Barrett 1980, 15; Capes n.d., 8–9). This was gradually resolved and in

1487 they were allowed to hold other benefices without residing in them (ed. Bannister 1919, 15–18). Although chantries were dissolved by Act of Parliament in 1547, the Hereford college survived having asserted that they 'were and had been founded, taken, admitted and allways hath been both reputed and called by the names of Vicars of the Quyer and not chantries' (Barrett 1980, 16). However, the chantry funds, that had supported the vicars in part, would have been subject to confiscation.

From 1575, details of life in the college can be gleaned from the college Act Books (*Hereford Acts*). In addition, Archdeacon Pate of Worcester Cathedral issued *Injunctions for Hereford Cathedral*, on behalf of Cardinal Pole, Archbishop of Canterbury (1556–8). Thus, when visiting the town, vicars were expected to be accompanied by an 'honest person' and should avoid 'all suspicious houses and often frequentynge of alehouses and taverns' (eds. Frere and Kennedy 1910, ii, 392). Edwardian *Injunctions for Cathedrals* issued in 1547 dealt with 'offences of morality' such as allowing 'suspected women' into their chambers, assaults on other vicars, and doubtful accounting (*ibid.*, ii, 136).

In 1583 *Statutes* were published following a Royal Commission in the previous year. Some 50 years later those *Statutes* were expanded and refined. The main effect was to reduce the college from 27 to

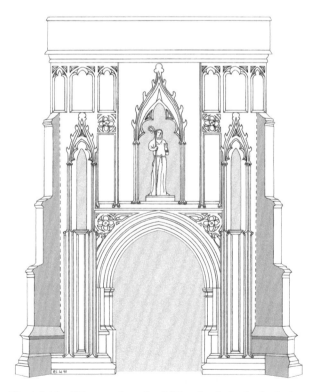

Fig. 6.11. Vicars choral of Hereford Cathedral. Reconstruction of the front of the porch (drawing and copyright, City of Hereford Archaeology Unit)

twelve vicars. The *Statutes* also limited the vicars' hospitality 'in order that the lavish extravagance, especially in drink, which has so reduced the means of the said College, as almost to exhaust them' could be curtailed (Marshall 1938, 22; Barrett 1980, 19). This was not altogether successful and in 1634, in an account of a survey of 26 counties undertaken by 'a Captain, a Lieutenant and an Ancient', Lieutenant Hammond recorded:

> 'Next came wee into a brave and ancient priviledg'd Place, through the Lady Arbour Cloyster, close by the Chapter House, called the Vicar's Chorall, or Colledge Cloyster where 12 of the singing men, all in orders, most of them Masters in Arts, of a Gentile garbe, have their convenient several dwellings, and a fayre hall, with richly-painted windows, Colledge-like, wherein they constantly dyet together, and have their Cooke, Butler, and other officers, with a fayre Library to themselves, consisting all of English books, wherein (after we had freely tasted of their Chorall cordiall Liquor) we spent our time till the Bell toll'd us away to Cathedral prayers' (Havergal 1869, 101).

Shortly after Hereford fell to the Parliamentary forces in the Civil War, the college was dissolved and the vicars were expelled. When Colonel Birch took up residence in the Bishop's Palace in 1649 he permitted the beggars, who were no doubt numerous at that time, to occupy the rooms in the college (Webb 1873, 154). The buildings were to suffer damage and decay for over ten years and it is not surprising that following the Restoration in 1660 they needed extensive repairs. It took several years to sort out the finances of the reformed college and it seems clear that it was during this time that a decision was taken to demolish the medieval hall on the south side of the cloisters and build anew. Large expenses are shown in the Account Book for 1670–71 when the hearth was mended and boards were laid in the dining room and a 'balcony', apparently held up by pillars, was erected (*Hereford Accounts*). There was also a large expense in 1674–75 and on 1st September 1676 the Act Book notes:

> 'Whereas Mr. Humphrey Fisher, Vicar of the Colledge of Hereford, hath taken great care and paines in finishing the building of the hall belonging to the said colledge and is thereby out of purse £4 13s. Therefor wee the custos and vicars ... doe order that the said Humphrey Fisher be repayed ... and that he be returned the thanks of the house.'

The work was apparently completed by 1676 (*Hereford Acts* 1676).

The College Hall

A hall such as this, built in the late 17th century, would have incorporated a Renaissance design in which symmetry was an important factor (Fig. 6.12). Dingley, writing in 1684, provides some additional evidence for he related that the College had 'belonging to it a very fair and square Refectory or HALL

looking into their Garden and towards the River Wye. Over the screen whereof it carried this rebus painted carved and Guilded' (ed. Winnington 1867, cciv). The screen mentioned by Dingley may well have been towards the northern end of the Hall. The rebus survives (Fig. 6.13); inscribed *HORTVLANVS RIGAT DAT FRVCTVM 16 DEVS 70*, and initialled *RC*, it was apparently the gift of a Dr. Richard Gardiner. It is possible that the new hall had been finished by 1670, and the rebus may even commemorate its completion. North of the partition there would have been service rooms; had the adjacent portion of the south cloister still been in use as lodgings, then access to these services, other than from the hall, may have been difficult. If there was an entrance to the 17th-century hall from the cloisters then it must have been adjacent to the former lodgings, and possibly in the same central position as the present doorway (Fig. 6.3). However, the doorway towards the north end of the west wall indicates that there was an access to the hall from a path leading from the college entrance down the outside of the west range.

The new hall is mostly faced with good quality ashlar blocks, traditionally said to be derived from the nearby castle after it was dismantled following the Civil War. The quality of the ashlar is such that had it come from the castle then it would have all been re-dressed before use. There is a moulded plinth running around the hall and, above the level of the windows, a thinner course of stone appears to have faint signs of being cut back. This may have been a levelling course or, possibly, a former moulded string course.

The main part of the hall was heated by a fireplace in the west elevation associated with an external stack. The stack is constructed of the same ashlar blocks as the rest of the building, and has the same moulded plinth. It is topped by a chimney made up of small, hand-made bricks that could be primary. The fireplace, once blocked but now exposed again, is wide and deep with rounded sides and a four-centred head (Fig. 6.14). The surround is of three shallow orders, the inner ones plain and flat. However, the outer moulding appears to have been decorated, but this decoration was probably chipped off when the fireplace was blocked and replaced with one further north as part of the Georgian remodelling of the hall in 1753. The position of the fireplace, which is to the south of the centre of the present hall, suggests that the Restoration Hall was shorter than the present one. The range of lodgings to the north may either have continued in use or could have been converted to become ante-rooms to the hall or, possibly, to contain services. Such a conversion seems to be borne out by the fenestration. The east side is now lit by four large windows, but the northernmost one was

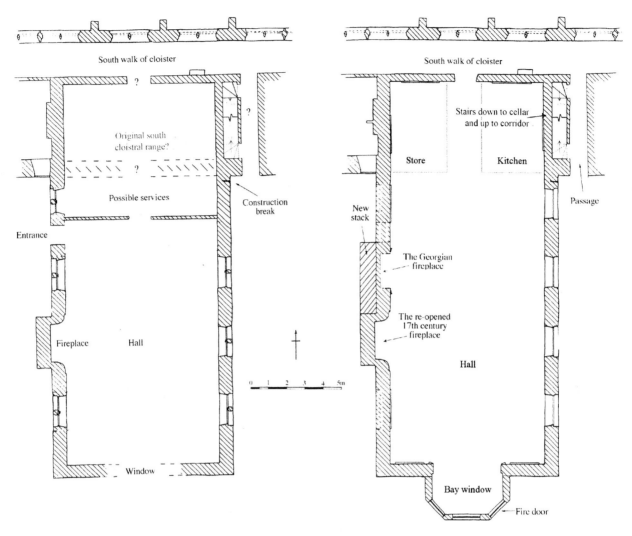

Fig. 6.12. Vicars choral of Hereford Cathedral. Plan of the hall in the late 17th century (left) and in 2002 (right) (drawing and copyright, City of Hereford Archaeology Unit)

evidently inserted at a later date. The windows now have fairly new balanced sashes that probably replaced earlier sashes fitted during the mid 18th-century refurbishment, but the original late 17th-century openings would presumably have contained typical cross-window casements.

There are no surviving window openings in the west wall, but one certainly existed towards the south end of the wall, facing one in the east wall. It is likely that there was another window in the position of the 18th-century fireplace, to match another in the east wall, but external evidence is totally obscured by the new stack. There are traces of the lower part of a smaller blocked window at the north end of this wall, but the upper portions are covered in ivy which impedes a thorough investigation. There was also a doorway, probably primary, to the north of the later stack. In all cases the blocking

material is similar to the 18th–century stack.

The side wall windows were all apparently of the same shape as the present openings, but the shape of the window (or windows) in the south wall is unknown. The style of the present bay window in the south gable is more typical of the mid 18th century than the Regency period (Fig. 6.15), and the 1757 Taylor map of the city (Fig. 6.16) shows a bay window. However, the masonry base and plinth around the bay are tied into those in the south wall of the hall and appear to be of the same period. Above this level everything associated with the bay window appears to be later than the south wall. However, two areas of patching could well have held the springers for an arched opening which would have been lower than the present opening. This opening could have been associated with an earlier bay window set on the present base, but not

Fig. 6.13. Vicars choral of Hereford Cathedral. The plaque of 1670 (photo Ken Hoverd, copyright City of Hereford Archaeology Unit)

as high as the present one, with windows in three or even all five sides. The design and shape of these windows are unknown.

There is sufficient evidence within the roof space to suggest that the original medieval roof trusses in the centre of the south cloister range were removed during the 17th century and that the three central lodgings were radically rebuilt with an inserted loft floor supported on spine beams laid between new trusses. The new trusses were clearly added at a time when the original medieval lodgings were amalgamated either into one larger lodging or, possibly, into a communal area of some description related to the hall. The main portion of the hall was ceiled in its Restoration phase and the roof structure was hidden. However, even in its original phase it was never meant to be seen, unlike the quasi-medieval roof over the remodelled chapel in the east range.

In the years after the Restoration the vicars began to join in the social life of the city and there were many card parties in the coffee house in Milk Lane (now St John Street), and 'frequent carousals' at the Black Lion Club Room (ed. Cooke n.d., 10) – was this the room that is still adorned with 16th-century wall paintings depicting the breaking of the ten commandments (RCHME 1934, 227 and pls 186–7)?

Even in the early 18th century the college hall was being used for concerts, a use that had become so popular that proposals were put forward in 1750 to rebuild and extend it. The re-modelled hall was back in commission in time for the Three Choirs Festival of 1753 (Barrett 1980, 23–4). In 1796 it was described as 'a large and handsome hall of modern structure' and in 1804 as 'a spacious hall' (Price 1796, 133; Duncumb 1804, 588). The main work had involved extending the hall northwards into the south range of the college, together with considerable alterations to its internal appearance. The north wall of the hall now butted directly onto the cloister walk and the only entrance to it was from the cloister. This extension meant that the earlier fenestration and the fireplace were no longer symmetrical to the enlarged room. To rectify this, the old fireplace was blocked and a new fireplace was inserted to the north of it, almost central to the enlarged room. This fireplace, which probably occupied the site of one of the original windows, has a fairly plain moulded surround with ears. A new stone-rubble stack was installed against the earlier stack to serve the new fireplace and at the same time the door in the west wall was blocked.

The window pattern was then in need of revision and the remaining windows in the west wall were blocked. A new window, of the same dimensions as the others, was added at the northern end of the east wall. This window was almost certainly a balanced sash, and the remaining openings were probably also replaced with identical sashes at the same time. Internally, the window surrounds consisted of heavy, moulded frames. To preserve the internal symmetry, blind frames of a similar design were fixed to the walls to create a integrated pattern of windows and frames on both sides of the hall. Thus

Fig. 6.14. Vicars choral of Hereford Cathedral. The two fireplaces in the hall (photo Ken Hoverd, copyright City of Hereford Archaeology Unit)

Fig. 6.15. Vicars choral of Hereford Cathedral. The bay window in the hall (photo Ken Hoverd, copyright City of Hereford Archaeology Unit)

there was one blind frame in the northern-most portion of the east wall – actually within the extension into the cloister range – and five similar frames along the window-less west wall, the central one being shorter as it was above the new fireplace. Similar blind frames flanked the main door in the north wall and the new bay window in the south gable. The door case of the new main entrance had a plain moulded frame with ears.

A reference to the replacement of the south window in 1817 seems to run counter to the architectural evidence from the bay, for Venetian work of the type surviving here is typical of mid 18th–century Palladianism (Fig. 6.15). In addition, the glazing bars of the windows are quite thick, again typical of early or mid 18th-century work and certainly not typical of the Regency period. It seems likely, therefore, that the 1817 replacement was

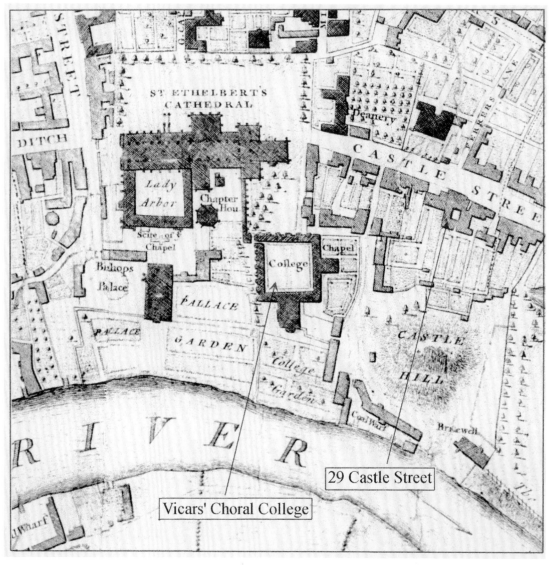

Fig. 6.16. Vicars choral of Hereford Cathedral. No.29 Castle Street and the college, as shown on Taylor's 1757 map of Hereford (source, Taylor 1757)

modelled on the original, rather than on the new, balanced sashes.

It is difficult to assess whether the present ceiling, with its heavy cove, is entirely the result of a rebuild after the 1828 fire or whether the earlier ceiling was simply repaired. Certainly the size of the coving is very similar to that in the former common room, now the chapter room, at the east end of the south range, and that it is the part of the college that had been so badly damaged during the fire that it had to be rebuilt.

During renovation work in the 1930s the hall's original fireplace was uncovered and re-opened (Marshall 1938, 28). The blind frame that had been in position since the 1750s was reduced in size to accommodate it, and the adjacent section of dado rail was removed. The result is somewhat unusual, with two large fireplaces set almost side by side, totally destroying the symmetry of the hall (Fig. 6.14). The hall has recently been refurbished and the symmetry has been restored by inserting a screen in the simplified classical style of the early 19th century within the northern part of the Hall.

Decline

The reduction in the number of vicars choral towards the end of the 16th century meant that over half of the lodgings were disused and the Act Books have numerous references to electing commoners to the college and allowed them to use some of the excess accommodation (*Hereford Acts*). Thus in 1581 William Jones, a commoner, was allotted a chamber, and from 1660 many lay commoners (described as 'esq.') are mentioned in the Act Books. Well before this time several pairs of lodgings had been joined together to make larger houses. The earliest one may have involved the two lodgings immediately to the south of the chapel, which appear to have been amalgamated in the first half of the 16th century. On the ground floor a simple doorway was cut through the partition, but on the first floor a timber-framed partition formed a corridor on the claustral side of the two first-floor halls. Both upper rooms have panelled ceilings with moulded and stopped beams at wall-plate level and attics above.

The two lodgings in the north-western corner were also joined together in the late 16th or early 17th century. Here a new partition of large panels filled with wattle and daub was built to create a spacious stairwell. Following the insertion of ceilings in the two halls, the attic space was also brought into use.

The northern half of the west range, which incorporates three original lodgings, had a more complex history. The central lodging was the first to be altered, probably in the late 16th century. A partition of wide, square panels with wattle-and-daub infill was inserted in the first-floor hall above the close-studded frame of the cloister walk. Closely set joists above this partition and across the whole hall supported a ceiling, but early in the 17th century a new ceiling was inserted at lower purlin level in the reduced upper hall. It was at this time that this lodging was apparently united with the one to the north to create a larger house. More alterations took place during the 19th century and by the end of this period the southern lodging had also been incorporated to create one large house.

The insertion of ceilings in most of the first-floor halls continued throughout the 17th and 18th centuries, and it is evident that several further amalgamations took place from time to time. Two examples are evident in the north wing, but the evidence for any which may have occurred in the south-east and south-west corners has been obscured by the 1828 fire and by later alterations.

The postulated *custos* lodging adjoining the passage in the north-western corner had a variety of uses before it was demolished. In the latter part of the 16th century the upper chamber was used as the singing school until the choristers were moved into the chamber beyond the hall. The college then granted it to 'Mr Crump, ye Chancellor's register, for ye use of his office' (*Hereford Acts*, 13 May, 1592). The lower chamber then became the porter's lodge (*Hereford Acts*, 9th June, 1608). In the 18th century this building was leased to the cathedral school while its premises were being rebuilt (*Hereford Acts*, 17th July, 1760); it was probably demolished during the 19th century.

At the beginning of the 19th century the library and chapel were 'in a state of delapidation' (Duncumb 1804, 589). Conditions worsened, and by 1835 the walls were bulging and it was decided that the eastern extension should be demolished and rebuilt (*Hereford Acts*, 26th October, 1835). The books were removed to the Common Room in the south-east corner of the cloister, which had just been rebuilt after the fire, and the necessary demolition then took place. The reconstruction was some 4m shorter than before and involved the total removal of the first floor, apart from the section above the cloister walk which became a passage linking the first-floor rooms to north and south of the chapel. The walls of the new extension, of roughly-coursed stone rubble, sat on the lower courses of the old north and south walls, but the original side windows were not replaced. The new east wall contains a large two-light window. The western wall was replaced with timber-framing incorporating early 17th-century turned balusters and a central door. The doorways that had led into the lodging to the north were both blocked off. A false, three-bay roof, aligned at right angles to the east range, was inserted underneath the original roof and continued into the short extension; it is loosely based on the style of the original lodging roofs with two arch-braced trusses, but the scantling is very thin and the trefoiled pattern is little more than shaped planking. The 'trusses' carry two pairs of thin, chamfered purlins and a ridge piece.

The rebuilding was completed in 1842, but by 1844 the chapel was described as being damp and seven years later it was disused. By 1938 it was in total decay (Marshall 1938, 26), but a little later it was repaired and was then used for a while as the chapter room.

In 1828 there was a serious fire in the college when 'a great portion of the building was materially injured and the buttery, cellar, larder, kitchen and servants' bedrooms totally consumed' (*Hereford Acts*, 9th August, 1828). A contemporary account in the *Hereford Journal*, dated 30th July 1828, said that, as well as the service quarters and part of the cloister range, 'the roof and ceiling of the great room are also extensively injured'. The servants occupied the eastern part of the south range, apart from the first-floor room in the corner, which was used as a common room. The 1828 fire started in the butler's room, which was on the ground floor in the south-eastern corner, and by half-past two in the morning...

> 'presented a terrific appearance; the offices in the south-east angle of the square and the roof of the centre part of the southern side, were enveloped in flames and burning furiously whilst the destructive element appeared spreading with fearful rapidity'.

Many townsfolk helped the various fire engines and by five o'clock the fire had been brought under control. The *Hereford Journal* reported on 6th August 1828 that the college butler, John Constable, died as a result of the injuries he received when he tried to rescue property from the building during the fire.

The fire more or less destroyed the three original lodgings to the east of the hall, although parts of the roof trusses survived and remain *in situ*. It also caused minor damage to one or two lodgings at the south end of the east wing. It was probably contained to this corner by one of original full partitions which prevented the fire from spreading through the roof space. However, to the west, the roof space was open to that above the Hall, as a result of the rebuilding works in the mid 18th century.

The reconstruction after the fire was mainly in brick and the whitewashed brick wall, which replaced the close-studding in the south-eastern corner of the cloister walk, is a permanent reminder of this near disaster. It was at about this time that the first-floor wall of the southern range above the cloister arcading was rebuilt with regular window openings,

and chimney-stacks were incorporated within the range to replace those assumed to have been present on the south wall. Brick was also used to build a small brewery for the benefit of the vicars, to the south of the eastern part of the south range. Not surprisingly, this building is no longer used for its original purpose, but its conversion to a song school helps to perpetuate the memory of the vicars choral.

Demise

The 1840 *Cathedrals Act* reduced the number of vicars choral to six and led to the practice of appointing lay clerks, some of whom were ordained. However, it was difficult to sustain a communal life with so few and the common table was discontinued in 1875. By this time the vicars each had three or four lodgings allocated to them, thus providing each with a reasonable suite of rooms.

In 1897 a new Ecclesiastical Commissioners' scheme reduced the number of vicars to four, with eight lay clerks being employed. Vacancies were not filled during the First World War and by the 1920s there were only two vicars left. In 1925 it was agreed that the property should be handed over to the Ecclesiastical Commissioners. The end was in sight and a cathedral commission in the 1930s recommended that all such minor corporations should be dissolved. Hereford received its new *Statutes* in 1937 and under their terms the vicars choral were no longer to exist as a separate entity, but the dean and chapter had discretionary powers to appoint up to two vicars choral if they so desired. The last meeting of the vicars choral took place on 4th June 1937 and thereafter the vicars choral, or minor canons as they were called in this period, were stipendiaries of the dean and chapter.

The dean and chapter took over the building and goods of the college and sold most of the plate, which had been deposited in the bank for safe keeping, to finance repairs. The college buildings are still in use. The combined lodgings provide accommodation for various people including the dean, the organist and vergers. The north range contains the cathedral offices and those of the recently formed perpetual trust. College hall is used for talks, meetings and concerts, especially during the Three Choirs Festival. The chapter meet in a large first-floor room in the south-eastern corner and the Sunday School in the chapel. The dean and chapter exercised their discretionary power to employ two minor canons and vicars choral until fairly recently. Philip Barrett was the last vicar choral at Hereford, serving between 1976 and 1986, after which he moved to a living in Hampshire. He died in April 1998.

7

'A Small Quadrangle of Old Low-Built Houses': The Vicars' Close at Lichfield

Warwick Rodwell

The cathedral precinct at Lichfield was traditionally, and for most purposes still is, known simply as 'The Close'. By contrast the use of the term 'Vicars' Close' at Lichfield is of recent vintage, and the latter is often taken to refer only to the northern of the two courts. The Close comprises a compact quadrilateral, which was well fortified in the middle ages with a wall, ditch and gatehouses. The cathedral stands alone near the centre of the enclosure, without a cloister or other attached structures, while the bishop's, dean's and canons' residences occupy a series of regularly planned plots around the perimeter of The Close (Fig. 7.1). Both the degree of fortification and formality of layout are unusual in English cathedral closes. Intruded into this plan are the residential complexes of several subsidiary medieval institutions, principally the communal lodgings of the vicars choral (1315), the college of chantry priests ('New College', 1411), and the choristers' residence (1527).

Substantial remains of the collegiate-style lodgings of vicars choral survive at the west end of The Close, between the West Gate and the north-west angle (Figs. 7.2 and 7.3). Here, two conjoined courtyards of medieval and later buildings comprise what was known as 'The Vicarage', or sometimes (for example, by Leland) as the 'College of the Vicars' (ed. Smith 1964, II, 102). Only the northern quadrangle is called 'Vicars' Close' today, but in the present work the term 'vicars' close' embraces both courts. In 1998 the southern court, previously a jumble of back gardens, was redesigned and named Darwin Close. Down to the end of the 19th century the usual term for all the vicars' dwellings was 'The Vicarage', and the two parts of it were generally referred to as the 'Upper Court' and 'Lower Court'. Although little known, the former is an attractive court, which retains medieval timber-framed lodging ranges in a good state of preservation on two-and-a-half sides.

The buildings of the Lichfield vicars have received little study, and very few antiquarian illustrations of them are known. Remarkably, no attempt seems to have been made to study the architectural history of the Vicarage in the 19th or earlier 20th centuries. A brief inventory has survived from 1649 (Tringham 1984), and there is a ground plan of the Vicarage dated 1805 (LRO, VC/A/21, cc17529) (Fig. 7.4).

A programme of historical research into the cathedral in the 1960s by Ann Kettle and D A Johnson, for the *Victoria County History*, included the study of much material relating to the vicars choral (ed. Greenslade 1970). Subsequent research into the history of the buildings of the cathedral Close in the 1980s by Dr Nigel Tringham, again for the *Victoria County History*, yielded further information on the vicars' close (ed. Greenslade 1990).

In the mid 1980s a measured survey of many of the buildings in the cathedral Close was undertaken by Jeremy Milln for Staffordshire County Council's Sites and Monuments Record. Various opportunities have arisen since 1990 for archaeological recording in the vicars' close, during renovation works, and much has been learned from these.

Outline history

Lichfield was besieged three times during the Civil War, when the cathedral and buildings of the cathedral Close were bombarded relentlessly. Massive destruction ensued, not only of historic fabric but also of muniments. Consequently, surviving records of the vicars choral are scarce before the mid 17th century, and neither are the later ones voluminous.

Vicars are mentioned in the first statutes of Lichfield Cathedral, which date from the episcopate of Hugh de Nonant (1185–98) and were probably

Fig. 7.1. Vicars choral of Lichfield Cathedral. The Close defences and principal buildings (drawing and copyright, Warwick Rodwell)

Fig. 7.2. Vicars choral of Lichfield Cathedral. Lichfield: the Vicars' Close seen from the cathedral west front. The gables in the foreground belong to Nos.7–10 The Close: these lodgings have been rebuilt, or re-fronted, and turned to face the cathedral. The set-back gable to the right is No.12 Vicars' Close. (photo and copyright, Warwick Rodwell)

drawn up in 1191 (Savage 1920, 15–16). The statutes provided for four dignitaries and twenty-two canons (or prebends) and, under rules of residence laid down in 1195, each canon was required to reside in Lichfield for at least three months a year. The number of vicars is not specified, but is unlikely to have been less than twenty; in the 15th century the maximum recorded was 27. However, the number of prebends eventually rose to 32, and the complement of vicars may have increased commensurately. The statutes laid down that the dean was responsible for the direction and correction of canons and vicars.

The first statutes for the vicars were made in 1241, effectively denoting the formation of an unincorporated college (eds. Caley, Ellis and Bandinel 1846, VI (3), 1257–8; ed. Greenslade 1970, 148). The vicars were required to be permanently resident in Lichfield and were compelled to attend services; absence was punishable with expulsion, and one member of the community was charged with recording absences. At least five vicars had to be priests ('priest vicars'), and these were attached to the resident canons. There were also some secular clerks ('clerk vicars') amongst the company. The two principal

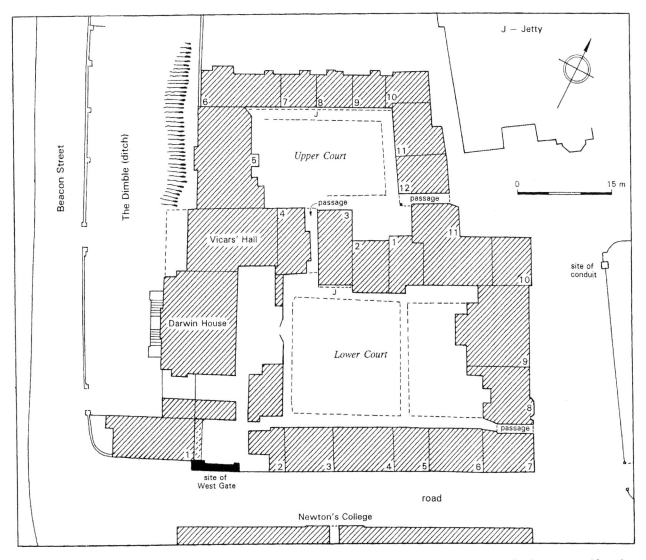

Fig. 7.3. Vicars choral of Lichfield Cathedral. Plan of The Vicarage, with the modern house-numbering system (drawing and copyright, Warwick Rodwell)

vicars were the subchanter (deputy for the precentor) and sacrist (deputy for the treasurer). The former had responsibility, in the precentor's absence, for arranging all cathedral services. The latter was responsible for the supply of candles, bread and wine for the services. During periods of prolonged canonical absenteeism, the vicars virtually ran the cathedral.

Ordinary vicars were to be paid at least 20s. *per annum* by their canons, and priest vicars received more. In addition, an allowance (commons) of 1*d.* was paid twice daily by the chapter. That was raised to 1½*d.* in 1311, and to 3*d.* in 1374. Newly appointed vicars were presented to the dean and tested by the precentor in singing and reading. Other sources of funding are recorded; bishops and canons, for example, frequently left lands in trust to provide income for the vicars who observed their obits. Thus in 1208 Bishop Muscamp (1198–1208) left one mark

per annum to the vicars for this duty. In 1249 Dean Mancetter made provision for the payment of 40s. to the vicars who kept his obit.

At least thirteen chantries were founded in the cathedral in the 13th century, and most of the chaplains who ministered at these were vicars. The college of chantry priests had not yet been established. Three vicars had permanent responsibilities for chantries: the subchanter had that of Bishop Pattishall (founded 1254); the sacrist had that of Canon Ralph de Chaddesdon; and the Archdeacon of Chester's vicar was responsible for Canon Thomas de Bradford's chantry. Other duties performed by the vicars included being Keepers of the Fabric of the cathedral, the earliest recorded being in 1283 when the task was shared by two vicars (ed. Greenslade 1970, 150). Vicars also variously fulfilled the tasks of chapter clerk, communar and scribe, and even represented the chapter at papal courts (e.g. in

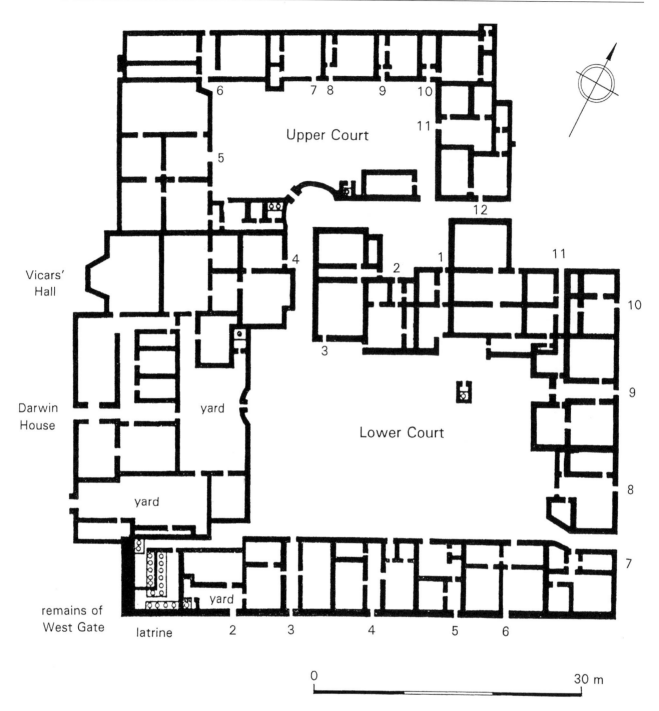

Fig. 7.4. Vicars choral of Lichfield Cathedral. Ground plan of The Vicarage in 1805, with modern house numbering added. Based on a redrawing of the plan published in Gould 1976a (fig.5) (drawing and copyright, Warwick Rodwell)

1325 – ed. Greenslade 1970, 156).

Additional rules and enforcements were introduced from time to time. In the 1240s the statutes required that any canon who had no vicar was to pay to the chapter a sum equivalent to a vicar's salary. In the early 1290s it was necessary for Bishop Meuland (1256–95) to order that every canon, whether resident of not, was to appoint a vicar, and in 1294 chapter ordered that new vicars should not be required to make gifts to existing vicars. Clearly,

dishonourable practice involving some form of extortion had been allowed to develop. This was again exposed in 1531 when some vicars protested about illegal practices that were impoverishing them; newly admitted vicars were required by the others not only to provide a feast but also to pay an 'entrance fee' of 20s., followed by two further payments of 26s. 8d.

It is unclear when the vicars were first brought together to live in a communal residence, although there is an unsubstantiated reference to the chapter's providing them with a house in the 1240s (Wharton 1691, 446). In the late 13th century Bishop Meuland assigned a house at Stowe for the residence of elderly and infirm vicars. Stowe was formerly a separate parish immediately adjoining Lichfield on the east, and with which the cathedral had close connections throughout history. One of the principal vicars, the subchanter, had a house of his own in Lichfield in the 13th century.

It was Bishop Walter Langton (1296–1321) who caused a communal residence for the vicars to be established within the cathedral Close. He was concerned about the dangers, presumably moral, of vicars lodging amongst lay-folk in the town. Therefore, in 1315, he gave them a plot of land inside the north-west corner of the Close. This was evidently a former canonical residence (LRO D. 30/K2). Unlike at Wells (chapter 11 below), there is no indication that the bishop himself instigated the construction of a communal residence akin to an Oxbridge college. Instead, we hear of building operations being initiated by individual vicars. Thus in 1330 John of Ashton was granted permission to complete the house that he had begun, and two other vicars were allowed to rebuild their house. The implication of the latter is there was already an aging property here. In both cases, conditions were imposed whereby the houses reverted to the chapter upon the deaths of the respective vicars.

Other references seem to imply that the vicars were allotted lodgings by the chapter in a college-style building, and that there was an implicit pecking order. Thus in 1326 a vicar complained that his lodging was not appropriate to his status. Moreover, vicars seem often to have lived in pairs, something which was expressly forbidden at Wells. References to communal structures also imply that a collegiate existence had been established well before 1329: in that year the vicars were ordered to repair their kitchen and common hall. Nevertheless, not all lived communally, because in 1374 the vicars' daily commons was doubled to 3d., on condition that they gave up the right to dine with their canons. Clearly, there was hitherto no prescribed domestic protocol, and various arrangements obtained.

Improvements were made to the vicars' accommodation in the early 15th century: the houses were repaired and a new common hall was built at the instigation of Canon Thomas Chesterfield with the assistance of Bishop William Heyworth (1419–47) and two Oxford burgesses, a curious combination of benefactors (Savage 1925, 7). This process was continued by Dean Thomas Heywood, who completed the repairs to the houses, and in 1474 built an infirmary chamber, chapel and muniment room. He stipulated that the building was to remain in common use, and could not be let to, or occupied by, any single vicar.

The size and status of the 'college' developed in the 15th century, the number of vicars rose to 27, and the subchanter became their *ex officio* president, a position not found elsewhere in similar English institutions. Statutes of 1428 required the principal vicars, now four in number, to wear special amices trimmed with fur, and they were given an annual allowance of 6s. 8d. to pay for these. The same statutes dealt with the prompt filling of vacancies, and required all new vicars to be examined to ensure that they could chant to an organ. Subsequently, a probationary period of one year was introduced for new recruits.

In an attempt to gain greater independence from the chapter, the vicars applied for a royal licence of incorporation in 1528. The application was made without the knowledge of the chapter, which subsequently exercised its influence to block the granting of the licence.

As in other cathedral closes, the unseemly behaviour of individual vicars was a constant source of concern to the bishop and chapter. The earliest record of the dean exercising his duty of control over unruly vicars occurs in 1321, when he delivered a stern lecture in their common hall. Examples of troublesome behaviour included Richard of Elmhurst who, in 1324, was indicted before the king's court of attacking royal officers in a lane just outside the cathedral Close; in 1330 he was reprimanded by the chapter for dealing in chickens and cattle and for having a fire in his lodging which might endanger other vicars. As usual in all-male institutions, sexual misdemeanours were rife amongst the vicars, and in 1359 seven were accused of them. They included the subchanter, whose activities involved no less than five women. Fines were levied for inappropriate behaviour, payable to the fabric fund.

In 1383 the chapter laid down new rules governing the behaviour of vicars. These included attendance at services, forbidding them to leave the cathedral Close after 9pm or to entertain any dubious woman (*suspectam mulierem*) in their rooms, and requiring them to dress in a seemly manner. The rules were not obeyed: in 1465 a fine of 2d. was imposed for absenteeism, and in 1496 there was a fine of 12d. for those found outside the Close at night, after the gates had been shut. The stringency of that ruling seemingly led to attacks on the porter, to persuade him to allow errant vicars into the Close after curfew, and consequently measures had to be taken to counter that abuse.

Statutes were drawn up by the vicars themselves governing their conduct in the communal buildings in the 15th century. They were to be well behaved at table and not to refuse the food served to them;

gambling was not permitted in hall, except for ale; they were required to keep their lodgings dry and in good repair, taking precautions against fire; women and hunting dogs were not to be kept in the vicars' close (ed. Greenslade 1970, 164). Charitable funds were made available to assist poorer vicars with attaining these objectives.

In addition to their vocation in the church, at least some vicars pursued other gainful activities. Some bred dogs for sport, and went hunting at night, practices which the chapter tried to stamp out in 1512. The following year there was a short-lived strike by the vicars, who complained that they were being unfairly treated, and overworked. The latter complaint arose from the fact that the chapter had reduced the number of vicars from 27 to 21, and consequently increased their individual duties.

From the early 13th century, vicars owned and managed their own corporate property. One of the earliest records of this occurs in Alexander de Stavenby's episcopate (1224–38), when they assumed control of the lands attached to the chapel of St Chad's Head adjacent to the south choir aisle of the cathedral (Rodwell 1985; 1989, 285–8). The management of this property was kept separate from all others, and the vicars who administered it were known as 'keepers of the martiloge'. In 1348 the vicars acquired their first appropriated church, at Penn (Staffordshire). Grants of property, mainly burgages in the town of Lichfield, were made to the vicars, usually coupled with a requirement to keep the obit of the donor. Various pensions were also granted to them in recognition of prescribed duties. Consequently, the vicars gradually built up a property portfolio together with sundry sources of regular income. However, this was still insufficient to meet their needs, and in 1412 a second church, at Chesterton (Warwickshire), was appropriated to them to boost their income.

Records have not survived to show how the vicars managed their property in the early days, but they certainly had a common seal by 1315 and were appointing proctors to act for them by 1324. In 1535 the vicars' gross income was just over £200 *per annum*, of which £100 was contributed by the chapter for commons. Much of the remainder came from property rents, the vicars owning about 250 houses and an even greater number of parcels of land in and around Lichfield (ed. Greenslade 1970, 164). They were important land-owners, and employed a bailiff and receiver-general to manage their properties.

The Reformation opened a new chapter in the history of the vicars choral, and an attempt was made to bring them under closer control. In 1539 a Royal Commission drew up a new set of statutes for their governance, and ordered that henceforth all additional statutes were to be introduced by the dean and chapter. Previous statutes drawn up by the vicars themselves were abolished. Perennial problems featured in the new regulations, such as absenteeism, attendance at services and immoral liaisons with women. Vicars were also forbidden to lease property for terms of more than fifteen years; nor could they act as debt collectors or bailiffs. A new regulation forbad the sale of water from the cathedral conduit, a supply from which was piped into the vicars' close. The new statutes were evidently not adhered to, and a warning was issued in 1544 that they would be applied with full vigour if the vicars did not mend their ways. They did not, and a steady stream of misdemeanours continued to be recorded well into the 17th century.

Under legislation abolishing the chantries of 1547, the vicars were threatened with the confiscation of their property, a case being made out against them that they were 'incorporated by the name of a college'. However, the chantry commissioners reviewed the position and determined that they were `united and consolidated to the corporation of the dean and chapter', and their possessions were subsequently confirmed by letters patent (ed. Greenslade 1970, 168).

As the 16th century wore on the number of vicars decreased and in particular the proportion of priest vicars to lay vicars dwindled. Some even held posts as sinecures and did not reside in Lichfield. After the Restoration the number of vicars remained steady at twelve, five of whom were priests.

The Civil War brought widespread devastation to Lichfield, and the cathedral Close was besieged three times. The *Parliamentary Survey* of 1649 described the cathedral as 'exceedingly ruinated' and recorded that the vicars' common hall and their communal 'boghouse' had been destroyed, and five of the twenty houses in the vicars' close were in ruinous condition. They also lost 52 houses in the town. Two inventories were made of the condition and use of buildings within the vicars' close, one in 1649, the other probably in 1660; they provide further details of the damage inflicted (Tringham 1984).

In 1649 there were ten houses each in the Upper and Lower Courts. The common hall 'with all houses and outbuildings thereto belonging' was described as `much demolished and spoiled, not worth repairing. The materials ... to be sold'. In 1706 the number of houses was still twenty, and in 1756 the common hall was rebuilt. Surely the latter cannot have lain in ruins for more than one hundred years before being rebuilt? The enigma remains.

Layout and topography

The cathedral Close was initially defended by a bank and ditch, which was almost certainly in place by the middle of the 12th century, and a description is preserved in an undated, 13th-century survey (Wharton 1691, 459). By the late 12th century the Close had been supplied with piped water from a conduit house at Maple Hayes, 1½ miles west of Lichfield (Gould 1976b). The two vicars' courts were fed from the conduit head which stood between them and the west front of the cathedral (ed. Smith 1964, ii, 100) (Fig. 7.3).

In 1299 Bishop Langton was granted a licence to erect a crenellated stone wall around the cathedral Close (*Cal Pat Roll* 1292–1301, 408). It survives in part on the east and north, and much of the rest of its course is readily traceable in later boundaries; only on the south is there some uncertainty (Fig. 7.1). Within the wall, the Close was divided into a regular series of plots, numbering 26 in all. Three corners of the Close evidently contained substantial medieval houses that were structurally integrated with the defensive wall. Thus, the Bishop's Palace occupied the largest plot, at the north-east corner, a 14th-century house (now St Mary's House) lay in the south–east corner, and a house with a tower occupied by Bishop Langton's nephew was built into the south-west angle (ed. Greenslade 1990, 67). Langton House, a Georgian brick building, probably occupies the site of the latter medieval residence.

Whether there was another integral house at the north-west corner, to which the Vicarage was subsequently attached, is unproven, albeit highly likely. There is, however, an early reference to a tower in this area, and one is shown on John Speed's map of 1610 (Speed 1616). In the siege of 1643, the tower was undermined by Parliamentarian sappers and a massive gunpowder charge laid which blew asunder the entire north-west corner of the Close wall (Clayton n.d., 44–5).

Almost certainly, the canonical plot given to the vicars by Bishop Langton in 1315 contained an existing structure which would have served initially as the nucleus of the new residence. Excluded from the gift were a barn and a dovecote, the latter subsequently reported as having lain in what is now the Lower Court. This perhaps points to the vicars' initial property being in the north-west angle of the Close, rather than alongside the road entering from the West Gate. According to Wharton (1691, 447), however, the vicars took over two canonical houses, which may indicate that a second grant of property was made. This may have been the land on which the dovecote and barn lay, thus extending the vicars' holding southwards.

Hence, the vicars' residence must have occupied much, if not all, of the western margin of the cathedral Close, from the West Gate to the north-west corner of the walled *enceinte*. However, no structural remains dating from the 14th century have been identified in the Vicarage, a complete rebuild

having taken place in stages during the course of the 15th century. This led to the creation of a college-style plan comprising two rectangular courtyards (or quadrangles), surrounded by lodging ranges. The southern court, or Lower Vicars' Court, is the larger unit and is bounded on the south by the road entering the cathedral Close from the west. The court incorporated one flank of the West Gate in its south-west corner.

Adjoining the Lower Court on the north is a second, smaller one, the Upper Vicars' Court. Both units abut the defensive wall of the Close on the west. To the north of the Vicarage, and extending as far as the northern wall of the Close, is a plot of land which was open until modern times. It was held by the vicars and could mark the site of the 14th-century canonical house that was integral with the defensive circuit.

Today, the entrances to the courts are visually insignificant, merely narrow gaps between buildings, with no substantial gates; and they are all bridged over at first-floor level. They are suitable only for pedestrian access. The Lower Court has an entrance on the east side, adjacent to the southern corner, where it faces the west door of the cathedral. There was formerly another entrance, now blocked, which lay immediately inside the west gate and was accessed from the main road into the cathedral Close. The Upper Court has a narrow opening on its east flank, giving on to the road which runs around the north side of the cathedral. There is also a passage between the houses on the north side of the Lower Court, communicating with the Upper Court.

The common latrine was in the Lower Court, in the south-west angle adjacent to the West Gate into the cathedral Close. It was hemmed in on two sides by lodging ranges, while the Close wall and north flank of the gate formed its remaining two sides. A chamber of unrecorded purpose lay above the latrine. On the plan of 1805 the latrine is shown divided into two compartments, doubtless for males and females, respectively, and one had eleven seats, the other seven. Unlike the vicars of Wells (chapter 11 below), those at Lichfield did not enjoy private latrines in their lodgings, discharging into a common drainage system.

The buildings of the vicars' close are extremely varied in construction and character, having undergone much alteration and renewal, particularly since the Civil War. They range from small timber-framed lodgings of the 15th century to substantial brick-built houses of the 18th and 19th centuries. The Upper Court still retains some sense of an institutional dwelling, comprising lodging ranges surrounding a grassy quadrangle. The Lower Court, however, imparts very little of that feeling, being essentially an agglomeration of gardens and outbuildings enclosed on all sides by the rear elevations of buildings which now look outward and not into the court. Since the mid 17th century, the Lower Court has literally turned itself inside out. By the end of the 18th century only the Upper Court was recognizable as 'a small quadrangle of old low-built houses' (Shaw 1798, 308).

Buildings of the vicars choral

The houses of the Upper Court have their own numbering system, and are identified as Nos. 1 to 12 Vicars' Close. Confusingly, the houses of the Lower Court are included in the general numbering system of the cathedral Close, being identified as Nos. 2 to 11 The Close; there is also Darwin House, which looks outwards from the Close on the west and forms part of the Beacon Street frontage. In the descriptions which follow, the numbers of properties in The Close are cited without a suffix, and those in the Upper Court of Vicars' Close are followed by 'Vicars' Close'

Lodging Ranges in the Lower Court

The court is rectangular, measuring overall *c*.52m by 36m (170 by 140ft) (Figs. 7.3, 7.5). The west side was defined by the early 14th-century defensive Close wall, which has entirely disappeared, having been damaged during the Civil War, although the line of the wall persisted as a major boundary until 1760. At its southern end lay the West Gate, the principal entrance to the cathedral Close. Only the northern flank of the carriageway survives, the remainder of the gate having been pulled down for road widening in 1800. Immediately inside the gate was apparently a passage leading into the Lower Court.

The south range (Nos. 2–6) displays a series of pleasant early 18th-century facades (built before 1732) fronting on to the road, and Nos. 2–4 are rebuilds of the period, replacing houses destroyed in the Civil War. No. 2 is identifiable as Richard Hinde's house which, in 1649, was described as 'all torn in pieces by granadoes and much of the materials carried away' (Tringham 1984, 41, item 4). However, the overall plan suggests that the south range was originally designed as a block of eight lodgings, and that the three easternmost were redeveloped for Dean Heywood's new block in 1474.

The best evidence, particularly of the original plan-form is preserved in No. 5, a late 15th-century timber-framed house, formerly jettied on the north but now underbuilt. It is independently framed, abuts No. 6, and has its own distinctive form of construction (Fig. 7.6). The width is 5.8m (19ft), and depth on the ground floor is 6.5m (11ft); the first floor is close studded and the jetty posts have

moulded detailing. The primary position of the chimney stacks in this and the adjoining houses is debatable; all are now incorporated in the party walls. Originally, it is likely that they formed a line of brick-built projections on the south side (cf. the north court).

No. 6 and its neighbour (No. 7), which turns the south–east corner, are also 15th century and archaeologically complex. It seems likely that they formed part of Dean Heywood's building campaign of 1474, when he constructed a two-storeyed block comprising a chapel, chamber or rest-room (*le drawth*) for infirm vicars, a muniment room, and other small rooms (*domicule*). It is not now possible to identify the specific spaces, although it is probable that the chapel was on the ground floor at the very corner; that way, it could have had an east window facing the cathedral. Since it is stated that the infirm vicars were able to hear mass, it seems likely that their chamber was also on the ground floor, west of the chapel. Hence, the muniment room and other unspecified chambers would have been on the first floor.

No. 6 originally comprised two jettied chambers of unequal width, 4m (15ft) and 3.7m (12ft), respectively, with oriel windows on the first floor. It has a purlin and collar-beam roof with raking struts. No. 7 again comprises unequal chambers, and on the ground floor incorporates the entrance passage to the Lower Court from the east. The house is cellared and, exceptionally, the ground floor walls are built of sandstone on the south and east. There is a chamfered plinth and, although much refaced in modern times, the ashlar masonry is apparently medieval (Fig. 7.7). No. 6 also has a heavily weathered stone plinth. The exposed timber framing on the first floor is arranged in square panels, and is clearly of 17th-century date. Without detailed archaeological investigation it is impossible to be certain whether the masonry construction belongs to the late 15th-century chapel, or is a post-Civil War reuse of medieval ashlar; considerable use was made in Lichfield in the 17th and 18th centuries of reclaimed medieval ashlars for plinths and lining cellars. The mid 17th-century surveys of the vicars' close do not mention a vicars' chapel, which must by then have been assigned to a new use.

Apart from the corner units (Nos. 7 and 10), the east range was entirely rebuilt as two houses (Nos. 8 and 9) in the 18th and 19th centuries. All that survives of the medieval range is part of the frame at the southern end of No. 8, where it looks as though a deep jetty was added, facing into the courtyard. One of these houses was previously the subchanter's (probably No. 9) which, in the 17th-century, had its own detached kitchen (Tringham 1984, 42, item 11). It was most likely the grandest residence in the Vicarage. The loss of the eastern

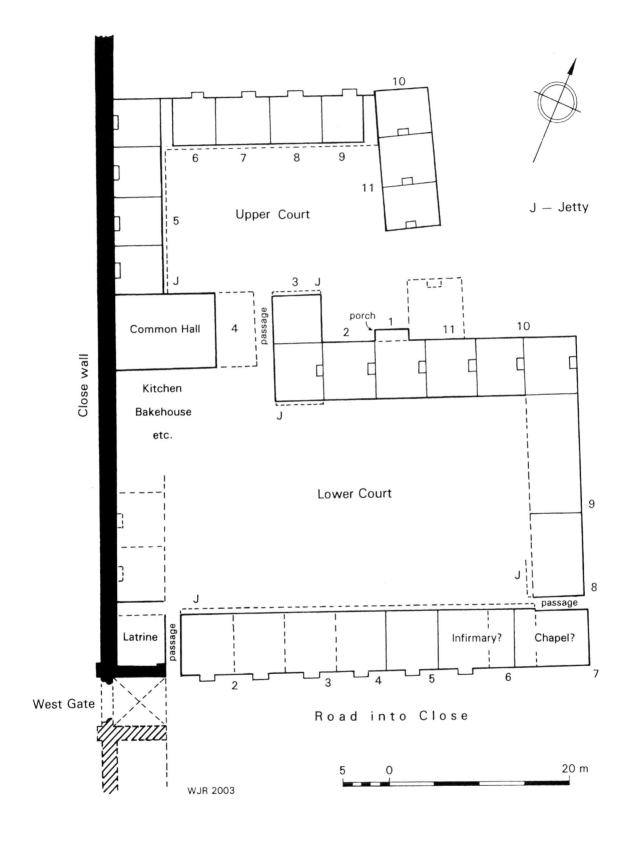

Fig. 7.5. Vicars choral of Lichfield Cathedral. Reconstructed plan of the upper and lower vicars' courts in the late 15th century (drawing and copyright, Warwick Rodwell)

Fig. 7.6. Vicars choral of Lichfield Cathedral. Timber-framed north elevations of No. 6 (left) and No. 5 The Close. Originally the jettied fronts of vicars' lodgings in the lower court, these are now rear elevations (photo and copyright, Warwick Rodwell)

Fig. 7.7. Vicars choral of Lichfield Cathedral. No. 7 The Close, from the south-east. Although much rebuilt after the Civil War, this was probably the late 15th-century chapel. Glimpsed to the left is the 18th-century brick façade of No. 6 (photo and copyright, Warwick Rodwell)

façade makes it impossible to determine whether there ever was a substantial gateway leading into the Lower Court. The tiny passage between Nos. 7 and 8 is so undistinguished that a more significant entrance, facing the cathedral, might be expected in the 15th century. Similarly, it cannot be determined whether there were more than two medieval lodgings here, but the plan dimensions would comfortably allow for three units and a gateway.

The north range is in two parts, interrupted at ground-level by the interconnecting passage between the two courts. The eastern part comprises a row of five timber-framed lodgings (Nos. 1–2, and Nos. 10–11 Vicars' Close), with a more substantial house (No.3 Vicars' Close) at the west end. The five two-storied, unjettied houses are of similar plan and dimensions, being 5.5m (18ft) wide by 6m (20ft) deep; they were potentially built as a unitary block, although there may be a structural break between No. 1 Vicars' Close and No. 11 The Close. They have tie-beam roofs with collars and side purlins; most of the collars are supported by a single strut rising off the tie-beam. Nos. 1 and 2 Vicars' Close have been studied in detail: they had oriel windows facing north and south on both the ground and first floors. Brick chimney stacks were sited internally against the east wall, and there was probably no original fireplace on the first floor. The stair lay at the north-east corner.

A gabled and double-jettied porch was added to the north side of No. 1 Vicars' Close, perhaps in the early 16th century (Fig. 7.8), probably in response to the internal extension on the north side of No. 11, which blocked the original doorway to No. 1 Vicars' Close. No. 10 was given an elaborate jettied facade on the east in the 17th century, a substantial, and purely decorative, piece of timber framing jointed on to the pre-existing gable-end.

No. 3 Vicars' Close is a difficult building to interpret without detailed investigation. It is two rooms deep, jettied on the south, built transversely to the axis of the range, and has the outward appearance of a cross-wing. It has lost a large oriel window from the south gable-end. The southern room has the same plan dimensions as the five adjoining lodgings, and may therefore represent the site of a sixth, which was subsequently rebuilt. The jetty posts bear the remains of engaged shafts with crenellated capitals, indicating a later 15th-century date. The house was possibly also jettied on the north, prior to 18th-century refacing in brick.

Parts of these structures have been dated by dendrochronology. The attic floor joists of No. 10 (at the east end of the range) have yielded a felling date range of 1453–78, but the floor is most likely to be an early insertion into a former open roof (*Vernacular Architecture* 30, 1999, 95). An attempt to date the roof trusses themselves was unsuccessful. The roof

Fig. 7.8. Vicars choral of Lichfield Cathedral. 16th-century two-storied porch added to the north side of No. 1 Vicars' Close. The first-floor jetty has been under-built, and the gable jetty has been cut back (photo and copyright, Warwick Rodwell)

framing of No.1 Vicars' Close has been dated to *c.*1451, and the frame of the transverse wing (No. 3 Vicars' Close) yielded a felling date range of 1448–68; the roof had evidently been repaired, the rafters dating to after *c.*1516 (*Vernacular Architecture* 33, 2002, 113–15).

West of No. 3 Vicars' Close is a passageway connecting the north and south courts, and this is contained within the footprint of No. 4 Vicars' Close, a house that was substantially rebuilt in the 18th century. At the north-west angle of the court is the much-altered common hall (known as Vicars' Hall). Adjacent to this, on the south, was the common kitchen and bakehouse, now entirely gone.

The west range is wholly occupied by a large, 18th-century brick building known as Darwin House, having been the residence of Erasmus Darwin from 1758 to 1781 (ed. Greenslade 1990, 64). When Darwin came to Lichfield, he 'purchased an old half-timbered house in the cathedral vicarage, adding a handsome new front' (LRO Anna Seward Mss.). Darwin must

have acquired the whole west range, which probably once comprised several separate lodgings, as well as structures ancillary to the common hall. These would have been built against the Close wall, which may already have been demolished before Darwin arrived on the scene, following damage during the Civil War. The houses, however, were not destroyed, and rebuilding after the Civil War included a transverse brick range, part of which still survives. In 1760 Darwin purchased a lease on,

> *'All those houses and buildings formerly called ... the Dovehouse and Bakehouse, and all that there common kitchen with chambers and Garretts, and all that low ground room adjoining the said kitchen with a door opening into the wall entry, and all those little gardens adjoining to houses, and ... a Draw well and then converted into a necessary House, and the little shop situated ... in the ... Nether Vicarage'* (LRO *Lease Book D30/XXXVIII, f.3v.*).

Darwin's new front range, erected in 1760–1, lay parallel to the existing range, straddling the former line of the Close wall and projecting westwards into the ditch outside (Figs. 7.3, 7.4 and 7.9). In order to expand into the ditch, which was and still is called 'The Dimble', Darwin had to obtain a separate lease from the dean and chapter. He built a bridge across the ditch which was removed in the early 19th century.

In *c.*1794 a subsequent owner demolished the old buildings behind Darwin's new range and replaced them with another brick range. In 1998–9 considerable evidence relating to late medieval timber-framed structures and 17th-century alterations was recorded during a major refurbishment of Darwin House (Meeson 1999). The line of the medieval Close

Fig. 7.9. Vicars choral of Lichfield Cathedral. Watercolour of c.1800, now presumed lost, showing Darwin House approached by a bridge across the Close ditch from Beacon Street. The west gable and oriel window of Vicars' Hall (1756) are seen to the left (sources, Anon 1897, 72–3 and ed. Greenslade 1990, pl.20)

wall was also traced. It is likely that the northern half of the site would previously have been taken up with communal structures, and it would not therefore have been possible to fit more than two vicars' lodgings on the remainder. The two lodgings had probably been combined in the 17th century to make one substantial house. That house is potentially identifiable in the 1649 survey as a property owned by Mr Braddoke, 'who has put [it] in good repair' (i.e. since the Civil War). The rental value of the house was given as £4 *per annum*, which was greater than any other in the vicars' close at this time.

Lodging Ranges in the Upper Court

This smaller, rectangular unit appears to have been annexed to the pre-existing Lower Court, but was not constructed as an entity (Figs. 7.3, 7.5). Like the Lower Court, it abutted the Close wall on the west, although reconstruction after the Civil War has removed all upstanding masonry of the latter. The court comprises three timber-framed ranges, of which the northern is almost entirely preserved in its original form. It was the last part to be built, and abutted the somewhat earlier façades of both the east and west ranges.

The primary east range (Nos. 10 and 11 Vicars' Close) comprised a block of three lodgings (No. 11 is a double unit) with a depth of 5.8m (19ft): two of the units measured 5m (16½ft) wide, while the third (southernmost) was only 4.6m (15ft). The frame is close studded, braced in the upper storey, and unjettied; the roof has side purlins, wind braces and collared trusses with pairs of upright struts rising off the tie-beams. The stacks were internal, set against the party walls. Only the lodging at the north end seems to have had oriels, one facing east on the ground floor, and another facing north on the first floor (and possibly also one on the ground floor).

The further development of the east range was piecemeal. To the three original lodgings was added a fourth (No. 12 Vicars' Close), and that seems to be much later. Adjoining that, on the south, is the entrance to the Upper Court, which in turn is flanked by a lateral extension to No. 11 the Close. That extension appears to have been an early addition, and was probably created as a separate lodging. The entrance, now only a narrow, ground-level passage, may well have been wider before infilling occurred.

The west range was 5.2m (17ft) deep and almost certainly comprised four lodgings, jettied on the east. Only the northernmost lodging survives, encapsulated in the western half of No. 6 Vicars' Close, while the eastern half forms part of the unitary north range. Part of the jetty, together with one closed truss and one arch-braced intermediate truss with butt-purlins survive (Fig. 7.11). Otherwise, the whole of

the west side is now occupied by a brick-built house of 1764 with an impressive façade on the west, and very plain back (No. 5 Vicars' Close). Nevertheless, the three-bay Georgian structure preserves some elements of the previous lodgings; the house was divided into flats in the 1970s, and the original staircase removed. The medieval lodgings must have backed directly on to the Close wall. Presumably the chimney stacks were constructed against, or even cut into, its masonry.

The north range (Nos. 6–9 Vicars' Close), which was constructed to fit between the existing east and west ranges, comprised four near-identical two-storied lodgings, jettied on the south and punctuated with large brick chimney stacks on the north (Fig. 7.10). The houses are 5.6m (17ft) deep on ground plan, and are of two different widths: the middle two measure 5.3m (18½ft), whereas the first and fourth are only 4.5m (15ft). The first-floor chambers, however, are all closely similar in size. The reduced ground floor area of the two end lodgings was caused by the construction of narrow lobbies that were necessary to facilitate access to the northernmost houses in the east and west ranges, respectively. Their entrances would otherwise have been totally obstructed. At the same time, the northern end of the west range was partly rebuilt to align with the new north range, and was evidently gabled.

A detailed study of Nos. 7–9 was carried out during refurbishment in 1990. They were erected as a single block with a continuous jetty. There were oriel windows to both ground and first floor rooms, and apparently no original windows on the north. All oriels have been lost from both courts, although the moulded aprons and mortices for their attachment to the main framing have survived in many cases. However, at No. 8 Vicars' Close moulded fragments of the oriel framing were found, reused in

Fig. 7.10. Vicars choral of Lichfield Cathedral. Nos. 7–10 Vicars' Close, after restoration (photo and copyright, Warwick Rodwell)

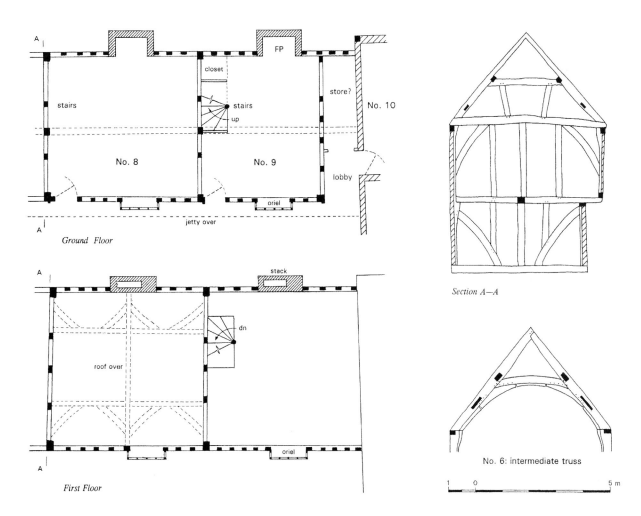

Fig. 7.11. Vicars choral of Lichfield Cathedral. Reconstructed plans and section of Nos. 8 and 9 Vicars' Close, based on evidence gathered during the restoration of Nos. 7–9. The intermediate, arch-braced truss is from No. 6 (drawing and copyright, Warwick Rodwell)

later features. Based on the evidence recovered, several oriels were reinstated in the 1990s.

The entrance to each lodging had a four-centred arch, and lay to the west of the window. The staircase was in or close to the north-west corner. The ground floor room had a large fireplace in the north wall, with a four-centred arch, all made in brick and lime plastered; the upper room was unheated and was open to the roof which is of clasped purlin type with one tier of wind bracing (Fig. 7.11). The closed trusses between lodgings each have a collar and two raking struts rising off the tie-beam. Each chamber was spanned at the mid-point by an arch-braced truss.

Over the entrance to the lobby between Nos. 9 and 10 Vicars' Close is a length of embattled cornice which retains red lead paint that may well be medieval. In No. 7 Vicars' Close there is a medieval painted inscription on the ceiling beam of the lower room, which takes the form of an invocation to the Virgin Mary. These are the only examples of medieval decoration so far recorded in the vicars' close.

While the north court seems to be entirely of the 15th century, it was not constructed as a unity. The north range, representing the last structural phase, may plausibly be identified as the work begun by Canon Chesterton (d.1452) and finished by Dean Heywood. There was presumably a boundary along the line of its northern edge, up to which the earlier east and west ranges extended. Dendrochronology was carried out on the framing of No. 8 Vicars' Close, yielding a felling date range of c.1450–75 (*Vernacular Architecture* 33, 2002, 115). When complete, the court would have provided at least eleven lodgings, and potentially twelve, and that total could be increased to thirteen if No. 12 Vicars' Close is in origin a medieval building rather than later infilling.

The Common Hall

The first common hall may well have been adapted from a hall that originally formed part of a canonical house. However, it would not have been large enough to accommodate twenty or more vicars for meals, and its replacement with a new, larger structure would have been inevitable as numbers increased. The earliest reference to the hall is in 1321, and to the common kitchen in 1329.

In 1334 a solar is referred to at the north end of the hall, indicating that the present hall, which is on an east–west axis, cannot have been built on exactly the same site. At the south end of the hall would have been a screens passage, separating it from the buttery and pantry. In 14th-century hall planning the kitchen frequently lay immediately beyond those service rooms, and was approached through them; in other words, the kitchen at Lichfield would have lain south of the hall.

When the vicars finally ceased to dine with their canons in 1390 the old hall was not large enough for the full complement, and a new common hall was built to accommodate their needs. It is uncertain exactly when this hall was erected, and there may have been a delay (ed. Greenslade 1990, 62). However, in due course, it was sited at the north-west corner of the Lower Court, remaining in use until the 1640s when it was badly damaged during the sieges, and had to be rebuilt.

The late medieval hall was aligned east–west, with its high end abutting the Close wall. A single roof truss belonging to the east gable has survived in the party wall between the present hall and No. 4 Vicars' Close; it has two sets of side-purlins, a collar supported off the tie-beam by a pair of struts, and is stiffened with curved braces. The span of the truss measures 7.6m (25ft), giving the width of the hall; it must have been *c*.11m (36 ft) in length. By turning the axis of the hall through 90 degrees, the screens passage could be entered from both the north and south courts, which was an obvious convenience. Since it is known that the kitchen lay to the south of the hall, in the southern court, there is a strong possibility that the 14th-century kitchen structure was still in use, and that it survived until the 1790s.

Presumably the hall was patched up after the Civil War bombardment, because it was not until 1756 that the vicars demolished the old structure and replaced it (on the same site) with a new red brick building, the shell of which stands today, albeit much altered. The new hall followed medieval precedent, being at first-floor level with an undercroft below; it measured 14m by 7.6m (46ft by 25ft) and was reached by an oak staircase which was destroyed only *c*.1979. The great window which lit the stair from the south still remains. At the west end, the hall projected slightly beyond the line of the demolished medieval Close wall. It had an oculus in the gable and an oriel window with a fine view over Beacon Street and beyond (Fig. 7.9). By 1800 the hall had been subdivided; it remains in use as flats today. The oriel does not survive.

The new hall was largely symbolic and clearly did not function for long, if ever, as the common dining room of the vicars. By this time many vicars had families, and they had their own cooking facilities in their enlarged houses. The hall was let out for civic functions, and its redundant kitchen was sold to Darwin in 1760. As part of the reconstruction in 1756 a new muniment room was provided at the east end of the hall, the vicars' records having previously been kept in a room, formerly the Chapel of St Chad's Head, in the cathedral, above the consistory court and canons' vestry (Harwood 1806, 271). They had probably been moved there in the 16th century from Dean Heywood's muniment room in the Lower Court.

Conclusion

The vicars' close at Lichfield was a piecemeal construction in the local vernacular tradition. By the late 15th century it comprised two college-style quadrangles enclosed by timber-framed ranges of lodgings and communal buildings.

Although the Lower Vicars' Court may have had its origins in the 14th century, none of the extant buildings is earlier than the 15th century. The oldest surviving fragment is a single roof truss at the east end of the block containing the pre-1756 common hall: that is likely to date from the late 14th or early 15th century. A little to the east, the jettied 'cross-wing' which is now No. 3 Vicars' Close is also early 15th century and was clearly a house of some pretension. It may have been occupied by the sacrist who was one of the two vicar principals. The subchanter, the other principal and eventually president of the college, lived in a sizeable house in the east range, which has not survived. By the late 15th century the Lower Court contained a hall, kitchen, bakehouse and other communal structures at the north-west corner, a chapel, infirmary chamber and muniment room at the south-east corner, and a communal latrine and probably a dovecote at the south-west. The Upper Court, which contained only lodgings, seems to have been built in the mid and later 15th century. Its three ranges were constructed separately.

A few vicars' lodgings were erected singly, but most were built in blocks: some were jettied, others not. Similarly, chimney stacks could be internal (against a gable end) or project externally from a side wall. Each unit comprised a ground-floor room of one bay with a fireplace and a stair. Under or beside the latter may have been a small closet serving as a garderobe, although there was no drainage. On the upper floor lay a single chamber, open to the roof which, in many instances, was of two bays separated by an arch-braced truss. Chambers were not, it seems, generally heated. Room dimensions and floor areas of individual lodgings varied slightly from block to block, but the average was about 5m square. In jettied houses the upper floor was obviously a little larger than the lower, and in five instances a passage was cut out of the ground-floor room, making it substantially smaller than the chamber above.

Considerable improvements were effected in the late 16th and 17th centuries, which included ceiling the chambers, subdividing rooms and installing more fireplaces. Some houses were modestly extended, others combined in pairs, and in a few instances cellars were excavated.

The total number of dwellings in the vicars' close has fluctuated through time. From 1549, vicars were permitted to marry and have families, and con-

sequently some units were combined (as at Wells). However, it is not now possible to ascertain the maximum number of lodgings created because whole blocks were rebuilt in the 18th century. The original Lower Court would have accommodated between eighteen and twenty lodgings, and the Upper Court eleven or twelve. Logistically, at least 30 units, and potentially 32, could have been fitted into the two courts.

However, three lodgings in the Lower Court must have been taken out of commission when Dean Heywood created a chapel and other special-purpose chambers at the south-east corner in 1474. Hence the total number of lodgings was reduced to about 30. Although there is no record of the company of vicars exceeding 27, the number of prebends eventually rose to 32; consequently, a minimum of 27 vicars' lodgings would have been required in the late 15th century, and perhaps a few more. The historical and architectural evidence are thus in close accord.

8

The Development of the College of Vicars Choral at Lincoln Minster

David Stocker

With an annex on recent survey and excavation by Naomi Field

Introduction

The college of vicars choral at Lincoln is still a beautiful group of honey-coloured limestone buildings loosely gathered around a sloping green lawn just to the south of the cathedral's east end (Fig. 8.1). Although this quiet court now contains only a small group of eccentric houses, during the later middle ages it was the powerhouse of the cathedral – the home of the priests and the senior clerks who managed the *opus dei*, the primary function of the medieval church. As was the case with many of the vicars' colleges in this volume, the Lincoln vicars were not recognised as a formal institution through separate incorporation until late in their development – Lincoln was not incorporated until 1441 (Maddison 1878, 3,10–11). But although the pen-ultimate incorporation at a secular cathedral, by that date the college buildings were largely complete and life 'in common' had been in progress for more than a century and a half. Despite the large number of canons serving the cathedral, Lincoln always had a relatively small college of vicars. Numbers of vicars here varied throughout the medieval period, but it is thought that there were usually about twenty-five in residence. This relatively small number is no doubt due to the fact that only non-resident canons at Lincoln were obliged to appoint a vicar to their prebendal stall (Edwards 1967, 264). As at several other secular cathedrals, at Lincoln from 1240, if not before, a distinction was maintained between 'Junior Vicars' and 'Senior Vicars', but the terminology used to distinguish particularly the Junior Vicars was sufficiently flexible to make counting total numbers difficult. Later on it is clear that the Senior Vicars were in priestly orders whereas the Junior Vicars were clerks in minor orders, but it is not clear if this

distinction existed from the 13th century. In 1501 there were fifteen Senior Vicars and ten Junior Vicars, but in 1558 the college was reformed and reduced to four Senior Vicars (all priests) and eight Juniors (in minor orders). This division amongst the ranks of the vicars choral at Lincoln was to have architectural consequences. Indeed, because the story of the vicars of Lincoln from the 13th century to 1558 is relatively thinly documented, much of our understanding of the institution has to be drawn from study of the remains of their buildings.

These remains have been the subject of three published studies. The earliest, a rather misleading account by the indefatigable Precentor Venables, was published in 1884, a survey of the south range was undertaken in 1950 by Mrs Wood (1951), whilst the excellent detailed analysis, deploying many new measured drawings, undertaken by Stanley Jones as part of the Civic Trust's survey of the Close was published in 1987. This latest account corrects many of Venables' more erroneous statements, and is so perceptive and all-embracing that only a little new work remains to be done to complete our under-standing of the college. Rather than superseding Mr Jones' excellent survey work, this paper seeks to build upon it and focuses on the development of the college as a whole. Although it proposes new dates for the west and north ranges, and a novel inter-pretation of the latter, the paper could not have been written without Mr Jones' survey, and even the changes proposed in our understanding of the complex are dependent on his initial survey work. It is a model of careful recording and we are all greatly in his debt.

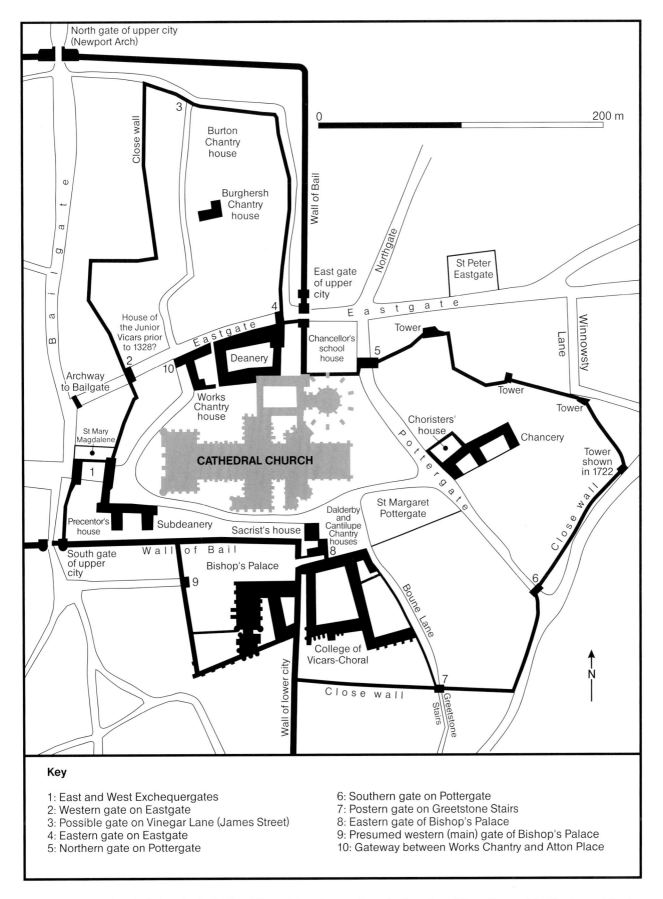

Fig. 8.1. Vicars choral of Lincoln Cathedral. Plan of the Close to show the location of the colleges of the Junior and Senior Vicars (source, Jones et al. 1987, Fig. 8.2. Drawn by Dave Watt, copyright English Heritage)

The earliest college building under Bishop Gravesend (c.1270)?

The first references to vicars choral at Lincoln occur at the end of the 12th century, when Bishop Hugh (1186–1200) required his prebends to provide vicars to substitute for them in the choir when they were absent from the cathedral (ed. Foster 1931, 260–1 no. 300; ed. Smith 1986, 66, no.93). There is also a licence for the foundation of a 'general fraternity' during Hugh's episcopate (ed. Smith 1986, 68, No.97). The licence was reissued by Hugh's successor William of Blois in 1203–6 (*ibid.* 166, No.257). Subsequently we have plenty of 13th-century evidence both for the establishment of vicarages by the canons, and for the vicars living in the canons' houses dotted around the close (Major 1974, 22–3). At some time before 1280 the vicars had also acquired the city hospital of St Giles in which their sick and infirm were lodged (ed. Foster 1935, 372, No.1049). An institution binding the vicars together with rules and officers existed by 1236, when a provost was appointed by the dean and chapter (Bradshaw and Wordsworth 1892–7, I, 57–9; II, xlv-vi). Then, between 1266 and 1272, land within the newly-expanded Close south-east of the Cathedral was given to the vicars (*ibid*, II, xlix-l; ed. Major 1973, 200, no.2870). Little attention seems to have been paid previously to this important grant, however, and credit for the 'foundation' of the vicars' college has been routinely given to Bishop Sutton (1288–99), a generation later. The site granted between 1266 and 1272 was known as the *boungarth* (the 'bean yard'- Cameron 1985, 17) and so was presumably an agricultural centre, although it also included the city ditch – the *werkdyke*. It was evidently a large trapezoidal plot bounded by the city wall on the west, the new Close Wall on the south, the canons' graveyard on the north and the street then called *Boune Lane* (now Greestone Place) on the east (Fig. 8.2a). The plot was on a steep slope, and included four terraces. The first, along the northern boundary of the site, meant that to enter the *boungarth* from this side a flight of steps down would be required. Later such steps would be incorporated into the passage through the gatehouse, but we don't know how access was managed *c*.1270. Although today Vicars' Court has a single slope, two further terrace walls ran across the college courtyard in the medieval period; the upper between the northern pairs of college buildings, and the lower between the southernmost lodgings in the east and west ranges. The locations of these two terrace walls are still marked by substantial steps in the string-courses and roof profile in both east and west ranges. As Venables observed, the terrace walls must have been broken by flights of steps in both east and west walks and he also says that there was a terraced walk across the centre of the court (1883–4,

243). It is not clear what his evidence for this was, but he had seen the substantial restoration work undertaken here in the 1870s and he may have seen the remains of these features. The south wall of the south range forms a fourth terrace wall across the site, and although at a different angle, and somewhat further to the south, the north wall of the 'Vicars' Barn' continues this line. Today the *boungarth* plot is also divided unequally north to south, but this division dates from the late 14th century and we will look at that in due course.

The 1266–72 grant of the *boungarth* to the vicars states that they can 'lawfully dispose of the land for their residence as seems best to them'. It seems clear, then, that the bishop, dean and chapter intended the vicars to establish themselves in a collegiate building or buildings at this early date. Hitherto it has been presumed that little building work was done for thirty years following the grant, but recent work on the ruined north range of the college suggests that it may represent an early building erected along the north side of the *boungarth*.

Today this north range is represented only by the lower parts of the north wall, alongside the road to the Bishop's Palace, and the west wall of the later gatehouse to its east. To Venables this range was the college hall, but Jones showed that this is most unlikely – and he placed the hall where it clearly belongs, in the south-east corner of the quadrangle. Jones correctly observed that north range does not follow the same layout as the others, but he went on to suggest that it might represent a college chapel. This seems equally unlikely, however; not least because we have absolutely no documentary evidence that the Lincoln vicars ever had their own chapel. The vicars at Exeter never acquired a chapel, and similarly at Chichester the vicars shared the ancient chapel of St Faith, outside their close, with another corporation (p.27 above). Tatton-Brown also rejects the claim made by the RCHME that the first floor chamber south-east of the hall at Salisbury was a chapel (chapter 10 below), whilst Hereford, Lichfield and, perhaps, Wells also did not acquire their chapels until the 15th century (p. 52, 68, 135–6). In the 14th century, then, dedicated vicarial chapels were rare – that at York (p.154 below) might be the only example. Consequently, we have no need to postulate that the Lincoln college had one at this date, and we will see, anyway, that the limited architectural evidence surviving for the north range makes such a function highly unlikely.

The lower parts of the north wall and the whole of the east wall of the north range survive above ground, and a well-constructed quoin in the north wall indicates that the range overlapped the north end of the west range by about half the latter's thickness. The present gatehouse, however, is clearly

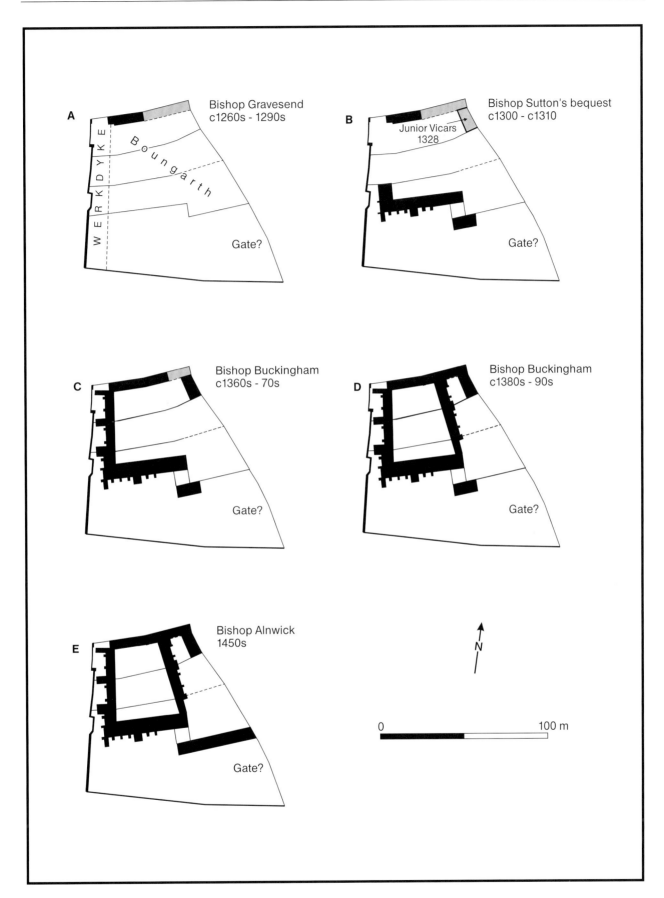

A   Bishop Gravesend
     c1260s - 1290s

W E R K D Y K E

B o u n g a r t h

Gate?

B   Bishop Sutton's bequest
     c1300 - c1310

Junior Vicars
1328

Gate?

C   Bishop Buckingham
     c1360s - 70s

Gate?

D   Bishop Buckingham
     c1380s - 90s

Gate?

E   Bishop Alnwick
     1450s

Gate?

N

0   100 m

Fig. 8.2. Vicars choral of Lincoln Cathedral. Block plan illustrating the proposed sequence of development of the vicars choral site (drawn by Dave Watt, copyright D Stocker)

of a later date and its west wall was evidently built on top of the existing east gable wall of the north range. We can use Jones' survey of this surviving wall (Fig. 8.3) to show that, in its first phase before the existing gatehouse was built, it contained two tall open arches. Furthermore, these arches rose through the two floors of the building. A once-moulded impost stone half way up the central pier between these openings indicates the location of a substantial timber floor at this level, apparently belonging to the original phase. A floor here would provide low headroom in the ground floor chambers and must imply that they were cellars.

The *Parliamentary Survey* of 1650, can be used to cast some further light on this range (Venables 1883–4, 247–9). Although scholars have been reticent to use the *Survey* to identify occupants of specific buildings on the vicars' site in 1650, this has been mostly because of Venables' false assumptions about the location of the hall. If we re-read the *Survey*, placing the vicars' hall where it certainly was, in the south-east corner of the court, the entries fall into a logical order – dealing with the occupied buildings in order round the court (as shown in Fig. 8.4). If the identification of properties proposed in Fig. 8.4 is correct, then, the Commissioners reported as follows on the north range:

> *There was auncientlie a Hall neare adioyning to the said William Ellis his house, with two pantrys and Cellerage under them (all very ruinous and unfitt for Use). There remains nothing but the Walls and some old Rotten Sparrs; The Covering was of Lead and taken of in the late Warr … xiii/- iiiid.*

This seems to provide confirmation that the north range was built over cellars created against the terrace wall along the northern boundary of the site. The pillar of masonry in the east wall, with its impost facing west as well as north and south, strongly suggests that the main floor was supported on a row of columns. We can reconstruct the plan of a long building on two floors, with a row of columns dividing the cellars below and supporting a large hall above (Fig. 8.5). In this reconstruction, the space at first floor level could be accessed directly from the south side of the street to the north, but it remains unclear what communication there was between the upper floor and the *boungarth* to the south. The first-floor space might have been accessed by means of a straight stair rising through the building from a doorway at the level of the courtyard but, had such an arrangement existed, we might have expected that stone walls defined the stairwell (as they do throughout the remainder of the college) and there is no evidence for such walls against the north wall. Furthermore there is no mention of such walls, or of any staircase, in the 1650 *Survey*. We have no reason to think, then, that this first floor space was divided by masonry walls

or by a staircase, and although it could have been divided by light-weight timber screens, it seems to have been an open hall, inaccessible from both the cellars below and directly from the courtyard. Presumably it would have been lit by windows in both north and south walls. It could have had fireplaces and flues within the wall-thickness (like that in the later gatehouse to the west), but elsewhere in the college such features were contained in large buttresses and there are no buttresses on the north wall of the north range. On balance, then, there were probably no fireplaces heating this first floor chamber. It seems clear, also, that the first floor space lacked the lateral garderobe towers that are such a feature of college accommodation in the south, west and east ranges, which were divided into individual chambers. At its western end, however, where the north range overlaps the west range, the surviving elements of the plan suggest an extension, and this may have been occupied by a garderobe – especially as it projects westwards over the presumed line of the *werkdyke* (Fig. 8.2a).

Although it subsequently became an integrated part of the layout of the college, then, the north range clearly did not resemble its other buildings. The lower floor was probably occupied by cellars and the upper floor seems to have been a single hall, perhaps without fireplaces, and it may have had only a single (possibly communal?) garderobe at its western end. The accommodation in the north range presents a marked contrast with the provision made for the vicars elsewhere in the college in the 14th century, who had not only individual chambers, but also individual fireplaces and garderobes.

Nor were these the only eccentricities of the north range. The evidence from the surviving east wall seems to show quite clearly that both the cellars and the chamber above communicated directly with a contemporary building to the east of the gable wall, on the site of the later gatehouse. We can make some deductions about this building but its character remains largely unresolved. Because the gable wall of the north range was constructed where it was, we have to deduce that the building to the east did not stand as high as the north range itself. We have no firm evidence how far to the east it extended, but we should note that the western wall of the gate passage of the late 14th-century gatehouse is markedly thinner than its eastern counterpart (Jones *et al.* 1987, fig.39). This detail might suggest that it belonged to our early structure – indeed it may have marked its eastern wall. It is highly likely that the vicars' gate into the *boungarth* was somewhere hereabouts, and this structure to the east of the north range might have been a part of it. From the limited evidence we have, it could be reconstructed as a single storey gate passage which opened directly off the street to

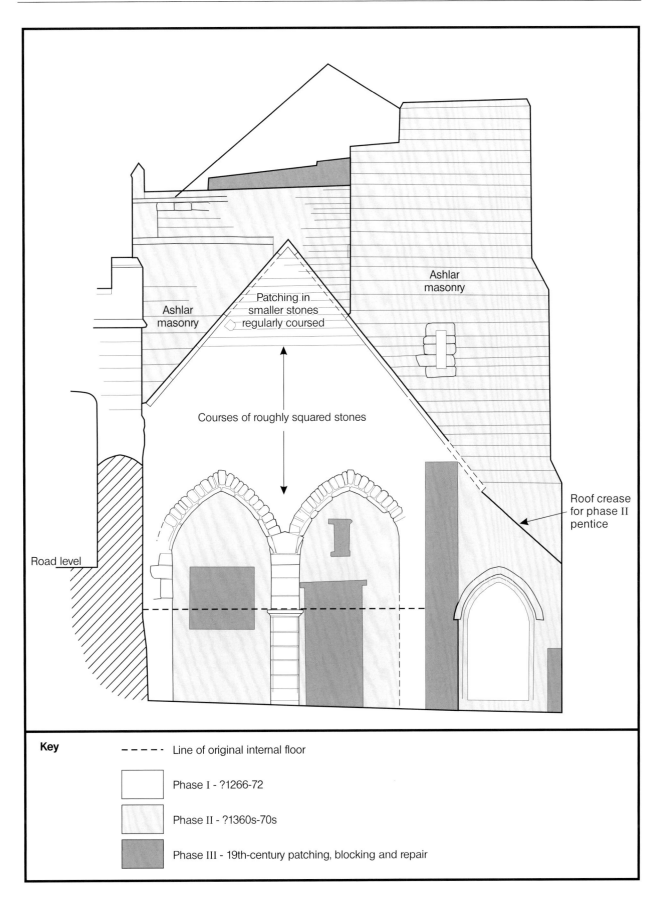

Fig. 8.3. Vicars choral of Lincoln Cathedral. West face of east wall of the north range, showing phases of masonry. Based on a drawing by Stanley Jones (source, Jones et al. 1987 fig.38. Drawn by Dave Watt, copyright D Stocker)

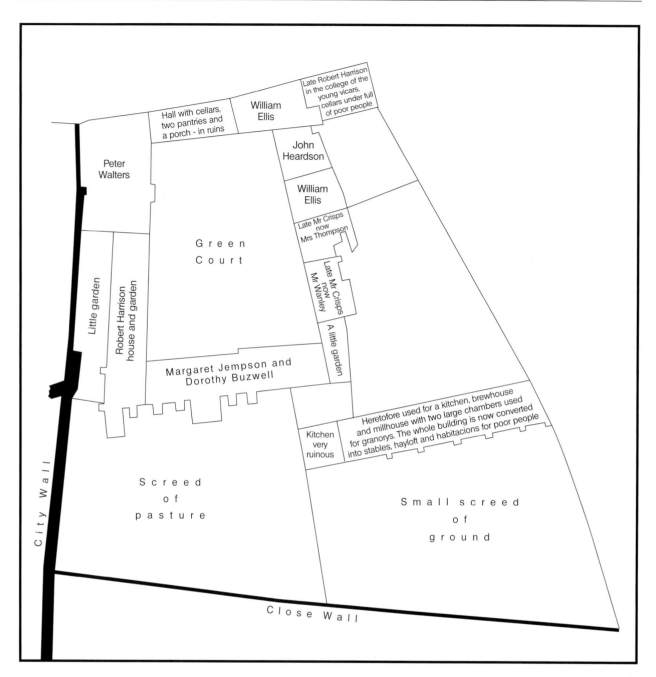

Fig. 8.4. Vicars choral of Lincoln Cathedral. Diagram to illustrate the disposition proposed here of the occupation of close properties reported in the 1650 Parliamentary Survey (source, Venables 1883–4. Drawn by Dave Watt, copyright D Stocker)

the north and which gave access to the *boungarth* down a flight of steps adjacent to its south wall. In such an arrangement the first floor hall to the west would have been directly accessible from the gate passage, but screened from it by the upper part of the open arcade. Similar access arrangements to this are sometimes seen in the (admittedly ground floor) access passages across the undercrofts of monastic ranges, for example across the laybrothers' under-croft at Kirkstall Abbey (West Yorkshire).

So, for whom was this specialised accommodation in the north range constructed, and when? Taking

the question of date first, unfortunately we find that direct evidence is largely absent. Although it was once moulded, the impost in the surviving arcade is now too weathered for precise dating, whilst the long broach stops on the chamfer-moulded arches are too generic to help us much, and this leaves us with circumstantial arguments alone. One possibility is that the north range was built as part of the evolving building programme around the college; this is the implication of Jones' account, although the date of the north range is not discussed specific-ally. This view would see it built following the west

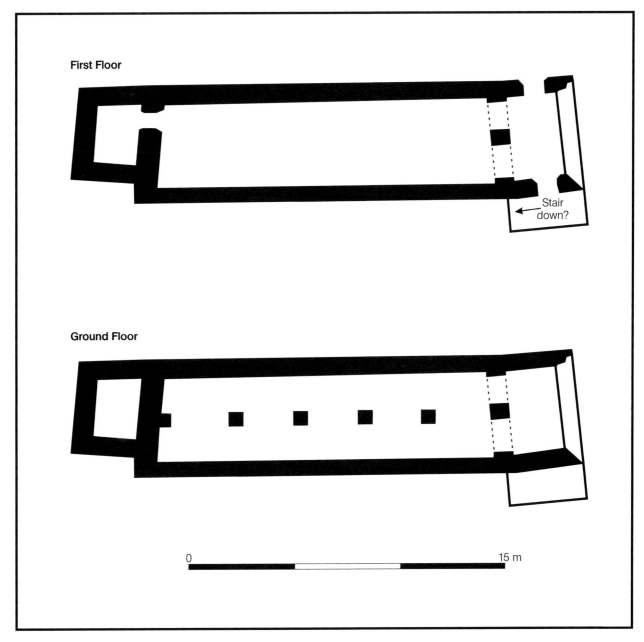

Fig. 8.5. Vicars choral of Lincoln Cathedral. Reconstruction of plans of north range at ground and first-floor level. North is at the top (drawn by Dave Watt, copyright D Stocker)

range and immediately before the gatehouse, which would place it in the 1360s. If it were built at such a late date, the north range is unlikely to have housed Senior Vicars, whose status by this date evidently justified single chambers with individual garderobes and fireplaces. Could it have been built for the Junior Vicars, who (it might be argued) would expect lower standards of privacy and comfort? It seems not – in 1328, the Junior Vicars had been given permission to build themselves a dwelling on the eastern side of the courtyard, along the *Boune Lane* street front. Consequently, the north range is unlikely to have been purpose-built for this group of clerks as late as

the 1360s. Could it have been built for Junior Vicars earlier than 1328? Again this seems unlikely – prior to 1328 (and probably since before 1307) we know that the Junior Vicars lived in houses near the inner gate on the north side of the Close (Maddison 1878, 28; Jones *et al.* 1990, 86)(Fig. 8.1). If it is of mid 14th-century date, then, the spartan accommodation of the north range is not easy to explain in terms of the relative status of its occupants.

Yet the accommodation provided in the north range was undoubtedly spartan, and this may suggest that it belongs to an earlier date when standards of accommodation in the college were not

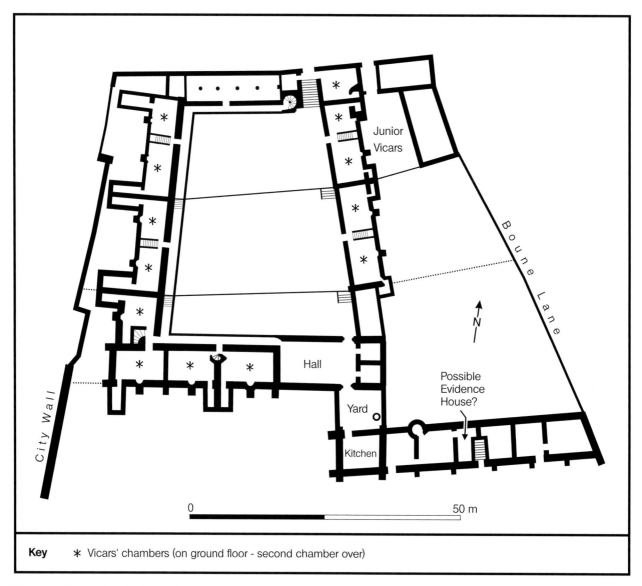

Key   ∗ Vicars' chambers (on ground floor - second chamber over)

Fig. 8.6. Vicars choral of Lincoln Cathedral. Reconstruction of the plan of the colleges of the Junior and Senior Vicars at ground floor level, as it might have appeared at its fullest extent in the late 15th century (sources, surveys by Edward Willson and Stanley Jones in Jones et al. 1987 and discussed here. Drawn by Dave Watt, copyright D Stocker)

as high as they later became. Certainly the interlocking plan of the north range and the west range (Fig. 8.6) probably suggests that the north range is the earlier and that the west range was built up against it. Indeed the north range may be nearly a century earlier in date because its architectural form can be readily explained as a common dormitory, over cellars. It may be a small version of the type of building which has now been identified through excavation at York (p.149–51 below) and which provided vicars' accommodation there from the mid 13th century until the mid 14th century. The Lincoln building's small scale relative to that at York might be the result of the relatively small size of its college of vicars. Furthermore, as noted in the discussion of the York building, it may only be because such

ranges at other cathedrals were replaced with more individual dwellings that they have not survived above ground at other English colleges. If we are correct to identify the north range as an early communal dormitory, it is likely to have been erected for the vicars immediately following the grant of the *boungarth* in 1266–72.

If the north range was an original vicarial building, built when they were first granted the *boungarth* c.1270, then it clearly must have changed function once the vicars moved into their individual chambers in the early 14th century. At that stage it could have remained as dormitory accommodation, perhaps for guests, or it could have been given over to storage. But whatever its use subsequently, it seems that the north range was not a favoured residence.

The mere fact that, along with the communal hall and kitchen, it had been abandoned by 1650, probably suggests that it was not a residential building during the late middle ages, and that it had no function once the vicars ceased to live in common after 1558.

If the north range is correctly interpreted as an early communal dormitory, the Lincoln college retains an important and rare survival. It may be the only vicarial dormitory in England of which anything can be seen today and it refers us to a period when vicars were expected to live in quasi-monastic buildings, as canons had been required to do by the original ordinances of Chrodegang of Metz. At York, it is suggested that the provision of a dormitory for the vicars might, itself, be further evidence for Archbishop de Gray's reform of cathedral clergy (p.151 below), and the same may be equally true of the putative Lincoln dormitory. Certainly Bishop Gravesend, during whose episcopate (1258–80) the *boungarth* was granted to the vicars, was interested in the reform of clergy. Although bound up in the turmoil of the Barons' War, Gravesend was remembered in Lincoln, not just for his grant of £10.00 per annum to the vicars in perpetuity, but also for his concern for the establishment of vicarages at both monastic and prebendal churches, such as Lincoln Minster (Owen 1994, 134).

The buildings of Bishop Sutton (1299–1309)

Thanks to Jones' work, much of the architectural development of the remainder of the Lincoln college is now understood, and using his surveys in combination with notes made during the first half of the 19th century by the important Lincoln antiquary Edward Willson (references in Jones 1987) it has proved possible to reconstruct the layout of the college as it must have been around 1500 (Fig. 8.6). According to his contemporary biographer, John de Schalby, new building work at the college was advocated by Bishop Oliver Sutton in the 1290s (eds. Bradshaw and Wordsworth 1892–7, I, 348; ed. Srawley 1966, 16). De Schalby merely states that 'later on' in Sutton's episcopate the bishop enjoined the dean and chapter to build a court for the vicars. Srawley (1965, 12) and Owen (1994, 148) both state that the bishop's injunction dated from 1293 but neither give a source. Like Gravesend, Sutton had been dean before he became bishop (Hill 1982, 3–5) and so had a clear idea of the administrative and disciplinary value to the cathedral of consolidating the vicars' status and establishing them within a well-endowed institution. It is not clear that any building work was begun during Sutton's lifetime, however. Indeed John de Schalby (*ibid*.) states quite explicitly that, although the dean and chapter had been considering the bishop's injunction, work did

not actually start until after Sutton's death in 1299. It seems that the dean and chapter were waiting for the bequest in Sutton's will, by the terms of which he left his executors the responsibility of building the college kitchen and hall and some dwelling chambers. The surviving architectural details of the south range accord with the content of Bishop Sutton's will, demonstrating that it was built before the east and west ranges and that it probably belongs to the first decade of the 14th century (Wood 1951, 281). The window tracery, in particular, contains distinctive pointed trefoils over each light, not bound within circles. In typological terms they represent one stage beyond the pointed trefoils decorating the Shrine of Little St Hugh in the Cathedral south choir aisle dating from the 1290s, but they lack the ogees first found in the central lantern tower, which was completed in 1311.

The south range is a massive structure with a hall (with buttery and pantry at the east end) and a group of six lodgings chambers to the west, all built northwards from the pre-existing terrace wall (Fig. 8.7). Unfortunately we know very little about the hall, but Jones used Willson's 19th-century surveys to demonstrate that it stood in this position. Including the cross passage at the low end, the hall was approximately 13.7m long by 7.6m wide; about the same size as the surviving hall of the 1370s at York. As we suspect was also the case at York, the Lincoln hall had a door leading directly to the high table end, and at Lincoln (where the door is in the north-west corner) this design detail is of some interest. It is clear from the reconstruction plan (Fig. 8.6) that the pentice, or covered way, in front of buildings along the south, west and north sides of the court was designed to read as their façade. The hall (and for that matter the later gatehouse at the other end of the pentice, against which it terminates) are projected forward of the

Fig. 8.7. Vicars choral of Lincoln Cathedral. South range from north-east. The original common hall was attached to the eastern (left hand) end of this range, where its abutments are still visible (photo and copyright D Stocker)

lodgings block. We don't know if the pentice was supported on a stone wall or a timber one, but this façade design clearly aims to imitate a monastic arrangement, with a prominent 'cloister' walk set in front of the residential buildings. This imitation is unlikely to be accidental; the buildings were probably intended to emphasise the monastic inspiration behind the vicars' common life. Bishop Sutton, after all, also began the cathedral cloister (i.e. the canons' cloister) on the north side of the Minster; presumably he was making the same architectural point about the importance of the common life to the canons there as he was to the vicars. We should also note that, by the time the east range was constructed in the final quarter of the 14th century, these quasi-monastic pretensions seem to have become less important. There is no evidence that there was ever any pentice, still less something resembling a cloister, along the eastern side (below).

We don't know, either, whether the high table of the vicars' hall was lit with a special window as seems to have been the case in some other halls (p.158 below), but as this building is relatively early in date, any such window is likely to have been a later insertion. One curious detail about it, however, is contained in the grant by the dean and chapter of income from the shrine of Robert Grosseteste in 1308 for the completion of the hall's 'vault' (*voltae eiusdem*). This important detail is provided by Precentor Venables (1883–4, 243) but he gives no source; it may come from the unpublished Chapter Acts in the Lincolnshire Archives Office (Williamson 1956, 25–9). But surely the hall was not to be vaulted in stone? Survey and dendrochronology work, undertaken by a team lead by Naomi Field in 1995, has suggested that the original wooden roof of the hall was cannibalised to provide a new roof for the western part of the range in the early 1660s (p. 93–5 below). Perhaps the word *voltae* applied to the completion of the cellars lying beneath the south side of the hall, similar to those that lay beneath the kitchen to the south-east. The word *volta*, however, can in certain circumstances also mean an arch (Latham 1965, 517) and it is just possible that an arch in the timber roof is meant here.

The cross passage at the east end of the hall opened to the south into a small courtyard. This contained a well on its eastern side, and had the kitchen on its south side. The kitchen was also an important element of the first phase of building and, as with the hall, money for its construction was left in Bishop Sutton's will. We know only slightly more about it than about the hall it served, but Jones drew attention to Edward Willson's drawing of the remains of a large kitchen fireplace preserved in the westernmost bay of the 'Vicar's Barn' (Jones *et al.* 1987, fig. 37). Although this wall was demolished in the mid 19th century, Willson's drawing shows that the main cooking area was set over an undercroft, perhaps stone-vaulted. The raising of the main kitchen to the first floor would have allowed direct access between the south door of the hall cross-passage and the kitchen without the need for steps or ramps. Willson's studies of this ruin also suggest that the kitchen was probably a cuboid building, perhaps with a major fireplace in each of the four walls. It may, therefore, have resembled the late 12th- to mid 13th-century kitchen of the Bishop's Palace just over the city wall to the west, which was also an irregular square in plan and was also raised above a stone-vaulted undercroft. The architectural similarity between the kitchens at the Bishop's Palace and at the vicars choral may not have been coincidental. The latter might have been imitating the former, although both represent a similar solution to the problem of building such a structure against a terrace on the Lincoln hillside.

The south range, including the hall and kitchen, was completed by the executors of Bishop Sutton in, or shortly after, 1309. (This is a date given by Venables – 1883–4, 243. It is not properly referenced and although it may come from Venables' reading of the unpublished Chapter Acts, it may be inference). As many have remarked, the range represents one of the most important surviving domestic buildings of this class. It is famous because it illustrates, at an earlier date than the earliest examples at Oxbridge, how an early collegiate plan worked (e.g. Pantin 1959, 243–6). The concept is straightforward – six similar chambers each with the same facilities are mounted on two floors. Each vicar was to have a single large chamber. Each chamber was provided with a fireplace and a garderobe (which is housed in a small second chamber). Each chamber had two windows (a small and a large one) facing north and, perhaps, two large ones to either side of the fireplace, facing south. This fenestration probably implies that the rooms were subdivided with movable internal partitions, perhaps to define a sleeping area or an oratory. Or perhaps each chamber was occupied by a senior vicar, with a more junior clerk under instruction acting as servant – as has been suggested was the distribution of space in similar chambers in the university colleges (e.g. Tyack 1998, 58).

The eastern four chambers in the south range were accessed by a spiral stair which opened off the pentice and led to small lobbies outside each chamber on each floor. Access to the westernmost two chambers was handled differently, however, *via* a doorway in the south end of the west range, but it is not certain whether the upper pair of chambers was reached by a vice or a straight stair. Jones provided two alternative reconstructions, both of which are credible. One incorporates a stair vice like that found in the southern block, whilst the other envisages a straight stair like those in the northern part of the west range and in the east range. As access to the chamber at the western end of the southern block must have been planned at the same time as the southern range itself, Jones' view that access is likely to have been *via* a vice is probably correct.

The southern part of the west range, below the third terrace (Fig. 8.8), was evidently planned at the same time as the south range, although it is now substantially ruined. Not only does it contain the access arrangements for the western pair of chambers in the south range, but the two chambers it contains to the north of the staircase have completely different dimensions from those further north in the west range. It seems likely, then, that the terrace wall marked a halt to the building campaign funded by Bishop Sutton's will. Further confirmation that the southern pair of chambers in the west range belong to this building campaign is provided by the surviving window in the east wall of the first floor chamber, which has the same tracery as those in the south range. But, unfortunately, little remains visible to help distinguish the four adjacent chambers to the north from it in date. The badly eroded remains of a two-light window, lighting the ground floor of the first chamber north of the terrace wall, seem to suggest tracery with a single quatrefoil – a feature not likely to be found as early as 1309. The single-light window in the first floor above sits under a square label and has cinquefoil cusping – again a feature unlikely to be found before the mid 14th century. Also the small single window to its south retains its original cusped, ogival head, which is similar to the surviving example in the east wall of the gatehouse and dates from Bishop Buckingham's work in the final third of the 14th century. Furthermore, not only are these four northern chambers considerably narrower than the two chambers at the south end, but they are of very similar dimensions to those in the east range. This similarity of plan form may also associate them with Bishop Buckingham's work at the college. In previous accounts it has been proposed that work on the west range continued northwards through the 14th century, following the flying start provided by Bishop Sutton's bequest, but these points of detail tend to suggest that work on this range stopped when it reached the third terrace wall and was not resumed until the episcopate of Bishop Buckingham (1363–98).

Even so Bishop Sutton's gift was of great importance to the development of vicarial architecture. The design clearly indicates that the Lincoln vicars were to live, not in self-contained houses, as was to be the case later at Wells, Chichester, Lichfield and Exeter, but in 'sets' of rooms off common staircases. So far

Fig. 8.8. Vicars choral of Lincoln Cathedral. The ruined southern and central parts of the west range from north-east (photo and copyright D Stocker)

York is the only other vicars' college where this style of accommodation is known to have been provided between the 1330s and the 1370s (p.152–5 below). It is possible, however, that some traces of this type of accommodation remain to be discovered at Salisbury and at the first college at Hereford. Although not as clearly monastic in its origins as the common sleeping arrangements suggested by the Lincoln north range, such accommodation emphasises, nevertheless, the collegiality of the institution. It still retains a 'quasi-cloister' and access to the vicars' individual rooms is common. At Lincoln, indeed, even the later phases of construction (the northern part of the west range and the east range) retained this emphasis on common access. At Lincoln the vicars were not allowed their own front doors until after the Reformation.

The early buildings of Bishop Buckingham (later 1360s or 1370s)

The central part of the west range, above the third terrace, is now partly buried and partly ruined; at the northern end, above the second terrace, the range was completely reconstructed in the 1870s (Figs. 8.8 and 8.10a). The arguments laid out above suggest that these parts of the range were built under the patronage of Bishop Buckingham (1363–98) who, like Gravesend and Sutton, had previously been dean of a secular cathedral, although at Lichfield rather than Lincoln (McHardy 2001, 13–14). Jones shows that the northern parts of the west range originally contained a total of four chambers on each floor – accommodation for eight vicars (1987, fig.47). As in the other ranges, each chamber had a large garderobe and a fireplace and several windows. The surviving garderobe projection at the north end of the block is the largest of those surviving and it is clear that it would have provided a substantial ancillary chamber measuring about 6.1m by 3.6m. The associated chamber is one of three in the college which retain elaborate drains worked into the sills of secondary windows – the others are in the chamber over the gatehouse and in chamber C in the east range (Jones *et al.* 1987, figs. 66 and 67). These drains are distinctive details, yet they lack a clear explanation. They could be explained routinely as being simply for the disposal of waste water, but they seem an over-elaborate detail for such a mundane purpose. Similar features exist in the Wells vicars' houses (p.132 below). The Senior Vicars, of course, were probably all priests, even in the 14th century, and each priest vicar would have had the obligation to celebrate mass once a day. Although employment at the cathedral provided opportunities to fulfil this obligation there, perhaps vicars were encouraged to perform a daily private mass in an oratory in their lodgings. If so, these drains might be interpreted as piscinae. We have already seen that internal screens might have existed in these chambers and it may be that parts were screened off to provide oratories. If these drains do represent private altars, they might be seen as further evidence that the Lincoln college was conceived as a quasi-monastic community.

When the new gatehouse was attached to the east end of the putative early hall and cellars in the north range, the pentice along the west range was extended to return along the south side of the north range. It connected with the doorway of the vice up to the first floor chamber over the gate (Fig. 8.6). The new gatehouse is an important but complicated building, which replaced the enigmatic building to the east of the original north range (already discussed), and it is clearly dated by the arms of Bishop Buckingham on its northern façade (Fig. 8.9). For reasons that will become clear, it is likely to have been built relatively early on in his episcopate – probably in the 1360s or early 1370s. We have seen that there was probably already a gatehouse or gateway in this approximate location, and the porter's lodge of Buckingham's new gatehouse may have incorporated some of its fabric. It also had a single vicarial chamber on the ground floor east of the gate-hall, with fireplace and garderobe, whilst on the first floor over the gate-hall was a very splendid chamber, accessed by the massive spiral stair opening off the pentice in the south-west corner. This was also the only chamber equipped with two fireplaces (one in the north wall and one in the east) and, whilst the single point of access makes it likely that the chamber was intended for single occupancy, we can suggest that it was intended for one of the most senior vicars – perhaps the succentor, or the vice-chancellor.

The later buildings of Bishop Buckingham (1380s or 1390s)

The east range, attached to the east end of the

Fig. 8.9. Vicars choral of Lincoln Cathedral. Gatehouse from north (photo and copyright D Stocker)

gatehouse, is stratigraphically later than the gatehouse; the mid-wall string of the east range crashes into the springing of the inner gate arch. There is no coursing through between the two buildings and the east range is seen to butt up against the gatehouse.

The entrances are also prominently badged with Bishop Buckingham's arms (Fig. 8.10a & b). Although it was built somewhat later than the individual vicarial houses at Wells, Buckingham's new east range at Lincoln did not break with Lincoln tradition. Like the earlier south range and the more recently built west range, the east range was also originally a block of independent chambers off common staircases – and not a row of houses. Like the northern part of the west range, but unlike the south range, the staircases here were straight. Like its fellows, each chamber was equipped with a fireplace and garderobe chamber (although the latter was a much smaller structure here than in the south and west ranges), and there were probably two windows in each wall, though this can no longer be easily demonstrated. Buckingham's new east range was intended, then, to provide eight further units of high-status accommodation, presumably for the Senior Vicars. It brought the total number of lodgings chambers in the institution up to 26 (excluding the north range) – about the same number as there were Senior Vicars at the height of the college's prosperity.

At the southern end of the new east range, where it met the pre-existing hall, was an awkward space, too small to have been a lodging, but perhaps a service building of some sort. Edward Willson thought he could see evidence that it had been a brew-house (ed. Jones 1987, 51) though it seems to have been a garden in 1650. At Exeter, Wells and York, the college 'evidence house' (i.e. the chamber where the college's jealously guarded muniments and other valuables were kept) is located conveniently close to the hall, presumably to facilitate the various payments of rents and dues which would have taken place there

Fig. 8.10a. Vicars choral of Lincoln Cathedral. College of the Senior Vicars looking north, showing the site of the early north range, the south wall of the mid 14th-century gatehouse to its east, and the abutment of the east range of the 1380s or 1390s (photo and copyright D Stocker)

Fig. 8.10b East range from south-west (photo and copyright D Stocker)

respecting the vicars' property (p.38, 128–31 and 159). These parallels prompt the suggestion that this space at the south end of the east range might have been occupied by the Lincoln equivalent of this building. If so the function may not have remained here long however, as an argument can be made that a new evidence house was provided in Bishop Alnwick's new building in the 1450s (below).

Whereas Buckingham's presumed work in the west range and gatehouse had followed the intended plan of the college established by Bishop Sutton, if not by Bishop Gravesend, the new east range represented a departure from this original conception. The new range was constructed running south-east from the gatehouse, at an angle to the other buildings of the college, and dividing the original space granted to the vicars between the city wall and *Boune Lane* into two unequal courtyards. Clearly by the date of the east range, then, the decision had been taken to make a physical distinction between the smaller eastern and the larger western part of the courtyard. The area to the east of the new east range is called the

'Young Vicars' in the 1650 *Survey*, confirming that this smaller rectangular plot east of the east range was the court of the Junior Vicars. This change in plan must represent a dramatic change in the concept of the college; it was no longer a single unit accommodating both Junior and Senior Vicars together, but one where the two classes of vicars were housed in different courtyards. The new east range thus turned the ideal that both Junior and Senior Vicars should live a 'communal' life in a single courtyard on its head. Yet this ambition had been reiterated as recently as 1328, when the Junior Vicars had been given permission to build their dwelling house along *Boune Lane*, presumably facing westwards onto the vicars' court (Owen 1994, 148; LAO, Chapter Acts DC A.2.23, f.9). This division between the Junior Vicars and Senior Vicars in the late 14th century was not merely physical. Although we know that the Junior Vicars' plot lay within the *boungarth* originally granted in 1266–72 (above), in 1390–1 the Senior Vicars mounted a legal case aimed at proving that it fell outside (Maddison 1878, 8–9, 29). The original eastern boundary of the *boungarth*, they said, was marked by Buckingham's new east range. The object of the Senior Vicars' mendacity was to obtain for themselves, exclusively, income from the churches of Kirton and Ravensthorpe, which was only available to those who dwelt within the *boungarth*. This dispute confirms that, by 1391, the Junior Vicars' view across the united courtyard had already been cut off by the new east range, and their own separate courtyard had been created. The east range must therefore be dated later than Buckingham's gatehouse (probably of the late 1360s or early 1370s), but before 1391. The will of Canon Geoffrey de Scrope made in 1382 (ed. Foster 1914, 14) distinguishes between bequests to the Senior Vicars living the *boungarth* and Junior Vicars 'living together', which suggests that the physical division of the court had already been undertaken by that date. A date *c*.1380 is perhaps most likely.

These disputes over the relative status of the different classes of vicar choral had obviously become much more pointed between 1328 and the 1380s and are of some importance for our understanding of the development of the cathedral hierarchy itself. In the earlier part of the 14th century the distinctions between the Junior Vicars and the Senior Vicars were not seen to be so great as to prevent them dwelling together in the same courtyard. But by the time the decision was made to construct the east range, perhaps *c*.1380, the single courtyard was no longer thought appropriate and considerable effort and expense was devoted to creating two colleges where there had originally been one.

One result of the decision to build the new east range dividing the two courtyards must have been to force the Junior Vicars to look to their own buildings,

Fig. 8.11. Vicars choral of Lincoln Cathedral. View of the north façade of the college in an engraving published in 1826 but based on a drawing made before 1811. This is a rare view of the north range of the Junior Vicars' close, to the left, east, of the Senior Vicars' gatehouse (source, Gentleman's Magazine October 1826, II, facing p.305)

for they would now need a separate entrance to their existing building along the west side of *Boune Lane*. Fortunately, this gatehouse range (now No.15 Minster Yard) was drawn before its complete reconstruction in 1811 and an engraving was subsequently published (Fig. 8.11). This engraving seems to show that it combined a gatehouse with two floors of accommodation (Jones *et al*. 1987, fig. 31). None of the accommodation was accessed directly from the street – so, like the Senior Vicars, the Junior Vicars also presented themselves as an enclosed institution. It seems that their gate arch went through the north range along the street into the court beyond, so presumably accommodation in the street range was accessed either from the south or from within the gate hall, or perhaps from both. This building also displayed at least two shields bearing the arms of Bishop Buckingham, which were reset in its north and west walls during the 1811 reconstruction. The reset shield in the north wall is presumably that shown in the engraving placed centrally (i.e. not above the gate) in the north façade. But this gatehouse range must date from late in Buckingham's episcopate, because the archaeological evidence shows quite clearly that it is later than Buckingham's gatehouse to what was now the Senior Vicars' court. The moulded plinth which runs around the north side of the Senior Vicars' gatehouse returns along its east face, and several original windows in the wall above were blocked by the superimposition of the new gatehouse building to the east. Like the construction of the east range,

then, the construction of the north range of the Junior Vicars probably dates from the 1380s, or even later. The construction of the new second gate is further evidence that, at the end of Buckingham's episcopate, the decision had been taken to divide the college; and because the second gatehouse was apparently unforeseen during Buckingham's work on the western gatehouse, we can also say that this division was not anticipated during the early part of his episcopate.

There were considerable numbers of Junior Vicars and, even though they may not have aspired to a chamber each, it is hard to see them all fitting into a building the size of this street range. Their original building of 1328, along *Boune Lane*, would certainly still have been required. Unfortunately we have very little information about this earlier building. Early leases relating to buildings on this site mention the 'poor clerks' and also an ancient stable along the eastern boundary of the site, but whether the stables were the final remnants of a medieval range here is unknown (Jones *et al*. 1987, 36–9). The stable building was evidently patched-up as a dwelling house in the 1730s and finally demolished in the 1820s. The view made prior to 1811 (Fig. 8.11) shows what might be a bell cote on the northern gable of this eastern range (above the roof of the north range). The west side of the Junior Vicars' courtyard was formed by the windows, garderobes and chimneys of the Senior Vicars' east range, and the southern boundary was presumably marked by the big terrace wall which still separates the Archdeaconry from

No.1 Greestone Place. Prior to the construction of the east range of the Senior Vicars, of course, this terrace had run across the site from east to west uninterrupted. Any building erected above this terrace would have greatly compressed the Junior Vicars' courtyard to the north and, consequently, none may ever have existed. South of the terrace wall is the large and attractive plot that was to become the site of the grand new Archdeaconry shortly before 1778. It is called a 'piece of ground' in the earliest lease (1703) and is not mentioned as part of the vicars' estate in the *Parliamentary Survey* of 1650. The plot was clearly part of the medieval vicars' close, but it was evidently alienated early on. We have no evidence that it was the site of any vicars' buildings in the medieval period, and indeed the fact that there seems to be no major communication route between this plot and the remainder of the college may suggest that it was always a marginal piece of land.

The buildings of Bishop Alnwick (1450s)

Below the fourth terrace on the eastern side of the *boungarth*, the vicars eventually erected a fine new building associated with Bishop William Alnwick (1436–49), a bishop who added considerably to many diocesan properties (Hayes 1994). Alnwick's arms are on the east gable, accompanied by the rebus of John Breton, prebendary of Sutton-cum-Buckingham (1448–65). If the building was constructed when both men were alive, therefore, it will have been built in 1448 or 1449. But it is probably more likely that it was erected in the 1450s, perhaps using bequests from Alnwick's will and under the guidance of Breton, who had a devotion to Alnwick (*ibid*. 17–8). This important masonry building, now known mis-

leadingly as the 'Vicars' Barn', is not well understood. It was built as a continuation to the east of the original kitchen of the vicars, though it is clearly much later in date. The kitchen itself had been demolished sometime after the *Parliamentary Survey* and before the early 19th century, but the next bay to the east was not demolished until after Edward Willson had made a survey of the structure in period between 1820 and 1850 (Jones *et al.* 1987, 62–4). Shortly after Willson's survey, and before J S Padley's survey published in 1851 (Fig. 8.12), the building underwent a complete reconstruction, during which most of the original internal features were swept away. It seems clear from these early sources, however, that it originally consisted of a range of six single chambers along the ground floor, terraced into the hill-slope. The central bay of the building housed a staircase which rose to a pair of large halls above. According to Willson's survey and his reconstructions of the openings, the ground floor was accessed by means of only two original doorways. One in the second bay from the east gave access to the two chambers east of the internal stairway, whilst a doorway in the extreme westernmost bay (that partly demolished in the mid 19th century) gave access to the three chambers to its east. The stairway itself, like those in Vicars' Court, rose straight from the front to the rear of the building and, according to Willson, it permitted no access into the chambers at ground floor. Each of the ground floor chambers was equipped with windows in the south elevation, but there are no windows at this level in the north wall because the building is terraced into the hillside.

The building's location, attached to the college kitchen, provides the best evidence for its original function. It was probably intended as a service range – a role it was still playing in 1650 when the

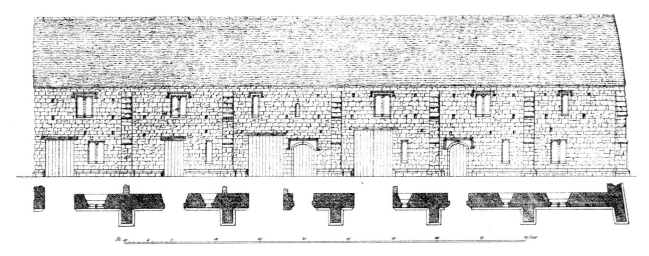

Fig. 8.12. Vicars choral of Lincoln Cathedral. So called 'Vicar's Barn' from south; a survey drawing by James Padley of c.1850 (source, Padley 1851)

parliamentary commissioners described it as:

a faire and large building 45 yards in length heretofore used for a Kitchen, Brewhouse and Millhouse, with two large Chambers in length 45 yards used for Granorys (the whole building now converted into Stables, Hayloffte and Habitacons for poore people)…

In such a location, beyond the college kitchen and close by the back gate, college residences would not be expected, but these service functions will have been conveniently sited here. We may, moreover, be able to say a little more about the function of the third chamber from the west on the ground floor, which had a number of distinctive architectural features when recorded by Willson. Unlike its fellows, it was lit only by a single window in the south wall. Access also seems to have been difficult – to get to it from outside the building, visitors were obliged to pass through the two chambers to the west. Finally, the single door (Willson shows that the second opening is a more recent alteration) which leads into it from the second chamber appears to be the wrong way round; it closes from the outside, not from the inside. These features suggest that this chamber was built as a strong-room and so it may have replaced an earlier building elsewhere in the college – perhaps the late 14th-century chamber at the south end of the east range (above). Indeed, the chamber in Alnwick's new building had an aumbry in its east wall as well as space for a press below the staircase landing, details which might have contained cupboards and pigeon-holes like the fittings still in place at Wells (p.130 below).

Although the location of this building within the college suggests a service role, we should also note that it is quite similar in scale and layout to the newly re-discovered north range – a large open first floor hall set over a group of substantial cellars. We have seen that the north range may have had a storage and/or a guesthouse role once the college's domestic accommodation was completed. However, set next to the gatehouse but away from the kitchen, the north range would not have been convenient for such activities as milling, or for storage of foodstuffs. Might we see Alnwick's new building here as a replacement of these storage facilities, and perhaps guesthouse facilities also, in a more convenient part of the college?

Summary

Although not as complete a group of buildings as at Wells, or the second college at Hereford, the remains of the vicars' college at Lincoln preserve evidence for a complex development – and this is highly informative (Fig. 8.2). In the ruins of the north range we may have the only standing fragments of an early 'monastic style' dormitory at any of the English colleges, though it was a small specimen compared with the building identified through excavations at York (p.149–51 below). Bishop Sutton's major investment around 1300, however, was in a distinctively 'collegiate' form of accommodation, with each vicar having his own 'set' of rooms off a common stairway and 'cloister'. This certainly represented a considerable rise in architectural status for the vicars over their communal dormitory, but the 'cloister' and dining hall preserved the appearance of a common discipline. Even more remarkable is the fact that when Bishop Buckingham built so extensively and expensively in the later 14th century, he retained Sutton's architectural philosophy and provided further 'sets' of rooms, rather than individual houses like those already in place at Wells and York by this date. Buckingham's later buildings, the east range and the gatehouse of the Junior Vicars, however, dramatically emphasised a novel distinction in status between the Junior Vicars (in minor orders) and the Senior Vicars (who were ordained priests). The inclusive courtyard in which both orders of vicars had formerly lived side by side was divided (and not very equally) and, whilst the Senior Vicars had comfortable prestigious accommodation subsequently, the inferior status of the Junior Vicars was emphasised through the cramped architecture of their new court. From a common dormitory to a divided close, then, the buildings of the Lincoln vicars choral demonstrate both the rise in social status of the minor clergy of the cathedral and, at the same time, the development of a rigidly defined hierarchy within their ranks.

Annex: Archaeological Investigation of the south range at Vicars' Court, Lincoln, 1993–4

Naomi Field

Introduction

The south range of the Lincoln college of vicars choral (now Nos. 3 and 3a Vicars Court) underwent a comprehensive programme of repair in 1993–4. This work focused on the stabilisation of the east garderobe tower and involved the insertion of a concrete ring beam inside and outside the structure, underpinning the foundations and grouting the wall core. At the same time stonework was selectively replaced on the range's west, south and east elevations, the south gutter was repaired and consolidated, the roof space was cleared and necessary repairs were made to the roof timbers. A programme of archaeological excavation and fabric recording was undertaken by Lindsey Archaeological Services as an integral part of the repair programme. It had three components, of which the first was the excavation of the garderobe pit and of a trench surrounding the east garderobe tower, and the excavation of two deep external soakaways nearby. Secondly, a stone-by-stone record of the external building elevations was produced, based on commercial 1:20 photogrammetric plotting commissioned by English Heritage in 1991; and, thirdly, the roof timbers were recorded in advance of, and during, repair. A detailed archive of the work is lodged at the Lincolnshire County Council Sites and Monuments Record; this note summarises the principal findings.

The environs of the south range

As we have seen (Figs. 8.1, 8.2 and 8.13), the south range south wall forms a fourth terrace wall across the vicars choral site, and the Close Wall, which marks the southern boundary of the vicars' site is, in effect, a fifth terrace wall, with a steep drop to the south. Evidence for extensive landscaping was found in the garden between this wall and the south range during the excavations in advance of the two soakaway pits, *c.*13m south of the

Fig. 8.13. Vicars choral of Lincoln Cathedral. The south range from the south-west before restoration. Note the two large garderobe towers projecting from the south wall (photo and copyright, N Field, ref: 93/21/25)

building. Substantial deposits of soil containing 13th- to 15th-century pottery were also found dumped over the old ground surface, *c.*1.8m below the medieval ground level inside the garderobe tower. The gradient of the site, prior to the terracing, was in the region of 1 in 7 (14.3%).

The layout of the south range

As noted above the south range of the college was probably built between 1299 and 1309, and was the earliest of the ranges at Lincoln to provide individual accommodation for the vicars. The two-storey building is divided into three lodgings on each floor, separated by two thick cross-walls. Each lodging had its own garderobe located in one of the two towers projecting from the southern wall of the range (Figs. 8.6 and 8.13). The west tower served the two westernmost lodgings with a single chute. The east tower had two chute systems and served the central and eastern pairs of lodgings on the ground and first floors.

The survey showed that there is a marked difference in size between the building's three structural bays, and this has lead to problems in synchronising the layout of the fenestration and the roof (Fig. 8.14). The cross-walls between bays occur at irregular intervals and the eastern wall is no more than a continuation of the cross-wall in the asymmetrically-placed east garderobe tower. The result of this poor layout is the cramping of some windows in the south elevation and the overlapping of other architectural features. The incompatibility of window, cross-wall and roof bay positions may have been the result of a fundamental error in setting out the ground plan, perhaps partly due to the difficulties of building on such a steep site.

Roofing the south range

a) The surviving high-pitched roof

The range has three broadly similar sets of five trusses, corresponding to the three main bays of the building, but within each bay the five trusses varied in detail and in interval dimensions (Fig. 8.14). Some had shortened wall-pieces to avoid window openings, whilst others were set into window jambs. The five trusses of the central bay formed only four roof bays, as the final truss was laid against the western cross wall, and the easternmost bay in the roof contained only a single common rafter (and not the usual three). Every fourth pair of rafters in the surviving roof was fitted with a collar that supported a clasped purlin in a mortice in its upper surface. These purlins were mostly re-used rafters from an earlier roof. The common rafters were joined at the ridge in a simple lap joint. The chaotic layout of the existing high-pitched roof structure retains clear evidence that the majority of the roof timbers have been re-used from an earlier roof, which was also of high pitch and coupled-rafter construction (Jones *et al.*

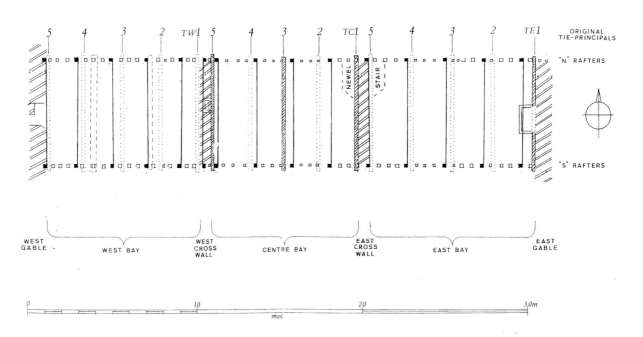

Fig. 8.14. Vicars choral of Lincoln Cathedral. Plan of roof of south range (drawing Mick Clarke, copyright Lindsey Archaeological Services)

1987, 57). Furthermore the disordered, rotated, and possibly shortened rafters which support the surviving roof were fitted over the remains of an earlier low-pitched roof, four trusses of which were utilised *in situ* as makeshift tie-beams (see below).

Tree-ring samples from the high-pitched roof indicate that the timbers over the central and east bays were felled between 1296 and *c.*1332. The rafters and collars of the west bay, however, were evidently newer timber, although they formed a roof of identical design to that further east, for they produced a combined felling date within the period 1663–1678. The archaeology and dendrochronology combine to demonstrate, therefore, that the high-pitched roof was constructed of re-used timbers from a roof which was originally constructed at the same time as the south range (i.e. *c.*1299–1309), but that it was actually erected in this formation and in this location in the 1660s or 1670s, following the depredations of the Civil War and Interregnum (Jones *et al.* 1987, 42, 57).

Where did the Restoration builders obtain their roof parts? Jones thought the timbers may have come from the Bishop's Palace (*ibid.*), but the bishop's hall was constructed was under the direction of Bishops St Hugh (1185–1200) and Hugh de Welles (1209–1234), far too early for the felling date obtained through dendrochronology. Instead, as the dendro-date demonstrates that the timbers were felled so close to the date for construction of the south range itself, the vanished hall to the east of the surviving range (see above) presents itself as an obvious candidate. The hall is not mentioned separately in the *Parliamentary Survey* of 1650 (Fig. 8.4) and this may suggest that it was already out of use by this date. If the roof had been taken down and stored before or during the Civil War, for example, its materials would have been available for

repairing the adjacent lodgings after the Restoration. Common ownership of the two properties would have facilitated such a transfer, and we know that, in 1650 at least, the houses created in the south range were in the same ownership as the site of the hall – that of either Dorothy Buzwell or Margaret Jempson. Furthermore, although the hall has not been excavated, we have seen (above) that Willson's records show that it was broader than the surviving part of the south range and this means it will have been roofed independently of the western parts of that range. As it was a 'formal' open hall of broad span, its roof would probably have been of high pitch and coupled-rafter construction, like the roof from which the south range timbers mostly came. Recording of the modern east gable wall of the south range in 1993–4 (Fig. 8.15) provided clear evidence that the vanished hall to the east was roofed independently and that its roof was of steeper pitch than that of the western part of the south range.

The lower part of the east face of the wall is built of carefully coursed ashlars, like the original fabric of the range; above this is a zone of carefully coursed squared masonry of smaller grade, which is probably also part of the original fabric. This original work extends upwards as far as the line of the surviving crease of the flat-pitched roof, which is more clearly expressed on the western face of the wall. Above this line, the apex of the gable was evidently rebuilt when the existing high-pitched roof of the south range was reconstructed in the 1660s or 1670s. On the west (now interior) face of the wall (Fig. 8.16) the crease at the junction between the original gable and the reconstructed apex, marked by a simple dripstone, clearly relates to an earlier flat-pitched roof, now represented by the four *in situ* tie-beams, and it is to the remains of this early roof that we must now turn.

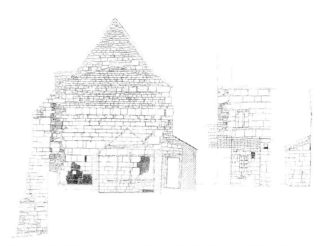

Fig. 8.15. Vicars choral of Lincoln Cathedral. Elevation of east face of east gable of the south range (formerly the west wall of the vicars' hall) (drawing Mick Clarke, copyright Lindsey Archaeological Services)

Fig. 8.16. Vicars choral of Lincoln Cathedral. Upper part of east gable of south range, looking east (the other side of the wall shown in Fig. 8.15). Note the early 'low-pitched' roof truss (TE-1) in situ against the east wall, the contemporary dripstone or crease above, and the later high-pitched roof (made of re-used timbers) over all (photo and copyright, N Field, ref: 94/3/25)

b) The low-pitched medieval roof

Evidence for the form of the earlier flat-pitched roof was confined to the survival of the four trusses which had been re-used in the high-pitched roof. Three of these had survived against the cross-walls whilst the fourth was in the centre of the central bay. It is suggested that there were originally fifteen such trusses in the range. The irregular spacing of north and south windows meant that the corbels supporting this roof could not be positioned at precisely regular intervals. Most of these corbels have been removed during subsequent alterations, but it is probable that all three bays contained five trusses at slightly irregular intervals (Fig. 8.14).

Each truss was formed from a 'cranked' or 'canted' tie-beam (i.e. a beam carefully selected to provide a flat arch

shape). The beam was supported on a pair of curved arch-braces let into wall-pieces set on stone corbels in the walls below. The spandrels created by these arched braces were originally filled with nailed planks (presumably originally painted) of which remains were recorded in the central truss of the central bay by Stanley Jones (*ibid.*, 57). Mortices in the surviving trusses show that the remainder of the roof was very simple, with a ridge-piece and a pair of purlins butted into sockets in the ties. The wall plate itself was concealed behind a cornice beam, for which the sockets survive near the terminals of some of the cranked ties. All the main components have edge-chamfers, which terminate in broach stops carved at the bases of the wall-pieces immediately above the stone corbels. The corbels themselves are simple semi–pyramidal forms; a table of rectangular section is supported by a hollow chamfer above a fillet, below which the concave-sided base reduces from three sides to a single point. A worn but complete corbel block of this type was also recovered from the garderobe shaft fill (below). Corbels of this type supported all the trusses except the north ends of those on either side of the east cross-wall. Here the braces terminated, not at the wall-pieces (which were shorter than standard) but at the upper surface of short projecting sole-pieces which also supported the wall-pieces. This device was made necessary by the protrusion of the upper surface of the stone newel stair head. Incomplete elements of the ridge plate, purlins and beams of this flat-pitched roof were later re-used as lengths of wall plate in the surviving high-pitched roof.

Samples for tree-ring dating were taken from the three surviving trusses in the centre bay. The estimated felling dates of two of them are consonant with the range suggested by the documentary evidence for construction between 1299 and 1309, while the third may have been felled at a somewhat earlier date (Groves and Hillam 1996).

These remains represent a relatively simple, low-pitched, domestic roof, covered in lead, of a type that had become standard for high-status ranges by the end of the 14th century. The early date for the roof, at the start of the century, is surprising, but the evidence for its date seems clear and the dendrochronological date accords well with dates derived from both architectural and documentary sources. The south range is a highly innovative building and, at present, this is the only explanation we can offer for its *avant-garde* design.

The eastern garderobe tower

The eastern (larger) garderobe tower is a rectangular structure projecting southwards from the south wall of the south range. It measures about 4.5m (north–south) by 6.3m (east–west), with walls some 1m thick (Fig. 8.6). It is divided internally by a substantial north–south stone wall and two east–west cross-walls, thus creating a chute for each of the four lodgings in the central and eastern bays of the building. The chambers in the garderobe tower were entered *via* arched doorways in the south wall of the lodging chambers. Ventilation was provided at first floor level by small trefoil openings set high in the south wall (now blocked). On the north side of the cross walls, in the north-west and north-east chambers, a single course of chamfered corbelling projects *c.*12cm beyond the wall faces and originally supported a timber floor at ground floor level. The floor in the south-east chamber was supported by a line of three joist holes in the east elevation and rested on a ledge at the top of the central spine wall. Below the joist holes is a blocked arch; limited trimming of its voussoirs on the north side suggests that the internal east-west partition wall was secondary. The arrangements for flooring in the south-west chamber are hidden by an inserted ceiling.

The north wall of the garderobe tower is the south wall of the south range and is built in regular, roughly-dressed stone courses, bonded with yellow sandy mortar. The wall foundations of both the tower and the south range wall were examined in 1993–4 and found to be of the same, stepped, construction, suggesting they are of the same build. Although, externally, the relationship between the south wall fabric and the tower has been masked by re-facing, it was clear from the internal elevations that the garderobe tower superstructure was secondary, added only after the south range south wall had been completed. It may be that work on the main south wall was required to be one storey in advance of the walls of the tower, to ensure correct positioning of doors, windows and cross-wall.

The north–south cross-wall, which divided the garderobe tower into two chambers on each floor, was simply an in-line extension of the cross wall extending through the range to join its north wall. Consequently it was the position of the cross-wall which predetermined the position of the tower; an observation which goes some way towards explaining the asymmetrical locations of certain windows in the south façade. Construction levels beneath the garderobe pit floors contained pottery dating between the early and later 14th century, slightly later than construction date (1299–1309) obtained for the south range from architectural, documentary and dendro-chronological sources. The garderobe pit floor itself contained mid 14th- to 15th-century pottery; it may have been a replacement for an earlier surface.

To facilitate emptying the garderobe pits, at basement level four arched doorways, two on the south elevation and one each on the south-east and south-west elevations, provided access points from outside to the bottom of the chutes. Only the south-west arch is currently open – the other three were blocked prior to infilling the chambers. Three internal arches connected the four chambers (there was no direct access between the two northern chambers).

An arch which connected the north-west and south-west chambers is now largely missing, though its west side, just below the apex, is still intact. The opening had been crudely blocked after the removal of a drain that carried water from beneath the south range and emptied into the south-west chamber of the garderobe. It was only re-opened in 1974 when the son of the tenants carried out the first exploration of the north-west chamber. His discovery of a group of tightly dated later 17th-century material led to further investigations by Andrew White and Tim Ambrose of Lincoln's City and County Museum in 1978. As the chamber was inaccessible from above, the chamber was entered from the garden and material was removed from the bottom of the deposit upwards. A

group of pottery and other artefacts closely dated to the 1660s was retrieved (White 1979).

The entire fill of the eastern pair of chambers was removed in 1993–4 to enable access for underpinning (Fig. 8.17). In contrast with the north-west chamber, the chambers on the east side of the garderobe tower appear to have been largely filled in during the mid 18th century. Conjoining pottery sherds found in both upper and lower deposits indicate that numerous tips of rubble and soil were probably thrown into the chambers from above in one operation, with only a few earlier layers below. A large number (148) of architectural fragments were found in the fill, including five large voussoirs from a single 13th-century arch of considerable proportions as well as a corbel of the type supporting the original roof of the south range (above) and window fragments which probably also came from the building. This assemblage points to a major programme of refurbishment in the building at this time. Prior to blocking of the eastern chamber arches, both chambers must have been thoroughly cleaned, as there is a total absence of material datable to between the 15th and 17th centuries.

Fig. 8.17. Vicars choral of Lincoln Cathedral. The 1993–4 excavation in progress in the two eastern pits in the eastern garderobe tower, from above (photo and copyright, N Field, ref: 94/6/9)

Discussion

Although limited, the 1993–4 investigations provided several important insights into the development of the south range. Tree-ring dating confirmed that the surviving trusses from the low-pitched roof were indeed part of the original fabric, and have given us a very early date for this type of roof. A similarly early low-pitched roof, with an almost identical pitch, has been tentatively identified from a roof crease on the south side of the gatehouse at Newark Castle. This has been connected with a phase of remodelling here by Bishop Sutton; who was, of course, also the (posthumous) patron of the work at the south range of the vicars choral (Marshall and Samuels 1997, 32,34–5). Another early roof of similarly low pitch, has been tree-ring dated at Walsingham House, one of the most important domestic buildings of the Ely monastery. There dendrochronology confirmed the date provided by the documentary sources, which indicate that it was built between 1333 and 1336, some twenty to twenty-five years later than the Lincoln vicar's south range (Howard *et al.* 1993, 41).

No damage was found in the south range fabric that might be associated with the Civil War, but it is likely that the original low-pitched roof was already affected by subsidence (visible on the north elevation) caused by an underlying Roman defensive ditch – the north wall was sinking around the newel stair, which pivoted northward, taking with it the north wall of the range, the east cross-wall and the roof trusses above. The south wall was largely unaffected by these movements, since a fissure developed between it and the cross-wall. Any stripping of the roof for lead during the Civil War and Interregnum would have contributed further to the damage, since the building was already in poor condition and the north parapet had either fallen already, or was in imminent danger of doing so. However the chambers here were inhabited in 1650 and the documentary evidence suggests the roof still survived with its lead intact. The only evidence of possible military activity was the chance find (during inspection in 1989) of a paper-twist cartridge of 17th-century date, discovered in a cavity in the external wall of the eastern garderobe tower. The north-west chute in the eastern garderobe tower was filled with rubbish in the third quarter of the 17th century, presumably as part of repair works in the aftermath of the Civil War and the siege of 1648, for which considerable documentation survives (Jones *et al.* 1987, 57). We should not be surprised that building materials were also recycled from other parts of the site during these works. Dendrochronology has confirmed that the present roof of the south range dates from this same period of refurbishment of the college buildings, and also that it was built re-using timbers from an earlier roof of the same date as the range itself. Detailed analysis of the fabric of the east gable wall has provided further physical evidence, which complements antiquarian and documentary evidence, that the vicars' hall was located immediately east of the surviving part of the south range. It now seems likely that this hall building was the source of the timbers re-used in the new high-pitched south range roof in the 1660s or 1670s. The fills of the eastern chutes in the eastern garderobe not only produced artefacts of intrinsic interest but provide evidence for a further programme of refurbishment in the Vicars' Court in the mid-18th century.

9

The Vicars Choral at St Paul's, London, and their Context in the Churchyard

John Schofield

Introduction

Much concerning the early history of the lesser clergy at St Paul's is uncertain. About 1300 it was argued that the 30 vicars of St Paul's, later known as the vicars choral, along with the 30 canons and the twelve minor canons, constituted the primitive foundation of the church, presumably that established by Bishop Maurice (1085–1107) before his death. Each of the vicars was responsible to one of the canons and they appear to have been an integral but subordinate element in the body of the clergy that maintained the service in the choir. By the late 13th century there emerged a third group of lesser clergy: the priests serving chantries and other altars outside the choir. Following a dispute they were accorded precedence over the vicars (Edwards 1967, 252–63; ed. Simpson 1873, 134–9; ed. Gibbs 1939, xxvi–xxviii). This paper is concerned with the vicars choral and their accommodation in the churchyard, which has to be distinguished from that of the minor or petty canons. We also have to sketch in the history of the second Bishop's Palace, which from the 13th century lay between the sites of the vicars choral complex and the hall of the minor canons.

In the case of St Paul's, also, some basic orientation is required; we have to first find the medieval cathedral. That is in fact comparatively easy. From the work of its Surveyor, F C Penrose, in the 1870s and 1880s we know that the pre-Fire cathedral occupied a slightly larger space than that of the Wren building, and though much damaged by the Wren building and associated works, it projects underground at both east and west ends, and minimally at the ends of the transepts of its replacement. It is also on a different alignment by a few degrees. Although we have sightings and fragments of these fairly fixed points, there is however much which is currently

being debated about the internal plan of the building. The outline of the pre-Fire cathedral used here, that of Hollar in 1657 rationalised by Penrose in the 1880s, is therefore provisional and the current best proposal (Fig. 9.1).

The present paper concerns the area north-west of the medieval cathedral, where three complexes of buildings were to be found: from west to east, the vicars choral, the second Bishop's Palace, and the joint complex of the Pardon Cloister (with the Becket Chapel within it) and the hall of the minor canons. In describing each of these, the evidence will be reviewed up to the Great Fire of 1666 and shortly after, since at certain points reconstruction of medieval details is possible from post-Reformation documents and later maps. A final section describes the sites today.

The western boundary of the precinct, to 1200

Little is known about the origins and development of the precinct, including this western part, from the foundation of St Paul's in 604 until the 13th century. The precise site of the Anglo-Saxon cathedral, which was rebuilt several times, is not known; there is faint support for it being beneath the nave of the medieval cathedral (Schofield forthcoming). Radiocarbon dates between the late 8th and late 10th century have recently been obtained from human burials excavated immediately north of the medieval nave in 1997. Before it moved in the 13th century, the Bishop's Palace was south-east of the cathedral, an area also distinguished by the discovery (in 1852) of the famous Ringerike-style tombstone dating to the second quarter of the 11th century (Tweddle *et al.* 1995, 226–8). Consequently we can point to two discrete

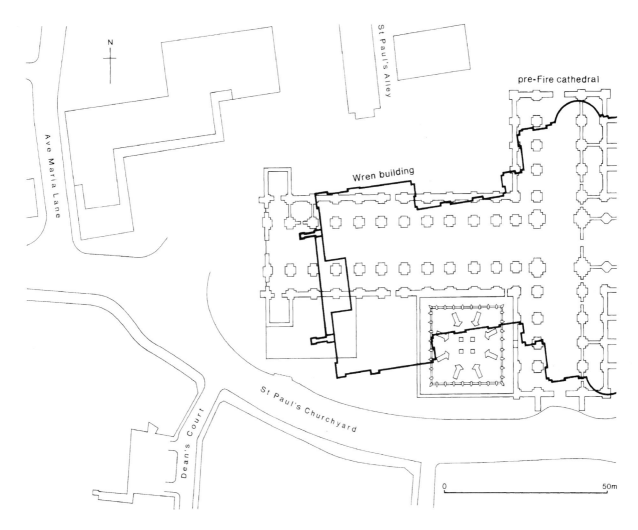

Fig. 9.1. Vicars choral of St Paul's Cathedral London. An overlay of the present Wren cathedral on the current 'best fit' plan of the pre-Fire cathedral, as surveyed by Hollar in 1657 and made to fit by Penrose in the 1880s. This is subject to revisions in progress (drawing Tracy Wellman, copyright Museum of London)

indications of an area of high status activity on the edge of the precinct (the palace and Viking burial site), south-east of the Anglo-Saxon and medieval cathedral, adjacent to a grid of streets probably laid out by Alfred or his successors in the late 9th century.

The most relevant elements to a reconstruction of the west part of the precinct or churchyard in the 12th century are given in Fig. 9.2. The west end of the medieval cathedral was built by about 1190, from the little evidence available, and presumably by this time the parish church of St Gregory was in its medieval position attached to the south end of the west front. St Gregory's church is first mentioned in 1010, and this may relate to the site of the Anglo-Saxon cathedral. It is possible that the medieval west front of the cathedral marks the west front of the late Anglo-Saxon cathedral also.

Probably in 1111, Henry I granted to the cathedral and to Richard, Bishop of London, so much of the

fossatum of the royal *castellum*, near the Thames, on the south side [of the church], as was needed for 'a wall of the church' (*murum eiusdem ecclesie*) and a road outside the wall, and, on the other side of the church northwards, so much of the same *fossatum* as the bishop has already destroyed (*diruit*) (eds. Johnson and Cronne II, no.991; Gibbs 1939, no. 28). The rubric to the copy of the grant in the cathedral cartulary adds:

> tantum de fossato castelli sui ad claudendum muro et viam extra murum versus australem et ad aquilonem,
> *'so much of the ditch of the castle for enclosing with a wall and a way outside the wall towards south and north'* (ibid.).

This indicates that the wall mentioned was a precinct wall, not part of the church building itself. Moreover, about 1140 Richard was remembered as having acquired the broad streets (*placeas*) around the cathedral previously occupied by the houses of the

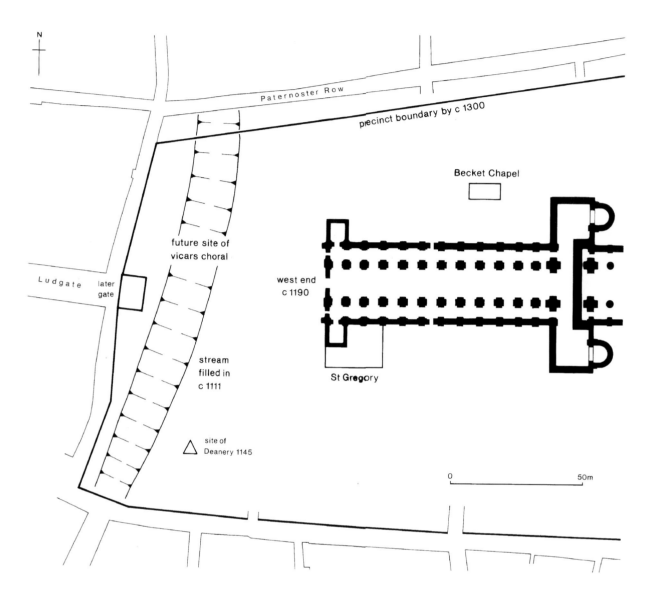

Fig. 9.2. Vicars choral of St Paul's Cathedral London. Reconstruction of the west part of St Paul's churchyard in the 12th century (drawing Tracy Wellman, copyright Museum of London)

laity, and for having enclosed them with a strong wall (Whatley 1989, 128–31).

A wide stream or managed watercourse found on several sites north-west of the cathedral contributed to this ditch, and ran south along the line of the modern (and late medieval) St Andrew's Hill to also form part of the ditch of the first Baynard's Castle (Schofield 1999, 38–9, fig. 26). Since the stream was there in Roman times, the Castle must have adapted it as a defence in the late 11th century. The stream has been found most recently in an excavation immediately north-west of the cathedral, in the southernmost part of the large redevelopment of the Paternoster Square complex. This vast area had been dug out in 1961 with minimal archaeological observation, and much was lost; in 2000–1 the small

remaining islands of stratigraphy were excavated in modern conditions. These three limited blocks of strata comprised one in the area of the vicars choral and two in the area of the Bishop's Palace. The excavation is called Juxon House, after the building of 1961 that was being removed.

The stream was aligned approximately north–south, at least 5.97m deep and ran in a hollow at least 22m wide (Fig. 9.2). The lower fills of the feature consist of fine sands and loose sandy gravels, probably deposited by fairly fast flowing water. These deposits are sealed by humic sands and silty clays containing dumps of organic material, perhaps indicating slackening water flow or the disuse of the feature. A layer of peaty sand and silt may point to soil formation or vegetation growth on top of these deposits. The upper fills of the feature consist of massive dumps of gravely, silty clay, intermixed with tips of organic refuse, representing a concerted attempt to infill the feature and consolidate the ground. These fills had slumped to form a large hollow on the eastern side of the feature, which continued to be used as a tip for organic refuse (cess, straw, plant remains, leather, bone and wood, including two bucket staves). Present evidence suggests the backfilling dates to the 11th or 12th century, and thus can be equated with the 1111 works at the cathedral.

By 1300 most of the precinct, like others of its type in London and elsewhere, was surrounded by a wall, which had gates to the major streets. One of these was on Ludgate to the west, but no trace of it has ever been seen or found. By 1400 or shortly after,

the elements within this part of the churchyard which form the focus of this paper were all in place (Fig. 9.3).

The vicars choral

By 1273 the vicars choral had a hall in which they were bound to take their food unless specially invited to the canons' houses (ed. Simpson 1873, 68). This hall probably lay within the site of their complex of buildings recorded at a later date, and may have originated long before 1273 (ed. Page 1909, 422, 427–8).

Very little is known about the vicars' buildings. The property of the vicars choral is mentioned in 1318 as being east of a Bridge House property which is placed on the east side of Ave Maria Lane (ed.

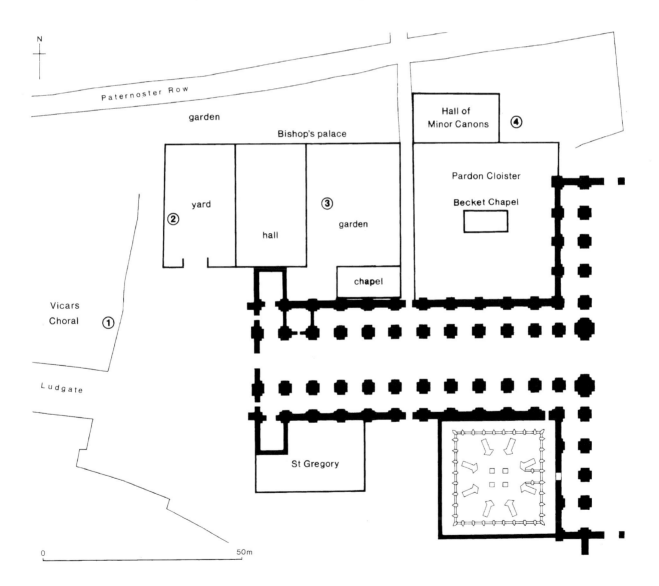

Fig. 9.3. Vicars choral of St Paul's Cathedral London. Plan of the north-west part of the churchyard in the early 15th century (after ed. Lobel 1989). The three parts of the 2001 excavation at Juxon House are shown as sites 1–3; site 4 is the works department ramp (drawing Tracy Wellman, copyright Museum of London)

Lobel 1989, 92). In Dean Colet's *Epitome of the Statutes* (written between 1505 and 1519), he notes that the vicars *in domo una manserunt* (ed. Simpson 1873, 234). In 1599 the 'mansion for the vicar' was called *Purlewe*, and contained a house, buttery, kitchen, shop, chambers, garden yard and a well (Macleod 1990, 8).

Letting out some of the vicars' houses had started before the Reformation. In 1532 the dean and chapter demised to Andrew Smythe a tenement 31ft 3in (9.52m) long north–south which lay on the north side of the east entry to the vicars choral, then called 'Doctors' Commons'; Smythe's building butted, on the north side, the Commons kitchen and wellhouse, to which he was to have access (Historical Manuscripts Commission 1883, 11, no. 456). In 1649 a parliamentary survey of all lands belonging to the dean and chapter described, with simple measurements of their grounds, sixteen units, but they cannot be reconstructed into a meaningful plan (GL, Ms. 25632, f. 243–61). The mansion house and hall of the vicars choral are mentioned as abuttals of two of the pieces, and there was at least one paved yard; but the dimensions of the hall are not ascertainable. The secular leases then in force went back into the 1620s; the arrangement was probably by then well established.

In the Juxon House excavation of 2001, the ditch along the precinct boundary had been filled in. No medieval ground surfaces survived, but a number of refuse pits were recorded in the centre and east of the site. Several inhumation graves indicate the use of the eastern part of the site as a cemetery (Fig. 9.4), although it is notable that refuse pits disturbed graves while the cemetery was still in use. Presumably these

Fig. 9.4. Vicars choral of St Paul's Cathedral London. A human burial being recorded on the Juxon House site in 2001. Although three burials were found in the area of the vicars choral, they may have preceded the 13th century and be ordinary burials in the churchyard before the vicars choral were established in this area (photo and copyright, Museum of London Archaeology Service)

skeletons (which have still to be dated accurately) indicate general churchyard burials before the vicars were established here sometime in the 13th century.

Little evidence for later medieval activity survived. Cut into the backfilled ditch was an isolated pier-base foundation. A chalk-lined cesspit, containing a copper alloy candlestick in its primary fill, must relate to a building. It was finally infilled in the later 16th or early 17th century. The only post-medieval features to survive were one brick lined cesspit, a drain and a small refuse pit. Future analysis of these remains will in due course throw limited light on the site development.

The Bishop's Palace

East of the vicars' accommodation, adjacent to the west end of the cathedral, lay the Bishop's Palace (Fig. 9.3) which had moved to this site in the 13th century. In 1461, during his coronation banquet, Edward IV received the major and aldermen there. The palace was also used during the 16th century for royal receptions and royal guests, for instance in 1551, when Henry Machyn records that Mary de Guise was entertained there. When the Pope issued a bull against Elizabeth I in 1583, copies of it were posted on the bishop's house.

About 1660 the bishop set up his palace a quarter of a mile away, in Aldersgate Street. By this time the site of the former Bishop's Palace had been let out, and apparently as a result largely rebuilt into over 40 small units comprising shops with houses (GL, Ms.12191). Many of the units have names, which would be their sign. The Black Raven, comprising four rooms, a cellar and a shop, was 'near the Portico' (i.e. Jones's portico of 1633–41). Presumably this indicates that during the Commonwealth period the bishop was not able to use his palace, and the site had been broken up and sold off.

Little is known about the medieval palace; we presume it was on the scale of bishop's palaces at other cathedrals, though it does seem to have been comparatively small in extent. The roof of the hall is probably shown on the anonymous 'View of London from the north', drawn between 1577 and 1598 (Schofield 2001). This range has crenellations, at least on the west side. An outline of the main buildings of the palace is given by an anonymous plan in the Wren drawings archive at the Codrington Library, All Souls College Oxford (volume II, no.1), though evidence for its sources is lacking and it is uncorroborated. The 'Codrington' plan is of the whole cathedral, apparently before the addition of the portico at the west end by Jones in the 1630s (Gem 1990, pl. IXb). Its accuracy is currently being tested against the surviving fragments of the medieval cathedral and other plans, including Hollar's of 1657.

The Codrington plan is the only one to show what seems to be the main range or hall of the palace, at right angles to the nave and joined at its south end to the north-west tower of the cathedral. The hall is of six bays, with buttresses on both sides; one doorway (presumably the main entrance) at the north-east corner, and perhaps two doors in the east wall. To the west is an open area, presumably the court, and a square building protruding into the atrium of the cathedral, but the expected gate in this area is not shown before the edge of the plan.

On the other side of the hall the plan shows another open area, presumed to be a garden, with a small rectangular building at its south-east corner, against two bays of the nave, with an entrance at its north-west corner. This is usually presumed to be the bishop's chapel; traces of a building were seen here in a trial hole of 1933, and documentary references suggest that a gallery led to it. The chapel seems to have been on two floors (or possibly one formal floor over a ground-floor undercroft), as would be expected for a bishop at his cathedral. Another long narrow garden stretched along the north side of the vicars choral for 110ft, according to the *Parliamentary Survey* of the latter in 1649 (GL, Ms.25632, f.261). These elements of the palace are shown on Fig. 9.3.

Becket's Chapel, the Pardon Churchyard and the hall of the minor canons

East of the Bishop's Palace were three features which are best explained together: Becket's Chapel, the Pardon Churchyard (also called Pardon Cloister) and the hall of the minor canons (Fig. 9.3). Remains have been seen here on four occasions: for two phases of construction of the underground cathedral works department in 1909 and 1969, the observation of a narrow drain trench in 1997 in a corridor at basement level of the part built in 1909, and a small excavation of 2001 of remaining strata in the open and immediately east of the Wren Chapter House, as the access ramp into the works department (a construction of 1969) was lowered. The following is an interim summary based on plotting of the various discoveries and assessment of the artefactual material, though much of it is unstratified by modern standards.

This area was a cemetery from the late Anglo-Saxon period; not only were stone coffins and stone-lined graves found in 1909, but observations at a lower level in the same area in 1997 recorded 29 burials, the lowest intruding into Roman strata beneath. Radiocarbon sampling of long bones from five burials has given dates ranging from AD 773–883 to 894–986 (at two levels of confidence). The burials were of men and women, so this was a lay cemetery, not that of the canons. The cemetery lay north of the Romanesque nave, and a building later known as Becket's Chapel was eventually placed centrally within it. This was the burial place of Archbishop Thomas's parents, and the chapel itself may have been founded in the mid 12th century by Thomas's father, the sheriff Gilbert Becket. In the later middle ages their tomb played an important part in civic ceremonial and was visited each year by the mayor at the commencement of his term (ed. Riley 1859, I, 26). Dean More (1406–21) rebuilt the chapel; or possibly built it for the first time, since the early references are to Gilbert's tomb, not to the chapel (ed. Kingsford 1971, I, 328). The whole area here was bulldozed in 1969, and the salvage records made at the time by Robert Crayford which are now being re-analysed indicate the chapel may have been a rectangular structure of stone, but little else could be recorded. It had stone coffins around it on at least two sides. During the later medieval period the chapel stood in the middle of the Pardon Cloister, and the area was also known as the Pardon Church-yard. The Pardon Cloister was also built or endowed (i.e. rebuilt) by Dean More (*ibid.*, I, 327).

Observations of 1909 and 1969 recorded a cloister that was basically square, and lay in the angle of the nave and the north transept. It had a back wall on the north and west, and the internal arcade on all four sides was supported on foundations of chalk piers which included fragments of earlier grave covers. In two of the pier foundations of the inner side of the cloister, that at the north-east corner and the next to the south, were parts of a large Purbeck marble slab bearing the indent of a cross brass, very similar to one of 1408 at Hildersham (Cambridge-shire). The stepped base, two pairs of trefoils sprouting from the stem and the octofoil head correspond closely. In the octofoil was placed a full-length priest in mass vestments (similar to the full-length priest in a cope in Hereford Cathedral, dated 1386, and to the full-length priest in mass vestments at Stone, Kent, dated 1409). The London monument appears to have dated from *c*.1410 (Page-Phillips 1969–74). It appears that the inner arcade, at least, of the cloister was rebuilt in the 15th century, presumably by Dean More. There is thus no independent evidence of the form of any cloister before this date, and no archaeological evidence for a cloister before 1410.

The Pardon Cloister as rebuilt by More was decorated with a remarkable wall painting (on boards) of the Dance of Death, sponsored by John Carpenter, town clerk, in the reign of Henry VI. Stow noted that the monuments in the cloister 'in number and curious workmanship passed all other that were in that church' (ed. Kingsford 1971, I, 327–8). In a rare comparison of his subject-matter with foreign cities, Stow also observed that the wall painting of the Dance of Death was modelled on that painted in 1424–5 in the cloister of the Saints-Innocentes, Paris. This was the main and largest cemetery in Paris, measuring about 6800m2 in area. An arcaded and vaulted walk surrounded it, and there were prominent tombs within the garth (a painting of it of around 1565 is in the Musée Carnavalet, and is reproduced in Harding 2002, 103). The Saints-Innocentes furnishes a significant parallel for the function as *campo santo* (as at Pisa) of the Pardon Cloister. Here was an alternative to the choir of the cathedral for luxury tombs; and the archaeological evidence now suggests that men and women had been buried here since the 8th century. In 1549 the Pardon Cloister and Becket's Chapel were pulled down to furnish materials for Somerset House. The area was quickly colonised by bookshops which already functioned in the churchyard to east and west.

The minor canons are traditionally thought to be of pre-Norman origin. They are referred to in 1162 as the 'prebendary clerks of the choir', as distinct from the canons themselves. They lived in separate lodgings near the cathedral, assigned to them by the dean and chapter. Their occasional extra duties included performance of chantries and individuals could hold the office of Keeper of the Old or New Work (i.e. a minor canon could be in charge of the building funds for the two parts of the cathedral) (ed. Page 1909, 422).

In 1353 Robert of Kingston, a minor canon, bequeathed his hall in *Pardonchurchhaugh*, with the adjoining houses, to his brothers, that they might have a common hall in which to take food together. The minor canons obtained a charter in 1356, a bull of confirmation from Urban VI in 1373, and finally a charter of incorporation as the 'College of the Twelve Minor Canons' in 1395–6 (ed. Page 1909, 426). A chamber adjoining the west end of their hall was to be a treasure house, in which the seal of the college would be preserved (Simpson 1871). The mayor and commonalty granted the college 'their watercourses' and other easements (ed. Kingsford 1971, I, 327). This is interesting as it refers to the otherwise totally unknown, but presumed, water system for the cathedral and its buildings. The college of minor canons had gates, which were to be closed at nine in the evening (ed. Simpson 1873, xxxvi). The minor canons lived in houses, presumably – though not certainly – one canon to a house. In 1598 eleven houses are mentioned, whereof three are said to be outside the precinct of the petty canons. At this date all had subtenants, and most of them had several; in one house there were five subtenants 'and no room reserved for the incumbent' (ed. Simpson 1873, 235, 274).

A survey plan by Henry Bond, dated April 1666, of property belonging to the dean and chapter (in Guildhall Library Print Room) shows a triangular block between Paul's Alley on the west, the 'alley next the Petty Cannons Colledge' on the north, and the New Alley which went diagonally across the site of the Pardon Churchyard, by now demolished. This places the minor canons' hall on the north side of the Pardon Churchyard or Cloister. The position of the individual minor canons' houses is not known at all; it seems probable that most of them lay in the narrow space between the hall and Paternoster Row to the north, on the site of the later Chapter House Court.

There has been one small recent excavation of relevance, on the present ramp into the works department (by the Museum of London Archaeology Service; being analysed as part of the work on the Paternoster Square development; Fig. 9.3, site 4). This small excavation recorded a succession of medieval timber-lined pits (one of which was dated by pottery in its fill to *c*.1270–1350) which culminated in the south-east corner of a chalk cesspit. It had eventually been backfilled in the 19th century, as shown by the inclusion of white china in the backfill. From its position, this cesspit appears to be part of the complex of buildings on the north side of the Pardon Cloister, and therefore probably part of the buildings of the minor canons. Thus of the three complexes considered here, only the hall of the minor canons was still recognisable, and presumably still largely in its medieval form, in 1666.

After the Great Fire

By the time of the Great Fire in 1666, the sites of the vicars choral, the Bishop's Palace and the Pardon Churchyard were all secularised and built over. Wren's new Chapter House of 1711 stands on the site of the hall of the minor canons. Some houses were erected over the site of the Pardon Churchyard, respecting the diagonal line shown on the Bond plan of May 1666, but these were removed in 1710 because they were too close to the new cathedral, and to provide a cleared site for the Chapter House.

By 1900, the outer margins of St Paul's Churchyard were just another part of the City of London (Fig. 9.5). By the 1950s there were several banks on the site of the vicars choral, the foundations of which would have badly damaged any remaining deposits. The site was again developed in 1961, with very little archaeological recording. The three fragmentary areas recorded in 2001 survived because they were in open space, outside the footprint of the buildings of 1961. But in 2001 the building line was pushed out to its limit and these last remains were also excavated.

Fig. 9.5. Vicars choral of St Paul's Cathedral London. Looking west down Ludgate Hill from the west end of the Cathedral c.1900, with the site of the vicars choral covered by the buildings on the extreme right. There was to be at least one further generation of buildings on the site before the rebuilding of the 1960s (photo and copyright, GL)

Conclusions

The vicars choral at St Paul's remain shadowy figures and the site of their complex at St Paul's has now been totally destroyed. We know that, like the other colleges in this volume, they had a hall and probably houses by the late 13th century, on a site near the west door of the medieval cathedral – a strikingly similar position to the vicars choral at Lichfield (Fig. 7.1 above). The vicars of St Paul's have survived as a body, though in different form, to the present day;

but their buildings were already only a memory in 1649. Even so, much survived below ground until 1961, and the remaining fragmentary archaeological features from the college were excavated in 2000–1 as part of the consequence of the redevelopment of the 1961 Paternoster Square development. The results from these latter excavations will be published in due course and it is possible that more intensive documentary study in the future will elucidate the topography of the vicars' close.

10

Where Was the Vicars' Close at Salisbury?

Tim Tatton-Brown

When John Leland visited Salisbury Cathedral in the 1540s, he recorded that 'the vicars of Saresbyri hath a praty college and house for their loggings' (ed. Smith 1964, 267). If one looks around the Close at Salisbury today there is no sign of the 'praty college', though a visitor with sharp eyes might notice a very worn brass plate on the front door of No.12 The Close (on the south side of the North Walk) naming it as the hall of the vicars choral.

At many secular cathedrals, including Chichester, Exeter, Hereford, Lichfield, Lincoln and especially Wells (and at St George's Chapel, Windsor), vicars' halls and their associated neat rows of houses for vicars within an 'inner' close survived long after the Reformation; but not at Salisbury. It has, therefore, been concluded by some that, despite Leland's statement, there never was a separate Vicars' Close at Salisbury, only a common hall. This seems un-likely, and a study of the documentary material and of the remaining fabric suggests that there was, from the early 15th century, a separate college or com-munity of vicars living on the south side of the North Walk of the Close, between St Ann's Gate and the Bishop's Walk (Fig. 10.1). This college not only had its own common hall and chapel (situated over St Ann's Gate), but also a series of small houses or lodgings at the western end of the site, most of which were destroyed by the middle of the 17th century. There does not, however, seem to be any evidence for regular rows of houses around an inner court, or for a separate close wall around the college.

As is fairly well-known, the vicars' common hall at Salisbury was probably not in existence until around 1409 (the year the vicars received their charter of incorporation), and was the last to be set up in England (Edwards 1949, 284; RCHME 1993, 13 and 88). When a new set of Statutes were drawn up in

1442, for the 'proctor and community of the vicars', it was stated that all vicars of non-resident canons must live together at the hall. At this time the vicars cannot possibly have been literally living in the hall, which was only 23ft wide by 29½ft (7m x 9m) long (this common hall was not demolished until 1814 – RCHME 1993, 90); instead they must have been living in chambers nearby. Documentary evidence for several of these houses exists, but only at one building today (No.10, The Close), does anything survive above ground (RCHME 1993, 83–4). Here a small part of a 14th- and 15th-century two-storied building survives on the north-west corner of the site (Fig. 10.2). No original doors or windows can be seen, but a medieval fireplace and its chimney stack survive in the west wall and opposite this a small area of painted wall-plaster, on a lath and plaster internal wall, has been discovered. The decoration is painted false ashlar work, with five-petalled flower-heads on curved stalks, possibly of the 14th century (illustrated in RCHME 1993, 85). This fragment of a building (sadly the roof has been replaced) has masonry outer walls and timber-framed internal walls, and it is just possible that this is all that now remains of a regular series of lodgings around an internal courtyard. The building remained a vicar's house, though often leased out, until the later 18th century. The houses on either side of this medieval fragment (now Nos.8, 9, and 11, The Close) were totally rebuilt in the 17th and 18th centuries, but we know from the documentary evidence that there were various vicars' houses on these sites from at least the 14th century. No.11, now a fine 18th-century house with a stable yard to the east and a large garden running back from it, was built on the site of four separate small tenements, amalgamated into one large property between 1547 and 1660. These earlier tenements had each contained

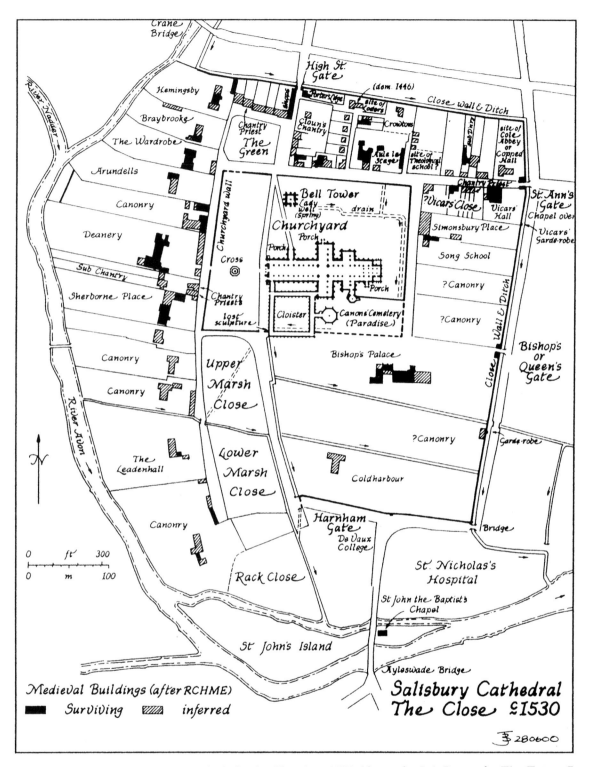

Fig. 10.1. Vicars choral of Salisbury Cathedral. The Close in c.1530 (drawn by J A Bowen for Tim Tatton Brown, copyright J A Bowen)

a chantry priest's and a vicar's house, from at least the late 15th century; and we know also that the vicars' orchard (said to be 51ft (15.5m) wide and 138ft (42m) long) was added to the site sometime in the Commonwealth period (RCHME 1993, 85). It seems likely, therefore, that in the 15th century there was a series of vicars' houses at Salisbury in neat

rows around one (or possibly two) courtyards as at other cathedral closes.

By the time of the *Parliamentary Survey* of 1649 (Malden 1893), when there were only six vicars remaining, their houses were spread around the northern and north-eastern part of the Close at Salisbury. The common hall had last been used

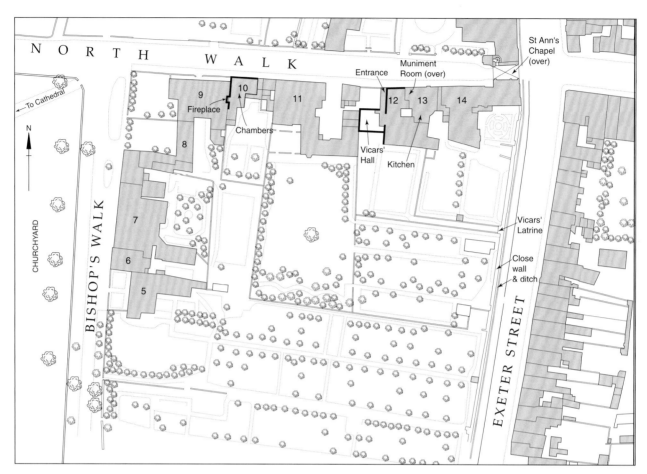

Fig. 10.2. Vicars choral of Salisbury Cathedral. Ordnance Survey map of 1881 (1:500), showing details of the houses south-west of St Ann's Gate, upon which is superimposed a reconstruction of elements of the plan of the vicars' close (drawn by Lesley Collett, copyright YAT)

communally in about 1620, and in 1679 it was given to one of the vicars as a single house (RCHME 1993, 89) 'being now much better than any of our present dwelling houses'. It is still called 'Vicars' Hall' today though, as we have seen, the hall itself was demolished in 1814 (Figs. 10.3, 10.4 and 10.5). All that now remains is the principal north door to the hall and the three doors on the east side of the screens passage leading to an L-shaped 13th-century canon's house that was given to the vicars in the 14th century. A kitchen (or kitchens) remains to the south (and east) of a small inner court, and on the first floor of the north range over the larder is the vicars' muniment room (rebuilt in about 1605). It is possible that two or three vicars could have had small lodgings above the buttery and pantry range, to the east of the hall, but no more. The building, which has been fully described by the RCHME (1993, 88–96), was divided into two houses (Nos.12 and 13, The Close) and a vicar was still living in the western house when the college was finally dissolved in 1934. All the vicars' property then passed to the dean and chapter.

East of the service wing and kitchen of the vicars' hall is another house (No.14) which was built by the

vicars in the 1660s on their own land. Much of the site in question must have been a garden, but it is likely that in the 14th century there was a building immediately to the south of St Ann's Gate in the north-eastern corner of the site. This would have contained a staircase leading up to the chapel of St Ann above the gateway, and to the crenellated wall-walk on top of the Close wall to the east. St Ann's Gate was probably built in the early 14th century, but by 1354 the side walls to the gate passage had been extended westwards to allow a chapel, dedicated to St Ann and the Blessed Virgin, to be built above it (Fig. 10.6). By the later 15th century it appears to have passed into the ownership of the vicars, so that they could use this as their own chapel. At this time a spiral staircase was added to the north-west side of the gate to allow the vicars to have easier access to the chapel. The original door to this staircase still survives, protected by a 17th-century brick porch. Until relatively recently the chapel still contained its 14th-century roof (though mutilated). Sadly this has now gone, though the openings for the original east, west and north windows still survive. The reticulated tracery in the

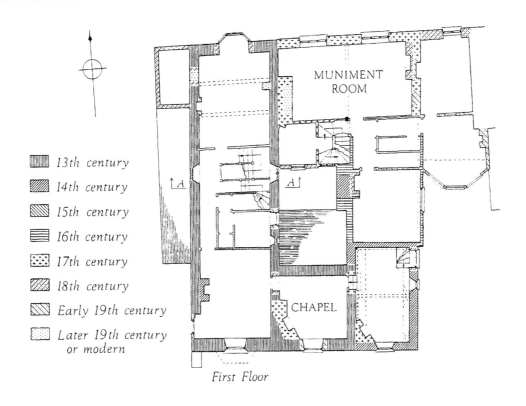

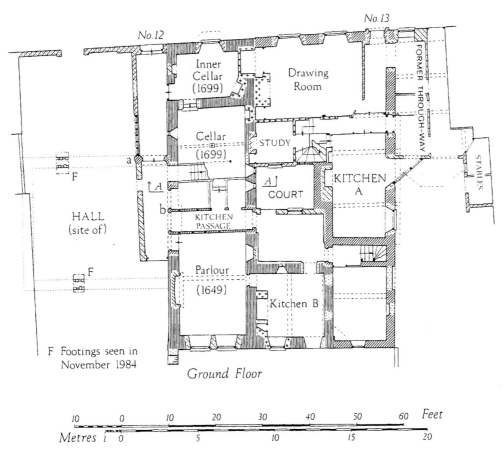

Fig. 10.3. Vicars Choral of Salisbury Cathedral. Composite plan of Nos.12 and 13 The Close, identified by RCHME (1993) as the college of the vicars choral. This interpretation is disputed in this paper (drawing and copyright, English Heritage)

First floor
*c.*1300

Ground floor
14th century

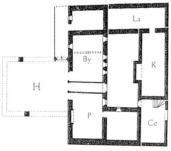

Late 14th, and
15th centuries

1668

Fig. 10.4. *Vicars Choral of Salisbury Cathedral. Plan illustrating the development of Nos.12 and 13 The Close, according to RCHME (1993). This interpretation is disputed in this paper (drawing and copyright, English Heritage)*

Fig. 10.5. *Vicars Choral of Salisbury Cathedral. Contemporary view of Nos.12 and 13 The Close (photo and copyright, English Heritage)*

Fig. 10.6. *Vicars Choral of Salisbury Cathedral. The east gate of the Close from the west. It is suggested here that the chapel of St Ann, over the gate, served as the chapel of the vicars choral college, which is located to the south (right) (source, Cook 1949)*

east and west windows only dates, however, from the mid 19th century (RCHME 1993, 47–9). No other medieval features survive in the chapel, which is now used as an architects' office.

The garden of No.14 has a wall on its south side (now partly destroyed) behind which was a narrow passage leading from the garden of the vicars' hall to the vicars' common latrine on the Close wall. When originally built the latrine must have emptied directly into the Close ditch, but unfortunately it appears to have been destroyed in the 19th century, perhaps when the Close ditch was infilled in 1860.

It remains, therefore, to ask why the Vicars' 'Close' at Salisbury was such a late and insubstantial affair, even though the corporate body was a large institution owning much property. When this institution came into being in 1409 there were 52 vicars, and even in 1442, when the new statutes were drawn up, there were still 48–49 vicars. This was an interesting time, when the vicars were at the height of their power. Much is recorded about them, and their wrong-doings, in episcopal visitations which took place every seven years between 1394 and 1475 (Edwards 1956, 180). The visitations in 1440 and 1447 by Bishop Aiscough suggest that much more discipline was needed, as Dr Edwards has shown. There were many complaints about vicars who were often absent from choir, or who, when present, were noisy and irreverent. They were also said to have neglected their masses, and caused many scandals in the Close and city by having relationships with women. (In the early 14th century one vicar, when charged with concubinage, said that every vicar kept a mistress, either in the Close or out of it.) One exceptional case was of John Wallope, who was not only accused of quarrelling with other vicars and having liaisons with three women, but was also accused of heresy at discussions with other vicars in their common hall. This, as Dr Edwards says (1956, 180), is a rare reference to heresy among the cathedral clergy before the Reformation. Only after the mid 15th century did the numbers of vicars start to drop, and in 1468 there were only 31 vicars (*ibid.*). In parallel with this the number of residentiary canons,

normally about ten to thirteen, started to drop until it reached seven or eight by the early 16th century. By the early 17th century the number of resident canons and vicars had reached its final figure of only six of each.

Dr Kathleen Edwards, the historian of Salisbury Cathedral, as well as of secular cathedrals in general, suggests that the reason for the late provision of a vicars' college at Salisbury was probably a result of the manner in which the close was planned in the early 13th century. The laying out of the new house plots at this time provided both spacious houses for the resident canons (where their own vicars also lived), as well as many other smaller plots for vicars and chantry priests houses (Edwards 1939, 82; 1949, 284). Senior vicars also later held posts such as subdean or succentor, and separate houses were provided for them. The situation of the vicars in the early 14th century is very clearly spelt out in the statutes of Bishop Roger de Martival (1315–30), who also finally completed the building of the cathedral (the spire). In one statute, for example, the vicars were told that if they lived in a canon's house at any time, they must not make it unsuitable for a canon's use 'by making lodgings or little chambers there'. All the canons' houses had their own chapels, which the vicar used and, when a canon died, or was away, the vicar often acted as custodian of his master's house, and was expected by the dean and chapter to keep it in good condition. As time went on more and more vicars (especially those of absentee canons) were also chantry priests, and on 24th September 1395, 31 of them who held chantries and other houses had to appear at chapter with titles to show 'how and from whom they held their houses and by what right'. Soon after this the vicars' common hall was built, at a time when most other cathedrals already had one, and this was presumably followed by the building of the new lodging chambers west of the common hall, already described. By the early 16th century Leland's 'praty college' inside St Ann's Gate in the north-east corner of the Close must have housed the majority of vicars, and have been a flourishing, if still somewhat unruly, institution.

11

'Begun While the Black Death Raged…' The Vicars' Close at Wells

Warwick Rodwell

With a contribution on the outline history by Frances Neale

The Vicars' Close at Wells is the most completely preserved and architecturally impressive monument of its type in Britain. It comprises a gatehouse, hall with undercroft, kitchen, chapel, library, treasury, muniment room, exchequer and forty-two individual houses, enclosed by a high wall, and lying within the northern part of the cathedral precinct which is known as the Liberty of Wells. It is partnered by an equally complete archive, which extends unbroken – except for the years of the Civil War and Commonwealth – from the foundation of the College in 1348 right up to its end as an independent entity on 30th September 1936, in conformity with Statute XIII of the 1936 Wells Cathedral Statutes, drawn up following the *Cathedrals Measures* of 1931 and 1934.

The Vicars Choral archives at Wells remain a largely unrealised resource. Walter de Gray Birch catalogued the vicars' charters in 1882, and Linzee Colchester (Cathedral Archivist 1976–1989) undertook much transcription and a short study of the development of the close buildings (Colchester 1974; n.d.; 1986a; 1986b); a complete handlist of the archives was produced as recently as 2001, and a properly classified catalogue is only now in hand. The more readily accessible dean and chapter archives have frequently been mined for vividly worded statutes, liturgical detail, and snippets about 'naughty vicars' (*HMC Cal* 1, 2). They provide an essential complement to the vicars' own archive; but as the dean and chapter were, apart from paying allowances and fees, mostly concerned with discipline, this gives a very one-sided view of the vicars choral. The Rev. H. Parnell (Priest Vicar 1922–33) made considerable use of original documents; but his opposition to the proposals in the 1931/1934 *Cathedrals Measures* became so embittered that it coloured his approach to the evidence, giving his

work an opposite bias to that of the chapter archives (Parnell n.d.). A recent study of some vicars choral estates between 1591 and 1936 marked a beginning in modern, objective historical examination of one aspect of the vicars' history (Hill 1998, 287–309). A complete, balanced history of the college at Wells, and of the tensions between college and chapter, which form a constant thread throughout their long history, has yet to be written.

Outline history

Origins

Although the present college buildings date from the mid 14th century and later, the institution was already more than two centuries old when they were erected. During the episcopate of Robert of Lewes (1136–66) the chapter was refounded and given a new constitution based on the Salisbury model (Gransden 1982, 25–8). Vicars choral, performing duties as deputies for the canons, are mentioned in the earliest extant cathedral statutes and ordinances (before 1165), but few details are recorded (Watkin 1941, xxv-xxvi, 1–4; D&C Wells, *Liber Albus* I [DC/CF/2/1], f. 26, 31 item cviii – *HMC Cal.* 1, 27, 33). The numbers of prebends and vicars fluctuated: Bishop Robert's foundation provided for twenty-two prebends, but by 1263 there were 53, and there must have been almost as many vicars.

Vicarages were not automatically assigned to every prebend, but Bishop Jocelin (1206–42) instituted them in all but three instances. In 1241 he issued a set of statutes, including one that 'the vicars, in regard to their places in choir, shall follow the prebends for which they have been admitted as vicars' (*ibid.*). In another ordinance dated 17th October 1242 he amended the statutes to give each vicar a cash allowance of one penny per day instead of bread (D&C Wells, *Liber Albus* I [DC/CF/2/1], f.51, also DC/CF/3/1/41A – *HMC, Cal.*1, 162; *Cal.* 2, 555). Vicars also received income from attendance at special services. The vicars choral of Wells are by this time clearly established as a body. As Dom. Aelred Watkin (1941, xxvi) observed, a vicarage was often regarded 'merely as a stepping-stone to higher things, or as a refuge for the unsuccessful', and consequently vicars often exhibited a lack of commitment. The statutes of 1273 tried to raise the standard of candidates with voice trials and a probationary year (D&C Wells, *Liber Ruber* [DC/CF/2/2], f.3 – *HMC Cal.* 1, 530[1]), while statutes of 1298 and 1338 were much concerned with discipline.

There is no mention in these early statutes of where the vicars choral lived. The original intention was that a vicar should lodge with the canon whom he served, but that proved impracticable in the case of non-residentiary canons, who were in the majority. Hence, vicars generally lodged in the town, an arrangement which it seems proved unsatisfactory and led to frequent quarrels and unseemly behaviour. In 1243 chapter decreed that no vicar was to live on his own, but must share his lodging with two others (Watkin 1941, 13; D&C Wells *Liber Albus* I [DC/CF/2/1], f. 217v. – *HMC Cal.* 1, 254, citing an earlier statute of 1243 which does not survive, and an injunction of 1295 in *Liber Albus* I, f.125v. – *HMC Cal.* 1, 162). Attempts to enforce this ruling were not entirely successful.

Early schemes

Consequently, in the early 14th century the provision of a communal living place for the Wells vicars was considered by the dean and chapter on several occasions. There were in fact three attempts to get a proposal off the ground. The first is a back-reference to an undated previous chapter decision 'that houses shall be built for the vicars to live in together', noting that nothing had been done (D&C Wells, *Liber Albus* I [DC/CF/2/1], f. 143, article 7 – *HMC Cal.* 1, 181). The second occasion was a special chapter meeting, also undated but *c.*1318–23, in the time of John Godelee, Dean of Wells 1305–1333. On this occasion chapter agreed that the site of 'the dwelling be from the house of Sir William de Cherlton to the penthouse where the masons work', and that a part of the churchyard be taken for the house and grounds 'for the recreation of the inhabitants', with the suggestion that it might all be at the cost of the dean (*idem.*). The site under consideration was part of a plot known as 'The Camery', adjacent to the east cloister of the cathedral, where the masons' yard lay (Fig. 11.1).

The Camery adjoins the grounds of the canonical

house now known as 'The Rib', which was perhaps the house held by Canon William de Cherlton, who was succentor and very active in cathedral affairs between at least 1292 and 1327 (ed. Greenway 2001, 24–5, 39; ed. Jones 1964, 26n.; *HMC Cal.* 1, 152, 215). This would have been a very convenient location, lying within the precinct wall, and having ready access to the cathedral *via* the east cloister walk. Projecting into The Camery from the cloister was the ancient Lady Chapel-by-the-Cloister, which could have served the vicars' needs, although there was also nearby a chapel of All Saints-by-the-Cloister with which the vicars had close connections by the 14th century (Rodwell 2001, 161–98, 320). Moreover, under the provisions of a statute of 1243 the ground around the cloister Lady Chapel was designated as the place of burial for vicars choral (*ibid.*, 358–9). In all probability, a small secondary cloister or courtyard arrangement was envisaged in the south-east part of The Camery. The intention was simply to provide the vicars choral with accommodation; there is no mention of collegiate status. The scheme did not materialize and nothing further is heard of it.

It was followed, thirdly, by a grant made on Friday 25 September 1332, in which more precise detail is given. Chapter made a grant to Dean John de Godelee and his brother Canon Hamelin de Godelee, of a plot 'within the churchyard next to the highway on the west side of the said churchyard, lying between the churchyard wall on the north and the other church-yard wall on the south', 8 perches long and 2 perches 8 feet wide, on which the dean and his brother 'shall cause a house to be built for the dwelling of the vicars of the said church' (D&C Wells, *Liber Albus* [DC/CF/2/1], f. 178 – *HMC Cal.* 1, 219). This strip of land, 132 feet (40m) long and 41 feet (12.5m) wide, apparently lay north–south between the churchyard walls at the western end of what is now Cathedral Green, parallel to Sadler Street (the highway) (Fig. 11.1). The plot is considerably smaller than the vicars' college eventually built.

His personal involvement in *c.*1318–23, and the inclusion of his brother in 1332, seem to suggest that Dean John de Godelee was the driving force behind the proposals. If such a plan for the vicars' accommodation, built by the dean on the Cathedral's own property, had come to pass, the history of the vicars choral and their relations with the dean and chapter might have been very different. As it was, the 1332 plan too came to nothing; quite possibly because Dean Godelee died little more than four months later, before 9th February 1333, and presumably before any work had begun (ed. Jones 1964, 3; ed. Holmes 1895, 137). He was followed by three deans in rapid succession, not conducive to any major building development.

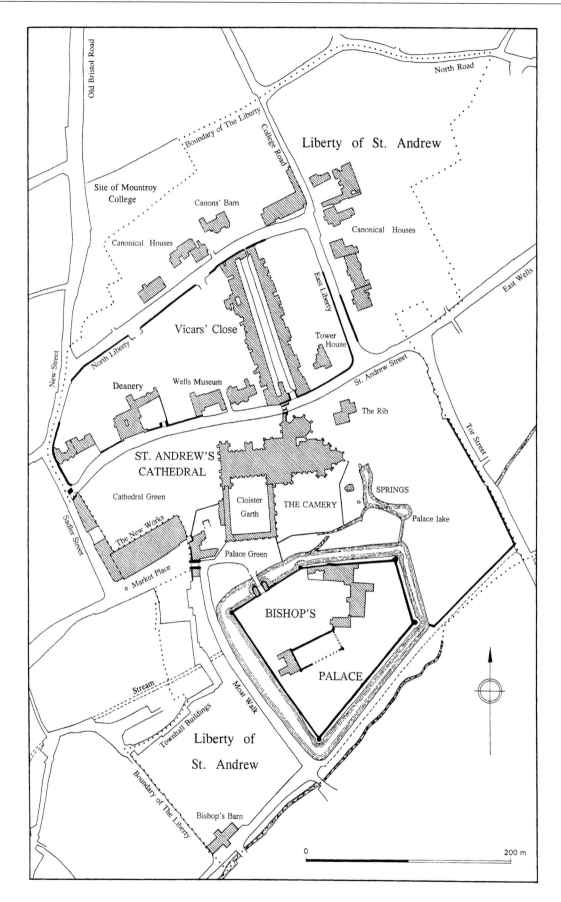

Fig. 11.1. Vicars choral of Wells Cathedral. Plan of precinct and Liberty of St Andrew (drawing and copyright, Warwick Rodwell)

1348 – foundation and construction

Fifteen years later, the initiative was taken up by the Bishop, Ralph of Shrewsbury (1329–1363), who embarked upon an ambitious scheme for housing the vicars by constructing the close that exists today. In December 1348 the Bishop incorporated the 'College of Vicars Choral at Wells' (VC Wells, Charters, VC/CF/2/2), having first obtained a licence in mortmain from King Edward III (VC Wells, Charters, VC/CF/2/1). Both these charters are in fact confirmations of an earlier preliminary grant by Bishop Ralph which does not survive. This earlier grant would have marked the start of building work on the site, some time before 1348.

The new foundation was styled *Collegium novi Clausi Vicariorum infra libertatem Wellensis*. Here, he observed, the vicars 'might be freer to serve God, live more respectably and nearer the church, attend divine service constantly, and meet together for meals in a companionable way, but without idle and scurrilous gossip' (Watkin 1941, 139–49; Gransden 1982, 38). Ralph then handed over the site *una cum domibus in eadem placea iam de novo constructas & construendas* ('together with the houses in the same plot now of new by us built or being built') and with an endowment of £10 *per annum* derived from estates at Congresbury and Wookey. Although further endowments were progressively acquired from Somerset estates, the college never became rich; on the contrary, it was nearly bankrupt by the mid 15th century (Hill 1998, 288).

Ralph of Shrewsbury's original statutes have not survived, but they were copied and incorporated in Bishop Thomas Bekynton's statutes in 1459 (Watkin 1941, 139–49). The College was under the control of the dean and chapter, but its day-to-day running was entrusted to two principals, who were elected annually by the vicars from amongst their number. The College elected other officers, including two bursars; it conducted its own financial business, audited its own accounts, and then or shortly after acquired a fine circular seal with the vicars' arms upon it, impressions of which survive on a number of their documents.

The plot assigned to the vicars for their college was one of the canonical houses in the bishop's own gift. Facing on to Cathedral Green opposite the chapter house, and conveniently near the north door of the cathedral, it was one of the row of principal canonical houses with long gardens extending northwards behind them. The shape of the plot dictated the shape of the 'New Hall' or 'New Close', as it was called from 1348 until the early 20th century. The house had been held by Canon John de Everdon in the early 1300s, passed to Canon Richard de Alresford in 1325, and then to Canon Alan de Hothum (or Hothom) in January 1328. Alan de Hothum was still alive and in Somerset in 1344 (ed. Jones 1964, 40, 42; ed. Hobhouse 1887, 222, 254, 279, 293; Holmes 1896, 515). In 1350 and 1351, however, he was in London, and official receiver of monies to be collected for the papal nuncio (Parnell n.d., 219). This suggests he might have left Wells for London in or after 1344, although still retaining his prebend and its income. He was presumably dead by March 1352, when a successor was appointed to his prebend. By 1348, therefore, his house may have been empty and available with the minimum of disruption to the other canons. The first grant could have been made, and building work commenced, about 1345. It seems highly likely that the vicars took over the existing canonical buildings for communal use so that effort could initially be concentrated on erecting their individual lodgings. The 13th-century features incorporated into the undercroft supporting the Vicars' Hall suggest that it could have held its own as a handsome building alongside the adjacent canonical houses on Cathedral Green. Features dated to the 13th or early 14th century survive in standing buildings, or have recently been excavated, at the former canonical houses now occupied by Wells Cathedral Music School, Wells Museum and the Tower House.

The principal evidence that building work was well under way, and the Vicars' Hall itself completed by the time of the 1348 charters, comes from a copy of the will of a wealthy Bristol widow. Alice Swansee was the mother of Philip Swansee, a vicar choral of Wells, who had predeceased her. She made her will on 7th November 1348. It seems very possible that both she, in Bristol, and her son, earlier in Somerset, may have been victims of the plague, which reached the southwest in the autumn of 1348. Alice desired to be buried at Wells near her son, in the Palm Churchyard or cloister garth which was normally reserved to those in holy orders; and besides leaving two silver cups and a maser to the high altar of the cathedral, she left a large brass vessel 'for the use of the Vicars ... dwelling in the new building which the Bishop has built', together with a basin with hanging ewer, and a table for their hall (D&C Wells, *Liber Albus* I [DC/CF/2/1], f.175 – HMC Cal. 1, 215). This probably indicates that by November 1348 the communal buildings were completed and the vicars were in the early stages of furnishing them. There are no extant accounts which shed light on the progress of building, or provide any clue as to the effect upon it of the Black Death; but Alice Swansee's will further demonstrates that although Bishop Ralph's foundation of the college took place during the Black Death, it was not a response to it. The plan and the building were under way before the arrival of the plague; however, since

47.6 percent of the clergy in the Bath and Wells diocese died of the plague between December 1348 and spring of the following year, work on Vicars' Close cannot have been unaffected (Ziegler 1970, 132). It has been suggested that, as at Chichester, the hall could have served as a dormitory as well as a refectory while the rest of the buildings were completed (Rodwell 1982, 212; Colchester 1987, 166).

Bishop Ralph's foundation charter appears to distinguish between the *domûs*, the communal buildings, comprising the hall, kitchen and bakehouse which are specifically mentioned and were more or less completed; and the *camerae*, the two rows of 42 bachelor 'sets' extending the length of the plot, where building was still in progress (Colchester 1974). There is, or is to be, 'to every vicar … a chamber with his appurtenances.' The vicars are to live in the *prefatas cameras*, 'the aforesaid chambers', and have the hall, kitchen and bakehouse 'to their common use', 'living together at meat and drink at [their] common costs and charges' (VC Wells, charters, VC/CF/2/2; Colchester 1986a, 2–3). The vicars of Wells were apparently the first vicars choral in England to be thus fully incorporated (Edwards 1967, 284). As the site and the foundation were the gift of the bishop, he and his successors had the right to collate new vicars to specific houses in the close.

Further endowments were given, on 12th December 1353 'to the vicars … living together in the new work … and taking meals in their common hall', and on 17th April 1354

> 'to the vicars … dwelling together in the new building erected by the said Bishop [Ralph] and taking meals in the common hall of the said building' (D&C Wells, charters, DC/CF/3/1/327, 331 – HMC Cal. 2, 618–9; Colchester 1986a, 4).

Both grants imply that by 1353–4 construction is complete, the Close is thought of as one unit of building, and the College is fully functioning. Likewise, Bishop Ralph in his will of 12th May 1363 (LPL, Islip 244; ed. Weaver 1903, 286–7) leaves grain and livestock 'to the vicars of Wells dwelling in the houses built by me', firmly in the past tense, so that the whole was apparently completed in Bishop Ralph's lifetime.

Later references to houses, in the plural, are the norm and indicate the beginnings of a numbering system. Thus in 1412 collations were made of vicars to the first, fourteenth and eighteenth houses on the east side of the close, and to the third, sixth and fourteenth houses on the west side; and it has been possible to make a tentative reconstruction of the occupants, house by house, in the 15th century (Holmes 1913, 120; Colchester 1974). A problem that has been aired by several past commentators is the generous amount of private accommodation provided for the vicars, given that they were required to

live singly prior to the mid 16th century, and they had no need for individual cooking facilities. Not only did each house have a ground floor 'hall' and first floor chamber but certainly on one, and possibly both, levels there was a separate small room at the southern end. At least some vicars had servants, and the small rooms could have been for them. It has also been suggested that when rural prebendaries were in Wells they lodged with their respective vicars, which could explain the provision of what were effectively accommodation suites on two levels.

With the bishop as their chief benefactor, and their collegiate status, the vicars had a degree of independence from the dean and chapter which they would otherwise never have acquired. At the same time, they were essential to the dean and chapter for their liturgical role, in singing the daily round of services and the many additional festival, chapel and funeral services; and dependent upon them for the allowances and fees essential to augment their own very modest endowment income. This complex relationship set up a tension which is a constant thread through their history.

15th-century developments

The vicars did not live up to Bishop Ralph's ideal, and when Bishop Thomas Bekynton (1443–65) made a visitation in 1459 he found much wanting. Consequently, he reissued and enlarged upon the statutes of 1348 (Watkin 1941, 139–49). He found the close in a run-down state and insisted that the vicars must keep their houses in good repair. Under the rules of communal living, which had to be enforced by the principals, undesirable persons were not allowed into the close; the gate had to be kept shut after the curfew had sounded; violence, discord, swearing, abuses of privilege, and making a noise after the curfew hour were to be prevented. Respect was to be shown towards the principals, who were charged with reprimanding those who committed offences. There were set fines for certain types of misbehaviour, such as 20s. for striking a servant. Vicars were commanded not to argue but to converse in a peaceable and orderly fashion at the table, and were to pay weekly for their food and drink; any who failed to discharge their debts were punished. Keeping dogs or horses was punishable by the 'great excommunication'. By contrast, sexual misbehaviour, which was obviously rife, was less seriously penalized. Vicars were ordered not to receive women of dubious reputation (*mulieres diffamatas*) into their lodgings, and if a vicar persisted in so doing he would be deprived of his house after the third warning. The fine for two vicars found cohabiting was 40s. Strangers were not permitted to reside in the Close for more than three days, unless sick. Other rulings related to correct tonsuring and the wearing of seemly clothes; Bekynton was particularly vexed by the sight of vicars wearing fashionable secular clothes.

As well as disciplining the lives of the vicars, Bekynton resuscitated and augmented the college buildings. He is often credited (incorrectly) with having built the chapel. The earliest extant mention of the vicars' chapel is in 1447, when a formal oath was taken there before a large assembly of vicars (VC Wells, Vicars Choral Register 1393–1534 [VC/CF/1/1], 11; Colchester 1987, 177; n.d., 13). In a charter of 1479 its dedication is recorded as being in honour of the Assumption of the Virgin (D&C Wells, charters DC/CF/3/1/703 – *HMC Cal.* 2, 690–1), and at a re-dedication in 1498 it was referred to as honouring the Assumption and St Katherine (VC Wells, Vicars Choral Register 1393–1534 [VC/CF/1/1], 20; Colchester n.d., 22–3). None of these dates, however, relates to the construction of the chapel, which can be assigned on heraldic evidence to the 1420s. It may also be noted that as early as 1351 Bishop Ralph had arranged for a chaplain to celebrate the divine office daily in the vicars' dwelling-place, which could be taken to imply that a chapel was already in existence in the close (ed. Holmes 1896, 679). Alternatively, the chaplain could have celebrated in the common hall; a possibility is that the eastern bays of the undercroft served as a chapel, until they were removed by the construction of the great gatehouse, which in turn created the need for another chapel.

From 1348 onwards the archives of the vicars choral provide a wealth of detail about the vicars, their estates and their activities. Over two hundred charters and deeds extend from 1348 to 1840. Their first surviving Register (1393–1534) starts with their oath of admission, in Latin with a later version in English, and contains details of administration, copies of important documents, and their own disciplinary proceedings against their members. Their Act Books and Minute Books run from 1541 to the present day, dealing with admissions, elections of officers, administrative decisions and discipline. Court rolls of their estates in Wells and elsewhere in Somerset exist from 1382 to 1725, overlapping with a fine series of lease books 1557–1892, which include the houses in Vicars' Close, and a copious collection of 17th-, 18th- and 19th-century leases and other papers. In particular, there is an impressive and scarcely studied series of accounts 1354–1900, mostly relating to their estates but including the accounts for 'Close Hall', particularly from the 18th century onwards. As things stand, medieval references to the fabric of the college are few and elusive, buried amidst the sheer volume of other information.

Two such references, however, certainly relate to

Bekynton's time. It has been suggested from architectural details that the staircase block adjoining the hall is dated to *c*.1420, but an agreement to make the vaulted stone ceiling over the ground stage of the tower is dated 1448 (VC Wells, Vicars Choral Register 1394–1534 [VC/CF/1/1], 12; Colchester n.d., 13; Colchester 1974). This was associated with the provision of a secure treasury in the staircase block adjoining the hall. A major new work was the construction of the Chain Gate Bridge in 1459–60 by Bishop Bekynton. This carries a high-level passage over St Andrew Street, linking Vicars' Close with the cathedral, obviating the need for vicars to cross the public road. On 29th March 1459 the dean and chapter granted the vicars a right of way across the bridge and down the stairs, 'by reason of the hazard to the vicars of the way between the close and the church, especially at night and in rain and various other dangers which might happen to the vicars at such times, for their greater protection and security'. Details of access, doors, locks and keys are given (VC Wells, Vicars Choral Register 1394–1534 [VC/CF/1/1], 26; Colchester n.d., 23–4). The vicars record their obligation to Bishop Bekynton,

> *'inasmuch as the bishop, taking notice of the risks* (discrimina) *of the way hitherto used by them from their close to the cathedral, especially on nights of snow, hail and rain, and the perils and accidents which might often befall them in the said way at such times ...' for enabling, at his own cost '... a fair, strong and safe way to be made leading directly from the Common Hall of the Vicars' Close to the steps of the chapter-house' (Maxwell-Lyte 1934, 338–9).*

The entrance gatehouse has been dated to *c*.1460 from its resemblance to the arches of the Chain Bridge (Colchester 1974), but no written reference to what must have been a major undertaking to create the archways beneath the east end of the ancient hall has yet been found. It is clear that vicars were usually expected to 'maintain, rebuild and roof' their own houses as necessary (ed. Holmes 1913, 120, *passim*) so that there are few references in the official archives to physical changes in Vicars' Close. The only written evidence associated with the alterations to the famous chimney stacks, paid for out of Bekynton's estate, is Edward IV's discharge to the bishop's three executors – Hugh Sugar, vicar choral, and John Pope and Richard Swann, canons – for having done their duty (D&C Wells, charters DC/CF/3/1/683 – *HMC Cal.* 2, 686). It is their devices which appear, along with the arms of the dean and chapter and Bishop Bekynton, on the plaques affixed to the chimney stacks. About 1468 water was brought from Beryl Spring to Vicars' Close (VC Wells, Vicars Choral Register 1394–1534 [VC/CF/1/1], 15; Colchester n.d., 19). The gardens in front of the houses, which give the close its 'medieval street' appearance, were enclosed in the mid 1400s. John Cleve was ordered to cut down all the trees in his garden *c*.1446/7 (VC Wells, Vicars Choral Register 1394–1534 [VC/CF/1/1], 10; Colchester n.d., 12). It is, so far, unclear exactly when and why the late 15th-century wing, elaborately decorated with its tournament shields, was added to No. 14, adjoining the west end of the chapel, or who lived in it. The career of Richard Pomeroy, vicar choral in the late 1400s and early 1500s, who was unusually wealthy (a connection of the Devon Pomeroys?), had property interests in Wells, made extensive improvements to the Vicars' Hall where he is portrayed in a tracery light in one of his windows, and acted for many years as Keeper of the Fabric to the cathedral, remains tantalisingly shadowy. That Vicars' Close had essentially taken on its present aspect by 1480 is made clear by William Worcestre, who described it as 'a road built up on both sides ... with houses of the vicars. 22 houses are built on each side, with very high chimneys and walled gardens in front of the entrance doors' (ed. Harvey 1969, 288).

The Elizabethan charter

The Reformation and the Elizabethan Settlement brought considerable changes to both the vicars choral and the Vicars' Close. In 1534 Henry VIII's survey of ecclesiastical incomes, the *Valor Ecclesiasticus*, recorded the college at Wells as having an annual income of £208 11*s*. 2*d*., which was divided between the ten vicars who were then in post (eds. Caley and Hunter 1810, 137–9; Hill 1998, 290). The college was not materially affected by the Reformation, although its finances suffered a serious blow in 1547 when, with the suppression of chantries, obits and anniversary masses, the vicars lost a significant part of their work and their income. Two years later the medieval round of daily services was replaced by the first *English Prayer Book*. For the first time, too, clergy were permitted to marry, despite the survival, among the miscellaneous chapter archives, of a contemporary copy of Queen Elizabeth's injunction dated 6th August 1561 against keeping wives and families in cathedrals and colleges, copied from the York Act Book of 1543–72 (D&C Wells, ADD/7035). These changes profoundly affected the lives of vicars choral. With fewer and simpler services came the loss of fees, and a reduction in their numbers. In Vicars' Close, houses were amalgamated into pairs to make family homes for married vicars. A period of unrest, as well as of financial insecurity, ensued; relations between the college and the dean and chapter were strained. There seem to have been ongoing disputes, with some vicars failing to take communion; the cathedral needed their voices but did not necessarily approve their views. The vicars apparently felt, perhaps with justification, that the dean and chapter were seeking to increase their control over the college,

and petitioned Queen Elizabeth I for confirmation of their rights and privileges, as set out in their two previous charters.

By the 1590s tension between the two was high. On 25th November 1591 the dean and chapter obtained a new charter from Queen Elizabeth I, confirming their endowments and redefining their constitution so as to clarify their organisation and powers (D&C Wells, ledger G, 89–162). On exactly the same day the Queen also issued a new charter to the vicars choral to address 'some questions, doubts and ambiguities [that] have lately arisen' – a reflection of the tension and disputes between the vicars and the cathedral in preceding years (VC Wells, charters, VC/CF/2/241)[2]. The college of vicars was defined as 'one body corporate and politique for ever', and its ancient rights and privileges were confirmed. The administration of the college was updated. It was confirmed that the dean and chapter had the right to appoint a new vicar to a vacancy, subject to ratification by the principals and members of the college. The minimum number of vicars was fixed as fourteen, and the maximum as twenty. The bishop of Bath and Wells was nominated as college visitor. Their round medieval seal was replaced by the vesica seal with the same design which is still among their treasures. The 1591 charter and seal together constitute very pointed symbols of the vicars' independence. If, as seems possible, chapter had been seeking to dominate and control the vicars choral, with their reduced numbers, reduced role and inadequate incomes, that aim was thwarted by the two simultaneous charters. The two charters may have been intended to define the powers of the two organisations, and strike a balance between them. They certainly did not resolve the ill-feeling between vicars choral and chapter; and the vicars' continuing suspicious mood is apparent in many 17th-century writings, notably by Godwin, who, writing only ten years later, remarked pointedly that the vicars' royal charter safeguarded their revenues which were 'in danger to be spoyled of them by certain sacrilegious cormorants' (1601, 301). It was a mood of suspicion on both sides that never wholly died away and was still apparent when the powers and properties of the college were abolished in 1936.

Some of these tensions are expressed in the great painting which was originally fixed on the processional staircase from the Close up to the hall, and which since the early 19th century has hung over the hall fireplace (Fig. 11.2). It shows Bishop Ralph (1329–63) receiving a petition from, and handing his sealed charter to, a large assembly of vicars choral. The vicars fall into two groups. Those actually receiving the charter are in surplices, and their tonsured heads can be seen receding away into the distance. This upper quarter of the painting is naïve in style and rather

Fig. 11.2. Vicars choral of Wells Cathedral. Painting in the vicars' hall (of perhaps c.1591) showing Bishop Ralph (1329–63) exchanging documents with a group of vicars choral; a group of later vicars is in the foreground (photo and copyright, Richard Neale, courtesy of Wells Cathedral Chapter)

clumsily executed. Alongside and in front of them is a totally different group of seventeen vicars with characteristic late Tudor or early Stuart clothes, ruffs and hairstyles. They bear no relation to the Bishop Ralph scene in size or position, and their faces are clearly attempts at individual portraits. On the vicars' petition and Bishop Ralph's charter are painted Latin doggerel verses describing Bishop Ralph's gift to the vicars; below is a plaque of further doggerel celebrating the granting of Queen Elizabeth's charter. The verses, first translated by Godwin, have often been used as a historical source in their own right, which if they are genuinely contemporary with the episodes they describe might be justified; without proof, they remain intriguing. Godwin implied that the original picture might have been medieval, and have deteriorated and been replaced or overpainted in or around 1591 (1601, 301). The picture was reframed by Arthur du Cane, Priest Vicar, in 1862 (Parnell 1926, 10). It was examined at the Victoria and Albert Museum in the 1960s, but considered too fragile for close investigation. Fifty years on, the painting hangs in a room where temperatures can fluctuate considerably, and the state of its underlying boards gives cause for concern. Modern conservation and examination might reveal any underpainting, and would certainly contribute to the understanding of it, and its contribution to the history of the vicars choral.

Decay and restoration

Resuscitated, the college prospered until the middle years of the 17th century. This is the period during which the vicars acquired most of their silver and pewter, donated by wealthier members of the college. The one break in continuity, for the vicars choral as for the cathedral itself, came not as part of the English Reformation but in the aftermath of the Civil War. For fifteen years, between 1645 and 1660, the cathedral and college were closed, the buildings confiscated by the state, and the vicars were dispersed without pension or home. In 1649, almost exactly 300 years after their foundation, the *Parliamentary Survey* records a total of 38 houses, twenty on the east side and eighteen on the west, showing that the physical amalgamation of units had scarcely begun. Many houses were 'void'. Unfortunately the survey does not give any of the details of structure or rooms that are often found in surveys of bigger individual church properties; but it does serve as a benchmark to describe Vicars' Close as it was at the end of the first 300 years of its existence. What happened in the close during the Commonwealth period is unrecorded, since lease books are absent from 1643 to 1660 and account books from 1642 to 1662.

In 1660/61 the estates of the vicars choral were restored to their owners, by which time only five of the pre-Commonwealth vicars could be summoned up. The college buildings had been severely abused. A pathetic petition from the vicars choral to Bishop William Piers as their Visitor, on 15th June 1663, gives a vivid picture of the state of Vicars' Close, demonstrating the way in which the documents can supplement the archaeology (VC Wells, charters VC/CF/2/116). A long preamble gives an interesting 17th-century view of their history from their foundation to ...

> 'that unhappy & unnaturall Rebellion which (continuinge about Twenty Yeares) overturned the established antient Government both of the Church & Common wealth', during which time 'your peticioners did extreamely suffer & were turned out of doores plundred & imprisoned & were reduced to greate want & poverty ... in the tymes of the Late Troubles most of our howses in close hall were defaced uncovered & extreame ruinated.'

The vicars, unable to afford repairs, petition the bishop to allow them to lease out twelve of the most decayed houses for twenty-one years, with no fines [entry fees] and at a low rent, but on repairing leases. They argue that, of the 40 small houses, there are 28 for the fourteen vicars, each having a double house, and twelve left over,

> 'and soe there will remaine Twelve smale howses which lyinge scattered amongst the rest must of necessity be upheld & repaired or else the whole fabricke will have breaches and thother houses will be in danger by winds or otherwise beinge without support of the rest'.

Vicars Close in 1663 was in danger of collapsing like a house of cards.

Permission to lease out houses in Vicars' Close was given, and Lease Books of the late 17th to the 19th centuries show the close gradually becoming a desirable place for respectable widows and widowers to live. In the late 17th and 18th centuries, their small rents helped to maintain the houses occupied by the few remaining vicars. It was these tenants who inserted more modern windows and doors into most of the houses, leaving the chimney stacks and remains of blocked medieval doors and windows as a testament to the earlier layouts. The 18th- and 19th-century account books for the maintenance of Vicars' Hall and Vicars' Close are the most complete to survive, full of details which should be able to fill out the archaeological framework for this period. Overall, however, the period was one of gentle and genteel decay. Unfortunately, the vicars had neither the interest nor the acumen for managing their estates profitably, and they merely presided over a long, slow decline. House No. 13, at the north-east corner of the close, was still ruinous and unleased in 1670, when a resident in College Lane (now known as North Liberty) offered to take it on if he could breach the Close wall to gain convenient access from the north.

Vicars' Close was in a precarious state by 1832 when Augustus Charles Pugin and his son Augustus Welby made their superb set of drawings of the best of the surviving buildings and their features (Pugin and Walker 1836) – drawings which not only had a considerable influence on the Gothic Revival, but were a direct stimulus to the wealthy antiquarian John Henry Parker who undertook the massive restoration of the close in 1863/64 (Parker 1866, 27–30), which gave it the overall appearance it has today.

In 1835, when the Ecclesiastical Commissioners enquired into the circumstances of all cathedral estates, the college was staffed by only three priests and eight lay vicars choral. In 1852, being in dire financial straits, the vicars themselves approached the Commissioners and asked to be taken over, but this did not finally happen until 1866. Henceforth, Vicars' Close became the property of the Ecclesiastical Commissioners, which it remained until 1980 when ownership was transferred to the dean and chapter. Meanwhile, moves were afoot nationally to disband colleges of vicars choral, and on 30 September 1936 Wells College was finally dissolved.

Antiquarian studies

The first detailed drawings of Vicars' Close at Wells were made by John Carter between *c*.1784 and 1795. These comprise a general plan of the close, a plan and elevation of one house, elevations of the hall and chapel, and numerous pencil sketches of architectural details (BL Add. Ms. 29,932)[3]. Publication of a selection of these will be included in a study of Carter's work at Wells (Rodwell forthcoming). Amongst the other antiquarian artists who visited Wells in the early 1800s, John Buckler's work is especially informative as a detailed record (BL Add. Ms. 36,384, f. 167, 174–7, 179–80).

In 1832 Augustus Charles Pugin and his son, Augustus Welby, devoted considerable effort to making a measured and drawn survey of Vicars' Close, which was published in the series, *Pugin's Examples of Gothic Architecture* (Pugin and Walker 1836). Plans, elevations and cross-sections of the principal structures were published, along with various moulding profiles and other details (Fig. 11.10). They are, however, to some extent interpretive, Pugin's aim being to present as complete a picture as possible of the close, not a precise archaeological record. The general plan of the close (contributed by Walker) was idealized and, like other drawings, omitted anything that was not considered to be part of the primary medieval structure.

One of the mid 19th-century lessees of properties in Vicars' Close was John Henry Parker, architect, antiquary and family member of the Oxford publishing house of James Parker and Co. He acquired Vicars' Hall and several of the houses (Nos. 22, 27 and 28), and in 1863 set about a major restoration in which he attempted to recreate full-blown Gothic interiors. Parker employed William Burges to design suitable furniture, and he doubtless also had a hand in the flamboyant stencilling, tapestries and wallpaper designs, which appear in contemporary illustrations (Parker 1866). Supplementary to Parker's book, which was illustrated only with line drawings, two separate series of photographic plates were issued in folders, and these provide an important visual record of the close in *c*.1865.

No substantial account of Vicars' Close was published in the 20th century, but guide-books to the college and chapel by Hugh Parnell (1926; n.d.) are useful. An exceptional opportunity for archaeological study of the fabric occurred in 1978–81, when a major restoration of the exteriors of all the buildings was undertaken, and the roadway was reconstructed. Regrettably, very little recording took place; despite strong representations made by the Cathedral Archaeologist and the late Martin Caroe, architect for the restoration, the Department of the Environment (as predecessor to English Heritage) declined to accept that there was a need to make a record of the restoration, or of the archaeological evidence revealed during its progress. Even so, important new information on the architectural history of the houses was noted (Rodwell 1982). Subsequently, restoration of the interiors of several houses have been archaeologically monitored, and much fresh evidence has come to light. The least altered of all the houses is No. 22, which was illustrated as a model by Pugin and Parker, as well as being restored by the latter. In 1991 this house was thoroughly refurbished, providing the opportunity to investigate internal arrangements, and in particular to resolve uncertainties about the staircase and latrine provision.

The layout of the college

The new Vicars' Close of 1348 was constructed on a long, narrow plot of land to the north of the cathedral, but separated from it by a road (St Andrew Street – Cathedral Green) which traverses the precinct from east to west (Fig. 11.1). The plot was one of a series of at least six which had been laid out in the 12th century and upon which the houses of the residentiary canons were built (Rodwell 2001, fig. 110). The plots were bordered on the north by the Liberty Wall, which was part of the cathedral precinct boundary.

The college plot tapers slightly and the boundaries are not perfectly straight (especially on the east), but it is essentially rectangular in plan, the overall measurements averaging 145m by 54m (475 x 177 ft); the area is 0.78 ha (1.93 ac) (Fig. 11.3). Its northern and southern ends are delimited by North Liberty and St Andrew Street, respectively, while the east and west sides share boundaries with the adjoining canonical houses (Archdeaconry on the west, and Tower House on the east). The college is enclosed by a high stone wall, with a gatehouse in the centre of the south side (Figs. 11.4 and 11.5). Initially, that was the only point of access (apart from a service doorway), but two additional breaches were made in the north wall in 1670.

The asymmetrical positioning of the college buildings within the modern limits of the close, and the configuration of boundaries on the west, points to an enlargement on this side by c.11m (36 ft). Almost certainly, there was a north–south road running through a gap here between the original canonical house-plots, over which the gardens on the west flank of Vicars' Close subsequently encroached. Indeed, this is confirmed by Carter's plan of c.1795, in which he shows the old rear boundary on the west still intact, with a series of supplementary gardens having been colonized beyond it (Soc Ant, Carter drawings, Wells, Plan I).

The gatehouse is integral with a two-storied range occupying the southern end; adjoining the twin-arched gate on the west is a spacious undercroft, the fourth bay of which was apparently partitioned off to form a porter's lodge. Above the undercroft, and extending over the entire gateway, is the common

Fig. 11.3. Vicars choral of Wells Cathedral. View of Vicars' Close looking north from the central tower of the cathedral. The hall range and Chain Gate are seen in the lower right-hand corner (photo and copyright, Richard Neale, courtesy of Wells Cathedral Chapter)

hall with a two-storied service range adjoining on the west. At first-floor level lay the kitchen with another vaulted undercroft below. No sign of the bakehouse mentioned in 1348 can now be found.

Attached to the north side of the hall, at right-angles to it, is a further tall, narrow block, the far end of which is marked by a small tower (Fig. 11.6). This range, which is a 15th-century addition, contains the great staircase leading from the interior of the close to the first-floor hall. Above the stairway is the exchequer, where the college's rents were collected, while the tower houses the vicars' muniment room and treasury in its upper stages. At ground level it serves as a porch to the staircase.

Running north from the gatehouse, on a gentle incline, is the road which today forms the spine of Vicars' Close. The road is flanked to east and west by continuous ranges of two-storied lodgings, each with its own entrance (Fig. 11.7). The façades are set well back from the road, there being an individual

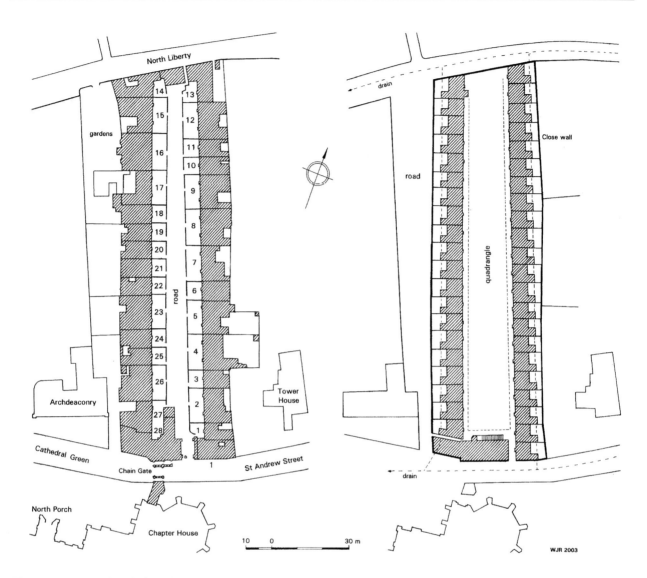

Fig. 11.4. Vicars choral of Wells Cathedral. Plans of Vicars' Close. Left As existing (after Ordnance Survey 1:500 plan, 1884). Modern house numbering has been added. Right Reconstruction of the plan in the later 14th century (drawing and copyright, Warwick Rodwell)

Fig. 11.5. Vicars choral of Wells Cathedral. The gateway to Vicars' Close. View from St Andrew Street (photo and copyright, Richard Neale, courtesy of Wells Cathedral Chapter)

walled garden in front of every house. Originally, the doors must have opened off a path running around the perimeter of the close, the plan being comparable to an Oxford college quadrangle. Wells has often been compared to William Wynford's work at Winchester, and at New College, Oxford (Harvey 1982, 90–1).

The present arrangement of walled gardens, all formerly with stone-arched gateways opening off an axial road, is a modification of the early 15th century. Five of those gateways survive. The backs of the houses do not present the same uniformity of appearance as the fronts, since numerous extensions and alterations have occurred. Likewise, the rear gardens are variable in extent, many having encroached into adjoining properties.

The two lodging ranges, with their façades un-

Fig. 11.6. Vicars choral of Wells Cathedral. The tower and staircase block forming the entrance to the vicars' hall. The Close gateway is seen on the left (photo A J Scrase, copyright University of the West of England)

Fig. 11.7. Vicars choral of Wells Cathedral. Reconstruction of the interior of Vicars' Close, looking south. Lithograph of a mid 19th-century drawing by F T Dollman. The individual gate-arches were mostly destroyed during Dollman's lifetime (1812–1900) (photo Richard Neale, courtesy of Wells Chapter Archives)

interrupted save for shallow chimney projections, extend for 134m (440 ft). They were not laid out parallel to one another, being separated by 20m (65 ft) at the bottom of the close and only 17m (56 ft) at the top. Coupled with the rising ground, a pleasing false perspective is achieved (best appreciated from the oriel window in Vicars' Hall), and this has been remarked upon by many writers, although whether the effect was achieved by design or accident is debatable. The employment of perspective as a component of architectural design was unknown in the mid 14th century, and almost certainly the tapering plan was merely a function of the original configuration of the plot.

The northern end of the close is occupied by the vicars' chapel, above which is the library (Fig. 11.16). This small building is wholly of the 15th century, and it is not known whether any other structure lay here previously.

The college was planned *ab initio* with its own drainage system. A well-built stone drain runs the full length of the close on both the east and west sides, just behind the lodging ranges. Where examined on the west (at Nos. 21 and 22), it was found to pass under the rear of each staircase projection, and segmental arches were incorporated in the foundations to span the channel, the cross-section of which is 60cm (2 ft) square. The channel is now largely infilled. The drain on the east side has been studied behind No. 11, where it is slightly larger in dimensions, barrel-vaulted and is still fully functioning. The drains were flushed by a continuous flow of water, channelled into them from a culvert in North Liberty, itself fed by springs at The Combe, some distance to the north of the town (Rodwell 2001, fig. 389).

A fresh water supply for Vicars' Close was provided by c.1468 by piping it from Beryl Spring, to the north-east of Wells. Given that Bishop Bekynton established a sophisticated water supply for the Bishop's Palace, cathedral and market place properties in the mid 15th century, it is likely that he was also responsible for the Vicars' Close supply. Excavation in the front garden of No. 14 revealed a clay-packed duct which must once have contained a lead water-pipe: it ran through the doorway into the house. Another section of pipe-duct was found under the road in front of No. 13. These features are similar to the 15th-century duct excavated in The Camery in 1978–79 and associated with Bishop Bekynton's piped water supply to buildings south of the cathedral (Rodwell 2001, 402–11). It would not be surprising if a conduit existed at the top of the close; here a lead cistern could have provided a gravity feed which would not only take piped water into all the houses but also up to the first-floor kitchen adjoining the common hall.

It is not known when the system broken down in the close, but there were two functioning wells with pumps in the 19th century, one at the south end and another at the north (outside Nos. 1 and 13, respectively).

Hall and gatehouse range

An impressive and complex range of structures occupies the southern side of Vicars' Close. Little archaeological investigation has so far taken place, and there are serious difficulties in both interpreting and dating the components of this range.

Undercroft to the hall

This four-bay structure (Figs. 11.8, 11.9 and 11.10) is undoubtedly the oldest element on the site, its detailing being indicative of a very late 13th-century date: hence, it is almost certainly part of the pre-existing canonical residence taken over by the vicars in 1348. It could have been a hall, or the undercroft to one, but it is remarkably lofty for the latter. Either way, it is difficult to understand why a hall should have been placed hard against the street frontage, when the canonical houses on the other plots were set back.

Internally, the walls are punctuated by deep window embrasures, and the bay divisions are marked by engaged shafts with moulded capitals and bases. Seated upon these are curved brackets supporting a 14th-century floor in the hall above. It is possible that originally the capitals supported arch-braced roof-trusses to a single-storey building.

The undercroft was originally longer by two bays, the east end having been truncated for the construction of the close gateway. There is reason to believe that the space was subdivided, on the line of the present east wall, and the possibility that the first vicars' chapel was located in the undercroft is worth considering.

The undercroft is lit by small, cusped windows of 14th-century date, all of which must have been inserted. The embrasures on the north side are much altered: three now contain doorways, and there had been a fourth (Pugin and Walker 1836, pl. 12). A major restoration was carried out in 1862–4 by J H Parker, who came to live here from Oxford. A Gothick stone fireplace was installed at the west end of the room, and the walls and timber ceiling were decorated to designs by William Burges. With the exception of the ceiling painting, Burges' decoration was almost entirely destroyed when the undercroft became the Wells Lodge of the Freemasons in the early 20th century. The room was recovered for cathedral use in 1997, and the painted ceiling has been conserved.

Common hall

The vicars' hall, of six bays, lay on the first floor (Figs. 11.9–11.12). It is partly over the undercroft, but the two easternmost bays are carried on the vaulted gateway to the close. All previous commentators have assumed that the present hall was built in 1348, although some have wondered whether it was initially only four bays in length, and was extended when the gateway was constructed later in the century (e.g. Parker 1866).

Although much altered, there is no reason to doubt that the hall is mid 14th century and was constructed with six bays; the insertion of the gateway beneath part of it must be secondary, but that is difficult to demonstrate archaeologically since it would appear that the entire exterior of the hall and undercroft was refaced at the same time. Apart from some of the windows, there is little primary masonry of the 14th century exposed; it is not even possible to be certain whether the building was buttressed (*pace* David Stocker's reconstruction in Richards 2001, fig. 192).

The hall followed the usual medieval plan, being divided by screens into two sections: the hall proper (three bays) lay to the east, while the buttery and thoroughfare to the kitchen (two bays) lay to the west of the passage bay. The principal entrance was from the north, *via* an external staircase which, in the first instance, is likely to have lain parallel to the hall. If so, when the close gateway was constructed a few decades later the steps must have been repositioned. They are now aligned with the hall doorway, but whether any of the existing masonry is 14th century (as opposed to early 15th) is a moot point. There could not have been a doorway on the south until the Chain Bridge was constructed, and thus no true screens passage. A small projecting stair-turret on the north, in the second bay, provided access between the service end of the hall and the undercroft below, as well as up to the roof. Immediately east of the entrance lay a small feature in the north wall: it may have been a lavabo or a cupboard. The feature was destroyed in the 15th century when a small doorway was opened here to a new staircase leading up from the hall. The doorway is partly framed by 15th-century mouldings, but still retains elements of a 14th-century opening with plain chamfers.

The hall was lit from both sides with two-light traceried and transomed windows, the surrounds of which incorporate a small wave moulding which is particularly associated with the work of William Joy, who was made master mason at Wells in 1329 (Harvey 1982, 100). Joy is thought to have perished in the Black Death. It is uncertain how the hall was initially heated, but it is perhaps most likely that there was a fireplace in the fifth bay where the

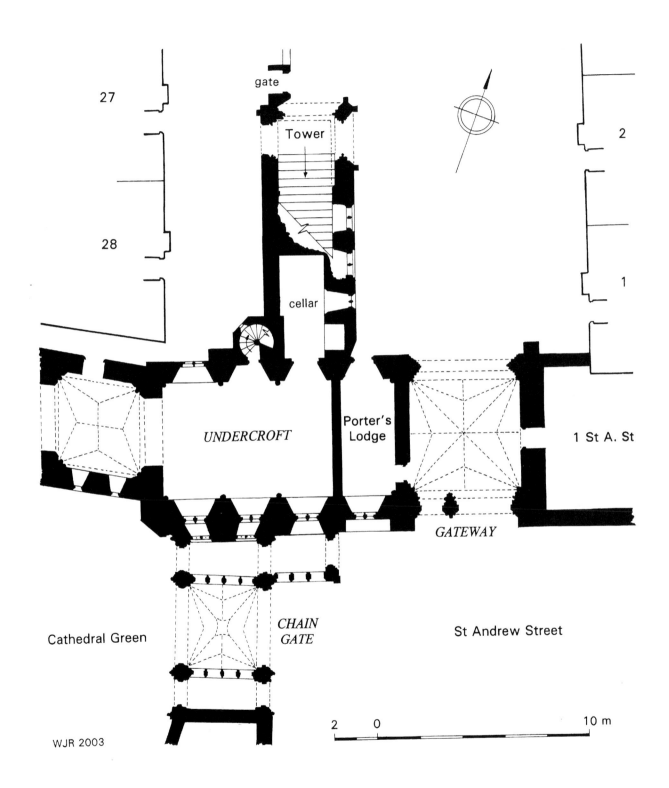

27

28

gate

Tower

cellar

UNDERCROFT

Porter's
Lodge

GATEWAY

2

1

1 St A. St

CHAIN
GATE

Cathedral Green

St Andrew Street

WJR 2003

2   0   10 m

Fig. 11.8. Vicars choral of Wells Cathedral. Ground plan of the southern end of Vicars' Close in the late 15th century, showing gatehouse, undercroft to the hall, staircase range and Chain Gate (drawing and copyright, Warwick Rodwell)

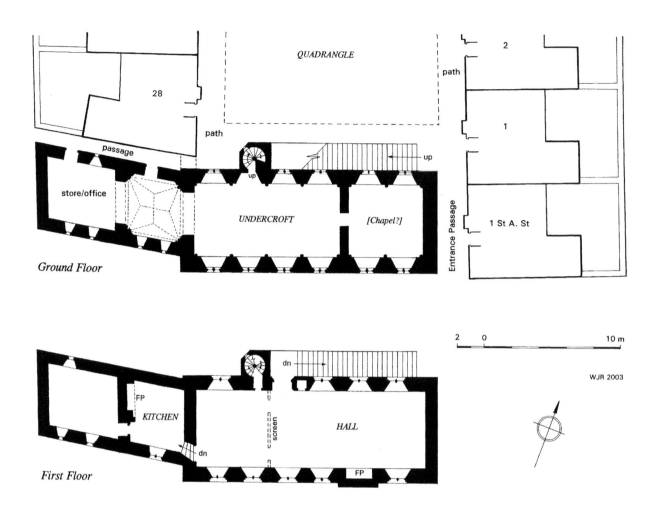

Fig. 11.9. Vicars choral of Wells Cathedral. Reconstructed plans of the hall range in the mid 14th century (drawing and copyright, Warwick Rodwell)

present Tudor one is. Since the vicars' lodgings were individually provided with lateral fireplaces, it is improbable that their common hall was unheated.

The hall has undergone alteration on several occasions. The first was probably the insertion of the three-light window in the east gable. However, major changes came in 1459–60 when Bishop Bekynton constructed the Chain Bridge, abutting the hall on the south. Henceforth, a functioning screens passage was created. The construction of the bridge caused three of the original windows on the south side to be lost, thus significantly reducing the light in the low end of the hall. This seems to have been ameliorated by inserting a new window in the west gable, for which 14th-century tracery elements were recycled; these were revealed when the window was dismantled and rebuilt in 1973.

One of Bekynton's contemporaries was Hugh Sugar, prebendary and later canon treasurer, and he is credited with having installed the pulpit which has been contrived within one of the window splays on

the south, and is also potentially of integral construction with the existing fireplace. Elaborated initials occur in the spandrels of the fireplace, which have been claimed as 'HS'. However, since the first letter is 'K' and the second is doubtful, the association with Hugh Sugar must be fallacious. Moreover, the fireplace is not mid 15th century: it has a distinctly Tudor appearance. It has been suggested that the initials might be those of Katherine Sugar, who is otherwise known only from the fact that she bequeathed 12*d*. to the cathedral fabric fund in 1500–1 (Colchester 1987, 167).

Although Bekynton's statutes of 1459–60 mention a pulpit, it cannot be certainly equated with the present one. A further complication is that the carved stone mantel-shelf cannot ante-date the death of Richard Pomeroy, in 1523, as an inscription on it records. Most likely, the present arrangement dates from the 1620s, when 'KS' rebuilt an existing fireplace, moving it slightly eastwards to accommodate a new pulpit. Pomeroy was a vicar choral, later

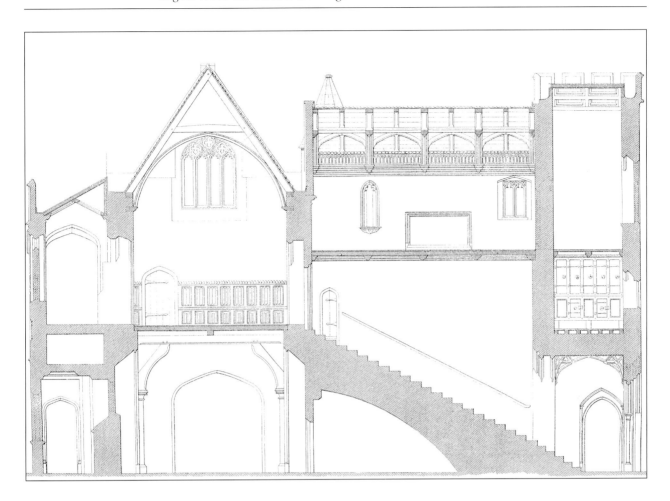

Fig. 11.10. Vicars choral of Wells Cathedral. Cross-section through the vicars' hall and adjoining structures, looking west. Principal elements, from left to right: northern pedestrian passage of Chain Gate, with lobby to hall from Chain Bridge above; hall with undercroft below; great staircase with exchequer above; tower, containing porch, treasury and muniment room. Drawn by A C Pugin, in 1832 (source, Pugin and Walker 1836)

Keeper of the Fabric, and was responsible for installing the two fine oriel windows which flank the high end of the hall. His arms and an inscription in the glazing testify to this. He seems also to have been responsible for the plainer oriel at the north-west corner of the hall. The introduction of such a window in what had been the service end of the hall must surely imply that its status had been upgraded (see Stocker's reconstruction: Richards 2001, fig. 192).

The date of the present collared roof structure is uncertain, but possibly 16th century. The hall is ceiled with a plastered barrel vault of nine and a half bays, and the ribs are plain-chamfered. The mortices remain that secured a full-height screen, west of the entrance, and scars of the second screen defining the east side of the passage are also pre-served. The eastern screen perhaps extended only up to wall-plate level.

Plain medieval oak panelling with V-jointed edges occurs on parts of the north and south walls, while the east wall is decorated with linenfold panelling, and some of the rails are carved with Renaissance detail. High up on the same wall, and mounted on two ornately carved timber corbels, is a pair of oak figures of exceptional quality. Dating from the mid 14th century, they are usually taken to represent the Annunciation (Alexander and Binski 1987, 429), but alternative identifications have been offered (Colchester 1987, 169). The figures were doubtless placed here to honour the high table. At the west end of the hall stands a medieval oak bread-cupboard with multiple compartments.

Service wing

This two-storied structure is attached to the west end of the hall range, but is not aligned with it, and the south wall is also set back (Figs. 11.8, 11.9 and 11.11).

A small, skewed doorway in the south-west corner of the hall led, *via* a few steps, down to the kitchen, which is rather a small room to serve some 40 men. Nevertheless, it seems to be part of the 14th-century arrangement. The stone floor is carried on a rib-vaulted undercroft, and a drainage channel runs diagonally across the room, its outlet discharging into the street below. There was probably a stone sink, fed by a piped water supply, in the north-east corner of the kitchen. The fireplace is on the west, beside which is a primary doorway leading to another service room beyond, potentially the pantry. A similar sized room on the ground floor, which is not vaulted, had a door and window facing north; this may originally have been either a store, or a domestic administrative office for the close. Later it probably became a brewhouse, and is likely the site of that mentioned in the *Parliamentary Survey* of 1649.

The rooms at the west end of the service range were partly reconstructed in the 19th century, and some details are uncertain; the west-facing oriel on the first floor is by Parker and dates from 1863. In the early 19th century the kitchen undercroft had wide openings (doubtless secondary) connecting it with the hall undercroft on the east, and the room on the west, respectively; there was also an external door on the north (Pugin and Walker 1836, pl. 12).

The two ground floor rooms of the service wing have become integrated with house No. 28, but in the 14th century they were clearly separate. The plan of the house is slightly distorted, its south wall and staircase projection apparently being skewed to reflect the orientation of the adjacent service range. However, there was initially a gap of *c*.1m between them, which provided a service passage for the communal buildings, accessed from the road that formerly ran along the west side of the Vicars' Close.

Close gateway

Vicars' closes were not always provided with prestigious gatehouses, and entry was sometimes through a modest opening at one corner (Figs. 11.5–11.8). Thus the presence of a major gateway at Wells is noteworthy but, archaeologically, it is also problematic.

The gatehouse is square in plan, rib vaulted, and comprises two four-centred arches on the exterior – a small one for pedestrians and a large one for vehicles – and a single, richly moulded, broad opening on the inner side; the medieval doors and the 18th-century gates that succeeded them have all been lost. Just inside the pedestrian entrance, on the left (west) is a small doorway giving access into the undercroft of the hall. The location points to a porter's lodge having been contrived in the first bay of the undercroft, and there was also a door leading out of the room to the close on the north side. In the middle of the east flank of the gatehouse is another doorway that gives access to the extended first lodging (No. 1 St Andrew Street).

The gateway is certainly not part of Ralph of Shrewsbury's work, and the complex mouldings of its arches have been associated with William Wynford, who was appointed master mason at Wells in 1364/5 (Harvey 1982, 90, 100). They have also been compared to the mouldings on the Chain Gate of 1459–60. There can be little doubt that the two easternmost bays of the original undercroft were destroyed, and the new entrance inserted beneath the high end of the hall above, but the date at which this occurred must remain uncertain for the time being. Integral with the construction of the gateway are several buttresses.

The position of the east end of the hall range remained unaltered. Between the end of the hall and the front of the first house originally lay a gap 2m (6½ ft) wide, which would have sufficed as the entrance passage to the close (cf. Lichfield and Hereford). When the new gateway was driven through, the old passage was no longer required and so was taken into the first house, to increase its accommodation. A new entrance to the house was formed in the flank of the gateway.

Staircase, tower, exchequer and treasury

Projecting northwards into Vicars' Close from the hall range is a narrow block terminating in a small tower (Figs. 11.6–11.8, 11.10, 11.11, 11.13). Essentially a 15th-century structure, some have argued for the lower parts being earlier, but that seems unlikely. The purpose of the range was to contain the great staircase, which initially seems not to have been enclosed, there being no former roof-line visible on the wall above the hall doorway. Beneath the stair, and accessed from the undercroft, is a rectangular, stone-roofed cellar lit by a window.

At the foot of the stair stands a square tower, the ground stage of which is open and arched on all four sides. The salient corners have slender clasping buttresses. It has been suggested that the tower began life as a porch to the staircase. However, there is no indication in the fabric that the tower has been raised, and the external masonry of the entire staircase block is uniform. Almost certainly the porch was built *de novo* in the 15th century, and it is structurally later than the garden wall and stone gate-arch to No. 27.

Nevertheless, there are several anomalies in the construction of the staircase block for which no satisfactory explanations have been offered. Thus, the east wall is considerably thicker than the west, up to floor level in the exchequer, where there is a

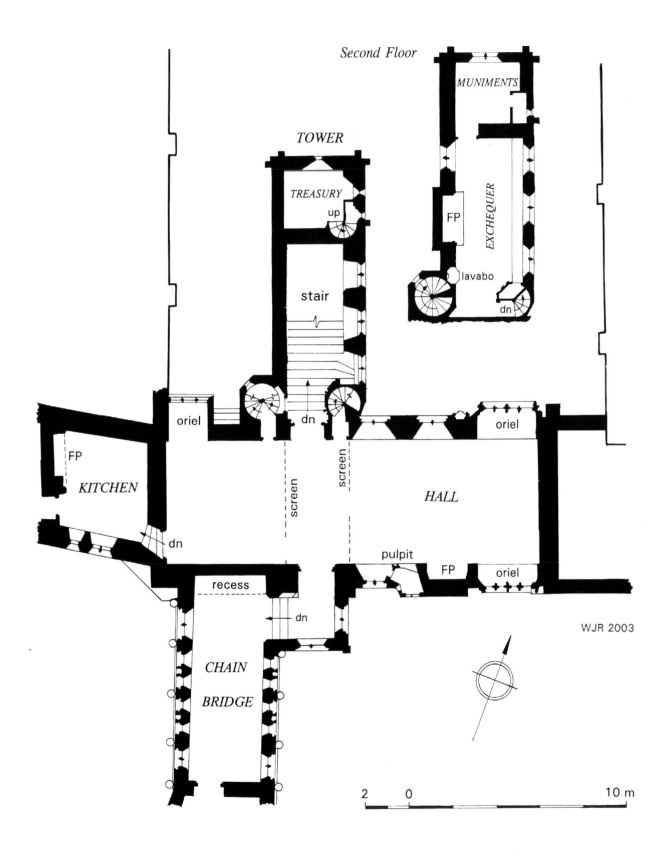

Fig. 11.11. Vicars choral of Wells Cathedral. First-floor plan of the southern end of Vicars' Close in the late 15th century, comprising the hall, kitchen, staircase range, treasury and Chain Bridge. Second-floor plan of the staircase range, containing the exchequer and muniment room (drawing and copyright, Warwick Rodwell)

Fig. 11.12. Vicars choral of Wells Cathedral. The interior of the vicars' hall, looking east. The furniture and pewter tableware belonged to the vicars choral (photo S W Kenyon, courtesy of Wells Chapter Archives)

Fig. 11.13. Vicars choral of Wells Cathedral. The vicars' exchequer, looking north, with the muniment room beyond. Note the ornate lavabo on the left (photo and copyright, Richard Neale, courtesy Wells Cathedral Chapter)

board offset at the point of reduction. Also, the windows on the staircase are typically 15th century, whereas those lighting the exchequer above have identical heads to mid 14th-century windows in the houses of the close.

Whether or not the great staircase itself was remodelled, an upper floor was constructed over it, providing secure office accommodation which was accessible only from the vicars' hall. A small spiral stair was erected to the east of the entrance to the hall (roughly balancing the one that already occupied a similar position on the west), its doorway being an enlargement of an earlier feature. The stair emerges, through its own tiny lobby of timber and stone, in the south-east corner of a long narrow room which was the vicars' exchequer, that is the office of the receiver, where rents from the estates were collected.

The cupboard for the receiver's writing instruments was incorporated in the stair-head structure, and built into the west wall opposite is a fine stone lavabo with a cinquefoiled arch and carved basin (Eames 1977, 20–1). There is also a fireplace in the west wall, and on the east are three windows with their original oak shutters. The medieval roof, although small in scale, is exceptionally elaborate: it is collared, with arched principals, embattled wall-plates above a small frieze of blind trefoil arcading, and two tiers of wind-braces, the upper inverted (Hewett 1985, 45, fig. 41).

A door at the north end of the exchequer opens into a square chamber within the top of the tower: that was the muniment room where the vicars' records were kept. Still in that room is a medieval oak multi-drawer armoire (effectively a filing cabinet) designed to contain rolls. Originally, there were 72 drawers arranged in six rows with open-topped bins below; each drawer has a finger-tab to facilitate opening, and a parchment label was affixed to the end with brass pins with decorated heads (Eames 1977, 40–1). A similar, but later, armoire survives in 'The Aerary' (i.e. the treasury) of the College of St George, Windsor.

In the south-east corner of the muniment room is a tiny spiral stair which descends to a chamber in the middle stage of the tower. Here lay the treasury, to which there was no other means of access. Its floor is the stone vault above the open-sided ground stage of the tower. A section of the timber floor of the muniment room has been made to lift out, thus enabling chests to be lowered into the treasury; this was a secondary modification. There is also an elaborate secret bolting device for securing the treasury door, using a long iron bar which was dropped through a hole in the floor of the muniment room.

Inside the treasury is another important item of furniture, an armoire of ten cupboards in two registers, assigned to the 16th century (Eames 1977, 251). The tall upper cupboards were probably designed to hold vestments, while the small ones at the base may have held mass vessels.

The date of construction of this remarkable suite of rooms for the administration of the college is not recorded, but is most likely to have been during Nicholas Bubwith's episcopate, or soon after his death in 1424, using funds bequeathed by him for a variety of projects (cf. the vicars' chapel). The secondary insertion of the vaulted ceiling under the tower is, however, recorded as having taken place in 1448.

Lodging ranges

The original scheme provided for 42 houses of near-identical size, split between two opposing ranges: twenty-two on the east and twenty on the west (Figs. 11.3, 11.4 and 11.7). William Worcestre was evidently mistaken in claiming that there were twenty-two on each side. Designed as bachelors' lodgings, the houses have been enlarged and adapted over the centuries to accommodate changing needs in vicars' lifestyles, and later secular uses. The present house numbering runs only to twenty-eight, the majority having been amalgamated in pairs, but twelve still remain as single units. Nos. 1–13 Vicars' Close are on the east, counting northwards; and Nos. 14–28 are on the west, counting southwards. No. 1 is actually the second house on the east, the first being known as No. 1 St Andrew Street, on to which it now fronts. Several houses were substantially remodelled in the 18th and 19th centuries, but in no case has all the medieval fabric been lost.

Interestingly, the plans, although conceptually the same, were 'handed', left and right: thus the house layout adopted on one side of the Close was a mirror-image of that on the other side. In practical terms, this meant that upon entering the front door one turned left to approach the staircase in houses on the west, or right in those on the east.

Each house was, *ab initio*, a self-contained lodging on two floors, with a rectangular staircase projection at the rear, and beyond that an L-shaped yard enclosed by high walls. The purpose of the yard is unknown, but it was presumably a convenient place to hang personal laundry and store fuel. The yard was the same depth (5.8m) as the house (discounting the staircase projection).

There were slight differences in size and other anomalies in the houses at the corners of the close, and No. 14, at the north-west, formerly had a stone porch in front of the entrance, the foundations of which were discovered during excavation in 1979. Insofar as we know, there is just one instance of a house with an original cellar beneath the principal room (No. 15).

All the houses have a shallow buttress-like projection supporting the chimney stack close to the middle of the front wall, and the entrance lay immediately south of the projection (Fig. 11.14). The doorways had pseudo-four-centred arches with plain chamfered mouldings, but no stops. Most of the original windows have been superseded on the front elevations, but fragments of a sufficient number remain to indicate that the fenestration was not rigidly uniform throughout the close. The principal room on the ground floor had a two-light transomed window with trefoil heads. Above, on the first floor, was a transomless trefoil-headed window of two, or in some instances three, lights. The presence of label-mouldings and details of their stops vary.

A greater variety of window types and sizes is found in the rear elevations, and more of these have been preserved, mostly as internal features within extended houses. There are single and double lights, some transomed and some cusped. The late Linzee Colchester observed that one element of the incised drawings preserved in the Wells tracing floor (in the room over the north porch of the cathedral; Colchester and Harvey 1974, 214) matches an ogival-headed, cusped window on the ground floor of No. 22.

Previous commentators have agreed on the general layout of a vicar's house, but there has been no consensus regarding the detailed workings of the staircase and latrine. No original staircase survives, although in many cases there is a much later replacement on its site. Pugin and Walker (1836, pl. 3) reconstructed a conventional stone newel, filling the entire staircase projection. That, however, ignored original windows in the east wall which would have been obstructed. Parker's plans (1866, pls. 26 and 27) do not indicate stairs at all, and he marked the rear projection at both levels as 'closet'. His plans are confusing since they show large sections of masonry (for which there is no physical evidence) partly obstructing the interior of the staircase projection. More recently, a new reconstruction of the stairs, taking account of all available evidence, and accommodating a latrine beneath them, was attempted (Rodwell 1982, plans 7 and 8).

Both Pugin and Parker based their studies on house No. 22, and when this was refurbished in 1991 the opportunity was taken to investigate the staircase projection carefully, as a result of which the previous reconstruction can now be refined.

Ground floor

The ground floor plan mimicked, in miniature, the hall and screens-passage arrangement of larger houses (Fig. 11.15). The internal dimensions are 6.0 by 3.9m (20 x 13 ft). A curious and unexplained feature is the main ceiling beam, which did not run across

Fig. 11.14. Vicars choral of Wells Cathedral. Front elevation of the best preserved vicar's lodging, No. 22. Drawn by Orlando Jewitt (source, Parker 1866)

the hall at the mid-point, as might be expected, but ran lengthways down its axis. The common joists ran from front to back.

The principal room, or hall, had a lateral fireplace and sizeable windows in both the east and west sides. The fireplace aperture was simple, with a plain, unstopped chamfer and cranked lintel. The windows also have cranked rear-arches and asymmetrically splayed reveals descending to floor level.

A timber screen divided the hall from a smaller room to the south. At least two screens survive in the close, one fairly certainly *in situ* but concealed by lath-and-plaster (No. 7), the other repositioned and now used as panelling against an end-wall (No. 17). Several more screens are suspected behind later plaster. It seems unlikely that there was a fully defined screens passage, and the entrance probably opened directly into the 'low' end of the hall, with the screen delimiting a small room, or closet, at the south end of the house. In the back wall, opposite

the entrance, was a narrower doorway skewed at an angle to give access to the rear yard, while at the same time avoiding the stair projection. Curiously, this doorway is slightly splayed and opens outwards from the hall, as though it were designed to give access to a subordinate space: it does not have the appearance of being an external opening, but it is difficult to find any other explanation.

Also in the rear wall of the hall, between the doorway and the window, a stone lavabo is preserved in some of the houses. The details vary: in No. 9 it is a relatively large and ornate feature, with an ogee head and cinquefoil cusping, evidently 15th century; in No. 17 the lavabo is built into the window reveal itself. Although the basin has not been preserved in No. 22, a drain, doubtless leading from it, has been found in the threshold of the adjoining doorway, connecting with the main drain in the yard to the rear.

The narrow closet at the south end of the house must have been entered through the screen, and was lit by a small, plain window in the front wall. Opposite, in the back wall, lay a broad, arched opening leading into the staircase projection. The surviving screen in No. 17 exhibits two doorways, perhaps indicating that access to the stair was separate from that to the closet.

Investigations in No. 22 showed that there had never been any stair tread-ends built into the walls of the rear projection, nor is there definite evidence of a stone newel-stair in any other house. Clearly, the staircases must have been of timber. Traces of a former window were found in the north wall, and a latrine had been situated in the north-west corner of the rear projection, alongside the stair. The latrine discharged into a short shaft which lay directly over the main drain, and the whole was constructed in a single operation. There is also evidence to indicate that a second shaft entered the drain in the south-west corner of the rear projection, potentially indicating a latrine on the first floor as well.

First floor

On the first floor in each house lay a fine chamber, open to the roof (Fig. 11.15). It too had a lateral fireplace and windows on opposing sides, towards the north end. In No. 22 the fireplace and rear-arches of the windows have plain, unstopped chamfers. The window at the front is of two trefoil-headed lights under a moulded label, while that at the rear is a plain rectangular light divided by a transom.

On the front elevation, close to the southern end, is a small rectangular window. Opposite, in the rear wall, is a broad opening under a segmental arch connecting with the stair projection. These features duplicate the arrangement on the ground floor, once

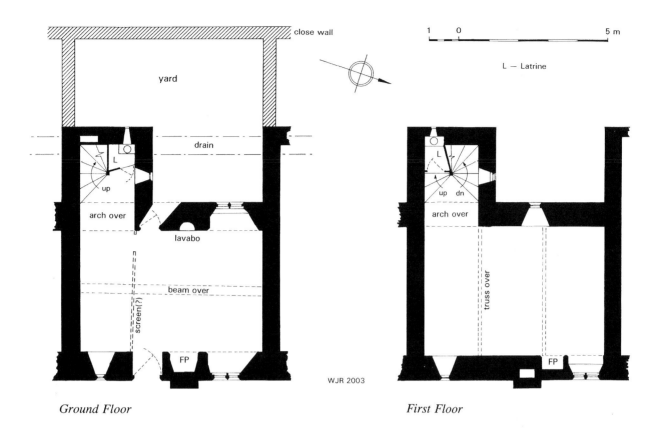

Ground Floor   First Floor

WJR 2003

Fig. 11.15. Vicars choral of Wells Cathedral. Ground- and first-floor plans of a typical vicar's lodging in the mid 14th century, based on house No. 22 (drawing and copyright, Warwick Rodwell)

again suggesting the possibility of there having been a small chamber or closet at the south end. If so, access to the main chamber, from the stairs, may have been through this antechamber. No surviving medieval partition has yet been identified on the first floor, and it is clear that any division must have been of an ephemeral nature. The roof space was not subdivided, and the crenellated wallplates are continuous for the full length of each interior.

The stair projection has its own tiny window set low down in the north wall. The position suggests that it was intended to light the middle part of the stair: the arrangement can be reconstructed with reasonable confidence, based on the survival of related features. Although mostly destroyed by a later doorway, it is apparent that in No. 22 there was a recess in the west wall at the south-west corner of the projection. This, and the evidence of the drain below, points to the likelihood of a first-floor latrine, probably with its own slit window in the west wall. Several of the houses exhibit recesses or secondary doorways in the rear wall here, potentially reflecting a former latrine.

The three-bay roof is of 'upper cruck' type with arched principals and a single collar. There is an embattled wallplate, two lines of butt-purlins, and a

square ridge-piece; pairs of curved wind-braces occur in the lowest register (Pugin and Walker 1836, pl. 3; Hewett 1985, fig. 46). The roof of each house is a self-contained unit, with stone-coped party walls rising between properties. The staircase projection was lower and gabled.

Additions and alterations

All the houses have been extended, often several times in succession, and many have been combined in pairs. A few houses received additions in the 15th century (e.g. at the rear of No. 14), but most date from the Tudor period, when vicars were first permitted to marry and have families. The least altered house is No. 22, where a diminutive wing was added in the 16th century to the stair projection, probably to serve as a kitchen; in the mid 19th century a new kitchen was constructed in what had hitherto been the yard.

The creation of a walled garden with a stone-built gate-arch in front of each house introduced a radical change to the morphology of the Close, essentially turning it from a college quadrangle bordered by lodgings into a street of houses. The garden walls were laid out parallel to the houses, and at a constant distance of 6m (20 ft) in front. Consequently, the road tapers towards the top of the Close, and there are unharmonious junctions between the garden walls and the chapel at the north end, and with the gateway and staircase tower at the south end. All four junctions are botched, and the problem is to decide whether laying out the road and building the garden walls antedated the erection of the chapel, or vice versa.

The configuration of the boundaries of Nos. 13 and 14 in relation to the chapel points to the garden walls having been there first, which would place them early in the 15th century. Moreover, there can be little doubt that the chapel never had a conventional buttress at its south-east angle, which was modified to articulate with the pre-existing gate-arch to No. 13 (north). Also the gate-arch to No. 27 was certainly in existence before the tower was erected at the foot of the staircase to the hall.

The garden walls were much higher than they are today, seemingly *c*.1.8 m (6 ft). The gate-arches were square topped and embattled: only five now survive (Nos. 5, 13 (north and south), 22 and 27). Drawings made by Buckler in 1811 and 1826 indicate that the walls and gate-arches were mostly then intact, and the main losses seem to have occurred in the 1830s (BL, Add. Ms. 36,384, f.175–7, 179). Some of the arches were subsequently fitted with *paterae* in the form of rosettes recessed into the spandrels.

The most flamboyant of the Tudor extensions is found on No. 14, where a shallow wing was added to the front of the house, filling the gap between it and the chapel. It has four-light traceried windows on both levels, separated by a series of panels containing shields of arms: one belongs to Bishop Stillington (1465–91), and the work can be dated to *c*.1490. Other houses retain evidence of inserted Tudor panelled ceilings and the creation of attic rooms.

Conservative improvements in the 17th century are evidenced by further extensions, simple boarded doors and oak wall-panelling. In the 18th century more rooms were panelled in pine and additional fireplaces installed. An extension was added to the front of No. 13 (north), filling the space between it and the east end of the chapel; it was demolished in the early 19th century, but replaced a few decades later.

A major refurbishment of Vicars' Close took place in the early 19th century, when sash windows were installed along with the present six-panelled front doors. Many of the houses have simple staircases, wall-cupboards and fire-surrounds of timber or stone dating from around the 1830s.

Decoration

Evidence of medieval decoration is scarce, but traces of polychromy have survived on the party walls in some attics. Vestigial remains of scrollwork and stencilled fleurs-de-lys, coloured red, occur in No. 9: this is likely to be a primary scheme. A 15th-century painting of stylized vegetation, also in red, has been uncovered in No. 23. Dark red and green paint, and traces of a black-line design remain on the concealed screen in No. 7.

Remains of Tudor painted decoration are more prolific, particularly in the added rear wing of No.9, where there is a fireplace with a running scroll design on the mantel-shelf, and ornamentation around window reveals. Fine wallpaper of Gothic design, *c*.1760, was discovered in No. 4, while Nos. 22 and 28 were elaborately painted and stencilled in 1863–64 by William Burges for Parker.

Sequence and dating

Some previous writers have supposed that the lodging ranges were entirely rebuilt by Bekynton in the early 1460s, being completed after his death in 1465 by his executors (e.g. Pantin 1959, 248; Wood 1965, 202). This view gained credence from the presence of heraldic shields adorning the chimneys of every house. There are two shields on each: one at the base of the chimney shaft, where the arms of Bekynton alternate with those of the See of Bath and Wells; and the other let into the face of the chimney projection just below the moulded eaves-course, where the arms of Bekynton's executors (Hugh Sugar, Richard Swan and John Pope *alias* Talbot) are found in succession.

An alternative view, popular until recent years, was that Ralph of Shrewsbury built the lodgings without fireplaces, and Bekynton provided the luxury of heating (e.g. Reid 1973, 120–1). Consequently, the chimney stacks and the shallow projections on the front walls from which they rise have been dismissed as secondary. While there has never been any doubt that the octagonal shafts with their louvred caps (all now renewed) belong to the 15th century, archaeological evidence shows that the fireplaces are unquestionably primary. The external projections are fully integrated with the masonry of the main elevations, and internally the ashlar of the fireplaces, on both levels, is integrated with that of the window reveals. In several instances, clear evidence can be discerned for the subsequent insertion of the heraldic panels just below eaves level.

Although a stone eaves-course frames the tops of the walls on the front elevations, imparting a strong sense of architectural unity, structural breaks can be detected between houses (e.g. there is a clear one between Nos. 25 and 26). More commonly, however, the masonry is coursed from chimney to chimney, passing smoothly across the line of the party wall. There is thus excellent continuity between chimneys in Nos. 21, 22 and 23; but the coursing is seldom in register from one side of a chimney to the other. This demonstrates that the chimneys were erected first, setting their ashlar quoins plumb and in line, and then the façade walling was infilled between them.

Excavations for drainage against the bases of the walls of several houses, on both sides of the Close, unexpectedly revealed different types of foundation construction. Each house was individually terraced into the sloping ground, and its foundations laid as an entity. In some instances there is a wide offset between the foundation and the wall standing on it, which provided a convenient base for the chimney stack, while in others there is little or no offset and a special projection was incorporated as a seating for the stack.

It is readily apparent that, although the house plots were carefully marked out to a predetermined plan, the foundations were not laid as one; nor were the façades erected in a single operation. Several teams of masons were involved, thus accounting for the differences in foundation construction, window position and detailing. If there were only a single break, it might plausibly be assigned to a hiatus caused by the Black Death, but that is not the case. Two or three teams of masons working simultaneously before, and again after, that cataclysmic occurrence might well account for the observed variations.

Although Bishop Ralph's charter tells us that some houses had already been erected by 1348, no independent dating was forthcoming until dendrochronological analysis was applied to the main ceiling beam in No. 20. Oxford Dendrochronology Laboratory reported that the tree was felled in the spring of 1349 (*Vernacular Architecture* 31, 2000, 109).

The roof construction is typical of the 15th century, although some scholars have sought to find precedents for its design in the 14th century, on the assumption that it was original to Bishop Ralph's work. For example, it has been pointed out that embattled wallplates occurred in the destroyed Great Hall at Windsor Castle as early as 1362–65, when William Wynford was master mason there (Colchester 1987, 175). But no analogues as early as 1348 can be cited, and Wynford was not appointed to Wells until 1364/5.

Archaeological study of the roofs, carried out when the slating was stripped in 1978–79, indicated that the oak framing was contemporary with the moulded stone eaves-course and the upper parts of the chimneys which are emblazoned with the arms of Bekynton and his executors. This implies that at the time of the bishop's death in 1465 major works were

in progress. Two timbers in the roof of No. 20 were therefore selected for dating by dendrochronology: one came from a tree felled in the spring of 1466, the other from a tree felled in the summer of the same year (*Vernacular Architecture* 31, 2000, 109).

The question arises: why would Bekynton be renewing roofs that had been constructed little more than a century earlier? The likelihood is that the eaves of the original houses were stepped, and the covering may have been thatch. The original party walls did not, it seems, project above roof-line, and therefore provided no fire-break. If the vicars had not maintained their houses in good repair – as we are told was the case – then the roof timbers could well have been in a serious state of decay by the 1460s.

Just before his death, Bekynton must have embarked on a comprehensive re-roofing of the vicars' lodgings, which brought not only practical benefits in terms of fire protection but also a considerable enhancement to the architectural aesthetics of the Close. The former was achieved by raising the party walls and covering the roofs with Treborough slates; the latter by adding the unifying eaves-course, the prestigious octagonal stacks with louvred caps, and the overt display of heraldry. The addition of fine chimneys was a fashionable pursuit in the mid 15th century: fourteen were built in the vicars' college at Exeter in 1459 (p.36 above).

Bishop Bubwith (1407–24) was almost certainly responsible for enclosing the gardens in front of the houses and providing them with stone gate-arches.

Vicars' chapel and library

The chapel stands at a focal point at the north end of Vicars' Close, with the road centred on it (Figs. 11.3 and 11.16). It is a simple rectangular building of two storeys and a parapet, in which the chapel occupies the ground floor and the vicars' library was formerly kept in the unheated upper room. The fireplace in the north wall was inserted in the late 19th century by Wells Theological College. The building is small, measuring 6.6 by 4.7m (21½ x 15½ ft) internally, being scarcely larger than a single vicar's house. The mean width is given since the front and rear walls of the chapel are not quite parallel, but taper by c.30cm in plan. The entrance is in the south wall, at the west end, and a projecting stair-turret at the north-west corner of the chapel provides internal access to the library (Fig. 11.17). An oak screen separates the body of the chapel from a passage across the west end. In the past it has sometimes been claimed that the chapel was built in the later 14th century, with the library added in the 15th. However, as a result of archaeological investigation it is clear that the structure is of a single build, dating from the 15th century.

Fig. 11.16. Vicars choral of Wells Cathedral. The vicars' chapel and library at the northern end of Vicars' Close (photo George H Hall, courtesy of Wells Chapter Archives)

The pre-existing Liberty, or Close, wall, which defined the north end of Vicars' Close, was used for the north wall of the chapel, for two-thirds of its height. However, this wall was skewed by eight degrees in relation to the axis of the close, and it was probably to correct the perspective that the ridge-line of the roof was made to descend towards the west. When viewed from the southern end of the close, the chapel appears to be squarely set within it and the ridge appears to be level. The adjustment of the roof construction in this manner is surprising but can hardly have been accidental.

The end walls of the chapel and the stair-turret are built of plain rubble, as is the Liberty wall, but the south elevation is of ashlar and is buttressed. Incorporated in its parapet, and in the spandrels between the lower window arches, is a series of 13th-century spandrel carvings derived from the cathedral (Rodwell 2001, 436–7). Their inclusion, the upper series inverted moreover, is a most curious piece of antiquarianism for which no explanation can be offered. All illustrations of the chapel, from the 1790s onwards, have shown them and there is no reason to doubt that they have been there since the 15th century.

The south wall is of two principal bays, with two-light Perpendicular windows paired in each; those in the chapel are under pointed arches, and those in the library under square labels. There are also east windows of three traceried lights on both the ground and upper floors. The doorway is contrived in a most awkward manner under the westernmost window, the lintel of which doubles as a sill at the base of the tracery lights. Superficially, it would appear that the

doorway has been broken through a pre-existing window, and that has often been claimed. Close inspection, however, indicates otherwise: the carving of the leaves and flowers which decorate both the hollow mouldings of the door jambs and the arches of the main windows is undoubtedly all by the same man. The entrance has never been in the west wall of the chapel, as has sometimes been suggested.

The oak door to the chapel is original and is carved with four shields which form an integral part of its design. The shields bear the arms of the See of Bath and Wells, Bishops Bubwith (1407–24) and Stafford (1425–43), and the family of Hungerford. The manor of Shipham, Somerset, was bought by Bekynton from the Hungerfords, and given in support of the vicars choral (Colchester 1987, 177). The heraldic evidence strongly suggests that the chapel was begun in Bekynton's episcopate and finished in Stafford's. Completion around 1425–30 is thus implied, although the first recorded mention of it is not until 1447. Other projects at Wells, initiated by Bubwith, were also finished by his successor.

There is a bellcote on the west gable which bears the arms of Bekynton, who was doubtless responsible for its addition. The roof structure was renewed in the 19th century (Pugin and Walker 1836, pl.7), but the oak panelled ceiling in the chapel and the screen, albeit restored, are both medieval. Remarkably, the medieval *mensa* slab has survived.

Chain Gate and bridge

Bishop Bekynton carried out a general reconstruction of the gates to the ecclesiastical precinct at Wells, culminating in 1459–60 in the erection of the Chain Gate and the bridge that it carries. The gate, which stands across St Andrew Street, at the point of entry to Cathedral Green, controls passage through the narrow gap between the stair-block of the chapter house and Vicars' Hall (Figs. 11.3, 11.8, 11.10, 11.18). The gate itself comprises a large vehicular arch which was supposedly closed by chains, but it has a rebated outer moulding which was clearly intended to receive a pair of doors. Detailed examination revealed no hint of fixing for chains. The entrance to the vicars' close at Chichester was also called Chain Gate (Fig. 4.4), and there was a similarly named gate in the precinct wall of Glastonbury Abbey. Flanking the central carriageway is a pair of small pedestrian arches, once fitted with wooden doors.

The gate passage is vaulted and the structure carries a gallery which is much grander than the name Chain Bridge might imply (Fig. 11.11). The gallery is entered from the south *via* a secondary flight of steps added to the top of the 13th-century

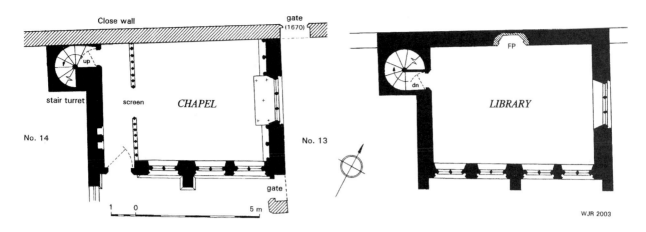

Fig. 11.17. Vicars choral of Wells Cathedral. Plans of the vicars' chapel and the library above (drawing and copyright, Warwick Rodwell)

great stair leading up to the chapter house from the north transept. The stairs are well provided with fenestration, and the gallery itself is four bays in length and fully glazed on both its east and west sides. Its medieval roof with an internal carved stone cornice remains and, externally, there is also considerable embellishment, including niches containing statuary.

As first built, it would appear that the gallery opened directly into the low end of the vicars' hall, where the two westernmost windows in the south wall were replaced by a single arch. However, a modification was quickly introduced, and a box-like annexe was constructed in the eastern angle between the Chain Gate and the hall. This abutted the bay containing the screens passage, where the window was replaced with the moulded door arch that had previously been installed a little further west. A lobby was thus formed, with a dog-leg entry into the hall. A true screens passage with opposing doorways had been created.

A possible explanation for relocating the new southern entry is that it was found inconvenient to allow the vicars to pass through the low end of the hall, where the buttery lay, on their way to and from services in the cathedral (Colchester 1987, 158). Since the lobby bears the arms of Bekynton – and he died in 1464/5 – it must presumably have been erected within four years of completing the Chain Bridge.

In this paper it has only been possible to provide a brief introduction to the Vicars' Close at Wells, the survival of which in such a complete form – both the buildings and the documents – is truly remarkable. Archaeologically, the structures are very complex, and a much fuller study is required to elucidate the numerous phases of extension and alteration exhibited by most of the houses. Also, many un-

Fig. 11.18. Vicars choral of Wells Cathedral. The Chain Gate and Chain Bridge above, looking east (photo George H Hall, courtesy of Wells Chapter Archives)

certainties still obtain relating to the architectural history of the hall and gatehouse complex.

Notes

1. This document is translated and printed in full, but wrongly dated, in Watkin 1941, 5.
2. The fact that the two charters were issued on the same date does not seem to have been generally noticed, and has long been confused by the fact that the date of the vicars' charter has often been given as 25 November 1592, an error that seems to have first appeared when a printed translation was published in 1889.
3. These drawings probably date from 1794.

12

The Vicars Choral
at Ripon, Beverley and Southwell

Philip Dixon

The three communities attached to the three great archepsicopal minsters of the medieval archbishopric of York at Beverley, Ripon and Southwell have much in common. Each was initially an Anglo-Saxon foundation. Each was responsible for providing ministry to a segment of the large archdiocese of York, and in each case almost all traces of the physical structures of the pre-Reformation community that served the churches have disappeared, to be glimpsed only in the archives. Only Ripon and Southwell eventually became cathedrals, in 1836 and 1884 respectively, Beverley Minster remains, somewhat incredibly, a parochial church.

Ripon

The earliest of these foundations was at Ripon, a monastery established as a Celtic house c.660, whose members included Eata, the disciple of St Aidan, and as guest-master St Cuthbert. After the Synod of Whitby the community withdrew from Ripon, and was replaced by monks following the Roman usage; a new church in squared stone with arcades and aisles was begun c. 669 by the new abbot, St Wilfred, Bishop of York (664–678)(eds. Colgrave and Mynors 1969, 294–309). Nothing is known of the location of the Celtic monastery, and little enough of that of St Wilfred, apart from the site of the principal basilica, below the nave of the present cathedral (Taylor and Taylor 1965,516–8). Cecil Hallett, on the other hand, conjectures that the 'Scottish' monastery stood below the site of the present building near *Stonebridgegate* beside the stream (1901, 5). The extent to which this early foundation provided the origin of the later college is uncertain, and the latter may have owed more to the reorganisation by St Oswald Archbishop of York (972–92) c.980, following the burning of the

Minster c.948 and the subsequent abandonment of the site. Hamilton Thompson (ed. Page 1913, III, 368) is inclined to identify the constitution of the ancient monastery with that of the later college, but notes how little evidence supports this position.

The permanent number of canons at Ripon was seven. They received rents from tenements, mostly in the parish of Ripon, but no canon held separate possession of such properties from which they received money. Despite this, the prebendaries eventually acquired local names mostly from the berewicks of the manor of Ripon, Littlethorpe, Monkton, Givendale and Skelton, Nunwick, Studley Magna, and Sharow, and were considered to have responsibility each for his area. One canon, who had duty of perpetual residence, held the prebend of Stanwick (Richmondshire)(ed. Page 1913, III, 369). As was normal, however, the canons were very irregularly resident. Indeed the visitations from 1291 to 1302 show a predominance of non-resident canons, as many as six of the seven in 1302 (ed. Fowler 1884, 16). It seems that the canons had been content to pay small sums for the cure of souls, and the archbishops had not been successful in changing this practice until Archbishop Corbridge (1300–4 – a former canon of Ripon), in a decree of 1303, set up a body of six vicars in the church of Ripon, with annual stipends of six marks each *per annum*. Each vicar was to be responsible for the cure of souls in one of the prebendary districts (ed. Page 1913, III, 369). These newly established priests formed the nucleus of a staff of resident vicars. They lived in common in a house, which became known as 'The Bedern', built on the site of two messuages given to the vicars in 1304 by Nicholas of Bondgate (ed. Fowler 1881, 119–21). The registers show that despite these measures, non-residency of both canons and vicars remained an issue, and in 1308 Archbishop Greenfield (1306–15) ordered the vicars to live in the Bedern, and in later visitations instructed them both to adhere to chastity and to avoid dancing and gambling (ed. Fowler 1884, 40, 56, 59–60). The situation was in part remedied by Archbishop Melton (1317–40), who in 1332 established by statute a sequence of residential terms of twelve weeks each year (the same number as was maintained at both Beverley and Southwell), and fixed the stipends for the vicars to be taken from the common fund of the canons (ed. Fowler 1884, 105–9). The six vicars were constituted into a college under a *proctor* in 1414, and Archbishop Bowett (1407–23) gave them the site for a new Bedern, the old house having been damaged by the Scots (*Cal Pat Roll* 1413–6, 267; ed. Fowler 1881, 125). By the middle of the 15th century there were 32 members of the body of religious, in addition to chantry priests. Thirty-one of these are named: seven canons, six vicars, six deacons, six thuribulers, and six choristers (ed. Fowler 1884, 148); the missing individual from this list was perhaps the *proctor*, although Hamilton Thompson suggested that the vicars were by error counted as seven (ed. Page 1913, III, 371). By the mid 16th century the prebends were valued at between £14 and more than £40 each, and the vicars received £6 per annum (eds. Caley and Hunter 1810–34, V, 250).

The dissolution of the chantries and the college in 1547 left Ripon with little revenue and few to serve it, until in 1604 a new college was created, consisting of six canons and a dean. This remained in being until the creation of a bishopric in 1836, when the establishment was reduced to four residential canons (ed. Fowler 1884, 258).

The layout of the Anglo-Saxon settlement at Ripon and its cemeteries have been the subject of recent detailed consideration (Hall and Whyman 1996, 138–144), whilst the later development of the town to the west of the Minster, away from the monastic precinct, has been dealt with by MacKay (1982). Neither of these studies, however, has much to say about Ripon's later-medieval colleges of vicars choral. Most of the vicars' buildings, referred to several times in the documentary sources, have now disappeared, with very little record of their appearance, or even of their location. It is clear, however, that we are dealing with two separate sites for the Bedern. The first, the two messuages of 1304, has been identified with some plausibility as being to the south-west of the Minster, on the street called Bedern Bank (Gowland 1943, 284) (Fig. 12.1), but excavations here in the 1980s revealed no clear traces of these buildings (*pers comm* Dominic Perring). The second Bedern was built in 1414 on a piece of land 140 ft broad, between the Archbishop's Palace and the house of the prebend of Monkton, to the north of the Minster. This area to the north of the church is now occupied by the Old Deanery of 1625: according to an early 19th century account, walls, vaulting and burials were noticed here during alterations, and these and fragments of an enclosing wall fronting on to Minster Road are taken to be part of the second Bedern (Gowland 1943, 285). A surviving building known as the Old Court House is probably medieval, and is sometimes said to have been part of the Bedern, but its distance from the Old Deanery makes it unlikely that both can represent structures of the Bedern, and it is perhaps better to view it as some element of the Archbishop's complex.

The Ripon canons themselves, at least after the 13th century, lived in houses set in a Close around the church, as indicated in Fig. 12.1, which is based largely on the discussion by Gowland. To the south of the Minster the prebendary of Thorp had a house, part of which still survives. Here a stone house, called St Agnes' Lodge, stood as late as 1901 (Hallet 1901, 136) and other prebendary houses are suspected among the old buildings which once stood here. Four prebends stood to the east of the Minster, completing the ring of buildings around the church.

Beverley

Like that at Ripon, the church at Beverley derives from an Anglo-Saxon foundation, and has been the recent subject of an extensive and comprehensive account (ed. Horrox 2000). Tradition identifies the place with an otherwise unknown spot called *Inderawuda*, where Bede says that John, Bishop of Hexham and York (705–18) was buried in 721, in the *porticus* of St Peter (eds. Colgrave and Mynors 1969, 457–9, 469). According to the later traditional account, John found here a church dedicated to St John the Evangelist, which he transformed into a monastery of black monks and nuns and seven secular priests (Hearne 1774, IV 99–104). This account was, however, treated with suitable scepticism by Hamilton Thompson in his discussion in the *Victoria County History* (ed. Page 1913, III, 353).

By the 12th century it was accepted that the monastery, burnt and abandoned during the Danish wars, had been re-founded as a college of secular canons by King Æthelstan, who gave land and privileges (ed. Raine 1879, I 263–4). No charters or other documentation of these claimed rights now exist, and much that came later may have been attributed to him; Æthelstan's earliest charters refer only to the granting of the privilege of sanctuary around the church.

The last three Anglo-Saxon archbishops of York were all engaged in works at Beverley. Ælfric Puttock (1023–50) began a refectory and dormitory for the canons, Cynesige (1050–60) continued the

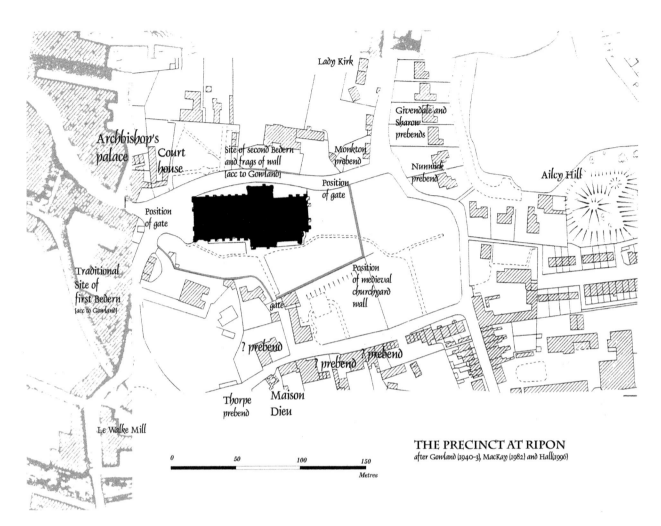

Fig. 12.1. Vicars choral of Ripon Minster. Plan of the precinct (sources, Gowland 1940–3, Mackay 1982 and Hall and Whyman 1996, drawing and copyright, P Dixon)

building of the church including a tall western tower, and Ealdred (1060–69) completed the refectory and dormitory and enlarged the church, particularly at the east end. By the time of Domesday the canons held a large amount of land from the archbishop. They may already have numbered seven, and they received their income from a single common fund under the control of a *provost*: their prebend consisted of the daily ration at 'The Bedern' along with an annual dividend from the fund, most of which came from the thraves of parishes in the East Riding. As Hamilton Thompson points out, this scattered allocation of income prevented the prebends becoming identified with specific locations, and the canonries were distinguished not by place, but by the name of an altar in the church: Sts Andrew, James, Martin, Mary, Michael, Peter and Stephen. By the 14th century an eighth canonry, St Katherine's, had been added, but the holder was not a member of the chapter, and his prebend was half the

daily offerings from the high altar (the other half and all the rest of the offerings falling to the other canons) (ed. Page 1913, III, 354).

The administrative structure of the church under these eight canons was complex. The *provost* appointed three dignitaries (precentor, chancellor and sacrist), who ranked below the canons, and had no voice in chapter. Seven clerks known as *berefellarii* (probably meaning bare-skins), were perhaps poor clerks taking alms from the canons. By the 15th century their status had improved and they had been incorporated as seven parsons in the quire of the church, appointed by the *provost*. The 'Statutes' of 1391 list, in addition nine vicars, seven chantry priests (increasing to fifteen by the time of the suppression), nine canons' clerks, one clerk of the precentor, a clerk of the charnel, seven clerks of the *berefellarii*, two incense-bearers, eight choristers, two sacrist's clerks, and two vergers (ed. Page 1913, III, 355; ed. Horrox 2000, 44–5).

The nine vicars (one for each canon and one for the archbishop, who had a non-chapter stall in quire) were the vicars choral. Each represented his canon at the appropriate altar, and the parishioners of each prebend came to be served at the altar of their prebend. In case of sickness the vicars choral attended to those in their prebend. In addition, the *berefellarii* provided choral service, at the canons' expense, to supplement the voices of the vicars.

Non-residence was as much a problem at Beverley as it was at Ripon and, indeed, at most of the other English institutions studied in this book. Archbishop Romanus (1286–96) agreed an ordinance enforcing twenty-four weeks residence each year for each canon, and continual residence for the dignitaries and *berefellarii*. In 1302 his successor Archbishop Corbridge decreed that at least one canon must be in residence (which shows a lack of compliance with Romanus' ordinance). Archbishop Greenfield reduced the canons' residence to twelve weeks in 1307, fulfilment of which obligation was necessary before the canon could receive his share of offerings at the high altar. By 1325 Archbishop Melton (himself sometime a canon of Beverley) had inveighed against those non-residents who, nevertheless, took a full share of the offerings.

The annual value of the prebends in 1535 varied from £31 to £48, whilst the value of each of the vicarages was £8 *per annum*, and that of each *berefellarii* post was £6.13s.4d. The provostship, however, was worth over £109 (eds. Caley and Hunter 1810–34, V, 130ff). The suppression fell more harshly on Beverley than on Ripon. One of the vicars choral was appointed vicar to the parish, with three assistant curates from among the inferior clergy, and the remaining body of the clergy was dispersed. Later, after the foundation of a grammar school, the lands and rights of the church came into the hands of crown grantees. What remained was given to the Corporation of the town, as patrons of the church, who have maintained the fabric into modern times.

Though little now remains of the collegiate buildings, something is known of them from excavation as well as documentary sources (Fig. 12.2). The Archbishop's Palace lay to the south of the nave of the church, in an area known as 'Hall Garth'. This was a moated enclosure, whose bank survives on the southern side, although most of the ditch was filled in during the 19th century. Excavations in 1980 located the abutments of a bridge at the north-west corner of this site (Miller *et al.* 1982, 12). The internal buildings were demolished for their building materials in 1548, but the platforms for them survived, and can still be seen as low banks (in Fig. 12.2 their layout has been adapted from the analysis by Miller *et al.* 1982). Part of the court house is believed to have stood in the Admiral Duncan Inn, also in Hall Garth, before its demolition in 1958. Other buildings were identified by excavation in 1947 as the Bedern tower and a hall; this is not likely, although apparently accepted by Miller *et al.*

The prebendarys' houses were scattered around the Minster (Neave 2000). The St Martin prebendal house lay to the north of the Minster, where in 1313/ 4 it was called 'small' and 'in poor repair'. It contained a hall, chapel, kitchen, brewhouse, bakery and a gate. The St Peter, St Katherine and St Mary prebendal houses seem to have lain close to the Wednesday Market also to the north of the Minster. Other prebendal houses lay to the east and south of the church. The St Stephen prebendal house stood next to a messuage in Lortegate, and a timber-framed building which once stood at the west end of Flemingate was perhaps part of the Bedern (Miller *et al.* 1982, 12), though it is more likely to have been the St Andrew Prebend. A 'hall garth' in Eastgate was 'commonly called St James prebend garth' (ed. Leech 1897, 353; Miller *et al.* 1982, 14). These buildings formed 'part of an almost complete circle of collegiate and Episcopal buildings around the Minster, an arrangement which would, in effect have constituted a Minster Close, although probably not a very well-defined one' (Armstrong *et al.* 1991, 249) and the point is nicely confirmed by Susan Neave in her recent study (2000, 204).

The location of the Bedern itself has remained obscure until recently. The documentary sources suggest that the Bedern complex contained a common hall and other chambers of the vicars choral in an enclosure, which (until the end of the 14th century) also contained the dwellings of other clerks, such as the *berefellarii*, and perhaps also the canon's clerks, whose residence and discipline are sometimes coupled with that of the vicars choral. The Bedern garden is named in Minster Moorgate, and the Bedern in Keldgate, which references have been used to place it in, or next to, the Hall Garth, on the south or south-western side of the Minster. Others have variously suggested both St John Street and the corner of Lurk Lane. Excavations between Hall Garth and Lurk Lane have, indeed, located a complex occupied from the late Saxon period until *c*.1600 (Armstrong *et al.* 1991). The site contained a complex of stone buildings in two phases built over a timber hall. These buildings were thought to represent housing for other members of the clergy, rather than part of the Bedern, however, and the excavators thought the Bedern most likely to be west, rather than east, of the Hall Garth. The excavated site east of Hall Garth has now been fairly conclusively identified as the St James prebendal house (Neave 2000, 206–7).

According to Leland the old Bedern had become the house of the *provost*, and the new Bedern was

THE ARRANGEMENTSOF THE BEVERLEY PRECINCT
after Horrox

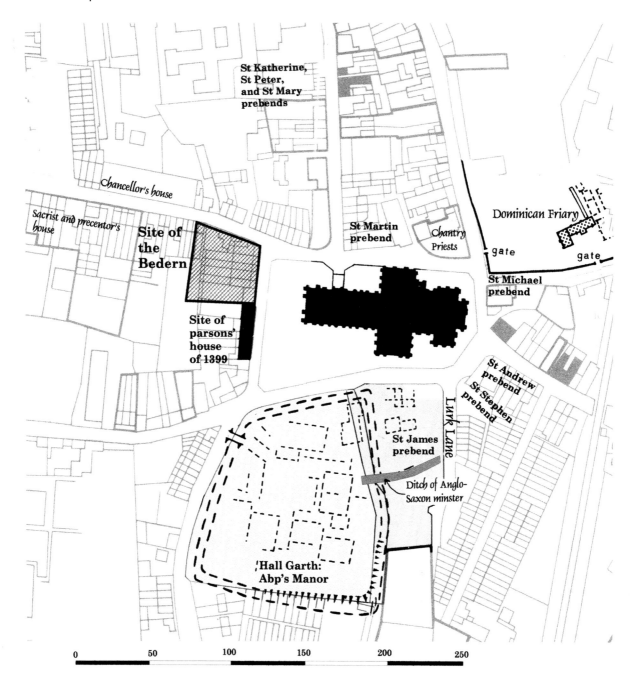

Fig. 12.2. Vicars choral of Beverley Minster. Plan of the precinct (source, Horrox 2000, drawing and copyright, P Dixon)

built adjoining.it. Further work on the documentary sources has now established the site of the Bedern lay immediately to the west of the Minster, fronting on to what is now St James Street, and extending between Minster Moorgate and Keldgate (Neave 2000, 199–202). The site contained great and small halls and kitchens, and other offices, dormitory and various chambers, with a tower added in the 1420s. This may suggest a courtyard arrangement, but the plan of the building complex is completely unknown. In 1399 part of the Bedern site was granted to the *berefellarii* for a separate house. This survived until the beginning of the 18th century, being transformed by the master of the grammar school after 1701 into a long narrow mansion, which still survives facing the churchyard. The shape of the structure and its internal walls suggests that the outline of the building represents the house of the *berefellarii*. The rest of the Bedern remained in use by the vicars until taken over by the *provost* as his house, probably later in the 15th century. A new Bedern was then constructed, probably in the garden to the west of the old site. Both *provost*'s house and new Bedern were granted out at the Dissolution, and nothing now remains of them.

Southwell

The minster at Southwell was, like those of Beverley and Ripon, of Anglo-Saxon origin, and may, indeed have had long roots back into the late Roman period, for the church was placed immediately to the west of a large Roman villa (Baylan 1901, 58; Daniels 1965–6). In *c*.956 Oscytel, Archbishop of York (956–72), who had then recently been translated from the see of Dorchester, received a grant from King Eadwy of the lands and jurisdiction in Southwell and seven other villages, and a fractional share of land and services in four more. The estate was to be explicitly held subject to an archbishop's court of justice. There seems little real likelihood that this dispersed assemblage of lands and rights had previously existed as a block (Stenton 1967, 13). It is more likely that it was an amalgam of properties which were at that moment available to the king in order to bolster the authority of the new archbishop at a particularly difficult time (immediately after the overthrow of King Eirik Bloodaxe of York, and the absorption of Northumbria into the Anglo-Saxon kingdom).

Though it is often assumed that this gift was intended as the foundation of a religious centre, this is far from clear. Nothing suggests that the estate was used at first as anything but as a financial resource for the archbishop. A church at Southwell is first recorded some sixty years later, in the *Liber Vitae* of Hyde Abbey compiled about 1014 (ed. Keynes 1996, f.37) where it is said that the minster of Southwell near the water called the Trent contained the relics of Eadburh, an otherwise obscure English saint, who may have been the East Anglian Eadburga who was daughter of king Aldwulf, and abbess of Repton *c*.660 (ed. Blake 1962, 19). The palace first occurs in 1051, when Archbishop Ælfric Puttoc died there. Archbishop Cynesige gave the church two bells shortly afterwards. As Stenton points out, nothing in the records suggests that at this period there was any 'elaborate religious establishment' (1967, 16), and the 11th-century estates of the church of Southwell itself were minute, since most of the land belonged

personally to the archbishop. At Domesday the church held only a tenancy in Southwell, the manor of Norwell (worth £6 per annum), the manor of Cropwell Bishop worth half that, and some pieces of land elsewhere. Even some of this was presumably of recent acquisition, the gift of Archbishop Ealdred, who is said to have bought estates with his own money and set up prebends at Southwell, and built a refectory for the canons to eat together (Stenton 1967, 17; Beaumont 1971, 8). It is clear, then, that Southwell's development as a minster church was proceeding on the same lines as both Ripon and Beverley, but about two generations later.

Furthermore, it seems relatively clear that the establishment of a great episcopal minster at Southwell, which is clearly recognisable in the records of the 12th century, was a relatively recent event, of the second half of the previous century.

How many prebends were established at this early date is not known, and there may well have been seven, as at the other York episcopal minsters. Southwell remained unusual in having no *provost* or other superior in chapter, the eldest canon in residence carrying out the duties of head. These arrangements were confirmed by Archbishop Thomas II (1108–14), who increased the numbers of prebends and encouraged the rebuilding of the Anglo-Saxon Minster. Eventually, through a papal bull issued by Alexander III in 1171, the Chapter was given independence of spiritual and temporal jurisdiction, owing allegiance to the Pope alone. By the end of the 13th century the number of prebends had increased to sixteen, a number maintained until the changes of the 19th century.

The 'peculiar' of Southwell, created by these privileges covered 28 parishes in Nottinghamshire, was independent of the Archdeacon, and was managed by the canons, whose prebends took their names from their estates. These were Oxton, Oxton Crophyll and Oxton Second Part, Norwell Overhall, Norwell Palishall, and Norwell Third Part, all of which were perhaps ancient endowments. Another prebend, Sacrista, completed the roll of seven prebends and was the income attached to the office of treasurer, which was paid from the common fund. Further prebends were established of South Muskham (created *c*.1110), Beckingham and Dunham (*c*.1125), Halloughton (1160), Rampton (*c*.1200), Eaton (1290) and North Leverton (1291). Some of Southwell's estates were managed in common; but the prebendal estates were controlled by the individual canons, and Summers notes that, although they were supposed to enter the leases of these lands in the chapter lease book, few actually did so. He considered that the leasing out of the town prebendal 'mansions was a cause of increasing non-residence amongst the canons' (1974, 23).

The papal bull of 1171 allowed the establishment of 'fit vicars' in the churches of the canons, and at the last prebendal creation (North Leverton in 1291) a stall on the north side of the choir 'next to the sacrist,...' was provided and the new canon was 'to have and to pay his vicar choral, as the other canons used' (*ibid.*). The payments made by the canons seem to have been inadequate, and so the chapter set up a fund administered by the chapter as a body, in order to pay for the support of the vicars choral. By 1291 it is clear that the canons (who had in the 11th century lived in common with a refectory) were occupying individual houses, regularly spaced around Minster Close. The vicars choral, on the other hand, were placed in a common hall with communal lodgings paid for by the chapter's trust fund, and remained employees of the chapter, with no incorporation or seal. The location of this common hall is not certainly known. From at least the 14th century the southern side of the Minster was occupied by the Archbishop's Palace, and it is presumed that earlier archbishops lived in buildings on the same site. The west and the north of the Minster were occupied by the prebendal mansions of the canons (Fig. 12.3). Thus it is likely that the vicars choral occupied a site to the east and, furthermore, it seems that it was

inconveniently far away – perhaps on the far side of Potwell Dyke. In the third quarter of the 14th century it was decided to move them closer to the Minster, probably near the present buildings of Vicars' Court to the east of the Minster. This was where the petition of 1379 to the archbishop by Richard de Chesterfield (Prebendary of Norwell Overhall) proposed to build a new college for the vicars choral, close to the house of the prebend of Beckyngham, where the school now stands (Summer 1974, 57). The allotted area was an irregular rhomboid measuring over 200 feet (60.96m) along its north and south sides, 146 feet (44.50m) on the west side, and only 100 feet (30.48m) on the east, a space similar in size to the present Vicars' Court. The complex consisted of a quadrangle with the lodgings on three sides, and a communal hall to the east. The entrance lay, as now, through a gate to the west. These helpful details are preserved in an *inspeximus* in Nottingham Record Office (DDM 105/44).

A watercolour of the western façade of the quadrangle viewed from beside the chapter house was made in *c.*1775, immediately prior to its demolition (Fig. 12.4). It shows a large building with a stone ground floor, and a timber-framed first floor. The roof trusses are crown posts and the framing seems

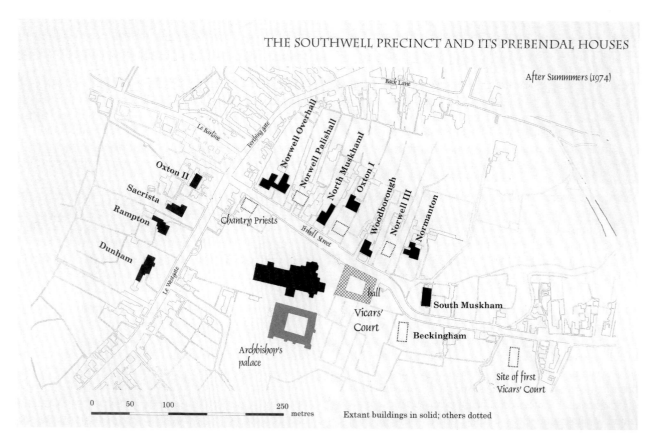

Fig. 12.3. Vicars choral of Southwell Minster. Plan of the precinct (source, Summers 1974, drawing and copyright, P Dixon)

Fig. 12.4. Vicars choral of Southwell Minster. View by S H Grimm of the college of vicars choral from the west made shortly before its demolition in about 1785 (BL Additional Mss. 15544, f.174. Copyright British Library)

Fig. 12.5. Vicars choral of Southwell Minster. Copy made by S H Grimm about 1785 of an earlier drawing 'belonging to Mr Bristoe', which seems to show the last surviving remains of the common hall of the vicars choral from the west, shortly before demolition (BL Additional Mss. 15544, f.172. Copyright British Library)

very suitable for the late 14th century. The position of the gate to the churchyard, shown on the left of the drawing, demonstrates that this new college for the vicars choral occupied exactly the same footprint as the present Vicars' Court. In its turn, this implies that the vicar's communal hall and its offices occupied the site of the present house known as The Residence, reconstructed for the dean in 1689–95 (Summers 1974, 59–61). Although Summers thought

this was a completely new building, a drawing made before a second rebuilding in or shortly after 1785 (Fig. 12.5) shows an irregular outline with a probable floored-in hall, which may have survived the 1689–95 reconstruction and preserved the remains of the 14th century common hall, and adjacent chambers. As rebuilt *c.*1785, however, The Residence, is a symmetrical structure, and an examination of its regularly laid-out cellars suggests that little or nothing can remain from its medieval ancestor. Similarly the rectangular layout of Vicar's Court precludes survival of any of the older buildings above ground in these 18th-century fabrics.

At the suppression of the chantries in 1547 the establishment at Southwell was extensive. Only three canons were in residence in 1545, but sixteen vicars choral and thirteen chantry priests were entered in the certificates, together with four deacons, six choristers, two thuribulers and two clerks. The *Valor Ecclesiasticus* estimated the worth of the richest prebend, Norwell Overhall, at nearly £50. However, the two poorest (Eaton and Sacrista) was thought to be worth only £2 per annum, though perquisites expanded Sacrista to more than £7. Each vicar choral received £4 a year. The total common fund at this point was valued at no more than £45 a year, but Summers pointed out that the total revenues of the college, at about £500, exceeded the wealth of many of the contemporary abbeys (1974, 25–6).

With the dissolution of the chapter in 1547, its funds passed to the crown, and the prebendary of Sacrista, with a stipend of £20, was appointed 'vicar', with two assistant priests. The remaining clergy were pensioned. This seemed to be the end of the college, but, after years of negotiation, in 1585 a new chapter and college was once more established with sixteen prebendaries, but without a dean and with only six vicars choral, six choirmen and six choristers. One of the vicars choral was to be parish vicar, and one to be schoolmaster, and one of the prebenaries was to be elected vicar general, to act as 'bishop' over the peculiar. This interestingly republican arrangement continued until 1840, when the church was again reduced to the status of a parish church (*ibid*. 26–9). The late 14th-century vicars choral buildings were increasingly dilapidated, and poorly adapted for the accommodation of married priests. By the end of the 17th century the building contained only four separate houses, whilst the old communal hall was surplus to requirements and had been partly demolished and partly reconstructed to form The Residence in 1689–95. In 1779 the chapter decided to remove the rest of the vicars' college, and replace it with four houses. This work, together with a re-facing of The Residence to bring it up to date, was completed by 1785.

Conclusion

This examination of the residences of the vicars choral at Ripon, Beverley and Southwell has revealed many points of similarity in the history, arrangements and fate of the institutions and their buildings. The physical similarities may be exaggerated. Only Southwell has preserved anything like a view of the structures, and the supposed layout of the colleges of Beverley and Ripon have been hypothesised on the basis of this single 18th century drawing (Neave 2000, 199). It is, however, interesting to note the increasing emphasis on collegiate and indeed courtyard planning in the later middle ages in the closes of the vicars choral in these episcopal minsters. In the general replacement of the older smaller Bederns by new houses based around courtyards we see an increasing dependence by chapters on their vicars, in the growing absence of their prebendaries.

13

The Vicars Choral of York – A Summary and Interpretation of Recent Archaeological Work

David Stocker

Introduction

Like the vicars choral at St Paul's London and Salisbury, the York vicars are not well represented by their surviving buildings in that part of the city still known as Bedern. Today only the hall and chapel survive of this, the earliest vicars' college to be established (Fig. 1.2 above), and both are truncated structures which give little indication of the complex development of this important institution. Yet a century ago the situation was even worse – at that time the chapel (though still standing to its full height) was propped up with raking shores, whilst the remains of the hall were deeply buried within the buildings of a factory and unrecognisable as a medieval building to all but the most diligent antiquary. The improvement in our appreciation of the college is due to the all-embracing *Esher Plan* (Esher & Pollen 1971) which recommended that what had been a run-down inner city area should be developed for housing. The adoption of this proposal by York City Council led to a substantial archaeological excavation carried out by York Archaeological Trust between 1973 and 1980, and to the restoration of the hall between 1981 and 1984 and of the chapel shortly afterwards. After the redevelopment, the street name Bedern was retained. Earlier it had described a narrow cul-de-sac, which was widened and extended through to a junction with St Andrewgate in 1852. In the present layout of the area the name refers both to the western end of the original lane – now an insalubrious service passage – and to the slightly re-aligned and pedestrianised extension, which gives access to a discrete backwater of modern housing.

All the archaeological data which follow are derived from the published report on this work (Richards 2001). This chapter seeks to take some of the archaeological conclusions further and, particularly, it attempts to understand the sequence of development of the college in terms of discrete phases of planning by the vicars and their masters. Many more archaeological periods were identified than are discussed here, and indeed these periods form a more or less continuous sequence of development. This was a correct and helpful approach to the recorded archaeology of the site, but we can now go further. By focusing on certain phases, it is possible to add depth to our understanding of the complex development of the York college of vicars choral as an institution, and this is the primary ambition of this chapter.

Unlike most of the other colleges, the vicars' court (or Bedern) at York was actually established outside the Minster Close (Fig. 13.1). Legally speaking, it formed an outlier of the Close, but that does not explain why such an important Minster institution should have been located in such a relatively remote place. Harrison (1952, 29) believed that the vicars' college had been attracted to this site because it had previously been occupied by a more ancient foundation, but there is no evidence for any such earlier institution, and no traces of any such foundation were found during excavation. It is more likely that by the time the college was established there was simply no room for a large group of new buildings within the Close and, to find sufficient space, the founders were forced to obtain land behind nearby commercial street fronts.

The earliest references we have to the canons of York appointing vicars to their stalls in the choir is *c.*1138–43 (ed. Tringham 1993, xvii), but (as seems to have been the case at all the other secular cathedrals)

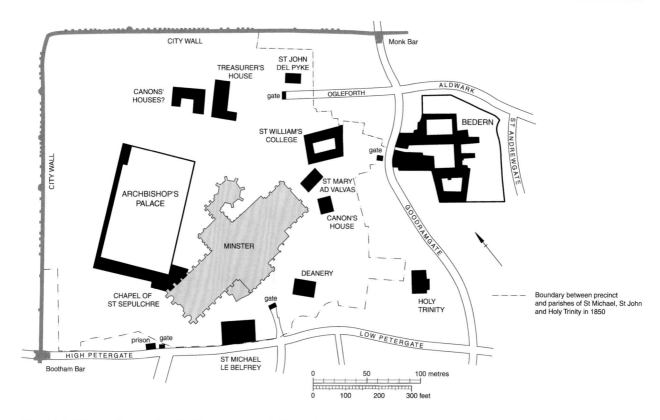

Fig. 13.1. Vicars choral of York Minster. Plan of Close, showing location of The Bedern (source, ed. Tillott 1961, p.340. Drawing, Lesley Collett, copyright YAT)

it was not for another century that steps were taken to found a college in which such vicars would live together. Sarah Rees Jones has skilfully demonstrated that the land on which the college was to be constructed in the mid 13th century had been mostly in ecclesiastical hands previously, as part of the Prebend of Wetwang (Rees Jones 2001). Even so, it seems that the canons who took responsibility for founding a college, notably William de Laneham and John Romeyn the elder, felt it necessary to purchase the land before donating it to the vicars. The land in question lay behind the street front of Goodramgate and had formerly consisted of long broad strips, presumably individual burgage plots, running back to St Andrewgate (Fig. 13.2). Romeyn was Treasurer of the cathedral and thus holder of one of the richest benefices in England. Matthew Paris said that he was 'crammed with rents and treasures' and it seems clear that he used the fabulous wealth generated by his prebendal estates for projects of ecclesiastical patronage (Dobson 1977, 51–2, 61, 73–5).

The early college – c.1250–c.1300

Rees Jones shows that the land that formed the southern 60 percent of what later became the precinct was given to the vicars, probably in a number of separate parcels, between about 1230 and about 1250.

Some of the properties along the Aldwark and Goodramgate frontages were not acquired until the 1270s and the plot later known as 'Little Bedern' was not acquired until *c.*1338. Much of this property in the northern part of the site remained in secular occupation during the later 13th century and was not brought into the college precinct until the mid 14th century. Because of this the first college buildings, begun in the mid 13th century, were laid out in the centre and south of the precinct area. Nigel Tringham has shown that these buildings must have been constructed by the 1270s, when the title *custos domus vicariorum* began to be used (1993, xix), but the material culture suggests that the first buildings had been put up a couple of decades earlier (Richards 2001, 413–5).

It seems highly likely that the entrance to the new college was always onto Goodramgate, in the position which it still occupies, facing the east gate of the Minster Close. The first buildings were laid out around an elongated three-sided courtyard (Fig. 13.3). The excavations recovered substantial remains of two parallel ranges, and some less coherent evidence that they were linked by a short range at the east end. Although these buildings were evidently not absolutely contemporary (and their construction extends over three structural periods in the report), it seems highly likely that they were laid out according to a

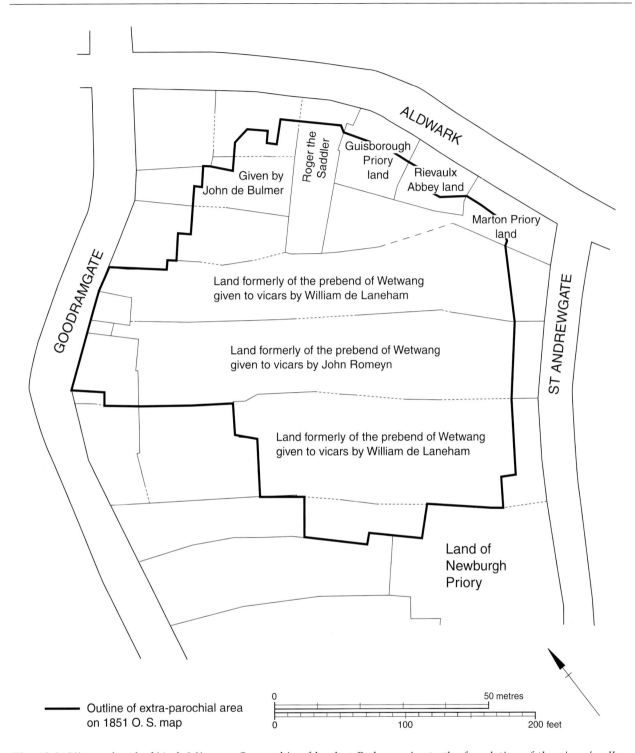

Fig. 13.2. Vicars choral of York Minster. Ownership of land at Bedern prior to the foundation of the vicars' college (source, Rees-Jones 2001, fig. 188. Drawing, Lesley Collett, copyright YAT)

single design, and took about a generation to complete – perhaps between *c*.1250 and *c*.1280.

The northern range, an enormous timber-framed building, was built first. Its slightly irregular frame was supported on posts with individually prepared foundations and post-pads; the infill between the frames was supported on sill walls of limestone rubble. With a minimum length of about 50m (the west end was not discovered in the excavations) and a width of 12m, it was at least as long as the nave of the late 11th-century cathedral (demolished *c*.1290). It may have been the second largest free-standing building in York that was not itself a church, surpassed only in size by the approximately contemporary dormitory of St Leonard's Hospital, which was about 70m by 12m (Benson 1919, 16–17,

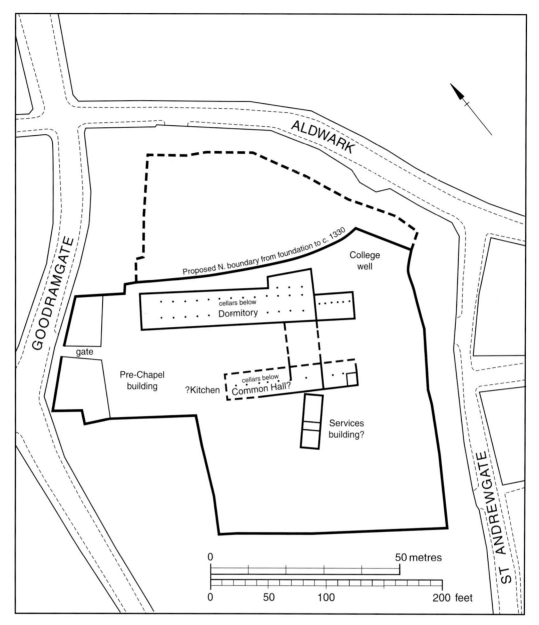

Fig. 13.3. Vicars choral of York Minster. Reconstruction of layout of college c.1250–80 (source, ed. Richards 2001, periods 2, 3, 4. Drawing Lesley Collett, copyright YAT)

fig.12; RCHME 1981, 93–5) – a building which provides several useful parallels for the newly discovered Bedern building.

Although the St Leonard's dormitory is a very expensive building of ashlar, whilst the Bedern building was timber-framed, both seem to have taken the form of a huge open dormitory on first floor level with a double-aisled undercroft below. It is likely that the Bedern building was also a two-storey structure because it was converted into a row of two-storey houses in Periods 6–7 (see below) with little structural alteration. Furthermore, whilst the additional row of posts in bays ten to twelve (from the west) would be very difficult to explain in a structure open to the roof, they make good sense as

additional supports strengthening floor joists at critical points in a two-storey building. Finally, if the Bedern building was two-storeyed we can suggest that the additional, contemporary, structure to the north (only partially explored during the excavation) could be a forebuilding, containing staircase access to the first floor. Although not impossible, it is much harder to explain this annex either functionally or structurally in the context of a single-storeyed building.

Using the parallel of the contemporary St Leonard's Hospital, we can propose that the Bedern building had an undercroft, with two aisles and a central nave, originally planned as an open, continuous, space – apparently at least seventeen bays long. The posts would have supported an enormous floor area above – presumably occupied by the dormitory, similar in scale to the largest hospitals of the day. If we presume that each vicar was allocated a bay along either the north or the south walls on the first floor, as in hospital dormitories, then it would have comfortably housed the 36 vicars who made up the complement by 1294 (ed. Clay 1958–9, vi).

The archaeology provides no reason to think that the space on either floor was originally subdivided into cubicles – that seems to have been a later and more piecemeal development (from Period 4 onwards). Consequently, when this building was designed, it seems that the canons had in mind a large communal dormitory; an arrangement that was, no doubt, influenced by the example of contemporary monastic and hospital dormitories. Our archaeological evidence, then, seems to suggest that the impulse to bring the vicars together into a college about 1250 was rooted in the desire amongst their patrons to provide them with a more regulated domestic regime, under which they were expected to sleep together in this huge open building. This must have had contemporary overtones of the monastic life, with the suppression of the individual to the common good being expressed in the architecture. More clearly than anything else, this huge communal dormitory demonstrates that the impulse behind the establishment of vicars' colleges at the secular cathedrals in the middle years of the 13th century owes its origins to movements for reform amongst the secular clergy, a movement which was lead by figures like Archbishop Walter de Gray of York (Dobson 1977, 46–52). Such dormitories were prescribed for the canons of prebendal churches by Chrodegang of Metz in the 8th century and we might see here some desire on the part of cathedral reformers like de Gray to emulate early forms of ecclesiastical discipline.

St Leonard's Hospital was built under the patronage of the same John Romeyn, who had been instrumental in establishing the vicars' college on its site in Goodramgate, suggesting that amongst the York clergy Romeyn, in particular, saw that spiritual benefits might be gained through the discipline of a common life in these great halls, whether as an inmate of the hospital or as a vicar choral of the cathedral. Furthermore, we might also suggest that timber might have been chosen as the principal building material for the construction of the Bedern because of the completion of the north transept roof at the Minster, of which Romeyn was also the principal patron. The transept roof was probably completed in the early 1250s (Gee 1977, 132–3; Brown 2003, 13–6), at precisely the same time that work started at the Bedern and, although we have absolutely no evidence to support the suggestion, it may be that the car-

penters moved from the transept directly to the Bedern; from one of Romeyn's projects to the next.

This great dormitory building at Bedern is an important discovery. It represents, almost uniquely, the first phase of development of the English colleges of vicars choral. Until recently such buildings were not known elsewhere in England, but it now seems likely that the ruins of a much smaller building of the same sort may have survived in the north range of Vicars' Court at Lincoln (p.78–85 above). By comparison with the Bedern building, the Lincoln hall was a very small specimen, being probably no more than 18.5m long. But with these two examples now identified, we should look for the remains of similar buildings at all of the vicars' closes in England. Warwick Rodwell (1982, 212) has pointed out that a 'habitation' (in the singular) was planned for the vicars at Wells in 1318 and that deeds of 1353 and 1354 seem to refer to the vicars living in a single building, which he takes to be the present hall (p.116 above). Could these be references to a single great dormitory building, preceding the famous close? Furthermore, Pantin pointed out that, for a brief period before the fine close of houses was built there in the mid 15th century, the vicars of Chichester slept in a common, first-floor dormitory at the west end of their communal hall (1959, 248). We might also reconsider the documentation of the 1320s and 1330s from Lichfield, which reports that vicars had a 'common hall' and a kitchen. Yet at this time the vicars there were dining daily with their respective canons, not in their 'common hall' and they were not enjoined to dine in common until 1390 (Tringham 1990, 62). Thus, at Lichfield also, there may have been a phase when the vicars lived in a single great dormitory, called the 'common hall'. However, even if the York building is no longer unique, we should still respect its great size, and its contribution to York's medieval roofscape must have been considerable.

In a second phase of development (Period 3), though probably one planned from the outset, the huge dormitory acquired a two-storey, timber-framed annex to the east. Unfortunately the floors below this building were not investigated at depth, but in plan it looks very much like a monastic reredorter, located where one might expect such a building – to the east of the 'dormitory'. The building had an asymmetrical division along its length, something which in stone monastic examples demarcates the latrine itself, and which in this case might mark a 'drop' from first floor. There was no sign of a drain in this building, but elsewhere on the Bedern site it is clear that latrines were not flushed but emptied by hand. Interpretation of this building remains controversial, however, as the excavators noted that it had plastered internal walls at ground floor (though no hearth) – and this prompted interpretation as a domestic building

(Richards 2001, 422, 424). If, however, this structure does represent an early reredorter, it would be neatly consistent with the proposal that the cathedral hierarchy had a monastic model in mind when planning the vicars' new buildings.

Unfortunately we know next to nothing about the short range which seems to have closed off the first courtyard because it lay below the road called Bedern, but to the south of it a second east-west range was constructed before the end of the 13th century (Fig. 13.3). It was not as large a building as the 'dormitory' on the other side of the court, but it was still quite substantial. The north and west walls of the building were not found but the remains we have indicate a structure at least 30m long and probably 7m wide. Again it was timber-framed, and had a line of posts down the centre of the undercroft. It is hard to see this as anything other than a two-storey building, consisting of an open undercroft below an open hall. The undercroft space was rapidly subdivided around the posts and, at least at this lower level, it seems that the eastern part of the building (east of the cross range) soon functioned as a separate structure. A clue to the building's original function may be provided by the apparent presence of a kitchen to the west, between here and the later site of the chapel. The references to this kitchen date from several generations later, in 1360 (Rees-Jones and Richards 2001, 575), but kitchens are amongst the less mobile buildings in such medieval complexes and it is possible that the kitchen was on this site long before its location was specified in the documents. If the kitchen was established on this site during the first phase of development, then we might expect this range along the south side of the courtyard to have contained the dining hall of the vicars. Certainly this favoured site, along the south side of the court, became the location for at least two later common halls (below).

Halls in which the vicars dined and conducted community business are thought to have been an important early requirement of the English colleges. Such a hall seems to have been amongst the earliest structures constructed at Lincoln, for example – although, as at York, the Lincoln hall on the south side of Vicars' Court seems to be later in date than the common dormitory on the north side. Unfortunately there are no references at York to a specific building called the common hall until 1319, but such a building is likely to have been provided at a date earlier in the life of the college (*ibid.*, 580–2). The archaeology suggests, indeed, that it followed about a generation after the construction of the dormitory, in the later 13th century, perhaps around 1280. The vicars' Chamberlains' Rolls report that the hall included cellars in 1328, and the archaeological evidence suggests that they were present from its first con-

struction (*ibid.*, 581). In its first phase the substantial first-floor hall indicated here would presumably have communicated internally with other first-floor chambers along the east side of the court. In such a layout, the vicars might have passed from the 'high table' end of the first-floor hall (i.e. opposite the kitchen) directly through the east range to the first-floor hall in the dormitory block. Although a reference to the monastic rule may have been intended in the initial character of the dormitory itself, its formal relationship to the common hall was that of the private chamber to the hall in secular households. We should presume that the proposed common hall was planned at the outset of the college, however, and that this relationship between the dormitory and the dining hall was intended from the start.

This putative common hall had a range of further service buildings to the south. Here a contemporary timber-framed building lasted for about a century, although rebuilt and altered many times. This building (Building 10) evidently accommodated a variety of service functions and, perhaps, workshops, for it contained at least one elaborate hearth, deposits of pure sand and, perhaps, clay moulds, all of which in concert suggest metal-working (Richards 2001, 422, 427–8).

The college between c.1300 and 1360

The results from the Bedern excavations show that the college buildings were in a constant state of change, with alterations often being undertaken very shortly after completion. It is quite possible, for example, that changes in the great dormitory were undertaken before work was completed on the putative common hall. Certainly by the 1330s the dormitory had undergone profound changes in its ground floor, which must suggest changes in the way in which it was used (Fig. 13.4). Most significant in this period (Period 5) is the clear evidence in the dormitory undercroft for a thoroughgoing re-design of the building. The undercroft was completely reorganised to provide a series of chambers of various sizes opening off internal corridors. This is also a development one sees, of course, in many monastic, and especially hospital, dormitories, but in this case the newly-established ground-floor cubicles were relatively large. Furthermore, it seems clear from the survival of hearths in these cubicles that they were occupied as dwellings. We can also presume that similar chambers were also created at first-floor level. For the first time, accommodation was available at both ground and first floor.

This process, which was evidently taking place in the early 14th century, must have gradually turned the great open dormitory at York into something very like the stone buildings at Lincoln, where each vicar

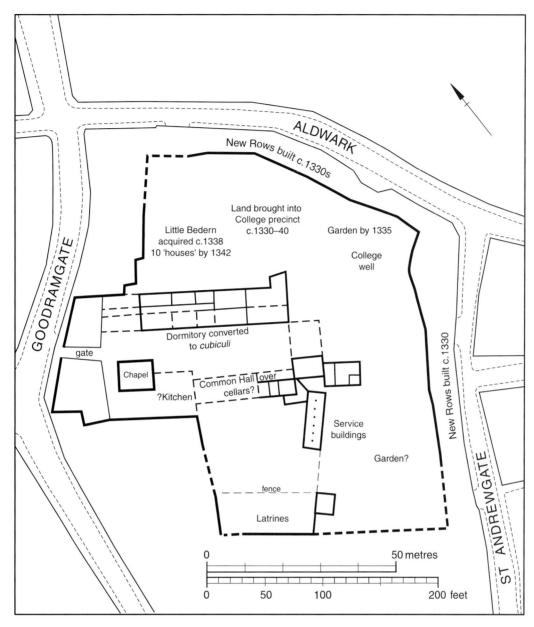

Fig. 13.4. Vicars choral of York Minster. Reconstruction of layout of college c.1300–60 (source, ed. Richards 2001, period 5. Drawing, Lesley Collett, copyright YAT)

had his individual chamber accessed from a common corridor. No doubt these are the *cubiculi* of which we hear a great deal in the 14th-century York documentation (Rees Jones and Richards 2001, 539, 579–80). Taking the average dimensions of the excavated examples, and presuming that they existed on both floors, the old dormitory building might have held as many as twenty-four chambers following its reconstruction. One of the ground-floor chambers along the north side contained a latrine pit, however, and this might suggest that each vicar was allocated more than one chamber (perhaps a dwelling chamber and a garderobe – as at Lincoln). On this basis, once rebuilt, the old dormitory block could not have held many more than twelve vicars. Perhaps it was

pressure on space caused by this rebuilding, reflecting an improvement in the facilities allocated to each individual vicar, which stimulated the college to acquire, finally, the plot of land called 'Little Bedern' *c.*1338 and, by 1342, to construct ten 'houses' on it (Rees Jones 2001, 390). This would bring the accommodation capacity on the north side of the close up to around twenty vicars – still short of the 36 spaces nominally required. However, the surviving rentals of these houses indicate that the tenants were not vicars (Nigel Tringham *pers comm*).

There also seems to have been a period in the early 14th century when there was no building attached to the east end of the dormitory and during which it was shortened by at least three bays. This phase seems to coincide with clear documentary and structural evidence for the construction of a deliberately designated latrine area, carefully fenced in but mostly in the open air, along the southern boundary of the site (Rees Jones and Richards 2001, 576–7). The principle of this communal facility was not lost, then, rather it was relocated. In its new location, however, it must have been a considerable inconvenience as it is a long way from the dormitory. It may be that this latrine was exclusively for the college servants, whilst those vicars with *cubiculi* used newly-partitioned private chambers.

Somewhat later on, perhaps in the mid 14th century, and allocated to Period 6 in the report (Richards 2001, 253–4, 449–5), the old dormitory block re-acquired a reredorter-like building to the east (Fig. 13.6). The possibility that this was a latrine block was not investigated during excavation, and there is no internal evidence to support this identification. By the second half of the 14th century, however, we have documentary evidence to suggest that the main latrine block for the college was known as 'the longhouse' (*ibid.*, 577) and the building east of the dormitory fits this description perfectly. There are continuous references to a longhouse from the 14th through to the 19th century, but the connection between the structure east of the dormitory and the longhouse in the documents was not made during the post-excavation process. This was because a diagram of 1851, drawn up when the whole area was being redeveloped, labelled a building close to Aldwark, well outside the area of excavations, as the longhouse (*ibid.*, 577, 636) and, understandably, this building has been equated with the 14th-century building. But the 14th-century structure east of the old dormitory was demolished during the 15th century (*ibid.*, 590), and it is not until the mid 15th century that we hear that the longhouse was located to the north-east of the college buildings, in a similar location to that shown in the 1851 plan. It is quite possible, then, that our documentary references to a longhouse could refer to two distinct buildings on two different sites. The 14th-century references could relate to the excavated building at the east end of the old dormitory, whilst later references, subsequent to this building's demolition, may refer to a second longhouse in the garden to the north-east, which replaced it and which was recorded in 1851. If the building built east of the old dormitory was the first longhouse, we might suggest that it was intended for the use of the vicars with *cubiculi* on the first floor.

If this is a correct understanding of the sequence and function of these latrine sites and buildings, they may point towards an increasing social stratification within the college. During the first half of the 14th century, apparently, some inhabitants used an open communal latrine, a long way from the dormitory,

although near the service buildings; these may well have been the college servants. Some of the vicars, perhaps those living in *cubiculi* on the first floor of the old dormitory block, may have used a communal purpose-built latrine at the east end of the building – the first longhouse. But other vicars, living on the ground floor, seem to have had their own individual garderobes adjoining their *cubiculi*. We are probably on safe ground if we argue that the social status of individuals using the out-door latrine at the southern end of the service yard was lower than that of those using facilities in the old dormitory. But did the different latrine arrangements on the two floors of the old dormitory mark a distinction between vicars of differing seniority?

The gradual conversion of the old dormitory into *cubiculi*, with all the implications that has for the rising status of the vicars, and perhaps also for their departure from the quasi-monastic ideals with which they had been first established, was only one element in the redesign of the college. The precinct as a whole was reorganised in the 1330s and the land behind the Aldwark street front, previously owned by the vicars but in private occupation, was now brought into the close (Fig. 13.4). A great garden had been laid out in the eastern part of the new land by 1335, which probably extended southwards to the southern boundary behind the vicars' buildings. Outside the new close boundary, which was probably marked by a continuous wall, the vicars rebuilt the properties along the Aldwark and St Andrewgate street fronts, replacing the mixed population of tenements, which they had acquired piecemeal, with long 'rows' built explicitly for rent (ed. Tringham, 1993, nos. 20, 467 and 468). This substantial exercise in speculative commercial development demonstrates, in itself, how rapidly the vicars college had developed as an institution.

And in the 1340s, for the first time, we think the college acquired a notable marker of its rising institutional importance – a private chapel. Not all English vicars colleges succeeded in ever acquiring this particular status symbol. We know that Exeter never acquired a chapel and neither, probably, did Lincoln (p.38 and p.78 above). Furthermore, the Chichester vicars always shared the chapel of St Faith, which stood outside their precinct, with other bodies in the close (p.27–8 above), and the Hereford, Wells and Lichfield vicars did not get theirs until very much later (p.117 and p.65 above). With a foundation date in the 1340s (Stocker 2001, 553–5), the York chapel is another early example of a very rare building type, although not an especially impressive one. Before its partial demolition in 1961 the building survived in an enlarged form dating from nearer the end of the 14th century, but in its first phase it was a tiny structure (Fig. 13.5). Yet

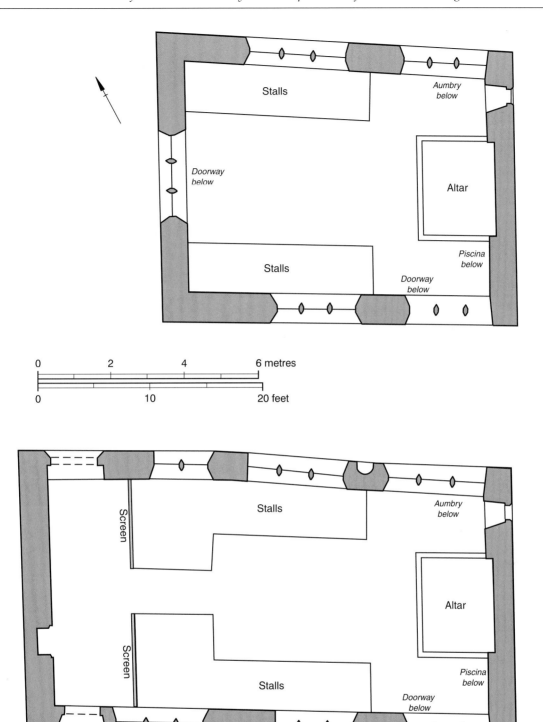

Fig. 13.5. Vicars choral of York Minster. Plans of the two phases of the vicars' chapel: above c.1340, below, following enlargement c.1370 (source, Stocker 2001, fig. 314. Drawing, Lesley Collett, copyright YAT)

although it was not an impressive building, the chapel had become the location of a chantry (*ibid.*, 555), and by the end of the 14th century it seems to have had a rich range of fittings. There was a superb set of stalls, although there must remain some question whether they were actually made for this building (*ibid.*, 549), and there was a fine sequence of historiated windows which, fortunately, were re-corded before they were lost at the start of the 19th century (O'Connor 2001). Probably the craftsmen employed to produce the stalls and the glass were employees of the dean and chapter loaned to the college. Moreover, like most masonry used in the Bedern college, that used to build the chapel was derived from demolitions and rebuilding work at the cathedral (Stocker 1999). The masonry was presumably given as alms by the canons – a gesture that emphasised, symbolically, the dependence of the vicars on the canons and the college itself on the Minster.

By the 1340s there had also been considerable alteration and reconstruction to the south range of the courtyard, but it is not clear from the excavation results whether this involved the reconstruction of the common hall. The hall itself may have been relocated to the east of the excavated area during this period, or it may be that the great complexity of the changes in the undercroft were not reflected in the hall above. The buildings further to the south continued to develop and the long service or work-shop range was reconstructed as a substantial two-storeyed hall with a row of central posts supporting the floor of the upper storey. During this phase there was evidence in the shape of a barrel stand and a brazier to suggest that craft activities continued there.

All the college's service buildings, no less than the domestic ones, underwent more or less continual adaptation and it is hard to pick out moments of comprehensive re-planning. Nevertheless, it seems clear that there was a decisive period in the 1330s and 1340s, when there was a major reorganisation of the college precinct. This reorganisation seems to be somewhat later in date than the division of the dormitory into *cubiculi*, but that division may have been a protracted process; the re-planning of the precinct might have been the inevitable result of a growing pressure on space, brought about by the allocation of more room within the dormitory to individual vicars. These re-organisations in the first half of the 14th century amount to a major change in the institutional emphasis of the college itself. In architectural terms, the college is no longer to be seen merely as the common dormitory for the cathedral, following a monastic inspiration. Now the vicars and their patrons wish to present the college as a self-contained institution with its own chapel, and running its own financial affairs which generate the wealth to support vicars living in some style, with their own servants, perhaps, and with their own individual rooms which have facilities that vary according to each vicars' status.

The close of vicars' houses c. 1360–1547

It is perilous to pick out further phases of general re-planning within the Bedern and distinguish them from routine repair and alteration, but nevertheless it is possible to identify within the excavation results a second round of re-organisation in the 1360s and 1370s (Periods 6 and 7). The two periods may represent the same planned building campaign spread over twenty years, or they may represent two quite distinct spells of activity, but in either case the result was another profound change in the character of the college.

The earlier parts of this phase (Period 6: Fig. 13.6) saw considerable tidying up of the east and south sides of the courtyard. There may have been a time when there was no eastern range to the court at all, but that state of affairs can't have lasted long and the range was reconstructed, along with a new east–west building lying to its east (Buildings 17 and 24). At this time, also, the site of the common hall was shifted to the south, making the court larger and closer to a square in plan. The excavation did not extend into the western part of this court area, but we should ask whether the intention at this time was to create a completely enclosed court, possibly even with a cloister walk, or something which imitated it. References to the walks around the edge of the courtyard occur frequently in the college records, although they start in the early 14th century (Richards 2001, 578).

We know very little about the timber hall that was put up along the new southern boundary of the court c.1360. It sat directly beneath its stone replace-ment (which was not excavated), but we can glean basic information from its surviving east wall and the excavated remains of its service block (Building 25). The fact that it was erected on a new site to the south of the earlier hall(s) probably suggests that the latter continued in use whilst it was being construct-ed, but the most distinctive change compared with its predecessors to the north was that it was re-orientated. Whereas it seems clear that the service end of the earlier halls was towards the west, the new hall had its service end towards the east. And, although the kitchen is mentioned in its old location, immediately east of the chapel, in 1360 (*ibid.*, 575), it must have been removed almost immediately after-wards to the south-east of the new hall, beside the new service block. This new timber common hall must have been short-lived. It seems to have stood for no more than 10 years, as it was replaced by the surviving stone building, on almost precisely the same footprint, in the early 1370s. Why the new timber hall was replaced so rapidly is not under-stood. Perhaps the most likely explanation is that some part of it was accidentally damaged in some way, perhaps by a fire, and accidental damage rather than deliberate re-planning may be implied by the fact that the footprint of the timber hall was re-plicated very closely by its successor. One altern-ative to the theory that the timber hall was rapidly replaced by the stone hall through damage to the former, of course, is that this haste was related to yet further, urgent, self-aggrandisement. To support this latter view we should note that, at approximately the same moment that the hall was reconstructed in

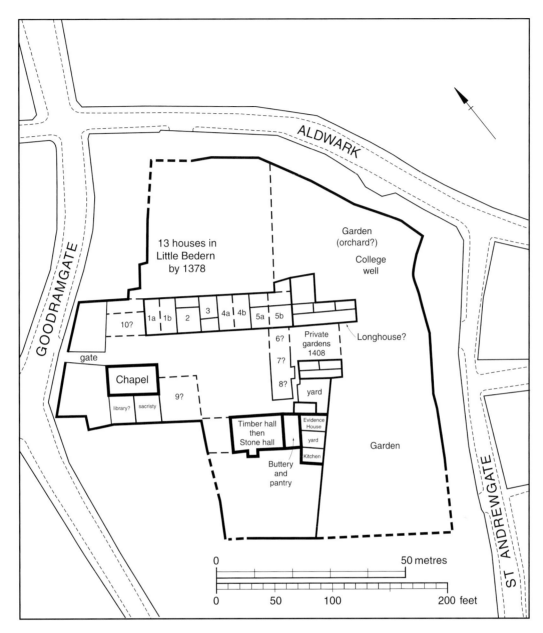

Fig. 13.6. Vicars choral of York Minster. Reconstruction of layout of college c.1360–90 (source, ed. Richards 2001, periods 6 and 7. Drawing, Lesley Collett, copyright YAT)

stone, the remains of the old dormitory building were also comprehensively reconstructed (below).

The archaeological evidence for the replacement of the timber hall with the surviving stone example is relatively clear. In the winter or spring of 1369–70 roof timbers for the new stone hall were being felled (Hillam 2001) and we can presume that the present stone hall building was under construction then or shortly afterwards (Fig. 13.7). The new building enclosed the east wall of the earlier timber-framed hall and re-used the service range of which it formed a part, no doubt because these were themselves relatively new facilities, but otherwise it was a relatively magnificent new building compared with the others in the close (Fig. 13.8). It had an elaborate

Fig. 13.7. Vicars choral of York Minster. Bedern Hall c.1370, from the north-west, following restoration (photo Simon I Hill, copyright YAT)

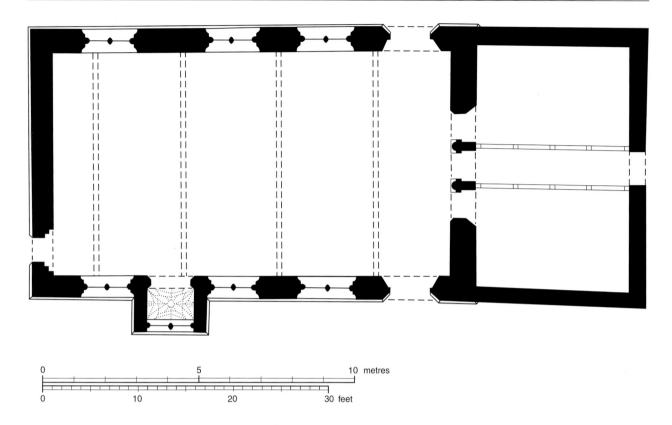

0   5   10   metres

0   10   20   30 feet

Fig. 13.8. Vicars choral of York Minster. Reconstruction of plan of stone hall and earlier service building, c.1370 (drawing Simon Chew, copyright YAT)

and beautifully designed roof, dramatic (if rather peculiar) window tracery and, most spectacularly, it has what seems to be the earliest firmly-dated stone-vaulted bay window in England. The designs for this bay (and perhaps all the hall's other architectural details) were probably made by Robert of Patrington, the Minster master mason, whilst the carving is from the hand of the best carver in the Minster workshop – the man who was also responsible for the carving of the tabernacle-work on the new Minster east end (Stocker 2001, 595).

The bay window has an interest beyond the local (Fig. 13.9). Although negatives are never easy to establish conclusively, research has yet to reveal an earlier, securely dated, example of a bay window of this type lighting the high table of a hall. The remains of an archway into a bay window survive at the Merchant Taylor's Hall in London, built following 1347 (John Schofield *pers comm*), and if the bay window was an original feature and not added later (as many bay windows were), this would seem to be an earlier example. There is, however, no evidence that the bay at the Merchant Taylor's was stone-vaulted. In the survey report it was suggested that this feature at Bedern Hall was intended to house a pulpit and a service (a sideboard on which meals were organised) because the vicars' statutes required that they were read to by one of their brethren

during meals and served by a second (*ibid.*, 594, 596–7). If it is true that this distinctive architectural feature was designed at York to cater for these specific activities, laid down in the vicars' statutes, then we might expect similar features at the other vicars' colleges. And indeed the halls at Lichfield (Tringham 1990, 64), Chichester and Wells (p.25 and p.124–7 above) all had such features. An argument can be made from the fabric that the hall at Exeter might have had such a feature, although John Allen believes that more credible alternative explanations can be given for the straight joins and transverse gable seen in the south wall of the Exeter hall prior to its destruction in 1943 (p.34 above). The structure of the vicars' halls at Lincoln, London, the first college at Hereford and Salisbury have not been investigated to the extent where such a feature would be revealed. Nevertheless, of the known vicarial examples, the York example is the earliest. Furthermore, as no certain examples have yet been found in other classes of hall dating from before 1370, it is even possible that the feature, having been first developed for a specific purpose at colleges of vicars choral, subsequently became fashionable across society more widely. Certainly, in the 15th century such windows became the norm at the high table end of almost all types of hall, and we should ask whether it is credible that the vicars choral in

may have been intended to house an organ or, perhaps, provide a platform for a band of musicians or the singing of responses. The apparent functions of the extension, then, indicate not increasing numbers of vicars attending services in the chapel but an increasing sophistication in the dramatic content of services undertaken – and thus, perhaps, the vicars' increasing liturgical skills and status within the cathedral community. Furthermore, this new structure communicated with buildings to the south, which may have included a library, like those at Wells, Exeter and Hereford (Rodwell 1982, 221, 224–5; Chanter 1933, 6–7; Morriss and Shoesmith 1995, 165) – another status symbol demonstrating the increasing sophistication of the college. A further sign of the college's developing sense of its own importance at the time is the construction of an 'evidence house', which was probably the structure excavated to the east of the hall and service range (Building 27). This building was also in stone and had unusual limited access arrangements so that it could be made secure; it had been constructed at the end of the 14th century or at the start of the 15th. An evidence house is first mentioned in the college documents in 1419, 22, by which time it had been standing long enough for repairs to be necessary (Richards 2001, 576). Here the vicars stored their valuables, and also documents relating to their extensive property portfolio, discussed by Dr Rees Jones in chapter 16 below.

Fig. 13.9. Vicars choral of York Minster. Reconstruction of the stone-vaulted bay window in south wall of Bedern Hall (drawing Simon Chew, copyright YAT)

York and elsewhere were sufficiently influential socially to popularise such an esoteric design detail amongst the building classes.

The grand new stone Bedern Hall conveys a sense of rising self-importance amongst the vicars, and the contrast with the cheaply built, cramped and poorly designed chapel, now thirty years old, would have been marked. It is not wholly surprising, then, that at about the same time as they began the reconstruction of the hall in stone, the vicars extended the chapel a further bay to the west (Figs. 13.5 and 13.10). Yet this was not done so that they would have more room to perform services – the space available within the chapel proper remained the same. The extension was entirely occupied with a new antechapel, and a loft over. The antechapel was presumably used for forming up processions and other comparable functions, and an aumbry in its west wall may indicate that it was used for storing service books. The loft

Fig. 13.10. Vicars choral of York Minster. Bedern chapel from north-east c.1960, prior to partial demolition (photo and copyright, English Heritage)

In 1396, right at the end of this period of institutional expansion and aggrandisement, the vicars applied to the king for a licence to build a bridge across Goodramgate (*Cal Pat Roll* 1391–6, 712), although we have no evidence that it was ever built (Richards 2001, 540). The bridge has frequently been interpreted as evidence of concern that vicars might be 'corrupted' as they passed through Goodramgate on their way from the college to the Minster, and indeed the licence was expressed in these terms. But seen against the near-contemporary self-aggrandising construction projects going on in the Bedern, it may be better viewed as evidence that the vicars wished to emphasise their exclusiveness and their connection with the rarefied world of the Close, rather than with the city, in the midst of which they were located. The bridge was to extend from the 'solar above the gate', which indicates that the medieval gatehouse was a two-storey structure (at the least). Strangely, we have very little evidence that the York vicars' college was ever approached through a major gatehouse. Such buildings were the most obvious opportunity for institutions to put on a brave public face, and it was an opportunity taken by many of the English colleges of vicars. We know that Lincoln, Wells, Exeter, Hereford and Chichester all provided their closes with distinguished gatehouses and Warwick Rodwell points out that there is room for a missing gatehouse in centre of the east range of the lower court at Lichfield (p.68–70 above). An imposing gatehouse offered the opportunity for displays of heraldry to demonstrate both the pride of patrons and the powerful allegiances on which the college could rely, and, consequently, its absence at York would be surprising. The present building on the gatehouse site, however, is said to date from the late 16th or early 17th century (RCHME 1981, 136) and it is possible that a more elaborate gatehouse was demolished to make way for it. The topographical map of York of 1610 published by John Speed (in 1616) seems to show a generic tower at the point where the Bedern gatehouse should stand and this may represent, however schematically, the medieval gatehouse of the college.

At approximately the same moment that the hall was being rebuilt in stone, the chapel extended and the evidence house built, the vicars' accommodation was also comprehensively reconstructed. This reconstruction in the shell of the old dormitory building, also partly in stone, was not intended to re-arrange the cubicles but to create independent houses, which the documentation suggests were probably of two storeys (Richards 2001, 579). Here at York between about 1360 and about 1390, then, we see a comprehensive rebuilding intended to bring the vicars' accommodation up to a similar standard to that seen in the close at Wells, begun in 1348. At last the individual vicars of York have reached the status, in their own eyes at least, where they should each be accorded their own individual house, with separate front door and all the symbolism of 'household' which that implied.

The excavations identified what seem to be the remains of at least five, and perhaps as many as eight, houses fashioned out of the old dormitory block (Fig. 13.6). The two buildings at the south end of the east side of the courtyard were probably houses as well, and an early 15th-century agreement suggest that there were three houses here (*ibid.*, 580). Once the old kitchen had been moved from east of the chapel to the service area south-east of the new hall, the former kitchen site became available and may have been occupied by a new vicarial house – as might the space between the old dormitory and the street range on Goodramgate. In this way we can count perhaps thirteen to fifteen houses in the main close, and we have documentary evidence that there were a further thirteen houses in 'Little Bedern' (outside the area of excavation) by 1378 (Rees Jones 2001, 390). This brings the total number of individual houses at Bedern to about 26, which would make the college about the same size as Exeter (which had about twenty-five houses), somewhat smaller than the 28 house close at Chichester and much smaller than the 41 house close at Wells. Although the twenty vicars who were reported by the chantry commissioners at York in 1546 could have all been housed within houses identified in this way, this was at least ten houses short of the full complement of 36 vicars, and it is possible that further accommodation existed within the close, perhaps in buildings grouped around a subsidiary courtyard to the south-east of the old dormitory block. As Sarah Rees Jones points out, however, there is no reason to think that all the vicars lived in the Bedern (Rees Jones and Richards 2001, 580). Occasionally some seem to have lived in other vicars' properties elsewhere in the city, and a number were accommodated in a complex of buildings owned by the vicars known as 'Cambhall Garth' on the west side of Goodramgate (*ibid.*, 580), which was rebuilt as a courtyard of houses in the early 1360s (ed. Tringham 1993, 99–100, no.162).

The second half of the 14th century was the high point in the fortunes of the York college and it is not co-incidental that these major building campaigns are contemporary with a period of substantial reform and re-organisation within the college itself (Rees Jones 2001, 384). From this date on, however, the archaeological record depicts an institution in a state of gentle decline. The only major new building later than *c*.1400 took place in the now fully developed service court to the south of the new stone hall and south and west of the new kitchen (Fig. 13.11). The court was established around a new well dug in 1401 and it contained a variety of service buildings including, probably, the brewhouse. However, the vicars' accommodation itself shrank through the 15th century. The eastern end of the old dormitory block was brought further westwards and re-organisations within this shortened building seem to have reduced the plan area of each individual vicar's house to a more uniform 5m by 12m (60 sq. m). We have seen that each house had two floors, each presumably with a room this size, suggesting that each house had a total floor area of about 120 sq. m, and this means that the York vicars were accommodated spaciously, compared with those at all the other English colleges. At Wells each vicar lived in approximately 64 sq. m, whilst at Chichester the figure was nearer 48 sq. m.

At Exeter each vicar had something like 54 sq. m, and although at Lincoln vicars retained their *cubiculi* and never acquired houses, the grandest chamber there contained about 74 sq. m. Does this considerably larger floor area available in each house to the York vicars suggest that they lived two to a house? Certainly this might explain the many subdivisions found within these structures during the excavation. It would also help to account for the fact that, following the final phase of re-development at the end of the 14th century, the York vicars still seem to have been some ten houses short of the number needed to accommodate their entire complement.

The post-medieval history of the college is even more richly documented than the medieval era and

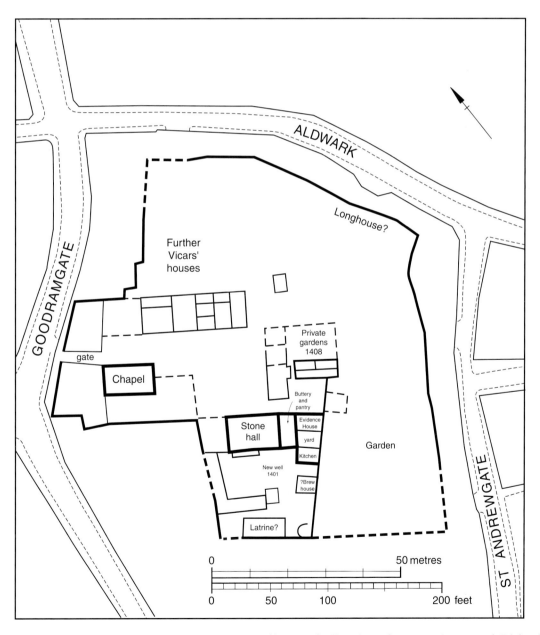

Fig. 13.11. Vicars choral of York Minster. Reconstruction of layout of college in 15th century (source, ed. Richards 2001, period 8. Drawn by Lesley Collett, copyright YAT)

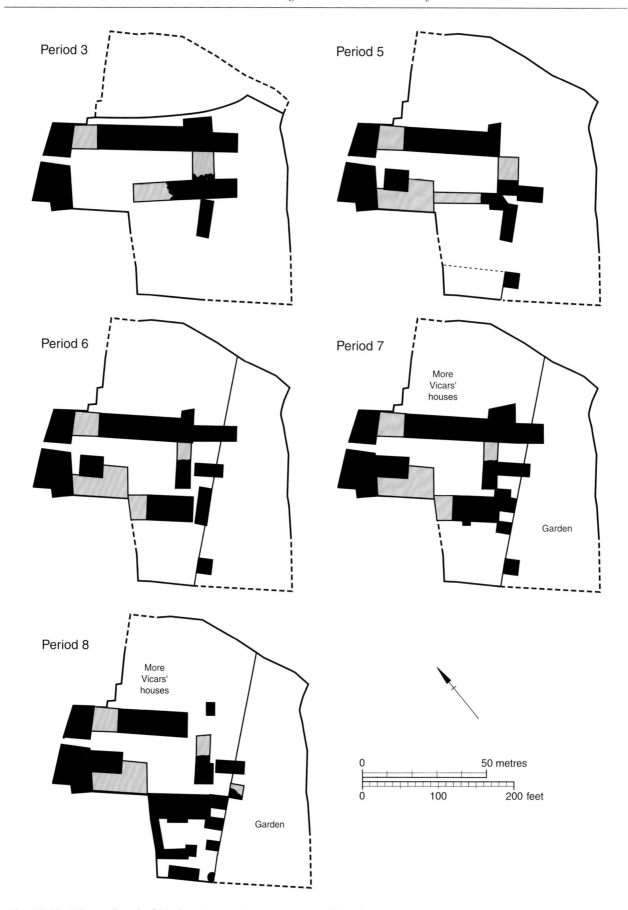

Fig. 13.12. Vicars choral of York Minster. Reconstruction of development of the precinct from c.1250 to 1547. The periodization refers to the excavation report (source, ed. Richards 2001. Drawn by Lesley Collett, copyright YAT)

both the documentation and the archaeology of this period has been summarised very carefully and fully in the excavation report. Like most of the other colleges, it is a story of decline, with fewer and fewer resident vicars living in larger and larger houses, with property let out to secular occupants and with a decline and extinction of the common life. At York, dining in common ceased in 1574, although the hall was still used for collegiate functions until at least 1628 and the chapel continued in use as a chapel of ease into the 20th century.

Conclusion

Although we are inclined to think that the colleges of vicars choral all resembled the surviving examples at Wells and Chichester, Hereford and Lincoln, the York excavations showed quite clearly that this is a misleading impression. York only reached this classic, late-medieval, layout of individual houses around a tight close, with a chapel and a hall, after 150 years of progressive development (Fig. 13.12). In its earliest stages, with its notable dormitory, the concept of collegiate life was clearly quite different from that which it later became, and York is unlikely to have been the only college which went through this early phase of dormitory living. Similarly, York went through a second, intermediate, stage during which the vicars occupied individual rooms (*cubiculi*), a layout which persisted in Lincoln until the end of the middle ages, before it finally evolved into a similar type of institution to those we can still see at Wells, Chichester and Hereford. These 'classic' colleges, then, represent only the final stages in an evolutionary pattern. Presumably they also retain a more complex history of development and evolution in their buried archaeology. But it is not the complex houses of the York Bedern, which were rebuilt and rebuilt over and over again, and which might have told us something more of this sequence of development in the college, that have come down to us. Instead, it is the two buildings which expressed the corporate identity of the college in the late middle ages that we can still see today, the hall and the chapel. And, although these two buildings have now been put in their correct, and complex, context by the survey and excavation work, perhaps the vicars themselves would have been content with the image of corporate simplicity, solidity and permanence that they still project.

14

'Wine, Women and Song': Artefacts from the Excavations at the College of Vicars Choral at The Bedern, York

Nicola Rogers

As so often, the title of this paper was conceived before the work was completed, and I was initially concerned that the impression of high living it conveys might not be borne out by the archaeological remains. However, as several of the other papers have noted, there are numerous documentary references to 'wine, women and song' in the lives of vicars choral, and a study of the artefacts recovered from excavations at the Bedern in York confirms that all three temptations were encountered here from time to time. This paper aims to discuss some of the most significant and interesting artefacts from an assemblage of over 3100 objects, many of which have already been published in several of the *Archaeology of York* fascicules (Volume 17 – especially Ottaway and Rogers 2002).

Craft and industry in the college and nearby

The 1970s excavations at Bedern (chapter 13 above) revealed a foundry along the southern boundary of the York college of vicars choral. In particular a large timber-framed building was recovered which had been used for non-ferrous metal working from the 13th to the 16th century, apparently producing vessels and bells and possibly other non-ferrous artefacts (Richards 1993). The foundry lay south of the college's precinct boundary, but nevertheless, there might have been connections between the two sites and manufacturing debris, of the sort produced by the foundry, was also found within the college. Some of it, particularly fragments of discarded or unfinished metal vessels, was concentrated in the south-west area, nearest the foundry, and there are other indications of material moving both ways across the boundary. Furthermore, the identification of a number of strips and bars suggests that some

working of copper and lead alloys definitely did take place inside the college precinct itself.

Other types of evidence for the casting of non-ferrous metal were also recovered from within the college, including fragments of crucibles in which the metal was melted, and also two chalk, 'multi-piece' casting moulds, both from 13th-century deposits (Fig. 14.1). These moulds apparently utilised both faces for casting various small decorative items, including beads, and they were probably used with metals of low melting-point, such as lead/tin alloys like pewter. Analysis of clay moulds indicated the casting of small artefacts in non-ferrous alloys. Unfortunately, no objects that could have been produced in any of these moulds was found, but some failed castings of other small metal objects were recovered, some at the foundry, and some within the college (Fig. 14.2). These castings are of metal fittings for belts that were never finished, as they still retain the casting flashes (i.e. extraneous metal extensions produced during the casting process and removed during the finishing process). A site nearby at St Andrewgate produced similar unfinished castings from similarly dated contexts of the 15th and 16th centuries (Finlayson 2004, 920–1).

Some of the metalworking debris, however, may have been left over from building works at the college. Both documentary and archaeological evidence shows that building work was more or less continuous on the site. There is some slight evidence of iron-working amongst the finds from the college, mainly in the form of bars, strips and plates, some of which are probably fragments of unidentifiable finished objects, but some of which are likely to be offcuts (or partly forged) items from the smithing process. Of particular interest is a very large misshapen bar (245mm in length) which is probably freshly smelted iron intended for use in a smithy. No smithy is known from documentary sources in the college, but smithing probably took place from time to time to service construction works. The bar comes from a late 14th- or early 15th-century context.

Ironsmithing tools used in metalworking were also found, including a pair of tongs, a basic smithing tool used for holding pieces of metal at all stages in the fabrication process (Fig. 14.3 a). Also found were a hammerhead, likely to have been used in non-ferrous metalworking, and punches of both tanged and non-tanged types (Fig. 14.3 b & c). The very large non-tanged type of punch was held in the hand but smaller examples were gripped below the head by tongs or wires, to protect the smith from the heat of the metal. Tanged punches had one arm set in a wooden handle whilst the other served as the working blade – similar tools were used by carpenters and by stonemasons. The incomplete blade of a metalworking file was also recovered (Fig. 14.4) as was a chisel which could have been used for either metalworking or wood-working. Like the bar iron, most of these tools come from later 14th- or 15th-century deposits.

Tools used in building work were also found. Two trowels, of similar form and also from later 14th or early 15th-century contexts, are of a type used by masons, bricklayers or plasterers (Fig. 14.5). Each has a cranked tang and a large triangular blade suitable for spreading mortar or plaster; one trowel was found in a mortar floor in Building 16. Two lead alloy plumb-bobs were also recovered – one from levels associated with the construction of a residential building (Building 11) in the late 13th or early 14th century (Fig. 14.6).

A total of twenty-one lead points, similar to pencils, were found at the college (Fig. 14.7), and although some may have been used in manuscript preparation (see below), an analysis of their forms and their find spots suggested that nineteen were more likely to have been used by craftsmen such as carpenters (Ottaway and Rogers 2002, 2936). At least five of these points were recovered from deposits associated with the construction of residential buildings during the 13th century.

Woodworking tools recovered include five spoon augers, used for boring or enlarging holes in wood and one of the medieval woodworker's most important tools (Fig. 14.8 a & b). Twelve wedges of various sizes were also recovered; these would be used for tree-felling, splitting wood and (in the case of the small ones) for securing wooden handles on iron tools (Fig. 14.8 c & d). Another tool fragment from a mid 14th- to early 15th-century context represents an incomplete saw blade with set teeth (Fig. 14.8 e). Other tools point to craft activities associated with the needs of the residents themselves. Leather-working for example is indicated by discovery of seven awls (Fig. 14.9), perhaps used in cobbling and the repairing of shoes and other leather items, and garments.

In addition to awls, several other types of tool used in textile production were recovered. These include part of a wool comb, used to straighten and align wool fibres prior to spinning, found in a 15th-century deposit (Fig. 14.10 a). There were also numerous iron spikes, which will have come either from wool combs or from flax heckles, used to process flax into fine individual filaments ready for spinning (Fig. 14.10 b & c). Spindle whorls, lathe-turned from chalk and limestone were found to be especially light, suggesting they were used for some very fine spinning (Fig. 14.11 a & b). Cutting and stitching was also carried out here – most of the iron and copper alloy needles are typical hand-sewing needles for ordinary needlework (Fig. 14.12 a & b). One copper alloy needle could be a sacking needle, and two copper alloy examples, with triangular sections at the tip, may have been used for leather. Four copper alloy thimbles were also recovered (Fig. 14.12 c & d), and two fragments from wooden beams found in late 14th- or 15th-century contexts may have been part of a frame for stretching an embroidery canvas (Fig. 14.13). Finally, nine pairs of iron shears were recovered, clustered in late 14th- and 15th-century deposits (Fig. 14.14 b). Shears were used for all sorts of household tasks, however, of which cutting cloth was just one. A pair of iron scissors, a comparative rarity in the medieval period, was also found in an early 14th-century deposit (Fig. 14.14 a). It seems, then, that the evidence points towards both yarn production and needlework at the college. These are the typical skills of the medieval housewife, and evidence for their presence at the college probably indicates that female domestic servants were working here. Here, then, are the women of my title.

A very commonly found iron tool type on all urban sites is the knife, and 66 were found in medieval deposits at Bedern. They are of various shapes and sizes and the collection includes a few particularly unusual examples. Two knives had incised and inlaid designs on their blades (Figs. 14.15 a & b and 14/16 a & b); the inlay has been identified as 'mercury-gilded silver' (Ottaway and Rogers 2002, 2756). Medieval knives inlaid with precious metals are not common, although other examples have come from London (Cowgill et al. 1987, 15). Their rarity may be an indication of the status and wealth of their owners, though we can't be certain that the Bedern knives actually belonged to vicars. Other unusual knives include an example from a mid 14th- to early 15th-century context with an inlaid cutler's mark (Fig. 14.15 c), and a possible folding knife, which was found in contexts of the same date. Like inlaid knives, folding knives are rare in medieval contexts, although two others, one in a boxwood case, have been found in London (*ibid.*, 106, nos. 309–10).

Used to keep knives sharp, a total of eighteen stone hones were recovered. Three were of local origin, but the remainder were made of stones possibly imported from Norway (Fig. 14.17). Such hones of metamorphic rock were first brought to this country by the Scandinavians in the 10th century and it was thought formerly that their use decreased from the 13th century onwards. However the hones found at Bedern represent part of the growing body of evidence indicating significant trade with Norway continuing from the Anglo-Scandinavian well into the medieval period in York. Apart from blades, the hones were also used to sharpen points of tools, such as needles and other craftsmen's tools.

Aside from knives the only cutlery recovered from Bedern was an unusual copper alloy spoon from a mid 14th-century post-hole in a residential building (Building 5) (Fig. 14.18 a). Metal spoons appear rarely in the medieval period; they would have been greatly outnumbered by wooden examples, although only one of these survived at Bedern (in a mid or late 13th-century context – Fig. 14.18 b). A few bowls and plates of wood were also found (Figs. 14.20 a & b) but undoubtedly many similar artefacts failed to survive deposition. Numerous non-ferrous metal vessels, on the other hand, of the type made at the foundry beyond the precinct south wall (above), were retrieved from the college and some of these may have been products of this foundry. The collection of such vessels includes fragments of three-legged skillets of 14th-century date (Fig. 14.19 a) and the leg of what may have been a 'tripod ewer' (Fig. 14.19 b). Other fragments were mainly from the rims or bodies of cast cooking vessels or dishes (Fig. 14.19 c-d).

Other domestic implements found at Bedern include mortars, used for pounding or grinding foodstuffs and other materials, perhaps including drugs. Fragments of twelve of these large durable stone vessels were found on the site (Fig. 14.21 a-b), as well as a possible pestle (Fig. 14.21 c). Most of the mortars are made of magnesian limestone, which is available locally, but the possible pestle and two of the mortars are probably of limestone from Dorset. Most of the mortars share features such as lugs and lips with runnels, as well as moulded projections and ribs on their exteriors; as well as providing strength to the mortar body, the ribs and lugs would have allowed the mortar to be let into a table top or bench and held firm, freeing both hands for grinding.

Domestic comforts in the college

Some of the most interesting artefacts found at Bedern are the remnants of glass vessels and cups – some of which may provide evidence for the wine of my title! In England, discovery of medieval glass vessels has been restricted to high-status sites, and the glass tends to be found in relatively small quantities, partly because it decays badly when buried. Glass of three types was made in this period – high-lead glass, soda glass and potash glass, and before *c.*1500, all high-quality table glass used in England was imported from the Continent. Manuscript illustrations of contemporary feasts suggest that glass drinking vessels were used in communal dining at this time, although it is likely that high-status vessels such as glass tablewares were restricted to the most important members of any given household or community. The Bedern excavations produced fragments from 48 glass vessels, including a stemmed goblet (Fig. 14.22 a), a jug or serving flask of yellow high-lead glass decorated with a painted trail in blue-green (Figs. 14.22 b, 14.23), two beakers with painted enamel decoration (Fig. 14.22 c-d), two colourless bowls with blue-trailed decoration (Fig. 14.22 e-f), and a blue painted bowl (Figs. 14.22g, 14.24). All these vessels date from the 13th and 14th centuries and the fragments from the jug or pouring flask were recovered in and around Building 10 – a service building close to the common hall. The stemmed goblet is represented by fragments from the lower part of the vessel's hollow stem, from the base, and from the rim, which is decorated with a blue trail. The vessel is of 13th- or early 14th-century date. Two fragments of colourless glass with enamelled decoration belong to a type of beaker also produced in the late 13th and early 14th century. The coloured enamel was painted on the inner and outer surfaces before firing in a kiln (Tyson 2000, 190). Often the decoration on such beakers included heraldic or religious scenes, and there is usually an inscription painted in a band around the lip .

The fragment of blue glass bowl comes from the flattened base in the centre of the vessel. This was ornamented with black painted decoration. A circular border with serrated outer edges contains a hexagram (or possibly a pentagram) within the border, which has foliate decoration within and between the points of the star. The centre of the star has not survived, but may have had additional decoration. Only two glass fragments with comparable decoration have been found in England, one in London, and the other from Weoley Castle, near Birmingham (Tyson 2000, 135–7, nos. g346–7), and no closely comparable vessels are known outside England. It is probable, however, that all three of these vessels are of western European maufacture, perhaps French, and were produced in the 13th century or the first half of the 14th century. There is little doubt that the York bowl would have been a distinctive and valuable vessel. Two more glass fragments come from very delicate colourless shallow bowls with a blue trail applied around the rim. Bowls of this type date from the late 13th and 14th centuries and may have been made in southern France or Italy.

Glass was also used at Bedern to make simple utilitarian vessels for lighting, storage, distilling and other industrial functions. These vessels were made of green potash glass at English glasshouses and it is likely that the vicars will have obtained such vessels from a relatively local source. Perhaps surprisingly, like decorated glass, utilitarian glass vessels are also found only on prosperous town sites, religious establishments, castles and manors. Fragments found at Bedern include a number of heavily weathered rim and base pieces of glass flasks and urinals. These distinctively shaped vessels were used in uroscopy, for examining the colour and consistency of urine – the principal method of medical diagnosis from the 13th to the 17th centuries (Fig. 14.25 a–c). Flasks with both wide and narrow necks had a variety of uses, including the preparation of herbal, alcoholic and medicinal recipes, and of colouring pigments. They were probably also used for general domestic purposes including storage, and possibly at table. On ecclesiastical sites some such vessels may have had liturgical uses. Such flasks are also sometimes found in combination with distilling equipment and a length of glass tubing from Bedern may have come from the spout of an alembic – the upper vessel in a distilling set (Fig. 14.25d). Glass and pottery distilling vessels were often used in combination and a number of pottery fragments recovered from Bedern have also been interpreted as parts of such apparatus (ed. Richards 2001, 402). Distillation was widely used in the preparation of alcoholic, herbal, medical and craft recipes. It is also known that distillation played a part in alchemy, which was practised in monasteries and castles (Tyson 2000, 168).

Dr Tyson concluded her report on medieval glass found at a group of York sites by saying, not only that the assemblage from York as a whole made the city one of the most significant British cities for this area of study, but also that 'some of the most prestigious decorative vessels of the 13th and 14th centuries were used at the college of vicars choral. The Bedern assemblage compares more closely with the glass from secular castles and palaces of the period than with the more abstinent monastic sites'. (eds. Ottaway and Rogers 2002, 2827).

Glass was also used to make medieval lighting equipment. Lamps would have been suspended from the ceiling by chains or by a harness around the base of the bowl, and fragments of such lamps were found at Bedern (Fig. 14.26 c & d). Substantial stone lamps were also recovered (Fig. 14.26 a & b). Both stone and glass types would have been filled with oil or fat, and were consequently more ex-

pensive than tallow candles or rush-lights. Both types are typical of ecclesiastical sites. More common, however, were lights supported by ferrous and non-ferrous metal structures. Iron candleholders were mounted in a wooden base, and came in various forms, two of which were seen at Bedern. The first has a socket (or cup) welded onto the head of a shank (Fig. 14.27a), whilst the second is the 'pricket', which has a spike on which the candle was impaled and two arms to hold it in place. In both types the tapering shank would have been inserted into the base to make the light stable. Another Bedern candleholder represents an unusual copper alloy type that is hinged and would fold up (Fig. 14.27 b). This came from an early 15th-century deposit in a building which was originally thought to be residential (Room 16A), but which Stocker now suggests may have been a reredorter (p.154 above). A socket from yet another type of candleholder represents an unusual two-branched candlestick, incorporating both pricket and sockets (Fig. 14.27c). This came from an early 14th-century internal deposit in a more clearly residential building (Building 11).

Security was clearly a preoccupation in the medieval period just as it is today, and fragments of both fixed door-locks and padlocks were found, the majority made of iron. One of the more unusual padlocks from the college is made of copper alloy, and has a swinging keyhole cover (Fig. 14.28 a). It was retrieved from an early 14th-century deposit in one of the buildings north of the common hall (Building 14), and was probably made for a casket. Two unusual small padlock keys of copper alloy were amongst the many keys for both fixed locks and padlocks and may have been designed for use in a padlock of this type (Fig. 14.28 b & c).

Clothing, accessories and activities

Buckles and brooches, being made of metal, always survive much better than the garments themselves, but (despite unfavourable soil conditions across most of the site) fragments of textiles were recovered from Bedern, mainly from the garden of the college and from the central area of the precinct. These fabrics included good-quality woollens, one a fragment of patterned wool textile with a narrow band of coloured stripes, from a mid or later 14th-century layer in a large cess-pit. This fabric seems to have been a Flemish import and was of a type often worn by the servants in wealthy households, as part of their livery. It may represent, then, the clothing of a male or female servant at the college. A linen fragment, probably made locally and perhaps from an undergarment, came from the college garden. It probably dates from the period between the mid

14th and early 15th centuries. More expensive fragments of silks and half-silks (i.e. textiles in which a silk weft has been combined with a linen warp yarn) were also found, as were the remains of two woven belts or straps from 15th-century deposits, and a silk cord from a 14th-century cess-pit. Unlike York excavations nearer the river Foss, such as Coppergate, soil conditions at Bedern ensured that very little leather was preserved. Only one medieval ankle boot was readily identifiable, recovered from an early or mid 13th-century deposit.

Metal fittings for belts, including buckles and their components (Fig. 14.29 a-q), belt loops (Fig. 14.30 a-g) and strap-ends (Fig. 14.31 a-g) were found in considerable numbers in the excavations, and exhibited a wide variety of forms and decoration. We have already seen that some strap-ends were incompletely finished, with unfinished spacer plates from composite strap-ends being found (see Fig. 14.31 f-g) and it is possible that the relatively large numbers of these and similar belt fittings result from their manufacture in the locality rather than from their use by those working in and around the college. Apart from the functional belt fittings, there were also numerous decorative fittings and mounts of various shapes that were applied to belts and straps (Fig. 14.32).

Although they were, of course, ornaments, medieval brooches had a more functional role than those we see today, being used also to hold garments together. Perhaps the most decorative was a small annular brooch of twisted, multi-strand, gold wire (Fig. 14.33a). This brooch was found in a mid to late 13th-century deposit outside a residential building (Building 9) and we can be sure that its original owner was someone of some wealth. A gilded silver brooch, found in a layer of mid or later 15th-century garden soil close to Building 27 (the 'evidence room' or library), is perhaps more likely to have been a vicar's personal possession (Fig. 14.33 b). It is inscribed with the standard formula *INRI* (for *Iesus Nazarenus Rex Iudeorum*) and may date from the 14th century. A second silver brooch was found in floor levels of mid 13th-century date (Fig. 14.33 c).

A beautiful gold ring set with a hexagonal blue sapphire in a closed setting was found in a mid 14th-century deposit in a residential building (Building 5) (Fig. 14.34). It was made in two parts; the head and shoulders and the shank are formed separately. Although a valuable ring, it has nevertheless been poorly finished, particularly at the junction between the shoulders and the shank (Fig. 14.35). Blue sapphires (Fig. 14.36) are found in the British Isles but have never been common, and the stone may possibly have come from Sri Lanka. Sapphire rings may have been particularly associated with ecclesiastics as at least a dozen have been found in the

graves of medieval bishops, some (if not all) being the ring with which the bishop was consecrated. An elaborate 13th-century example from York survives in the ring of Archbishop Walter de Gray (died 1255). Could the fine ring found at Bedern really have belonged to one of the vicars choral, or is it just too grand? We have to be cautious in ascribing possible owners to any objects found at the college. Although the vicars choral were resident, many other people worked here, and no doubt many more visited.

Some of these visitors may have come for the sport – we know, for example, that Rules of 1420–1 forbade games of chess and draughts, betting, gambling and throwing dice in the hall under a penalty of 3s. 4d. (p.190 below). The rules controlling gambling were clearly necessary because the excavations recovered numerous simply made counters (Fig. 14.37 a & b) and dice (Fig. 14.37 c), proving that games of chance were commonplace within the college, although none of the examples recovered were from the common hall.

Numerous horseshoes, several fragments of rowel spurs (Fig. 14.38 a & b) and bits from bridles (Fig. 14.38 c & d) show that residents and visitors alike were using horses. Several lengths of leather strap with decorative copper alloy mounts came from an early 15th-century pit in the college garden, and may be part of a harness (Figs. 14.39, 14.40). Also recovered were several harness pendants (Fig. 14.41), including a 13th- or 14th-century enamelled example with a white lion (Fig. 14.41 c), a commonly used heraldic device, and another enamelled mount possibly from a stirrup (Fig. 14.41 d).

The vicars' profession

It should be no surprise that objects associated with books and writing were recovered from the college. Bedern was not (so far as we know) a major centre of manuscript production, but a large archive of records written here does survive in the York Minster Library, and in the early 15th century the college erected a purpose-made building to house its documents (p.159 and p.190). Finds of two iron styli, one tin-plated (Fig. 14.42 a), twenty-two bone styli or parchment prickers (Fig. 14.42 b-h) and five bone ink pens (Fig. 14.42 i) testify to the fact that writing was being done here, and we have already seen that two lead points may also have been used in book production. Book clasps and hinges were found on the site (Fig. 14.43 a-d), and also part of a clip for holding the pages of a book in place perhaps whilst reading or singing from it (Fig. 14.43 e). Decorative mounts from book-bindings (Fig. 14.43 f & g) were also found. Many of these book-related items were recovered from excavations within the chapel and may support the suggestion (p.159

above) that the college library was located here-abouts.

Seal matrices are the objects pressed into wax to make a personal seal, in a less literate age than ours they were analogous to a written signature and thus the essence of business, both personal and professional. The Bedern excavations produced three matrices of copper alloy and one rather crude example of stone (Fig. 14.44 a-d). All the metal matrices are of the same faceted conical form, which first appears towards the end of the 13th century, and two retain looped handles. Unfortunately, it is unclear whether any of these matrices should be associated with individual vicars. One has the device of a squirrel with its tail curled up over its back, and the inscription running round it reads *i crake notis* or *nutis*, that is, 'I crack nuts'. Squirrels are sometimes seen in medieval art as women's pets, and a bawdy meaning could also be read into this inscription. It has also been suggested, however, that the cracking of nuts is an analogy for cracking open the seal (Alexander and Binski 1987, 277). This matrix was found in an early or mid 14th-century floor in one of the residential buildings (Building 11), so it may have belonged to a vicar. A second seal matrix is unfortunately incomplete, lacking the upper end of its handle; it has a crudely cut 'stag 'device, and an incomplete inscription. The best preserved example is a personal seal, with an oval matrix showing a robed man, perhaps Christ, and a crowned kneeling woman, the Virgin Mary, with a smaller kneeling figure, probably the seal's owner, below. The inscription reads *S'Thome de Swin Cementarius*, 'the seal of Thomas of Swin. Stonemason'. It has recently been suggested that *Swin* might be Swine, a village near Hull (P M Stell *pers comm*). Thomas of Swin may have been one of the many craftsmen who worked at the college. Although devices on seal matrices were sometimes tailor-made for the customer, none of those employed on the Bedern examples is unique, and it is likely that they were all selected from a pre-fabricated range of motifs at the die-cutters' shop.

Other items which cast some light on the vicar's professional work include a small gilded clapper from a bell found in a late 13th-century occupation level (Fig. 14.45 a). Although a number of uses for such bells might be envisaged, they were used by priests visiting the sick, in funeral processions, and during Mass. Rosary beads made of jet, amber and bone were also retrieved (Fig. 14.45 b-i) and two rock crystals may have been set into church metal-work, or even reliquaries. The only stratified gem-stone was found in an early or mid 14th-century deposit (Fig. 14.45 j).

As music was such an essential part of the vicars' professional life (chapter 3 above), it is no surprise that several parts of musical instruments were found, and finally, therefore, we get to the 'song' of my title. An iron 'Jew's harp' was found in an unstratified context, but 'Jew's harps' of this form found elsewhere frequently date from the later medieval period (Fig. 14.46 a). Also recovered were twelve tuning pegs of bone and antler (Fig. 14.46 b-f), which would have been used to tune harps, lyres or fiddles. An apparently unfinished peg of this type was found in excavations at Nos. 1–5 Aldwark, very close to Bedern (unpublished, YAT 1976.15. sf204), and although this is slender evidence for a workshop, it is tempting to suggest that they were being made in the vicinity, perhaps for the vicars themselves.

Conclusion

It is perhaps rather disappointing for us that the floors within the college appear to have been kept very clean, and few of the finds made there actually came from floors. Even so, there were a great many relevant finds from the Bedern excavations and some did come from deposits in residential buildings, even if they have not helped greatly in interpreting their functions. Many more finds were found in rubbish pits and in spreads of debris, although the apparent mixing of rubbish from the foundry and college, perhaps during periods when middens were shared, has also confused the picture. Nevertheless, some of the finds back up the documentary evidence that the vicars were possessed of both personal and institutional wealth, expressed most clearly, perhaps, in the quality of vessel glass used at their tables. We should note, also, that many of these particularly high status items derive from late 13th- and 14th-century contexts, i.e. from the period of the college's greatest prosperity. As an assemblage, the finds not only provide a glimpse into the maintenance and service industries required to keep the college functioning, but also provide the occasional insight into the professional life of the college, illustrating the performance of music and the use (and possibly preparation) of manuscripts. 'Wine, women and song' may have been a rash title to initiate this study, but the evidence of the finds from the Bedern excavations suggests that the vicars choral of York found time for all three distractions within their college.

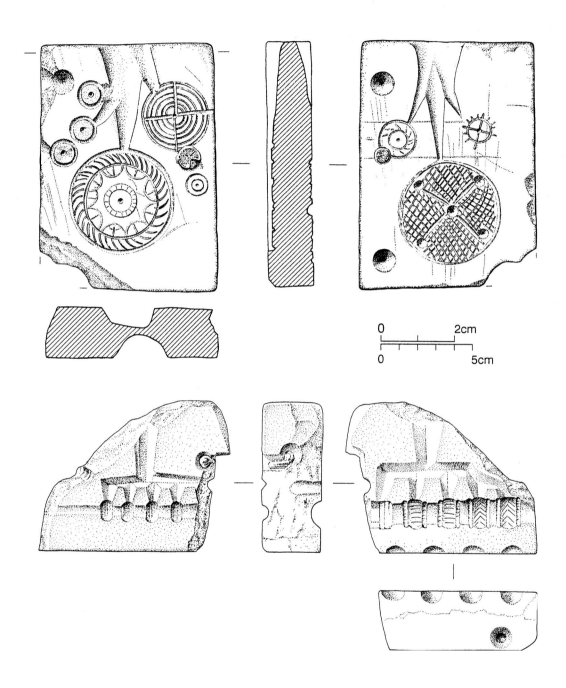

Fig. 14.1. Vicars choral of York Minster. Chalk moulds for casting non-ferrous metals (drawing and copyright, YAT)

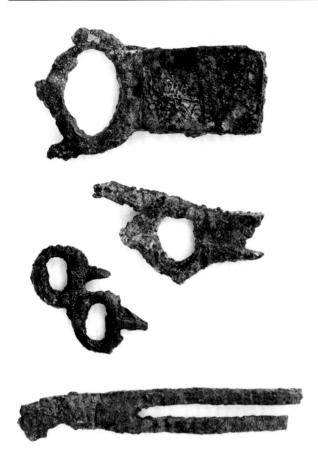

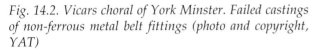

Fig. 14.2. Vicars choral of York Minster. Failed castings of non-ferrous metal belt fittings (photo and copyright, YAT)

Fig. 14.4. Vicars choral of York Minster. Detail of an iron blade from a metal-working file (photo and copyright, YAT)

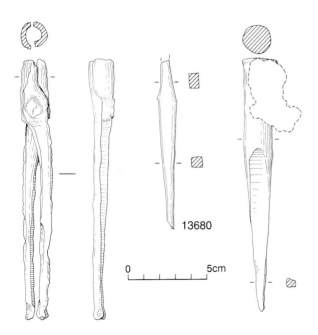

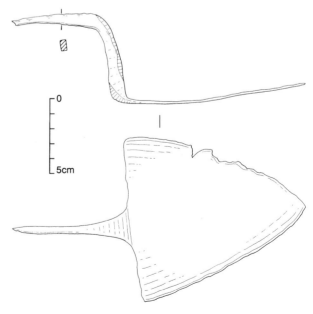

Fig. 14.3. Vicars choral of York Minster. Ironworking tools: a) iron tongs and b) and c) iron punches (drawing and copyright, YAT)

Fig. 14.5. Vicars choral of York Minster. Iron trowel (drawing and copyright, YAT)

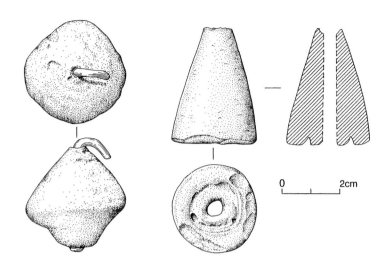

Fig. 14.6. Vicars choral of York Minster. Two lead alloy plumb-bobs (drawing and copyright, YAT)

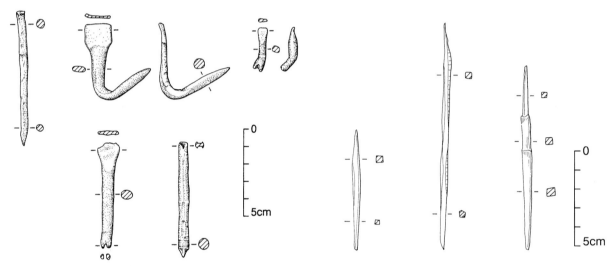

Fig. 14.7. Vicars choral of York Minster. Lead alloy points (drawing and copyright, YAT)

Fig. 14.9. Vicars choral of York Minster. Iron awls used in leather-working (drawing and copyright, YAT)

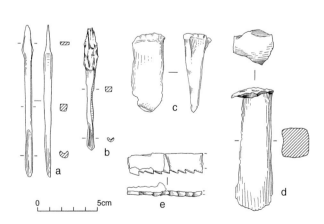

Fig. 14.8. Vicars choral of York Minster. Woodworking tools: a) and b) iron spoon augers, c) and d) wedges and e) fragment of saw blade with set teeth (drawing and copyright, YAT)

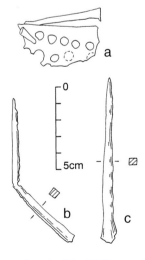

Fig. 14.10. Vicars choral of York Minster. Fibre processing tools: a) iron wool comb fragment and b) and c) spikes from wool combs (drawing and copyright, YAT)

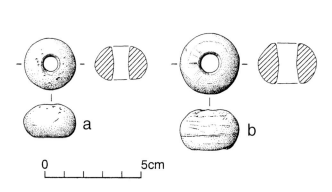

Fig. 14.11. Vicars choral of York Minster. Spindle whorls of a) chalk and b) limestone (drawing and copyright, YAT)

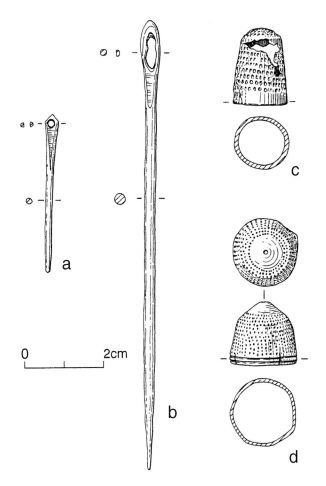

Fig. 14.12. Vicars choral of York Minster: a) and b) copper alloy needles and c) wand d) thimbles (drawing and copyright, YAT)

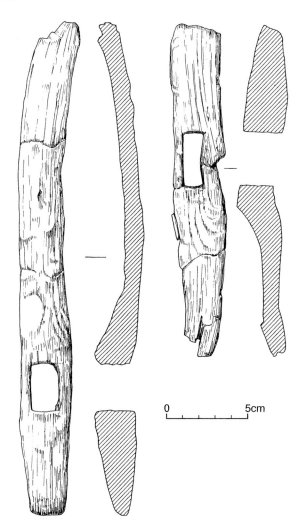

Fig. 14.13. Vicars choral of York Minster. Two fragments from an ash-wood, frame possibly used for stretching an embroidery canvas (drawing and copyright, YAT)

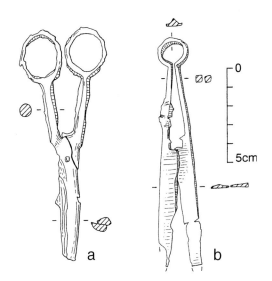

Fig. 14.14. Vicars choral of York Minster: a) iron scissors and b) shears (drawing and copyright, YAT)

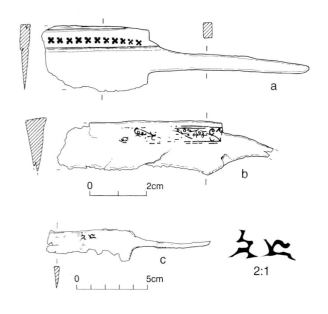

Fig. 14.15. Vicars choral of York Minster. Iron knives with decorated blades: a) and b) with inlaid mercury-gilded silver, and c) with a cutler's mark (drawing and copyright, YAT)

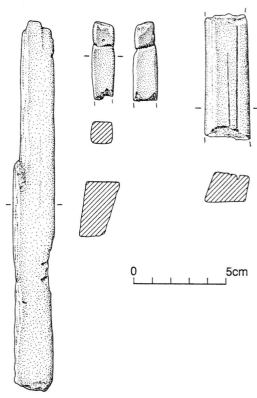

Fig. 14.17. Vicars choral of York Minster. Schist hones for sharpening knives (drawing and copyright, YAT)

Fig. 14.16. Vicars choral of York Minster. Detail of the inlaid knife blades 14.15a) and b) (photo and copyright, YAT)

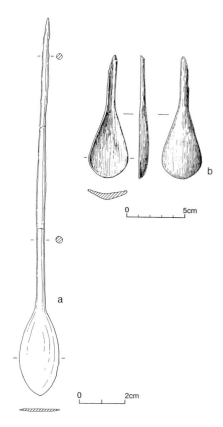

Fig. 14.18. Vicars choral of York Minster. Spoons: a) is of copper alloy, b) of cherry or blackthorn wood (drawing and copyright, YAT)

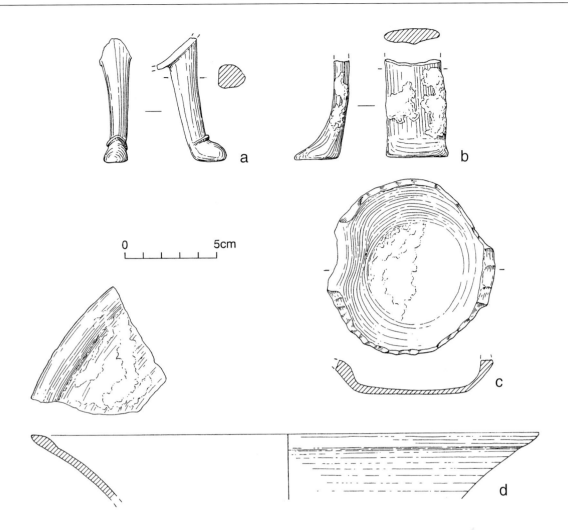

Fig. 14.19. Vicars choral of York Minster. Copper alloy vessel fragments: a) of a skillet, b) of a tripod ewer and c) and d) of cast cooking vessels (drawing and copyright, YAT)

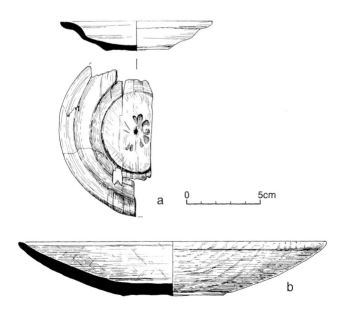

Fig. 14.20. Vicars choral of York Minster. Wooden vessels: a) bowl of field maple, b) plate of ash (drawing and copyright, YAT)

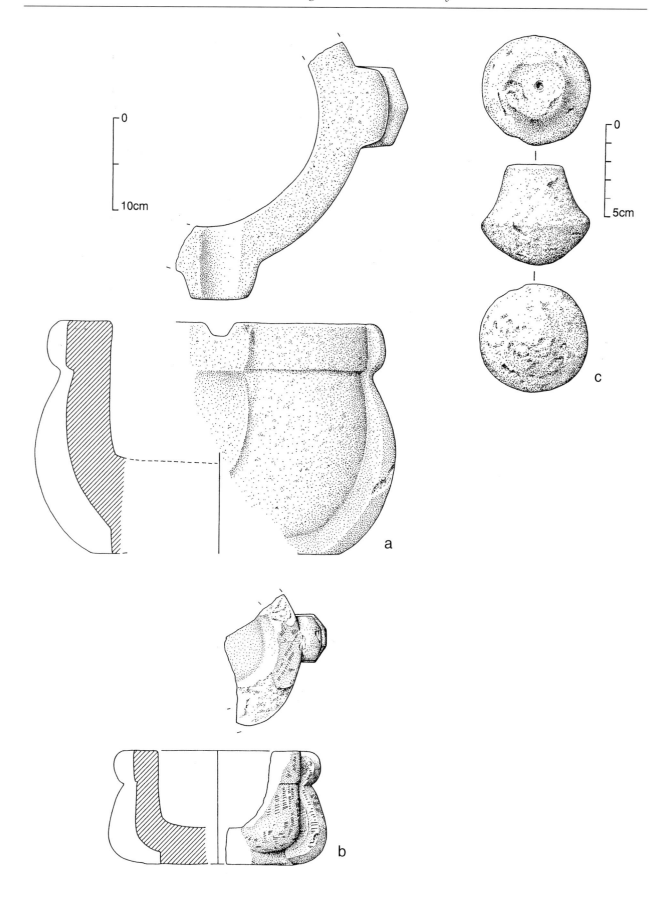

Fig. 14.21. Vicars choral of York Minster. Stone vessels: a and b) mortars and c) a pestle (drawing and copyright, YAT)

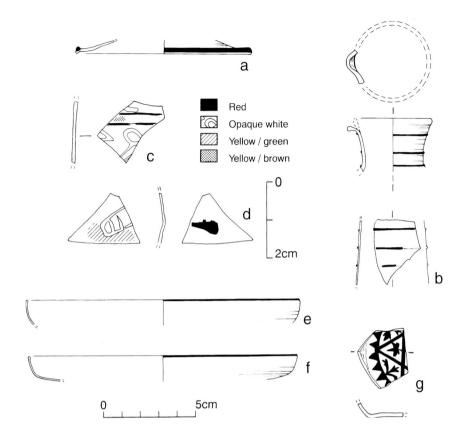

Fig. 14.22. Vicars choral of York Minster. Glass vessels: fragments of a) stemmed goblet, b) jug or serving flask, c) and d) two painted enamelled beakers, e) and f) bowls with trails, and g) blue painted bowl (drawing and copyright, YAT)

Fig. 14.23. Vicars choral of York Minster. Fragments of jug or serving flask decorated with blue-green trailing (photo and copyright, YAT)

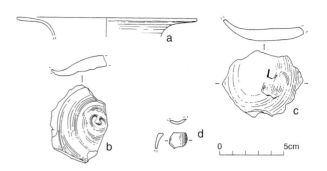

Fig. 14.24. Vicars choral of York Minster. Fragment of bowl of blue glass with blue painted decoration (photo and copyright, YAT)

Fig. 14.25. Vicars choral of York Minster. Fragments of glass urinals: a) rim and b) and c) two bases; d) is a possible alembic fragment (drawing and copyright, YAT)

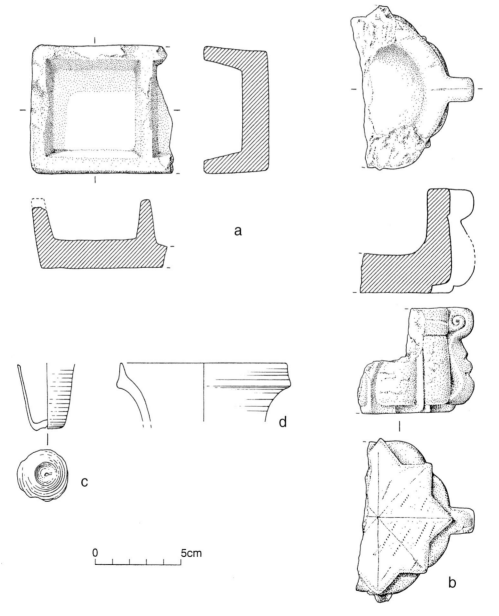

Fig. 14.26. Vicars choral of York Minster. Fragments of lamps: a) and b) of stone, c) and d) of glass hanging lamps (drawing and copyright, YAT)

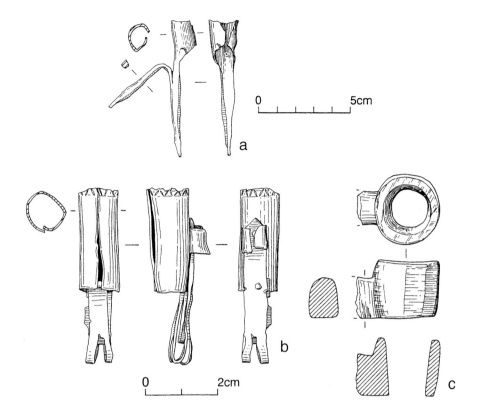

Fig. 14.27. Vicars choral of York Minster. Candle holders of: a) iron, and b) and c) copper alloy (drawing and copyright, YAT)

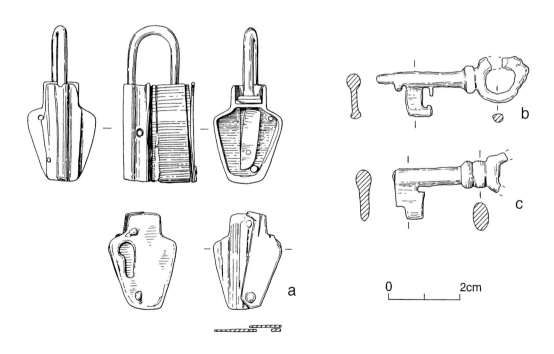

Fig. 14.28. Vicars choral of York Minster. Padlock and keys, all of copper alloy (drawing and copyright, YAT)

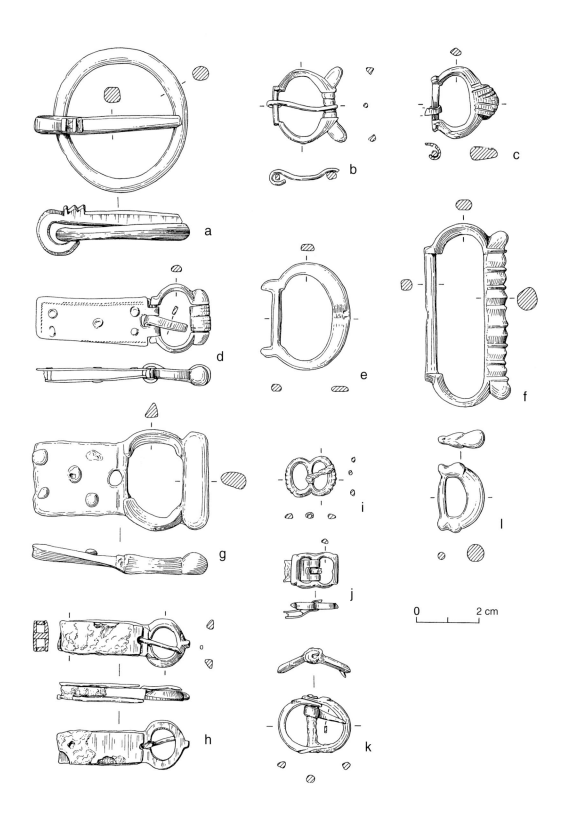

Fig. 14.29. Vicars choral of York Minster. Copper alloy belt fittings: a)-l) buckles (drawing and copyright, YAT)

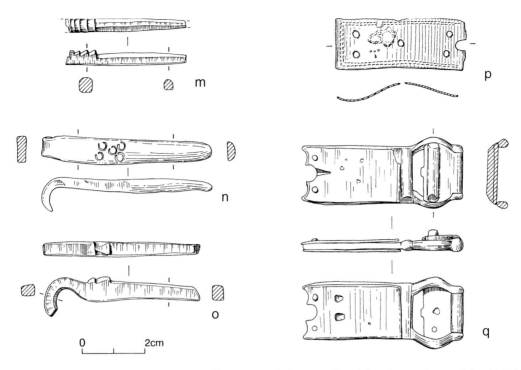

Fig. 14.29. (continued) m)-o) buckle pins, p) buckle plate and q) strap clasp (drawing and copyright, YAT)

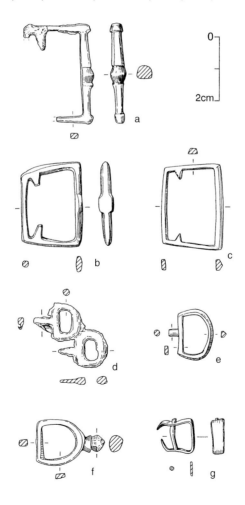

Fig. 14.30. Vicars choral of York Minster. Copper alloy belt loops including a failed casting of two loops (d) (drawing and copyright, YAT)

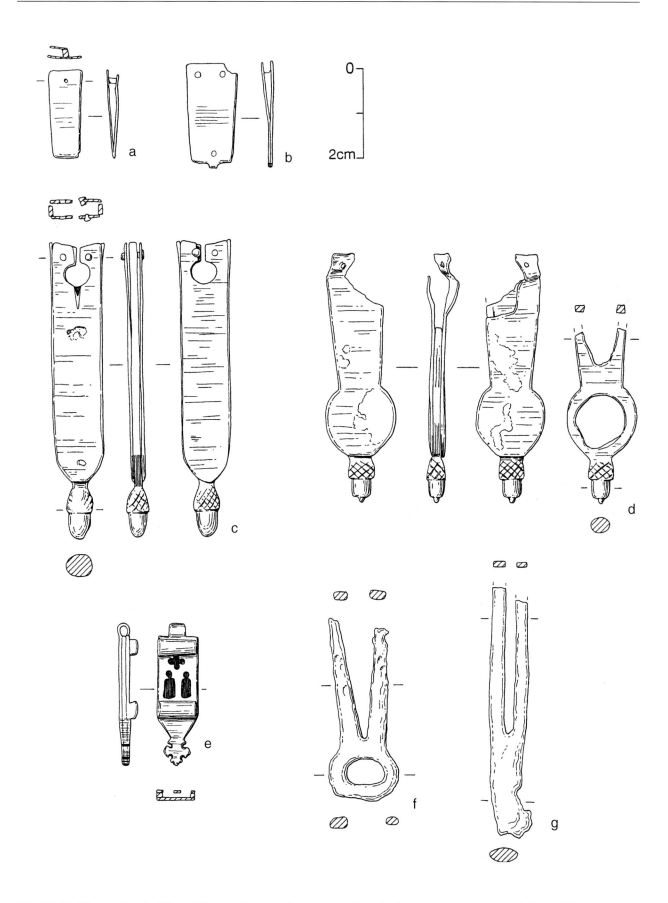

Fig. 14.31. Vicars choral of York Minster. Copper alloy strap ends including two-piece strap-ends (a and b), strap-ends with spacer plates (c, d and e), and failed castings of spacer plates (f and g) (drawing and copyright, YAT)

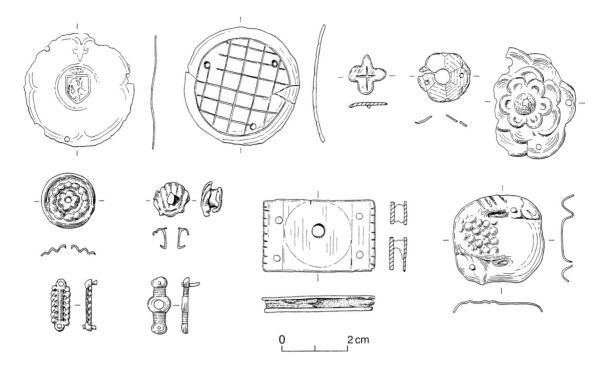

Fig. 14.32. Vicars choral of York Minster. Decorative fittings and mounts of copper alloy (drawing and copyright, YAT)

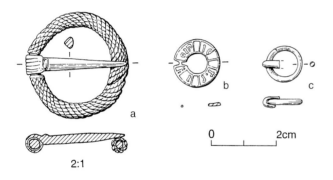

Fig. 14.33. Vicars choral of York Minster. Annular brooches: a) of gold, b) and c) of silver (drawing and copyright, YAT)

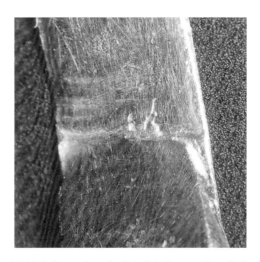

Fig. 14.35. Vicars choral of York Minster. Detail showing the join between the two parts of the gold ring shown in Fig. 14.34 (photo and copyright, YAT)

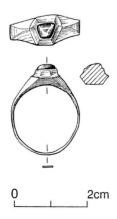

Fig. 14.34. Vicars choral of York Minster. Gold ring with sapphire setting (drawing and copyright, YAT)

Fig. 14.36. Vicars choral of York Minster. Detail of the stone set in the gold ring shown in Fig. 14.34 (photo and copyright, YAT)

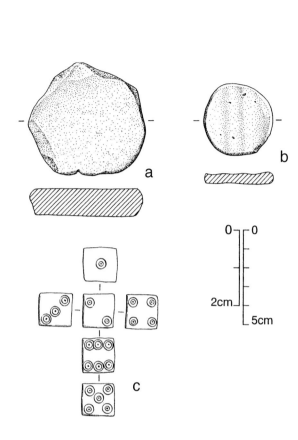

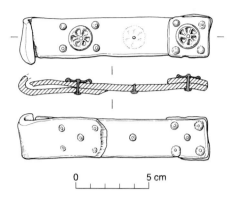

Fig. 14.39. Vicars choral of York Minster. Leather strap with copper alloy mounts, possibly part of a harness (drawing and copyright, YAT)

Fig. 14.37. Vicars choral of York Minster. Gaming pieces: counters of a) stone and b) ceramic, and c) a bone die (drawing and copyright, YAT)

Fig. 14.40. Vicars choral of York Minster. Detail of leather strap with copper alloy mounts shown in Fig. 14.39 (photo and copyright, YAT)

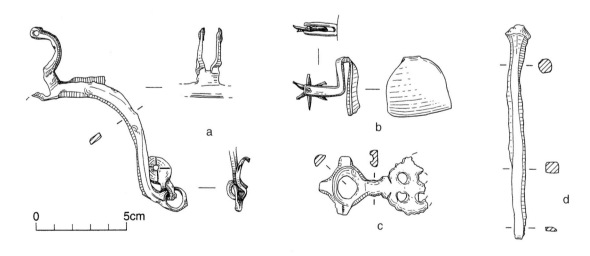

Fig. 14.38. Vicars choral of York Minster: a) and b) fragments of iron rowel spurs, c) and d) bridle bits (drawing and copyright, YAT)

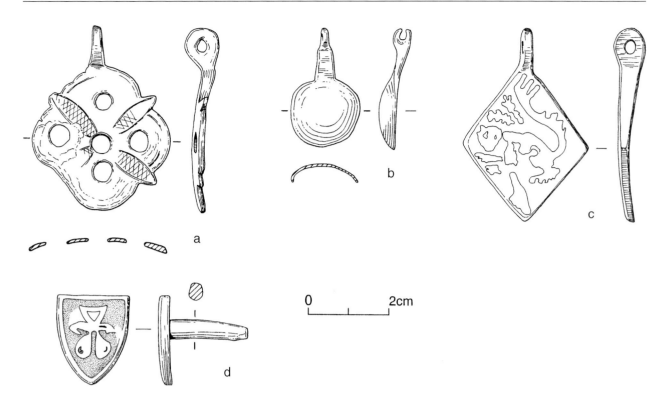

Fig. 14.41. Vicars choral of York Minster: a) – c) decorative harness-mounts and d) possible stirrup mount (drawing and copyright, YAT)

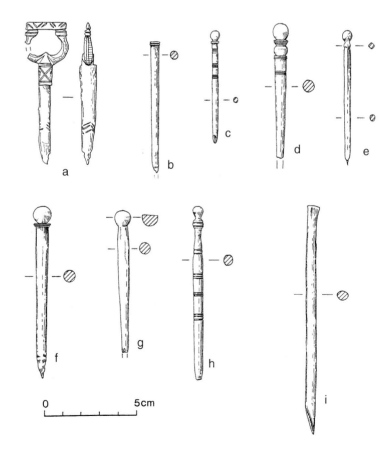

Fig. 14.42. Vicars choral of York Minster. Writing equipment: a) iron stylus, b) – h) bone styli or parchment prickers and i) bone ink pen (drawing and copyright, YAT)

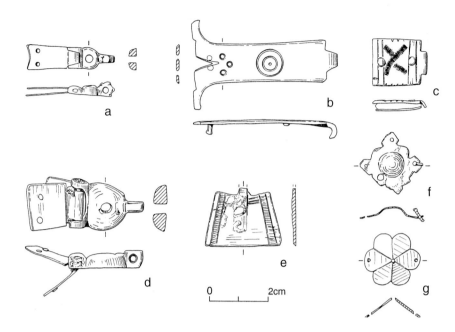

Fig. 14.43. Vicars choral of York Minster: a) – d) Copper alloy book-clasps, e) fragment of page holder and f) and g), book mounts (drawing and copyright, YAT)

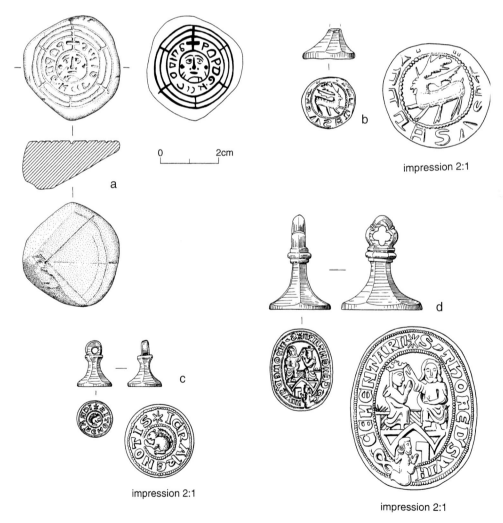

Fig. 14.44. Vicars choral of York Minster: a) seal matrices of stone and copper alloy (b – d) (drawing and copyright, YAT)

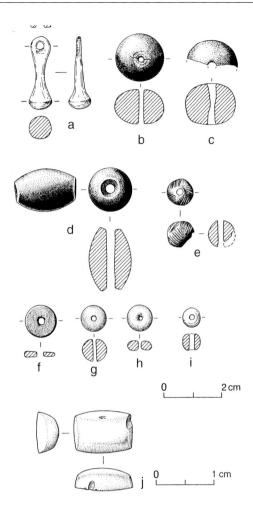

Fig. 14.45. Vicars choral of York Minster: a) gilded copper alloy bell clapper, b) – d) rosary beads of jet, and, e), of a jet-like material, of shale (f), of amber (g - h) and bone (i). (j) is a rock crystal gemstone (drawing and copyright, YAT)

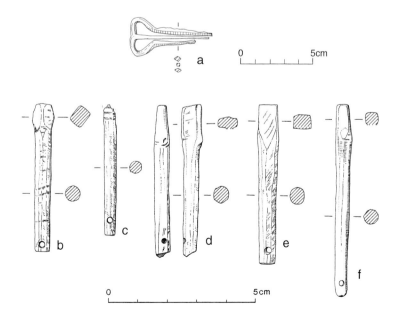

Fig. 14.46. Vicars choral of York Minster: a) iron Jew's harp, b) – f) bone tuning-pegs for musical instruments (drawing and copyright, YAT)

15

At Home in The Bedern: the Domestic Life of the Vicars Choral of York Minster

Nigel J. Tringham

The York vicars acquired their common residence, the Bedern, in the late 1220s or 1230s as grants from the subdean, John Romeyn the elder, and a Minster canon, William de Laneham (ed. Tringham 1993, nos. 137, 462 note; ed. Richards 2001, 388). No documentary evidence survives to describe how they organised themselves domestically in the early years, but the archaeological record has been interpreted by David Stocker, who suggests that the vicars were at first housed in a dormitory range, not dissimilar to the kind found in contemporary hospitals, notably St. Leonard's in York (above, p.149–51). Built perhaps in the 1240s or early 1250s that building was of considerable size and would have easily accommodated the full complement of 36 vicars that existed by 1294 (ed. Tringham 1993, xviii). Indeed, the dormitory's capacity rather confirms that the practice of each canon having a vicar assigned to his stall was in force about the time that the vicars acquired the Bedern site and certainly by 1252, the date when the dean and chapter regulated the manner in which the 40s. stipend which each vicar received from his canon was paid out (YMA, VC 3/1/1, f. 70v.–71v.).

The 1252 ordinance reveals that the vicars by then had a common fund administered by a chamberlain (*camerarius*) chosen by the vicars themselves with the consent of the dean and chapter. His main duty according to the ordinance was to supervise the payment of each vicar's stipend, in two lots of 10s. and the rest in the form of a weekly commons of 7d. The latter distribution, however, was dependant on a vicar's attendance at choir services, and the chamberlain had to note unauthorised absences for which fines were imposed. Charters of the mid 1250s refer to 'chamberlains' (that is , more than one) and on at least two occasions (one of them in 1261) grants of land by the vicars were authenticated with the chamberlains' seals (ed. Tringham 1993, nos. 61, 301, 463). Most probably, therefore, there were a pair of

chamberlains, one to deal with stipends and the other with the income from property and rent charges that the vicars were beginning to acquire in the form of pious grants (ed. Tringham 1993, xxiv–xxvii). At one point the 1252 ordinance refers to the 'chamberlain or warden', the latter being the head of the body of vicars and formerly known as the succentor (the deputy of the Minster canon who acted as precentor). That officer was confirmed as the vicars' 'perpetual warden' in an ordinance of the later 1260s (YMA, VC 1/3/3)[1], and by the 1270s the style 'warden of the house of vicars' (*custos domus vicariorum*) was coming into use (ed. Tringham 1993, no. 13). By the mid 13th century, therefore, the vicars had established a hierarchy of officers to deal with their affairs, and their leader's change of style from succentor (relating to liturgical duties in the Minster) to warden (emphasising domestic organisation) evidently reflects a growing sense of community amongst the vicars. Moreover, besides the dormitory the vicars also had what was almost certainly a common hall (above, p.152), presumably used for meals: indeed, the appropriation of half of each vicar's stipend to the common fund (as required by the 1252 ordinance) looks very much like a means of funding common meals.

It is, however, only with the survival of financial rolls of account from the beginning of the 14th century that the vicars' affairs can be investigated in any detail. The first surviving accounts date from the second decade (1304 and 1309: YMA, VC 4/1/1 and VC 6/2/1) and are a rental and a chamberlain's account, the latter giving totals of rental income and the distribution of any profit amongst the vicars; it also gives details of the doles paid out to vicars for attending obit services in the Minster, a responsibility which flowed naturally from the fact that much of the vicars' early rental income came from endowments for such commemorative services. Another set of accounts presumably gave details about the vicars' attendance at choir services, in compliance with the 1252 ordinance, but such accounts do not survive before the 1350s, when they were compiled by an officer called the choir bursar; his accounts took the form of a calendar listing all the vicars by name and noting week by week the total fine (if any) which had been incurred[2]. Summaries of the chamberlain's and choir bursar's accounts were included in the rolls of the vicars' warden, which survive from the late 1360s (YMA, VC 6/1). The warden was responsible for an overall statement of the vicars' income from property and stipends and how that money was distributed.

What is lacking from all these accounts, therefore, is evidence for how the vicars organised their domestic life in the Bedern. The only relevant set of medieval accounts is that starting in 1393 and compiled by the officer who purchased the malt and barley used in brewing ale in the vicars' own brewhouse in the Bedern (YMA, VC 6/5). The college brewer was accountable to the bursar of the common hall and it is the latter's accounts that would have covered expenditure on food consumed in the common hall; unfortunately they have not survived. Some information about living standards, however, can be gleaned from stray references in the archive. Luxury foods, for example, were served to important guests: when seeking advice from a lawyer in 1416, the vicars treated him to a meal of beef, pork, chicken, various fish (including pike), lobster, lamphreys, and eels, all washed down with red wine and a sweet wine (YMA, VC 4/2/FF & Hun/15), whilst a dinner of venison and swan was served to the chantry commissioners when they investigated the vicars in 1546 (YMA, VC 6/1/26). The vicars' own daily diet was presumably rather less interesting, although the archaeological record points to a varied and moderately high-status diet (ed. Richards 2001, 618–20), of which the venison pasty which a vicar stole from a college servant in 1474 and ate 'at his own pleasure' may not have been untypical (YMA, VC 1/1, 25).

The surviving financial accounts are also generally uninformative about college buildings in the Bedern, although a few references to repairs and *ad hoc* work are found in the chamberlains' rolls in the early 14th century. Those items include one in the late 1320s to work on the common hall, notably its doorway at the top of a flight of steps, and to a repair to 'the Bedern bell' which probably hung in the gatehouse facing Goodramgate (YMA, VC 6/2/10). The suggestion made by Stocker that the 13th-century dormitory had been divided by the earlier 14th century into sets of chambers on both the ground and upper floors (above, p.149–51) is supported by another stray reference to building work in the chamberlains' accounts: that for 1312 gives the cost of gravel for raising the path in front of the doors of pairs of named vicars, itself probably an indication that the chambers were shared (YMA, VC 6/2/8).

None of the stray items mentions a chapel in the Bedern, and although the archaeological report tentatively identifies an early 14th-century structure as a chapel (ed. Richards 2001, 436), it is almost certainly the case that the chapel (originally a very small building) at which a Minster canon celebrated solemn mass on St. Katherine's day in 1346 was the first one on the site (YMA, VC 1/3/8). Indeed, when in 1348 the vicars promised to celebrate a chantry for two of their number, they did so in return for a subsidy given towards the construction of the chapel 'newly situated in the Bedern' (YMA, VC 1/1, 102 and 107).

The chapel was built immediately after the vicars had successfully defended their rights and privileges in a series of disputes with the resident canons (YMA, VC 1/1/3, ff. 69–118) and it symbolised their corporate strength. Further evidence perhaps of the vicars' growing self-confidence is the construction, probably in the 1350s or 1360s, of a new timber-framed common hall to the south of the 13th-century hall, and then by the rebuilding of that hall in stone in the 1370s (above, p. 00). The funding for the latter work presumably came from the substantial cash bequests from two senior canons in 1366 and 1368 (ed. Tringham 1993, xxxiv), and the vicars' reliance on benefactions from superiors is a regular theme in their financial affairs (ed. Tringham 2002, xxvii–xxviii). Already in the later 14th century, indeed, a shortfall in disposable income from common property meant that the vicars faced problems in maintaining their common life.

In the 1380s, it seems, meals were no longer being taken together in hall and at least five vicars had been forced to abandon common residence altogether (ed. Tringham 2002, no. 250); it was in order to relieve this situation that Richard II, probably at the instigation of Archbishop Thomas Arundel, in 1394 granted the vicars the church of St. Sampson in York with its revenue. There was evidently some disagreement, however, about the desirability of restoring common life, and in 1396 and again in 1397 the king had to insist that the whole of the income from St. Sampson's should be applied to common expenses and not be shared out equally among the vicars; presumably that had been happening, with some vicars refusing to eat in common hall because it would have meant handing over some of their share of the new income (*ibid.*, nos. 248, 250). The dispute was arbitrated in 1399 by the dean and chapter, which stipulated that the bulk of St. Sampson's disposable income (over £6) should be paid directly to the common hall bursar. The only benefit to individual vicars would be a dole for attendance at the obits established in the Minster for the king and Queen Anne (*ibid.* no. 251). The scheme to restore a full common life coincided with the construction in the later 1390s of a stone room to the east of the common hall (YMA, VC 8/Metcalfe notebook VIa, no. 83). Called 'the counting house' in the early 15th century (*domus computacionis*: YMA, VC 1/1, 29–30), the room was almost certainly also used as a place of safe-keeping for the vicars' archive and valuables. It is probably that identified in the excavations to the east of hall (Building 27, p.159 above).

It was as a consequence of another benefaction *c*.1420 that the vicars embarked on a consolidation of their renewed common life. In 1417 a Minster canon, William Cawood, agreed to give them £334 in return for the maintenance of a chantry, and when the vicars received the money from his executors in 1420 they embarked on an ambitious programme of repairing their common properties in York, as well as on buying new houses (ed. Tringham 2002, xxvii). In 1421 they also acquired a charter of incorporation from the crown and commissioned a silver matrix for a new common seal (ed. Tringham 1993, xix, xxii). Moreover, the vicars drew up a set of Rules for the ordering of their common life, and it is this record which provides for the first time a detailed insight into the domestic life of the York vicars (YMA, VC 1/1, 1–11).

The first rule describes the duties of the bursar of the common hall: namely, to collect a weekly commons of 14*d*. from each vicar, in addition to half (20*s*.) his annual stipend, and to buy in all the necessary food and fire wood and to hire servants. He was to hold office for a year and was assisted on a fortnightly basis by a vicar who undertook duties as a steward. The provision of ale was the responsibility (as already noted) of the college brewer, and a following rule notes that on first coming into residence each vicar had to hand over 20*s*. and a silver spoon to the brewer in order to be allowed to eat in the common hall. (The brewer's accounts show that he bought utensils not only for the brewhouse but also for the bakehouse and kitchen.)

Next follow rules for eating and drinking in the hall. The mid-day meal took place immediately after the office hours had been completed in the Minster, with supper at five o'clock. The warden sat in the centre of the high table, which was probably situated in front of what was the hall's most exceptional architectural feature, a bay window (above, p.158–9). The other vicars sat to the right and to the left according to 'priority', which presumably meant seniority in service. One vicar served the food, whilst another read from a pulpit. Breakfast was also taken in hall, but that seems to have been an informal occasion and no special rules were laid down for it.

Vicars were not obliged to eat in common all the time. They could order food from the kitchen to eat in their own houses if they were entertaining friends, although on such occasions they had to pay extra for bread and ale. If a vicar was eating out with friends in the city, however, he lost his entitlement, as he did if it was his turn to eat with one of the residentiary canons.

The drinking of ale in hall outside mealtime took place only at certain specified times: in winter, once after the main meal and the Blessing and after the vicars had washed their hands next to the fire, and three times after supper (the first time after the Blessing and then twice up to eight o'clock at times nominated by the warden and senior vicars). Presumably at each drinking time measures of ale were doled out to each vicar, and if a vicar wanted a drink after eight o'clock he had to pay extra. On days of abstinence (when no meat was consumed), the vicars assembled in the common hall at five o'clock and were allowed to drink at three or four specified occasions until eight o'clock. In summer, hand washing took place at table and opening hours, as it were, were extended to nine o'clock. These times correspond to the change of hour when the Bedern gate was closed: in winter at nine o'clock and in summer at ten o'clock (YMA, VC 1/1, 99).

The remaining rules, along with supplementary ones added between October 1420 and January 1421, relate to the personal conduct of vicars, with fines being imposed on vicars who persisted in asking 'vain questions' which led to discord, who beat or verbally abused college servants (only the bursar or steward could do that), and who played chess or draughts or bet in the hall. Misdemeanours were to be corrected by the warden together with the 'six men', a group of senior vicars who are first recorded in 1351 when they were elected by the whole body of vicars (YMA, VC 3/1/1, f. 4). They feature in a number of memoranda about the correction of individual vicars which immediately follow the text of the 1420 Rules (YMA, VC 1/1, 13–23), including a case of physical assault when one vicar threw another against the kitchen grate; most other disputes involved only heated words.

Another matter which the 'six men' regularly investigated was the condition in which the vicars left their houses, either because of death or because they had moved to a new house in the Bedern. Vicars evidently moved house with some frequency, and at one point in the later 14th century they had to be forbidden from taking windows with them when they did so (*ibid.*, 109). The reason for all this moving about seems to have been that it became common for vicars to change their choir stalls in the Minster: when a vicarage attached to a stall became vacant, a vicar next in seniority might move into it rather than it being filled by a new recruit, and when a vicar moved stall he also moved house. Indeed, it might be the case that the reason for moving stall was in order to occupy a different house, as not all houses seem to have been of the same standard. In 1360 the warden argued that given his office he ought to be able to move into a house (actually 'houses': *domos*) that had recently become vacant following a death, and that it ought not to be assigned 'by priority' according to customary practice (YMA, VC 1/1, 93).

The claim only makes sense, perhaps, if the house was worth moving into.

Already by the later 14th century, it seems, the shared chambers in the dormitory range were being converted into individual two-storey houses (ed. Richards 2001, 579), an arrangement apparently reflected in the description of a house given in an inventory of 1454 which mentions goods in a hall, parlour, chamber, and chapel (ed. Stell and Hampson n.d., 223–5)[3]. The rooms were presumably on two floors: a later inventory of 1540 mentions the 'principal low chamber' (the living room) with a parlour above, along with a great chamber (ed. Cross 1984, 46–7). These inventories, however, may refer not to houses in the former dormitory but to individual houses elsewhere in the Bedern. There were at least three such houses at the east end of the site in 1408, when one vicar granted a parcel of his house plot to a colleague so that the latter could build himself a study (YMA, VC Box XII, misc. 6), and there were presumably other houses too in the un-excavated part of the Bedern. The 1408 document, moreover, states that the house onto which the study was to be added was assigned to a particular stall in the Minster, and that seems to support the notion that a vicar would vacate a house if he moved to a vicarage attached to another stall.

By at least the 15th century, therefore, the York vicars were living in their own houses in different parts of the Bedern, enjoying a degree of privacy not envisaged by their 13th-century predecessors. It was that privacy which enabled some vicars to indulge in what has usually been cited as an indication of moral laxity, the forming of what were evidently long-term relationships with concubines. There is much evidence for such sexual misconduct at York in surviving 15th-century church court records (Purvis 1943; Ryan 1995), but what is striking is the leniency with which the dean and chapter treated the offenders and the tolerance shown by fellow vicars: in 1461 a woman spent a month living with a vicar in his house in the Bedern and actually gave birth to a child there (Purvis 1943, 31). The York evidence still requires detailed study, but the general impression is of a state of affairs in which some vicars in the 15th century tried to create a kind of 'family life' that approximated to that enjoyed by the laity. On the other hand, although a few vicars 'opted out' of college life, most seem still to have retained a sense of community, and there was probably some attraction in living in an all-male environment where there was always a drinking partner at hand. It may also be the case that as the number of vicars declined during the 15th century, the college became less hierarchical with duties shared out more equally; the warden's office, for example, changed hands more frequently with men coming back after a break in service rather than staying in control for long stretches of time, as was the pattern in the 13th and 14th centuries.

The vicars by no means kept themselves isolated from the city at large. In the late 15th and early 16th century they enjoyed what seem to have been regular drinking sessions with monks from St. Mary's Abbey, usually in the Bedern hall but on one occasion in a local tavern (YMA, VC 6/1/10, 11 and 15). Indeed, slipping out in the evening to visit a tavern was not uncommon (e.g. BIHR D/C AB1, ff. 30, 220v.), and in 1422 a vicar and a chantry priest from the Minster were punished for wandering about late at night, dressed improperly and carrying poll-axes whilst visiting midsummer bonfires in the city (ibid., f. 61v.). More seemly opportunities for enjoyment may have been offered by the confraternity which the vicars established, probably in the 1360s: in 1370 each vicar was given 2d. 'for the reception of brothers and sisters' (YMA, VC 3/1/1, f. 142v.; VC 6/1/2). There are no further references to the fraternity, but some vicars were members of the York Corpus Christi gild (Crouch 2000, 165, 176, 178) and in 1414 the city gild of St. Christopher admitted vicars as brothers in return for the celebration of a mass for gild members on St. James's day (YMA, VC 1/1, 85). When the St. Christopher gild reissued the concession in 1485, it was further recorded that on that day the gild master would send the vicars two pasties and a gallon of red wine (YMA, VC Box XII, no. 2). Further connections with York citizens would almost certainly be revealed by a close study of surviving vicars' wills.

Much work still has to be done on the vicars' archive but a story emerges of a vigorous community striving to maintain a common life despite recurrent economic problems. Unlike a monastic community observing a common Rule, the York college of vicars choral to some extent had to fashion its own life, developing powers of self-government and on occasion having to fight the resident canons in order to protect its rights and privileges. Only comparison with the life of vicars choral at other cathedrals and with that of secular clerks in comparable institutions will reveal just how successful the York vicars were in that regard.

Notes

1. The title occurs in an undated ordinance, usually ascribed to Archbishop Walter Gray (d. 1255). The grantor, however, is referred to merely as Archbishop 'W.', and when the York antiquary Francis Drake saw the document in the early 18th century it still had its seal attached and that belonged to Walter Giffard, who became archbishop in 1265: (Drake, 1736, Appendix, lxxiii and plate facing ci (no. III)). The ordinance was confirmed by the king in 1269: YMA VC 1/3/4.

2. The main run of choir bursar's accounts (dating from the late 1370s) are in YMA, VC 6/4, but undated ones of the 1350s are in VC 6/2/24 and VC 6/4/2b and 2c.

3. The 1426 inventory of another vicar (eds. Stell and Hampson n.d., 114–19) probably refers to a house outside the Bedern.

16

God and Mammon: The Role of the City Estate of the Vicars Choral in the Religious Life of York Minster

Sarah Rees Jones

The college of the vicars choral of York Minster was one of the city's most important landlords in the later middle ages. Acquisition of the vicars' estate was made possible by the generosity of some of the senior canons of the cathedral and the archbishops of York, and reflected their determination to enhance the religious life of the cathedral. Yet the day to day running of the estate was entirely the responsibility of the vicars themselves, who, as a consequence, became more closely involved in the daily life of the city than did any other body of Minster clergy. Indeed individual vicars often developed an expertise that equipped them particularly well to take on other major administrative tasks in the Minster. By 1400 it was members of the vicars choral who were generally employed to manage the Minster's fabric fund, (which had its own city estate), and to oversee the continual work of maintenance and rebuilding in the Minster itself (YMA, E3). The city estate of the vicars choral did not just provide the material support necessary for their college and their worship in the Minster, but it also required them to engage, successfully or otherwise, in all aspects of the life of the cathedral city.

The Acquisition of an Urban Estate

The college of the vicars choral in York was something of a 'prayer factory'- as indeed the name of their college, the Bedern (meaning place of prayer), suggests. The origin of this college has been discussed in full elsewhere, and is only briefly recapitulated here (Harrison 1952; ed. Tringham 1993, xvii–xx; Rees Jones 2001, 380–396 etc.). York Minster was a secular cathedral staffed by canons. By 1300 there were 36 canons, but the majority of these were absent from York most of the time (Dobson 1977a, 52–8). Each

canon therefore supported a vicar who could deputise for him in the Minster's regular worship. The core part of the duties of these vicars choral thus lay in observing the offices of the day in the cathedral church. At first individual vicars may have lived with their canons, but in the early 13th century the vicars were provided with a collegiate residence in the Bedern in Goodramgate to the east of the Minster Close (Richards *et al.*, 2001, *passim*; p.148–52 and Fig. 13.1 above). By 1291 the canons' responsibilities for their vicars had been formalised into the provision of an annual stipend of 40s. paid by each canon to the college for their vicar and other limited contributions in kind (*YCS*, 13, 21, 27). However, these payments from the canons were soon exceeded by the colleges' other sources of income.

As Julia Barrow amplifies further in her paper in this volume (chapter 2), the origin and function of colleges of minor priests, such as the vicars choral, was much more complex than a simple requirement to deputise for non-resident canons. Vicars choral had other duties which augmented their financial resources and responsibilities considerably, and promoted their independence from the canons. In particular, from the later 12th century, the vicars choral gradually amassed a large number of endowments for the support of prayers and masses for the dead in the Minster (Rees Jones 1987, 117–27). By the later 13th century these endowments provided an annual income for the college which greatly exceeded the contributions of the canons. Indeed it was the steady growth of these independent endowments that provided the resources for the endowment of a new college for the vicars in the mid 13th century. As a result, in the later middle ages the vicars enjoyed the possession of a sizeable estate both in and outside the city of York – but primarily within it. Indeed, by

1304, they were one of the largest landowners in the city of York with about 80 city properties which produced an income of about £45 a year (YMA, VC/4/1). By 1395 this estate had trebled in size to over 240 properties producing and income of about £160 a year (YMA, VC6/2/36). The majority of this estate lay in the city centre and was developed with houses and shops. However the college also owned some agricultural and industrial properties in the city's suburbs, including mills and brickworks (Tringham, 2001). In addition the college also derived an income from some rural properties, from their ownership of the benefices, and thus the spiritual income, of some parish churches outside the city, and from various other enterprises, such as the sale of surplus building stores or the sale of surplus malt from their own brewery (ed. Tringham, 2002).

The development of these independent sources of finance secured the independence of the vicars from their canons. Nevertheless, it was the archbishops and senior members of the cathedral chapter of York who drove the process, and many of the properties they gave to the new college already formed part of the Minster's ancient estate in the city (Rees Jones 1987, 117–27; Rees Jones 2001, 385–91). Through the creation and endowment of the college of the vicars choral the dean and chapter were thus able to address three significant spiritual and administrative problems that confronted them in the early decades of the 13th century.

The first of these problems was the fact that the majority of the Minster's canons were not resident in York, but were often employed as senior administrators in the courts and chanceries of the pope and of the king of England (Dobson 1977a, 57). As a consequence, the considerable incomes from their prebendal estates (that is the official endowments of their canonries in the Minster) were more often applied to subsidising their papal and royal careers than to supporting the work of the Minster. This problem was appreciated in particular by Archbishop Walter de Gray (1216–55). Gray and his associates and successors, such as John Romeyn (1286–96), undertook a major reform of the finances and internal management of chapter and issued new Statutes governing rules of residence among the canons (Dobson 1977a, 48–50, 60, 81). It is therefore not surprising to find that Gray and Romeyn were also instrumental in founding the new college for the vicars choral, providing much of the land on which the Bedern was built (Rees Jones 2001, 381–90). The founders of the college gave the site of the Bedern in return for prayers for their souls. This established the common pattern for all later endowments to the college and confirmed a growing trend among the senior clergy of the Minster to entrust the observance of services for their souls to members of the vicars

choral. The endowment of further chantries in the Minster by other members of the chapter, enabled the canons to give back a significant portion of their prebendal estates to the support of the vicars choral (ed. Tringham 1993, *passim*; Rees Jones 1987, II, *passim*). The Minster thus won back the fruits of at least some of its ancient endowments for the support of the religious life of the cathedral, and placed their management in the hands of local clergy who were resident in the city. In the majority of cases the vicars were given the urban rather than the rural parts of these prebendal estates. Canons who were not resident in the city clearly had no need of the large city residences with which they had been provided in the 12th century. In particular the vicars choral acquired those prebendal properties which lay outside the original Minster Close, but that were immediately adjacent to it in the neighbouring streets of Petergate and Goodramgate (including the site of the Bedern). Certainly the college also acquired properties in other parts of the city and its suburbs, especially earlier in the 13th century before the foundation of the Bedern (ed. Tringham 1993, *passim*). However by 1309 about two-thirds of the vicars' urban rent income was drawn from houses in the immediate neighbourhood of the Minster Close (YMA, VC 4/1/1). Moreover their acquisition of properties in these streets next to the Close was not restricted only to those that already belonged to the Minster's canons. They were also given the last few properties in Goodramgate and Aldwark that belonged to the more ancient estate of the archbishops of York and, more controversially, they also gradually acquired several neighbouring sites in the same streets that had never belonged to either the Minster or the archbishop (Rees Jones, 2001, 389–91: Rees Jones, 1987, II, *passim*). In this way the endowment of the vicars choral secured for the Minster the economic control of its ancient endowments in the city centre outside the Minster Close and extended and consolidated their lordship in adjacent streets.

The second problem addressed by the endowment of the college of vicars choral was one that the dean and chapter shared in common with the majority of landlords in the late 12th and 13th centuries. They suffered from the fact that so much of their ancient estate had been granted to free tenants at perpetual rents that, by the early 13th century, income reflected nothing like the real economic value of the property. The development of royal law in the same period was also strengthening the legal rights of such free tenants, extending their rights of inheritance and weakening the traditional authority of their landlords (Clanchy, 1998, 99–112; Hudson 1994). Free tenants were in effect being turned into landowners at the expense of their nominal lords. Wealthy landlords reacted by trying to buy out such free tenants and re-let the land on more restrictive terms, especially in key areas of their estates. For York Minster the endowment of the vicars' college was one means by which the canons could deal with this problem on their York estate. Established free tenants, of both prebendal and other properties in the city, were bought out and the property given to the college. The property was then let on more restricted terms, often directly to the occupants, who as tenants-at-will, had no title of ownership in the property and only limited rights to use and occupy it. This reclamation of their property in the city was often a costly, time-consuming and contentious business. It took at least 50 years to secure full rights to the ownership of the site of the vicars' college at Bedern (Rees Jones 2001, 385–91). The contemporary repossession of a very important group of canons' houses on the corner of Petergate and Stonegate took even longer, involved some extremely protracted and high-profile court cases, and must have cost many times the recorded sum of £38 (Rees Jones 1987, I, 125; II, Tenements 15–17; ed. Tringham 1993, nos. 406–416). The vicars choral continued this policy of reclaiming maximum control of the properties in their city estate, and so extracting the largest possible income from it, almost to the end of the 14th century. Indeed from the 1290s, the impact of national legislation that was intended to limit the church's acquisition of new freeholds, made the full exploitation of existing property even more important, as access to new endowments was (at least from time to time) restricted and taxed by the crown (Raban 1982).

The third issue addressed by this strategic endowment of the college dealt with the political consequences of this changing legal climate for wealthy urban landlords. As we have seen the creation of the vicars' estates provided a buffer zone between the Close and the rest of the city. Traditionally the Minster claimed full rights of jurisdiction over all the tenants of their city estate whether lay or religious. Its estate in the city was therefore known as the 'Liberty of St Peter', and its tenants were able to avoid paying taxes to the city. As a consequence the Minster was often in conflict with the city council, especially as the powers of taxation and jurisdiction delegated to civic authorities by the crown increased from the later 12th century. This kind of conflict – between cathedral and burgess communities over the control of local government in cathedral cities – was far from unique to York. It was a feature of cathedral cities across Europe as the respective rights and powers of secular and ecclesiastical governments were being rapidly developed and defined in relation to each other through the development of new written codes of both canon and secular law (Nicholas, 1997, 141–68, 208–10).

The political implications of the creation of this new estate for the vicars are evident in its manifestly political repercussions. In the later 13th century there were no less than three major inquiries into the jurisdiction of the Minster in the city of York commissioned by the crown (YMA, L2/1, part IV, f. 37–43; l2/2a f. 30–31; PRO, JI 1/1111; eds Illingworth and Caley, 1812, 119). For the time being it was decided in 1276 that the vicars' estates did indeed fall within the jurisdiction of St Peter, even including those properties that had been acquired from outside the original fee of the Minster in the relatively recent past. This definition was later to change. However, in *c.*1300 the estate of the vicars choral provided the Minster with a zone within the city in which it remained able to exercise some control over its tenants. This zone lay between the inner *sanctum* of the Minster Close, which was itself being enclosed within stone walls and gates in this period, and those areas of the city governed by the commune of the citizens.

The scale of these projects, and the way in which they tended to be focussed (especially in the later 13th century) on acquiring properties in streets close to the Minster and Bedern , suggest that the whole enterprise must have been planned and co-ordinated to some degree. The dean and chapter must have regarded it as one of their most important projects, and not only the dean and chapter – for successive archbishops in both the 13th and 14th centuries, men such as Walter de Gray, John le Romeyn and William Zouche (1342–52) were involved as well. It was senior chapter officials in particular, such as the treasurers, precentors, sub-deans and deans, who were especially prominent among the college's patrons and took the lead in buying back the urban estates of the non-resident canons (Rees Jones 1987, I, 121–3). The foundation of the college of the vicars choral and the endowment of its estates were thus at the heart of reformation of the Minster community and its place in the city. The best-recorded aspects of this reformation are the legal and the financial benefits, because it is the legal and financial records that survive. Yet this should not blind us to the fact that the central purpose of this expensive undertaking was the reformation of the spiritual life of the Minster community and its spiritual contribution to the city of York. God and Mammon could be served at the same time – although I suspect that the both vicars and their patrons thought that God was more important.

The first college

How do these broader purposes of the college's founders and early patrons inform our understanding of the college buildings themselves? In the report on the excavations of the Bedern we argued that the first college buildings were much closer in form to the conventual buildings provided for monks or friars, than to the much later colleges built for vicars and university students in the 14th century and later (Rees Jones 2001, 391–5, esp. 395; Rees Jones and Richards 2001, 538–40, 579; p.86 and chapter 13 above). In particular the first college provided accommodation for the vicars in a communal dormitory, rather than in the individual cottages or rooms of later colleges. Like a conventional monastery one of the main functions of the newly endowed college of vicars choral was to perpetuate the memory of its patrons, and to ease their passage through purgatory by prayer, and so the choice of a quasi-monastic style of building was entirely appropriate. Yet, above all, the choice of a communal style emphasised the desire of the Minster to reform and strengthen the corporate organisation of its lesser clergy. In the early 13th century canon lawyers were refining new theories of corporate government for institutions such as cathedral chapters. These emphasised that collective and representative forms of organisation were more effective in promoting the common good of a community than were autocratic or individualistic forms of government (Brundage 1995, 103–9). The benefits of such corporate organisation extended beyond the walls of the institution itself. Corporate institutions better reflected the mystical body of Christ, and so they could more successfully represent the essential truths of the Christ's message to the world. Cathedral chapters, therefore, did not just govern their cathedrals but provided spiritual leadership for all Christians throughout their whole diocese (*ibid.*, 107). The reform of both the communal structure of the chapter undertaken by Archbishop de Gray and his colleagues, and the associated endowment of a new corporate college of vicars was thus perfectly in step with the contemporary reform of other new bodies of independent clergy, such as the friars. Like the friars, these vicars' services did not just enhance the internal religious life of the Minster, but they represented the Minster's spiritual authority in the community at large. Indeed it is surely telling that part of the site provided for the new college of vicars choral in Goodramgate had, only a few years previously, been given by Archbishop de Gray to the newly established order of Dominican Friars who had only just arrived in the city (indeed Gray's gift is the first notice of the Dominicans in York – ed. Tringham 1993, nos. 138, 83–4; Rees Jones 2001, 389). The friars relinquished this when they were given a new site for their house across the city at Toft Green in 1227, and Gray gave the Goodramgate houses to the vicars for their new college. The corporate form of the first college buildings at the Bedern was thus dictated by the wider spiritual aims of the Minster community, which in many respects they shared with the friars. Was it just a coincidence that the Minster's desire to impress their spiritual leadership on the city occurred at a time when other aspects of their secular authority were beginning to be challenged (cf. Miller 2000, 253–9)? After all, the new college of the vicars choral was not a modest building tucked away in a backwater of the Minster Close, but a large, architecturally adventurous, structure built on the very boundary of the limits of the controversial lordship of the Minster in the city.

The continuing contribution of the estate to college life

The foundation of the college and its initial endowment with a city estate was thus an integral, even central, part of a programme designed to reform and reassert the Minster's spiritual and secular lordship of the city in the 13th century. The ownership and administration of this estate certainly tied the college of the vicars more closely into the daily life of that city than any other clergy in the Minster community.

By the mid 13th century the vicars had established an administrative structure to manage this estate, and their various financial accounts, which survive in good, if broken, series from *c*.1303, provide a very rich source for historians interested in the social and economic history of York. They are particularly important as no other runs of financial accounts survive for landowners in the city before 1400. Bartlett was the first to appreciate the value of these records in his paper on the economy of York in the later middle ages (1959–60). He traced a pattern of growth and decline on the vicars' estate over the 14th and 15th centuries, which he used, together with other sources, to describe a narrative of the city's economic growth and decline in this period . The cycle he described is still very widely cited in urban histories and has been the basis for much broader discussion of urban and social crisis after the Black Death (Dobson 1977b; Palliser, 1988).

Bartlett's chronology needs some correction, however, for he did not fully understand how and why the rent accounts swelled and shrank over those two centuries. In particular he did not ask questions about the administrative context in which the figures were created, nor about the relationship between the vicars' estate in particular and the broader 'economy' (itself a difficult and diffuse term) of the city in general. He tended to assume that a growth in the rental, or a rise in the average value of rents, reflected a growth in the prosperity of the city and vice-versa.

If we look at the rent accounts from the perspective of the vicars' needs, and their management practices, however, a slightly different picture emerges. A detailed reconstruction of the growth and management of their estate suggests that in only two rather brief periods did the rental of the vicars choral grow because the value of rents on their estate was inflated (Rees Jones 1987, I, 202–224). The first was the period (1331–6) that coincided with Edward III's use of the city as a royal base during the wars with Scotland (Ormrod 2000). The second was the period 1364–84 and coincided with a general period of national inflation in a variety of rents and prices (Hatcher 1977, 32–3; 47–54). Other periods of growth in the value and size of the vicars' rentals can be attributed to changes in the way in which the vicars administered their city estate in response to the internal needs of the college.

First the vicars continued to receive new endowments for chantries, from archbishops and canons of the Minster, from members of the college itself, and even from some lay patrons. Increasingly these endowments took the form for cash, which enabled the college both to buy and to build many new properties. Secondly, the managers of the vicars' estate continued to strive to eliminate free tenants from their urban estate and to let more houses and shops on their estate directly to their subtenants, the actual occupants, themselves. As a consequence the vicars choral were able redevelop many of their city properties with new buildings. Particularly detailed accounts survive for their demolition of a redundant church and the old stone buildings of a former canon's palatial residence in the 1350s and the redevelopment of both these sites with rows and courtyards of much smaller timber-framed houses (YMA, VC 6/9). However this style of redevelopment was typical across the whole of their city-centre estate, including the perimeter of the college site around which they constructed six rows of small cottages in the later 13th and early 14th century (Rees Jones, 1988, 51–63). New endowments and the redevelopment of existing property thus both contributed far more to the growth of the vicars' income from rents in the 14th century than did inflation. The third factor that contributed to the increasing size of their rental was even more arbitrary and arose simply from technical changes in the administration of their accounts. In particular the amalgamation by 1409 of several series of chantry accounts, which had previously been kept separately, into a single set of

accounts was the major cause of the apparent increase in the size and value of the college's rental at the beginning of the 15th century. This administrative change in the keeping of the accounts in fact disguised a real fall in the value of individual rents on much of the estate.

When we take account of this administrative background to the management of the vicars' York estate it becomes apparent that, by and large, the vicars were only able to increase their income as a result of acquiring new endowments. The pattern of growth in the rentals closely reflected the pattern of endowments received by the college (Fig. 16.1). The growth of their estate in the 14th century is thus as much a measure of the demand for the vicars' spiritual services as it was a measure of demand for their houses in the city. Yet the costs imposed on the college by these new endowments were hard to meet. The Black Death in 1349, and repeated epidemics of plague thereafter, had a particularly negative impact on the college's financial solvency. The college undertook many new obits and chantries as a result of the plague, but could not expand their income from their estate fast enough to pay for them. After the Black Death the cost of supporting the chantries and obits, was actually rising faster than the colleges' ability to pay for them (YMA, VC 6/2/1–66; Rees Jones 1987, I, 220–223). Whatever the prosperity of the city at this time, the vicars were encountering significant financial problems in balancing the books (Fig. 16.2).

The college's response to this crisis was threefold. Firstly they looked for new sources of funding. They petitioned the crown for extra resources on the grounds that they needed to support and reform the common life of the college. In 1394 Richard II granted them the city church of St Sampson's, so that they might reform the common life of the college (Imbornoni 1999). This drive to reform the common life of the college coincided with the provision of the new dining hall for the college and the creation of a new set of statutes for the common life of the college (YMA, Vicars Choral Statute Book; Rees Jones 2001, 384). Other colleges of vicars choral elsewhere – at Chichester, Exeter, Hereford, Lichfield and Wells – were similarly experiencing attempts to reform their common life in the period after the Black Death, often through the provision of new or additional

	Number of rents	Total value
c. 1300	83	£40
c. 1400	240	£160
c. 1500	179	£70

Fig. 16.1. Vicars choral of York Minster. The value of the estate of the York vicars in York

	Number of Obits and Chantries	Cost (£)	Cost of Obits as % Chamberlains' Income.
1304	21	37	43
1358–9	36	26	64
1378	56	58	78
1421-2	109	143	84

Fig. 16.2. Vicars choral of York Minster. Number and cost of services for the dead. (source, York Minster Library Ms. VC 6/2)

college buildings, and this raises interesting questions about broader clerical attitudes toward these colleges at this time (Rees Jones 2001, 391–5, 581). More prosaically it may suggest that other colleges were experiencing similar financial problems to those experienced by the vicars in York. The example of the York vicars choral would seem to suggest that the aspiration to provide increasing numbers of spiritual services before, and especially after, the Black Death was not matched by the ability to raise resources to fund them.

Once again we can see the impact of this dilemma on the buildings of the York college themselves. The increase in prayers and masses for the dead produced significant increases in income for individual vicars. Although the college's endowments were managed collectively, by the college chamberlain, the payments for observing obits and chantries were made to individual vicars. While the college struggled to resource their growing obligations, individually each vicar benefited from the new sources of income available to them as numbers of services increased. Rising standards of individual living were perhaps not easily compatible with the expressed corporate goals of the college, and it is perhaps no surprise that many aspects of the common life, especially the dormitory, were abandoned in the middle decades of the 14th century and the vicars began to live, first in *cubiculi*, and then in individual houses instead (Richards *et al.* 2001, *passim*; p.152–5 above). This shift from an entirely communal to a more individual form of residence required considerable remodelling of the original college buildings. However the site was not large enough to contain individual houses for all 36 vicars and the evidence of their rent accounts suggest that some vicars were accommodated in houses owned by the college outside the Bedern. Certain closes and courtyards of houses near the college were consistently rented mainly to clerical tenants. The most expensive, including a row of houses within the Close itself were typically rented to ecclesiastical lawyers working in the Minster's courts, some of

whom were former members of the vicars choral. Others of their clerical tenants were probably priests serving at independent altars in the Minster, who were later accommodated in the new college of St William, but at least some of these clergy were vicars choral such as Thomas Britby, a former chamberlain of the college, who rented a house in 'Little Bedern' (alias *Hugaterent*) next to the Bedern in 1389–90, or the two priests William and Thomas Laveroke who rented various houses in Goodramgate in the second quarter of the 15th century (YMA, VC 6/2/59).

There was therefore an innate conflict between the financial solvency of the college as a corporation and the prosperity of individual vicars serving at the proliferating services for the dead. New endowments did not solve this problem, in some respects they only deepened it. Even the acquisition of the parish church of St Sampson made a negligible contribution to the college's needs, for it too was rarely solvent (Imbornoni 1999). An alternative solution for the college was to cut back on expenditure. As early as 1389–90 some services for the dead, originally founded in perpetuity, were no longer being observed and the money saved was instead put towards increasing the vicars' basic stipends (YMA, VC 6/2/33). This was clearly a way of redistributing income from individual vicars in order to raise the income levels of the community as a whole. From the 1390s, however, the college's financial position deteriorated still further. Houses on the college estate became harder to let and their rents began to fall in value (Rees Jones 1987, I, 215–7). The college responded by reducing the amounts it spent on building and repair work, but this only reduced still further the value of their estate. In the end their traditional patrons, the canons of the Minster, began to turn away from the college and to choose other, newer, agencies for their chantries. Increasingly they turned to independent parsons in the Minster and endowed the fabric fund, which encompassed a growing portfolio of chantry foundations, and which, ironically, was usually administered by two members of the vicars choral acting as keepers of the fabric (YMA, E3). In 1461, in a development which was bound to erode the attractiveness of the vicars choral still further, a new college, the college of St William, was founded for these independent priests (Dobson 1977a, 97, 107). Some potential patrons even looked outside the Minster community altogether. One prominent canon, Thomas Haxey, even chose the mayor and corporation to manage his chantry in the Minster in 1418, endowing the city, not the Minster, with a valuable estate of city property for its maintenance (YCA, C80).

The college of the vicars choral had apparently entered a spiral of decline, in which even the abandonment of services was not enough to balance the books. By 1449 it was no longer possible for the college to maintain the full complement of 36 vicars, and by 1484 their numbers had fallen to less than 30. From this perspective the success or failure of the maintenance of their city estate appears to be integral to the success or failure of the college, as a prayer factory. But this may be a false perspective. While it is true that the vicars were reducing the numbers of obits and chantries that they could effectively support, the evidence of the college

bursars' accounts (YMA, VC 6/4) suggest that their core functions (the singing of the daily offices in the Minster) were not so adversely affected by this financial crisis. An analysis of fines imposed by the college bursar for non-attendance in the Minster (Fig. 16.3), actually suggests (if it can be read at face value) that the early-to-mid 15th century was a period when attendance at the main liturgical offices of the day in the Minster was relatively good. Perhaps the mini-Reformation of the decades before and after 1400 was successful after all (or perhaps the college bursars were less inclined to punish non-attendance). At a time when new and different institutions were taking responsibility for many of the new obits and chantries in the Minster, the vicars choral seem to have been focusing upon and improving their core duties in the cathedral church.

It is impossible to say whether this was a conscious choice or one forced upon the college by circumstances. Once again however, we can set these developments in the financial management of the college in the context of the other changes that we see in the buildings and organisation of the college at this time. The decades between *c*.1370 and 1410 saw the rebuilding and elaboration of the college chapel and

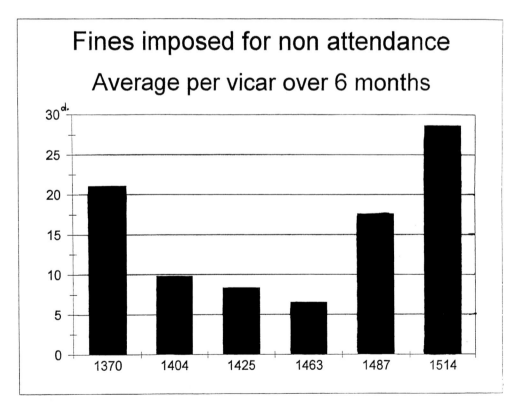

Fig. 16.3. Vicars choral of York Minster. Graph illustrating fines imposed on vicars for non-attendance in the Minster. Average per vicar over a period of six months. From 1449 the college bursars began to account for fictitious vicars, for whom maximum fines were recorded, as a means of redistributing income to the remaining members of the college. These 'fictitious' vicars are not included in these figures. (source, York Minster Library Ms. VC 6/4)

dining hall and the introduction of new college statutes emphasising the common life of the vicars. The same period may also have witnessed an elaboration in the musical role of the college, as Professor Harper discusses above (chapter 3), and it certainly saw the vicars given direct control of the management of the Minster's fabric fund so making them responsible for the shrine of St William and the massive new building programmes in the Minster. All these suggest that there was a deliberate effort in the years around 1400 to restore and emphasise those features of common life of the college that were most central to the principle religious services of the Minster.

Conclusion

So we may conclude that the financial management of the vicars' estates is revealing not just of the economic pressures under which the vicars laboured but of their spiritual mission also. Of course, their accounts also tell us about many more intimate aspects of the vicars lives in the city. We can see that at least some members of the college were recruited from their city tenants. For example, in the 15th century a family of weavers living in Goodramgate, the Laverokes, provided at least two recruits for the college. Many more of the vicars' tenants worked as servants of the college as porters, gardeners, builders, cleaners and washerwomen. Among these was Emma the laundress who, as rents fell, steadily moved her way up the housing ladder in Aldwark and Goodramgate, but never lived more than a stone's throw from the college. We know that some vicars kept concubines in their estate cottages, yet many other tenants were fellow clergy working elsewhere in the Minster. The estate thus, in many respects, provided an extended family for the vicars and the opportunity for all kinds of friendships and relationships in every area of business and domestic life. Whatever criticism they reaped for engaging too much in the secular pleasures of the world, in many respects it was an engagement in the world that had been deliberately engineered for them by a Minster which believed that its community should not remain detached from the city in which it was built.

Consolidated Bibliography

1) Abbreviations

A-D Aisne – Laon, Archives-départementales de l'Aisne, G1850 (13th-century cartulary of Laon Cathedral).

A-D Cher – Bourges, Archives-départementales du Cher, 8 G 23 (dossier of documents concerning the deanery of Bourges Cathedral).

ASC – G N Garmonsway (ed.), 1953, *The Anglo-Saxon Chronicle*. London.

BIHR – Borthwick Institute of Historical Research.

BL – British Library, London.

Cal Pat Roll – *Calendar of Patent Rolls*, various dates. London.

D&C Wells –Archives of the Dean and Chapter of Wells Cathedral.

EAO – Exeter Archives Office.

EC – Exeter Cathedral Library.

GL – Guildhall Library, London.

Hereford Acts – Hereford Cathedral Library, Ms. Act Book of the Vicars' Choral, HCA 7003/1/-.

Hereford Accounts – Hereford Cathedral Library, Ms. Account Book of the Vicars' Choral, HCA 7003/2/-.

HMC, Cal. 1 – W H B Bird and W P Baildon (eds.), 1907, *Calendar of the Manuscripts of the Dean and Chapter of Wells, Volume 1*, Historical Manuscripts Commission. London.

HMC, Cal. 2 – W H B Bird and W P Baildon (eds.), 1914, *Calendar of the Manuscripts of the Dean and Chapter of Wells, Volume 2*, Historical Manuscripts Commission. London.

LAO – Lincolnshire County Council, Lincolnshire Archives Office.

LPL – Lambeth Palace Library, London.

LRO – Lichfield Record Office.

OED – *Oxford English Dictionary*, 1971 edn.

PRO – Public Records Office (The National Archives).

RCHME, 1931, *Royal Commission on Historic Monuments, England. Herefordshire*, I. London.

RCHME, 1934, *Royal Commission on Historic Monuments, England. Herefordshire*, III. London.

RCHME, 1981, *Royal Commission on Historical Monuments, England. An Inventory of the Historical Monuments in the City of York, Volume V, The Central Area*. London.

RCHME, 1993, *Salisbury, the Houses of the Close*. London.

Soc Ant – Archives of the Society of Antiquaries of London.

VC Wells – Archives of the Vicars Choral of Wells Cathedral.

WCSL – West Country Studies Library, Exeter.

YCA – York City Archives.

YCS – The Dean and Chapter of York, 1900, *Statutes of the Cathedral Church of York*. Leeds, 2nd edn.

YMA – York Minster Archives in York Minster Library:
E3 Account rolls of the keepers of the fabric of York Minster
L 2(3)a Visitations and Miscellanea
VC 3/1/1 York vicars choral cartulary
VC 4/1 York vicars choral rent rolls and lease books
VC 6/2 York vicars choral chamberlains' account rolls and rent rolls
VC 6/4 York vicars choral bursars' account rolls
VC 6/7 York vicars choral tileworks accounts
VC 6/9 York vicars choral building accounts York vicars choral maltsters' accounts

2) Unpublished secondary sources

Collingwood, B, 2001, 'The Vicars Choral and secondaries of Exeter Cathedral 1468–1500'. MA dissertation, Music Department, University of Exeter.

Cooke, W (ed.), n.d. [*c*.1850], 'Biographical Memoirs of the *Custos* and Vicars', 2 Ms. vols., Hereford Cathedral Library.

Dyer, M J, 2000, 'Archaeological observation and monitoring during the installation of new gates and railings at College Hall, South Street, Exeter'. Typescript report (Project 3842), archive of Exeter Archaeology.

Erskine, A M (ed.), 1962, 'Catalogue of the records of the *Custos* and college of Exeter Cathedral'. Typescript, reproduced by Historic Manuscripts Commission for the National Register of Archives.

Greenway, D E, 2001b, 'Cathedral Clergy: Jobs for the Boys?'. Unpublished paper.

Groves, C and Hillam, J, 1996, 'Tree Ring Analysis of Oak Timbers from the roof of 3–3A Vicars' Court, Lincoln'. English Heritage, Ancient Monuments Laboratory Report 21/96.

Imbornoni, A M, 1999, 'The parish account rolls for St. Sampson's, York, 1405–1514'. MA dissertation, Medieval Studies, University of York.

Jenkins, H, 1956, 'Lichfield Cathedral in the Fourteenth Century'. BLitt. thesis (d. 538), History Faculty, University of Oxford.

Meeson, R A, 1999, 'Darwin House, Lichfield: An Archaeological Watching Brief, 1998–1999'. Ms. report, Lichfield Record Office.

Morriss, R K, 1989, 'No. 1a The Cloisters, Vicars Choral'. Internal report in the Hereford Archaeology Series, HAS 65. Copies in Hereford City Library, Hereford Cathedral Library and the National Monuments Record.

Morriss, R K, 1991a, 'No.1a The Cloisters, Vicars Choral – 2nd Interim Report'. Internal report in the Hereford Archaeology Series, HAS 108. Copies in Hereford City Library, Hereford Cathedral Library and the National Monuments Record.

Morriss, R K, 1991b, 'The College Hall, Vicars Choral'. Internal report in the Hereford Archaeology Series, HAS 111. Copies in Hereford City Library, Hereford Cathedral Library and the National Monuments Record.

Morriss, R K, 1991c, 'The Deanery, Vicars Choral'. Internal report in the Hereford Archaeology Series, HAS 114. Copies in Hereford City Library, Hereford Cathedral Library and the National Monuments Record.

Morriss, R K, 1991d, 'The Chapter Room, Vicars Choral'. Internal report in the Hereford Archaeology Series, HAS 115. Copies in Hereford City Library, Hereford Cathedral Library and the National Monuments Record.

Parnell, H, n.d. [*c*.1920s], 'The Vicars of Wells', Ms. vol., Archives of the Vicars choral of Wells.

Rees Jones, S, 1987, 'Property, Tenure and Rents: Some Aspects of the Topography and Economy of Medieval York'. DPhil thesis, History, University of York.

Ryan, A, 1995, 'Vicars and Prostitutes: sexual immorality in and around the close of York Minster, 1396–1489'. MA dissertation, Medieval Studies, University of York.

Shoesmith, R, 1988, 'Vicars Choral, Hereford – The Entrance Porch'. Internal report in the Hereford Archaeology Series, HAS 40. Copies in Hereford City Library, Hereford Cathedral Library and the National Monuments Record.

Shoesmith, R and Hook, R, 1987, 'The College of the Vicars Choral – an analysis of the historic development'. Internal report in the Hereford Archaeology Series, HAS 14. Copies in Hereford City Library, Hereford Cathedral Library and the National Monuments Record.

Stone, R, 1991, 'Watching Brief on Excavations South of the Brewhouse, Vicars Choral'. Internal report in the Hereford Archaeology Series, HAS 105. Copies in Hereford City Library, Hereford Cathedral Library and the National Monuments Record.

3) *Published secondary sources*

Alexander, J and Binski, P, 1987, *The Age of Chivalry. Art in Plantagenet England 1200–1400*. London.

Amiet, L, 1922, *Essai sur l'organisation du chapitre cathédral de Chartres du XIe au XIIIe siècle*. Chartres.

Armstrong, P, Tomlinson, D and Evans, D H, 1991, *Excavations at Lurk Lane, Beverley, 1979–82*. Sheffield, Excavation Report 1. Sheffield.

Anon. 1897, *An Illustrated Guide to Lichfield Cathedral ... with some Account of the Ancient and Loyal City of Lichfield*. Lichfield.

Aylmer, G E and Cant, R (eds.), 1977, *A History of York Minster*. Oxford.

Aylmer, G and Tiller, J, 2000, *Hereford Cathedral, A History*. London.

Bannister, A T, 1918a, 'The College of Vicars Choral in Hereford Cathedral', *Transactions Woolhope Naturalist and Field Club* 23, 82–4.

Bannister A T (ed.), 1918b, *Register of Bishop John Stanbury*. Hereford.

Bannister, A T (ed.), 1919, *Register of Bishop Richard Mayhew*. Hereford.

Bannister, A T, 1924, *The Cathedral Church of Hereford*. London.

Barrett, P, 1980, *The College of Vicars' Choral at Hereford Cathedral*. Hereford.

Barrett, P, 2000, 'The College of Vicars Choral', *Hereford Cathedral, A History* (eds. G Aylmer and J Tiller). London, 441–60.

Barrow, G W S (ed.), 1971, *The Acts of William I, King of Scots 1165–1214*, Regesta Regum Scottorum 2. Edinburgh.

Barrow, J, 1989, 'Vicars choral and chaplains in northern European cathedrals', *The Ministry: Clerical and Lay*, Studies in Church History 26 (eds. W J Sheils and D Wood). Oxford, 87–97.

Barrow, J, 1992, 'How the twelfth-century monks of Worcester perceived their past', *The Perception of the Past in Twelfth-Century Europe* (ed. P Magdalino). London.

Barrow, J (ed.), 1993, *English Episcopal Acta, VII, Hereford 1079–1234*. Oxford.

Barrow, J S (ed.), 2002, *Fasti Ecclesiae Anglicanae 1066–1300, VIII, Hereford*. London.

Bartlett, J N, 1959–60, 'The Expansion and Decline of York in the Later Middle Ages', *Economic History Review*, 2nd Series 12, 17–33.

Baylan, A M Y, 1901, 'Southwell, Pavement, probably pre-Norman', *Transactions of the Thoroton Society* 5, 58.

Beaumont, R M, 1971, *The Chapter of Southwell Minster*. Southwell.

Benham, H (ed.), 1984, *John Taverner III: Ritual Music and Secular Songs*. Early English Church Music 30. London.

Benson, G, 1919, *Later Medieval York: The City and County of the City of York from 1100 to 1603*. York.

Beyer, H, Eltester, L, and Goerz, A (eds.), 1860–74, *Urkundenbuch zur Geschichte der jetzt die preussischen Regierungsbezirke Coblenz und Trier bildenden Mittelrheinischen Territorien*, 3 vols. Koblenz.

Bidwell, P T, 1979, *The legionary bath-house and basilica and forum at Exeter*, Exeter Archaeological Reports 1. Exeter.

Bishop, H E and Prideaux, E K, 1922, *The Building of the Cathedral Church of St Peter in Exeter*. Exeter.

Blair, J, 1987, 'The 12th century Bishop's Palace at Hereford', *Medieval Archaeology* 31, 59–67.

Blake, E O (ed.), 1962, *Liber Eliensis*. Publications of the Camden Society, 3rd Series, 92. London.

Blaylock, S R, forthcoming, *Bowhill, Exeter Devon: The archaeological study of a building under repair, 1977–1995*, English Heritage Archaeological Monograph Series. Swindon.

Bormans, S and Schoolmeesters, E (eds.), 1893–1933, *Académie Royale des Sciences, des Lettres et des Beaux-Arts de Belgique, Commission Royale d'Histoire. Cartulaire de l'Eglise Saint-Lambert de Liège*, 6 vols. Brussels.

Bowers, R, 1994, 'Music and Worship to 1640', *A History of Lincoln Minster* (ed. D Owen). Cambridge, 47–76.

Bowers, R, 1999, *English Church Polyphony*. Aldershot.

Bradshaw, H, and Wordsworth, C (eds.), 1892–7, *Statutes of Lincoln Cathedral*, 2 vols. in 3 parts. Cambridge.

Brooke, C N L, 1957, 'The Earliest Times to 1485', *History of St Paul's Cathedral and the Men associated with it* (eds. W R Matthews and W M Atkins). London, 1–99.

Brown, S, 2003, *'Our Magnificent Fabrick' York Minster An Architectural History c.1220–1500*. Swindon.

Brundage, J A, 1995, *Medieval Canon Law*. London.

Caldwell, J, 1966, *Early Tudor Organ Music I: Music for the Office*, Early English Church Music 6. London.

Caldwell, J, 1992, 'Plainsong and Polyphony 1250–1550', *Plainsong in the Age of Polyphony* (ed. T Kelly). Cambridge, 6–31.

Caley, J, Ellis, H and Bandinel, B (eds.), 1846, *Sir W. Dugdale's Monasticon Anglicanum*, 6 vols. London.

Caley, J and Hunter, J (eds.), 1810–34, *Valor Ecclesiasticus* (Records Commission), 6 vols. London.

Cameron, K, 1985, *The Place-Names of Lincolnshire Part 1. The Place-Names of the County of the City of Lincoln*, English Place-name Society 58. London.

Capes, W W (ed.), 1908, *Charters and Records of Hereford Cathedral*, Cantilupe Society 3. Hereford.

Capes, W W, n.d., *The Vicars Choral and Chantry Priests of Hereford Cathedral*. Hereford.

Carus-Wilson, E M, 1963, *The expansion of Exeter at the close of the middle ages*. Exeter.

Chanter, J F, 1933, 'The *custos* and college of the Vicars Choral of the choir of the Cathedral Church of St Peter, Exeter', *Transactions Exeter Diocesan Architectural and Archaeological Society* 16 (3rd Series, 5/1), 1–52.

Chick, E, 1918, *The hall of the Vicars Choral, South Street, Exeter: its origin and history*. Exeter.

Clanchy, M, 1997, *Abelard: a Medieval Life*. Oxford.

Clanchy, M, 1998, *England and its Rulers*. Oxford, 2nd edn.

Clay, C T (ed.), 1935–65, *Early Yorkshire Charters, Volumes 4–12*, Yorkshire Archaeological Society, Record Series, Extra Series. Leeds.

Clay, C T (ed.), 1957, *York Minster Fasti*, Yorkshire Archaeological Society, Record Series 123. Leeds.

Clay, C T (ed.), 1958, *York Minster Fasti*, Yorkshire Archaeological Society, Record Series 124. Leeds.

Clayton, H, n.d.[*c*. 1990], *Loyal and Ancient City. The Civil War in Lichfield*. Lichfield (privately printed).

Colchester, L S, 1974, *Notes on the History and Development of Vicars' Close, Wells*. Wells (typescript booklet).

Colchester, L S (ed.), 1982, *Wells Cathedral: A History.* Shepton Mallet.

Colchester, L S, 1986, *Documents of the Vicars Choral of Wells, 1348–1600*. Wells.

Colchester, L S, 1987, *Wells Cathedral*, New Bell's Cathedral Guides. London.

Colchester, L S (ed.), 1987, *Wells Cathedral: A History.* Shepton Mallet (reprint).

Colchester, L S (ed.), 1996, *Wells Cathedral: A History.* Shepton Mallet (reprint).

Colchester, L S, n.d., *The Earliest Extant Register of the Vicars Choral of Wells, 1393–1534*. Wells.

Colchester, L S, and Harvey, J H, 1974, 'Wells Cathedral', *Archaeological Journal* 131, 200–14.

Colgrave, B and Mynors, R A B (eds.), 1969, *Bede's Ecclesiastical History of the English People*. Oxford.

Cook, G H, 1949, *Portrait of Salisbury Cathedral*. London.

Cowgill, J, de Neergaard, M and Griffiths, N, 1987, *Knives and Scabbards, Medieval finds from excavations in London 1*. London.

Crocker, J, 1886, *Sketches of old Exeter*. Exeter.

Cross, C (ed.), 1984, *York Clergy Wills 1520–1600: I, Minster Clergy*, Borthwick Texts and Calendars 10. York.

Crouch, D J F, 2000, *Piety, Fraternity and Power. Religious Gilds in Late Medieval Yorkshire 1389–1547*. York.

Daniels, C M, 1965–6, 'Excavation on the site of the Roman Villa at Southwell, 1959', *Transactions of the Thoroton Society* 69–70, 13–54.

Davis, F N, Foster, C W and Thompson, A H (eds.), 1925, *Rotuli Ricardi Gravesend Episcopi Lincolniensis A.D. MCCLVIII – MCCLXXIX*, Lincoln Record Society 20. Lincoln.

de Charmasse, A (ed.), 1865–1900, *Cartulaire de l'église d'Autun*, Société éduenne des lettres, sciences et arts, 2 vols. Paris and Autun.

Deedes, C (ed.), 1910, *The Episcopal Register of Robert Rede …Bishop of Chichester, Volume 2*. Sussex Record Society 11. Lewes.

Dobson, R B, 1977a, 'The Later Middle Ages, 1215–1500', *A History of York Minster* (eds. G E Aylmer and R Cant). Oxford, 44–109.

Dobson R B, 1977b, 'Urban Decline in Late Medieval England', *Transactions of the Royal Historical Society* 27, 1–22.

Dobson, R B, 1979, 'The Residentiary Canons of York in the Fifteenth Century', *Journal of Ecclesiastical History* 30, 145–74.

Dobson, R B, 1986a, 'The Bishops of late medieval England as intermediaries between church and state', *État et Eglise dans la Genèse de l'État Moderne* (eds. J-P Genet and B Vincent). Bibliothèque de la Casa de Velazquez, Madrid, 227–38.

Dobson, R B, 1986b, 'Recent Prosopographical Research in Late Medieval English History: University Graduates, Durham Monks and York Canons', *Medieval Lives and the Historian: Studies in Medieval Prosopography* (eds. N Bulst and J-P Genet). Kalamazoo, 181–200.

Dobson, R B, 1991, 'Contrasting Chronicles: Historical Writing at York and Durham in the Later Middle Ages', *Church and Chronicle in the Middle Ages: Essays presented to John Taylor* (eds. I Wood and G A Loud). London, 201–18.

Drake, F, 1736, *Eboracum, or the History and Antiquities of the City of York, with the History of the Cathedral Church*. London.

Duchet, T, and Giry, A (eds.), 1881, *Cartulaires de l'église de Térouane*, Société des Antiquaires de la Morinie. St-Omer.

Duncumb, J, 1804, *Collections towards the History and Antiquities of the County of Hereford, Volume I*. Hereford (reprinted Cardiff 1996).

Eames, P, 1977, *Furniture in England, France and the Netherlands from the Twelfth to the Fifteenth Century*, Publications of the Furniture History Society. London.

Edwards, K, 1939, 'The houses of Salisbury Close in the 14th century', *Journal of British Archaeological Association*, 3rd Series 4, 55–115.

Edwards, K, 1949, *The English Secular Cathedrals in the Middle Ages*. Manchester, 1st edn.

Edwards, K, 1956, 'Salisbury Cathedral', *Victoria History of the Counties of England, The County of Wiltshire* 3 (ed. G. Templeman). London, 156–210.

Edwards, K, 1967, *The English Secular Cathedrals in the Middle Ages*. Manchester, 2nd edn.

Ehmck, D R, and von Bippen, W (eds.), 1873–1902, *Bremisches Urkundenbuch*, 5 vols. Bremen.

Emery, A, 1970, *Dartington Hall*. London.

Erhard, H A (ed.), 1847–51, *Regesta Historiae Westfaliae: accedit Codex Diplomaticus*, 2 vols. Münster.

Esher, Lord and Pollen, F, 1971, *Aldwark: Renewal Project for the City of York*. London.

Eubel, K (ed.), 1913–23, *Hierarchia Catholica*, 3 vols. Munster.

Farrer, W (ed.), 1914–16, *Early Yorkshire Charters, being a Collection of Documents Anterior to the Thirteenth Century*. Yorkshire Archaeological Society, Records Series, Extra Series, 3 vols. Edinburgh.

Finlayson, R, 2004, *Medieval Metalworking and Urban Life at St Andrewgate, York*. The Archaeology of York 10/7. York.

Finnegan, F, 1979, *Poverty and Prostitution: a Study of Victorian Prostitutes in York*. Cambridge.

Fleckenstein, J, 1966, *Die Hofkapelle der deutschen Könige, II Teil: Die Hofkapelle im Rahmen der ottonisch-salischen Reichskirche*, Schriften der Monumenta Germaniae Historica 16/II. Stuttgart.

Flynn, J, 1995, 'The education of choristers in England during the sixteenth century', *English Choral Practice, 1400–1650* (ed. J T Morehen). Cambridge, 180–199.

Foster, C W (ed.), 1914, *Lincoln Wills Volume 1. AD 1271 to 1526*, Lincoln Record Society 5. Lincoln.

Foster, C W (ed.), 1931, *The Registrum Antiquissimum of the Cathedral Church of Lincoln Volume I*, Lincoln Record Society 27. Hereford.

Foster, C W (ed.), 1933, *The Registrum Antiquissimum of the Cathedral Church of Lincoln Volume II*, Lincoln Record Society 28. Hereford.

Foster, C W (ed.), 1935, *The Registrum Antiquissimum of the Cathedral Church of Lincoln Volume III*, Lincoln Record Society 29. Hereford.

Foster, C W and Major K (eds.), 1937, *The Registrum Antiquissimum of the Cathedral Church of Lincoln Volume IV*, Lincoln Record Society 32. Hereford.

Fowler, J T (ed.), 1881, *Memorials of Ripon Volume I*, Publications of the Surtees Society 74. Durham.

Fowler, J T (ed.), 1884, *Memorials of Ripon Volume II*, Publications of the Surtees Society 78. Durham.

Fowler, J T (ed.), 1886, *Memorials of Ripon Volume III*, Publications of the Surtees Society 81. Durham.

Fox, H, 2001, *The evolution of the fishing village: landscape and society along the South Devon coast, 1086–1550*, Leicester Explorations in Local History 1. Leicester.

Frere, W H (ed.), 1898, *The Use of Sarum Volume I*. Cambridge.

Frere, W H and Kennedy, W McC (eds.), 1910, *Visitation Articles and Injunctions of the Period of the Reformation*, Alcuin Club Collections 15. London.

Garbett, T, 1827, *A Brief Enquiry into the State of Hereford Cathedral*. Hereford.

Gee, E A, 1977, 'Architectural History until 1290', *A History of York Minster* (eds. G E Aylmer and R Cant). Oxford, 111–148.

Gem, R, 1990, 'The Romanesque architecture of Old St Paul's Cathedral and its late eleventh-century context', *Medieval art, architecture and archaeology in London*, British Archaeological Association Conference Transactions 10 (ed. L Grant). London, 47–63.

Gibbs, M (ed.), 1939, *Early Charters of the Cathedral Church of St Paul, London*, Publications of the Camden Society 3rd Series 58. London.

Godfrey, W H and Bloe, J W, 1935, 'Cathedral historical survey', *Victoria History of the Counties of England. Sussex, Volume 3* (ed. L F Salzman). London, 105–160.

Godwin, F, 1601, *Catalogue of the Bishops of England*. London.

Gould, J, 1976a, *Lichfield: Archaeology and Development*. Lichfield (privately printed).

Gould, J, 1976b, 'The Twelfth-Century Water-Supply to Lichfield Close', *Antiquaries Journal* 56, 73–9.

Gowland. T S, 1943, 'Ripon Minster and its Precincts', *Yorkshire Archaeological Journal* 35, 270–87.

Gransden, A, 1982, 'The History of Wells Cathedral, c. 1090–1547', *Wells Cathedral: A History* (ed. L S Colchester). Shepton Mallet, 24–51.

Greenslade, M W (ed.), 1970, *Victoria History of the Counties of England. Staffordshire Volume 3*. London.

Greenslade, M W (ed.), 1990, *Victoria History of the Counties of England. Staffordshire Volume 14*. London.

Greenway, D E (ed.), 1972, *Charters of the Honour of Mowbray 1107–1191*. British Academy Records of Social and Economic History, New Series 1. London.

Greenway, D E (ed.), 1991, *Fasti Ecclesiae Anglicanae, IV, Salisbury*. London.

Greenway, D E (ed.), 2001, *Fasti Ecclesiae Anglicanae, VII, Bath and Wells*. London.

Hall, R A and Whyman, M, 1996, 'Settlement and Monasticism at Ripon', *Medieval Archaeology* 40, 62–150.

Hallet, C, 1901, *The Cathedral Church of Ripon*, Bell's Cathedral Guides. London.

Hamilton Rogers, W H, 1877, 'The sepulchral effigies in the parish churches of north Devon', *Transactions Exeter Diocesan Architectural Society*, 2nd Series 3, 193–520.

Hanham, A (ed.), 1970, *Churchwarden's Accounts of Ashburton, 1479–1580*, Devon and Cornwall Record Society, New Series 15. Torquay.

Hannah, I, 1914, 'The Vicars' Close and adjacent buildings, Chichester', *Sussex Archaeological Collections* 56, 92–109.

Harding, V, 2002 *The Dead and the Living in Paris and London, 1500–1670*. Cambridge.

Harper, J, 1991, *The Forms and Orders of Mediaeval Liturgy: A Historical Introduction and Guide for Students and Musicians*. Oxford.

Harper, J, 1999, 'The British Church Organ and the

Liturgy: A Historical Review, 1480–1680', *The Organ Yearbook* 28, 91–97.

Harper, J, 2000, 'Music and Liturgy, 1300–1600', *Hereford Cathedral, a History* (eds. G Aylmer and J Tiller). London, 375–397.

Harrison, F, 1952, *Life in a Medieval College. The Story of the Vicars Choral of York Minster*. London.

Harrison, F L, 1963, *Music in Medieval Britain*. London, 2nd edn.

Harrison, F L (ed.), 1973, *The Eton Choir Book III*. Music Britannica 12. London, 2nd edn.

Harrison, F L, 1980, *Music in Medieval Britain*. Buren, 4th edn.

Harvey, J H (ed.), 1969, *William Worcestre: Itineraries*. Oxford.

Harvey, J H, 1978, *The Perpendicular Style 1330–1485*. London.

Harvey, J H, 1982, 'The Building of Wells Cathedral, I: 1175–1307'; 'II: 1307–1508', *Wells Cathedral: A History* (ed. L S Colchester). Shepton Mallet, 52–101.

Harvey, J H, 1987, *English Medieval Architects: a Biographical Dictionary down to 1550*. Gloucester, 2nd edn.

Harwood, T, 1806, *The History and Antiquities of the Church and City of Lichfield*. Gloucester.

Hatcher, J, 1977, *Plague, Population and the English Economy 1348–1530*. London and Basingstoke.

Hautcoeur, E (ed.), 1894, *Cartulaire de l'église collégiale de St-Pierre de Lille*, Mémoires de la Société d'études de la province de Cambrai, 2 vols. Lille and Paris.

Havergal, F C, 1869, *Fasti Herefordenses*. Edinburgh.

Hayes, R., 1994, 'The 'Private Life' of a Late Medieval Bishop: William Alnwick, Bishop of Norwich and Lincoln', *England in the Fifteenth Century*, Proceedings of the 1992 Harlaxton Symposium (ed. N. Rogers). Stamford. 1–18.

Hearne, T, 1774, *De Rebus Britannicis Collectanea*. Oxford.

Henderson, C G and Bidwell, P T, 1982, 'The Saxon minster at Exeter', *The early church in western Britain and Ireland: Studies presented to C A Ralegh Radford* (ed. S M Pearce), British Archaeological Reports (British Series) 102. Oxford, 145–71.

Hewett, C A, 1985, *English Cathedral and Monastic Carpentry*. Chichester.

Higham, R A, Allan, J P and Blaylock, S R, 1982, 'Excavations at Okehampton Castle, Devon: Part 2: the Bailey', *Proceedings Devon Archaeological Society* 40, 19–151.

Hiley, D, 1993, *Western Plainchant: A Handbook*. Oxford.

Hill, R G, 1998, 'The Somerset estates of the Vicars Choral of Wells', *Proceedings Somerset Archaeology and Natural History Society* 142, 287–309.

Hill, R M T, 1982, *Oliver Sutton Bishop of Lincoln, 1280–99*. Lincoln.

Hillam, J, 2001, 'Dendrochronological study of the timbers [from Bedern Hall]', *The Vicars Choral of York Minster: the College at Bedern*, The Archaeology of York 10/5 (ed. J D Richards). York, 598–602.

Hillaby, J, 1976, 'The Origins of the Diocese of Hereford', *Transactions Woolhope Naturalist Field Club* 42, 16–52.

Hilton, R H, 1966, *A Medieval Society: The West Midlands at the end of the Thirteenth Century*. Cambridge.

Hilton, R H, 1973, *Bond Men Made Free: Medieval Peasant Movements and the English Rising of 1381*. London.

Hingeston-Randolph, F C (ed.), 1901–6, *The register of Thomas de Brantyngham, Bishop of Exeter, 1370–1394*, 2 vols. London and Exeter.

Historical Manuscripts Commission, 1883, *Ninth Report of the Royal Commission on Historical Manuscripts. Part 1*. London.

Hobhouse, H (ed.), 1887, *Bishop Drokensford's Register, 1309–1327*, Publications of the Somerset Record Society 1.

Holmes, T S (ed.), 1895, 1896, *Register of Bishop Ralph of Shrewsbury, 1300–1363*, Publications of the Somerset Record Society 9, 10.

Holmes, T S (ed.), 1913, *Register of Bishop Bubwith, 1407–1424*, Publications of the Somerset Record Society 29.

Horrox, R (ed.), 2000, *Beverley Minster: an illustrated history*. Beverley.

Howard, R E, Laxton, R R, Litton, C D and Simpson W G, 1993, 'Tree ring dates: list 48. Nottingham University tree-ring dating laboratory results: general list', *Vernacular Architecture* 24, 40–1.

Hudson, J, 1994, *Land, Law, and Lordship in Anglo-Norman England*. Oxford.

Illingworth, W and Caley, J (eds.), 1812, *Rotuli hundredorum temp Hen. III et Edw. I in turr' Lond' et in curia receptae scaccarij West. asservati* 1. London.

Israël, F and Möllenberg, W (eds.), 1937, *Urkundenbuch des Erzstifts Magdeburg, Teil I, 937–1192*, Geschichtsquellen der Provinz Sachsen und des Freistaates Anhalt, Neue Reihe, 18. Magdeburg.

Johnson, C and Cronne, H A (eds.), 1956, *Regesta Regum Anglo-Normannorum 1066–1154, Volume 2*. London.

Jones, B (ed.), 1964, *John Le Neve: Fasti Ecclesiae Anglicanae, 1300–1541, VIII: Bath and Wells*. London.

Jones, J, 1867, *Hereford Cathedral, City and Neighbourhood; a handbook for visitors*. Hereford (3rd edn., 1878).

Jones M J, 1980, *The Defences of the Upper Roman Enclosure*. The Archaeology of Lincoln 7/1. London.

Jones, S, Major, K, and Varley, J, 1987, *The Survey of Ancient Houses in Lincoln II: Houses to the South and West of the Minster*. Lincoln.

Jones, S, Major, K, and Varley, J, 1990, *The Survey of Ancient Houses in Lincoln III: Houses in Eastgate, Priorygate, and James Street*. Lincoln.

Jones, T (ed.), 1952, *Brut y Tywysogyon. Penlarth version of the Chronicle of the Princes*. Cardiff.

Jones, T. (ed.), 1955, *Brut y Tywysogyon. Red Book of Hergest version of the Chronicle of the Princes*. Cardiff.

Jones, W H R (ed.), 1883–4, *Vetus Registrum Sarisberiense, alius dictum registrum S. Osmundi Episcopi*, Rolls Series 78, 2 vols. London.

Kemp, B R (ed.), 1999, *English Episcopal Acta, 18, Salisbury 1078–1217*. Oxford.

Keynes, S (ed.), 1996, *The Liber Vitae of the New Minster and Hyde Abbey, Winchester* (facsimile of *BL*, Stowe Ms. 944). Copenhagen.

Kingsford, C L (ed.), 1971, *J Stow, A survey of London, 1603*. London (1908 edn., reprinted with additions).

Knowles, D, 1963, *The Monastic Order in England*. Cambridge.

Knowles, D and Hadcock, R N, 1971, *Medieval Religious*

Houses: England and Wales. London, 2nd edn.

Lalore, C (ed.), 1880, *Cartulaire de Saint-Pierre de Troyes*, Collection des principaux cartulaires du diocèse de Troyes 5. Paris and Troyes.

Lander, J R, 1980, *Government and Community: England 1450–1509*. London.

Latham, R E, 1965, *Revised Medieval Latin Word List from British and Irish sources*. London.

Lawrence, C H (ed.), 1965, *The English Church and the Papacy in the Middle Ages*. London.

Le Neve, J, *see* Greenway, D E (ed.) and Jones, B (ed.).

Leech, A F (ed.), 1897, *Memorials of Beverley Minster: The Chapter Act Book, I*, Publications of the Surtees Society 98. Durham.

Lega-Weekes, E, 1915, *Some studies in the topography of the Cathedral Close, Exeter*. Exeter.

Lega-Weekes, E, 1933, 'Ryse's Rebus in vicars' college hall, Exeter', *Devon and Cornwall Notes and Queries*, 17/8, 359–60.

Lepine, D N, 1991, 'The Origins and Careers of the Canons of Exeter Cathedral, 1300–1455', *Religious Belief and Ecclesiastical Careers in Late Medieval England* (ed. C Harper-Bill). Woodbridge, 87–120.

Lepine, D N, 1995, *A Brotherhood of Canons Serving God: English Secular Cathedrals in the Later Middle Ages*. Woodbridge.

Lobel, M (ed.), 1989, *The City of London from prehistoric times to c.1520*, British Atlas of Historic Towns, 3. London.

Lottin, R J F (ed.), 1869, *Chartularium insignis ecclesiae Cenomannensis quod dicitur Liber Albus capituli*, Institut des Provinces de France, 2nd Series 2. Le Mans.

MacGregor, A, Mainman, A J and Rogers, N S H, 1999, *Bone, Antler, Ivory and Horn from Anglo-Scandinavian and Medieval York*, The Archaeology of York 17/12. York.

MacKay, W, 1982, 'The development of medieval Ripon', *Yorkshire Archaeological Journal* 54, 73–80.

Macleod, R, 1990, 'The topography of St Paul's precinct, 1200–1500', *London Topographical Record* 26, 1–14.

Macray, W D (ed.), 1891, *Charters and Documents Illustrating the History of the Cathedral, City and Diocese of Salisbury*, Rolls Series 97. London.

Maddison, A R, 1878, *A Short Account of the Vicars Choral, Poor Clerks, Organists and Choristers of Lincoln Cathedral, From the 12th Century to the Accession of Edward 6th*. London.

Magdalino, P (ed.), 1992, *The Perception of the Past in Twelfth-Century Europe*. London.

Major, K (ed.), 1940, *The Registrum Antiquissimum of the Cathedral Church of Lincoln Volume V*, Lincoln Record Society 34. Lincoln.

Major, K (ed.), 1950, *The Registrum Antiquissimum of the Cathedral Church of Lincoln Volume VI*, Lincoln Record Society 41. Lincoln.

Major, K (ed.), 1953, *The Registrum Antiquissimum of the Cathedral Church of Lincoln Volume VII*, Lincoln Record Society 46. Lincoln.

Major, K (ed.), 1958, *The Registrum Antiquissimum of the Cathedral Church of Lincoln Volume VIII*, Lincoln Record Society 51. Lincoln.

Major, K (ed.), 1968, *The Registrum Antiquissimum of the Cathedral Church of Lincoln Volume IX*, Lincoln Record Society 62. Lincoln.

Major, K (ed.), 1973, *The Registrum Antiquissimum of the Cathedral Church of Lincoln Volume X*, Lincoln Record Society 67. Lincoln.

Major, K, 1974, *Minster Yard*. Lincoln.

Malden, A R, 1893, 'Survey of the Close in 1649', *Transactions Salisbury Field Club* 1, 95–9.

Marshall, G, 1918, 'The Roof of the Vicars' Cloister at Hereford', *Transactions Woolhope Naturalist and Field Club* 23, 71–81.

Marshall, G, 1938, 'The College of Vicars Choral in Hereford and some recent discoveries', *Friends of Hereford Cathedral 6th Annual Report*. Hereford, 20–29.

Marshall, P and Samuels, J, 1977, *Guardian of the Trent: The Story of Newark Castle*. Newark.

Maxwell-Lyte, H (ed.), 1934, *Register of Bishop Bekynton, 1443–1465*, Publications of the Somerset Record Society 49.

Mayr-Harting, H (ed.), 1964, *The Acta of the Bishops of Chichester 1075–1207*, Canterbury and York Society 56. Torquay.

McFarlane, K B, 1952, *John Wycliffe and the Beginnings of English Nonconformity*. London.

McHardy, A K, 2001, *The Age of War and Wycliffe. Lincoln Diocese and its Bishop in the Later Fourteenth Century*. Lincoln.

Miller, K, Robinson, J, English, B and Hall, I, 1982, *Beverley: an archaeological and architectural study*. London.

Miller, M C, 2000, *The Bishops Palace. Architecture and Authority in Medieval Italy*. Cornell.

Millet, H, 1993, 'Les Chanoines des cathédrales du Midi', *La Cathédrale (XIIe-XIVe siècle)*, Cahiers de Fanjeaux: Collection d'Histoire Religieuse du Languedoc aux XIIIe et XIVe siècles. Toulouse.

Millet, H and Mornet, E, 1993, *I Canonici al servizio dello Stato in Europa secoli XIII-XVI*, Instituto di Studi Rinascimentali. Ferrara.

Monumenta Boica 1864, *Monumenta Boica 37*, Academia Scientiarum Boica. Munich.

Morgan, F C and Morgan P E, 1970, *Hereford Cathedral Libraries and Muniments*. Hereford.

Morris, C A, 2000, *Wood and Woodworking in Anglo-Scandinavian and Medieval York*, The Archaeology of York 17/13. York.

Morris, R, 1979, *Cathedrals and Abbeys of England and Wales*. London.

Morriss, R K and Shoesmith, R, 1995, 'The College of the Vicars Choral in Hereford', *Medieval Art, Architecture and Archaeology at Hereford*. Transactions of the British Archaeological Association 15 (ed. D Whitehead). Leeds, 157–172.

Muller, S and Bouman, A C (eds.), 1920, *Oorkondenboek van het Sticht Utrecht tot 1301*, i, *695–1197*. Utrecht.

Neave, S, 2000, 'The Precinct', *Beverley Minster: an illustrated history* (ed. R Horrox). Beverley, 202–7.

Niermayer, J F, with van Kieft, C and Burgers, J W, 2002, *Mediae Latinitatis Lexicon Minus*. Brill, Leiden and Boston, revised edn.

Newman, W M (ed.), 1977, *Charters of St-Fursy, Péronne*, Medieval Academy of America. Cambridge, Mass.

Nicholas, D, 1997, *The Growth of the Medieval City*. London.

O'Connor, D, 2001, 'The Bedern Stained Glass', *The Vicars Choral of York Minster: the College at Bedern*, The Archaeology of York 10/5 (ed. J D Richards). York, 559–575.

Orme, N, 1977, 'The kalendar bretheren of the city of Exeter', *Reports and Transactions Devonshire Association* 109, 153–69.

Orme, N, 1978, 'The Early Musicians of Exeter Cathedral', *Music and Letters* 59, 395–410.

Orme, N, 1980, *The minor clergy of Exeter Cathedral, 1300–1548*. Exeter.

Orme, N, 1981a, 'The medieval clergy of Exeter Cathedral: 1. The vicars and annuellars', *Reports Transactions Devonshire Association* 113, 79–102.

Orme, N, 1981b, 'Education and Learning at a Medieval English Cathedral: Exeter 1380–1548', *Journal of Ecclesiastical History* 32, 265–83.

Orme, N, 1986, *Exeter Cathedral As It Was, 1050–1550*. Exeter.

Orme, N, 1991, 'The charnel chapel of Exeter Cathedral', *Medieval Art and Architecture at Exeter Cathedral* (ed. F Kelly). London, 162–71.

Ormrod, W M, 2000, 'Competing Capitals? York and London in the Fourteenth Century', *Courts and Regions* (eds. S R Rees Jones, R Marks and J Minnis). York, 75–98.

Ottaway, P and Rogers, N, 2002, *Craft, Industry and Everyday Life: Finds from Medieval York*, The Archaeology of York 17/15. York.

Owen, D, 1994, 'Historical Survey 1091–1450', *A History of Lincoln Minster* (ed. D Owen). Cambridge, 112–163.

Padley, J S, 1851, *Selections from the Ancient Monastic and Ecclesiastical and Domestic Edifices of Lincolnshire*. Lincoln.

Page, W (ed.), 1894–5, *Certificates of Chantries, Guilds, Hospitals etc. for the County of York 1546*, Publications of the Surtees Society 91. Durham.

Page, W (ed.), 1913, *The Victoria History of the Counties of England: Yorkshire III*. London.

Page, W (ed.), 1909. *The Victoria History of the Counties of England: London I*. London.

Page-Phillips, J, 1969–74, 'An indent from Old St Paul's', *Transactions Monumental Brass Society* 11, 42.

Palliser, D M, 1988, 'Urban Decay revisited', *Towns and Townspeople* (ed. J A F Thomson). Gloucester, 1–21.

Pantin, W A, 1959, 'Chantry priests houses and other medieval lodgings', *Medieval Archaeology* 3, 216–58.

Parker, J H, 1866, *Architectural Antiquities of the City of Wells*. Oxford and London.

Parnell, H, 1926, *The College of the New Close of the Vicars within the Liberty of Wells*. Wells (N.B. numerous later edns. exist).

Payne, I, 1983, 'The vicars choral of Exeter cathedral: A disciplinary study *c*. 1540–1600', *Reports Transactions Devonshire Association* 115, 101–22.

Peckham, W D, 1937, 'The Vicars Choral of Chichester Cathedral', *Sussex Archaeological Collections* 78, 126–59.

Poole, R L, 1907, 'Muniments and Library of the Dean and Chapter of Exeter', *Report on Manuscripts in Various Collections, Historical Manuscripts Commission* 4. London.

Price, J, 1796, *An historical account of the city of Hereford, with some remarks on the river Wye and the natural and artificial beauties contiguous to its banks from Brobery to Wilton*. London.

Pugin, A C, and Walker, T L, 1836, *History and Antiquities of the Vicars' Close, Wells*, Pugin's Examples of Gothic Architecture, 3rd Series 1. London.

Purvis, J S, 1943, *A Medieval Act Book with some account of Ecclesiastical Jurisdiction at York*. York.

Pycke, J, 1986, *Le chapitre cathédral Notre-Dame de Tournai de la fin du XIe à la fin du XIIIe siècle: son organisation, sa vie, ses membres*, Université de Louvain, Recueil de travaux d'histoire et de philosophie, 6th Series 30. Louvain-la-Neuve and Brussels.

Quantin, M (ed.), 1854–60, *Cartulaire général de l'Yonne: recueil des documents authentiques*, 2 vols. Auxerre.

Raban, S, 1982, *Mortmain legislation and the English Church 1279–1500*. Cambridge.

Raine, A, 1926, *History of St Peter's School, York: AD 627 to the Present Day*. London.

Raine, A, 1955, *Medieval York*. London.

Raine, J (ed,), 1859, *The Fabric Rolls of York Minster*, Publications of the Surtees Society 35. Durham.

Raine, J (ed.), 1879, *The Historians of the Church of York and its Archbishops – Volume I*, Rolls Series 71. London.

Ramsey, F M R (ed.), 1995, *English Episcopal Acta X, Bath and Wells 1061–1205*. Oxford.

Rastall, G R (ed.), 1980, *Processionale ad usum Sarum*. Clarabricken.

Rawlinson, R, 1717, *The History and Antiquities of the City and Cathedral-church of Hereford*. Hereford.

Rees Jones, S R, 1988, 'Historical Background of the Aldwark/Bedern Area', *Medieval Tenements in Aldwark, and Other Sites*, The Archaeology of York 10/2 (eds. R A Hall, H MacGregor and M Stockwell). London, 51–62.

Rees Jones, S R, 2001, 'A Short History of the College of the Vicars Choral', *The Vicars Choral of York Minster: the College at Bedern*, The Archaeology of York 10/5 (J D Richards ed.). York, 380–396, 538–540, 575–582.

Rees Jones, S R, and Richards, J, 2001, 'The Plan of Bedern' and 'Other College Buildings', *The Vicars Choral of York Minster: the College at Bedern*, The Archaeology of York 10/5 (ed. J D Richards). York, 538–541, 575–82.

Reid, R D, 1973, *Wells Cathedral*, Publications of the Friends of Wells Cathedral. Leighton Buzzard.

Richards, J D, 1993, *The Bedern Foundry*, The Archaeology of York 10/3. London.

Richards, J D (ed.), 2001, *The Vicars Choral of York Minster: the College at Bedern*, The Archaeology of York 10/5. York.

Riley, H T (ed.), 1859, *Liber Albus*, Munimenta Gildhallae Londoniensis 1. London.

Rodwell, W J, 1982, 'The Buildings of Vicars' Close', *Wells Cathedral: a History* (ed. L S Colchester). Shepton Mallet, 212–26.

Rodwell, W J, 1985, 'Archaeology at the Cathedral: A New Study of St Chad's Head Chapel', *Friends of Lichfield Cathedral: Forty-eighth Annual Report*, 10–14.

Rodwell, W J, 1989, 'Archaeology and the Standing Fabric: Recent Studies at Lichfield Cathedral', *Antiquity* 63, 281–94.

Rodwell, W J, 2001, *Wells Cathedral: Excavations and*

Structural Studies, 1978–93, English Heritage Archaeological Report 21. London.

Rodwell, W J, forthcoming, *The Architectural Records of Wells by John Carter, c. 1784–1795*, Publications of the Somerset Record Society.

Roux, J, (ed.), 1897–1914, *Cartulaire du chapitre de la cathédrale d'Amiens*, Mémoires de la Société des Antiquaires de Picardie: documents inédits concernant la province 14, 18, 2 vols. Amiens and Paris.

Sandon, N (ed.), 1996, *The Masses and Ceremonies of Holy Week*, The Use of Salisbury 4. Moretonhampstead. (Antico Edition).

Saul, N, 1997, *Richard II*. New Haven and London.

Savage, H E, 1920, *Lichfield Cathedral. The Earliest Statutes of the Cathedral*, Festival of St Chad Address. Lichfield.

Savage, H E, 1925, *Lichfield Cathedral. Thomas Heywode, Dean*, Festival of St Chad Address. Lichfield.

Schofield, J, 1999, *The building of London from the Conquest to the Great Fire*. London, 3rd edn.

Schofield, J, 2001, 'The View of the City of London from the north', *Tudor London: a map and a view*, London Topographical Society Publications 159 (eds. A Saunders and J Schofield). London, 33–45.

Schofield, J, forthcoming , *The archaeology of St Paul's Cathedral, I: survey and excavation up to 2004.*

Shaw, S, 1798, *History and Antiquities of Staffordshire* 1. London (reprinted 1976).

Sheils, W J, and Wood, D (eds.), 1989, *The Ministry: Clerical and Lay*, Studies in Church History 26. Oxford.

Shoesmith, R, 1980, *Hereford City Excavations Volume 1, Excavations at Castle Green*. Council for British Archaeology Research Report 36. London.

Shoesmith, R, 1982, *Hereford City Excavations Volume 2, Excavations on and close to the defences*, Council for British Archaeology Research Report 46. London.

Shoesmith, R, 1992, *Hereford – History and Guide*. Stroud.

Shoesmith, R, 2000, 'The Close and its Buildings', *Hereford Cathedral, A History* (eds. G Aylmer and J Tiller). London, 293–310.

Simpson, W S, 1871, 'The charter and statutes of the College of the Minor Canons in St Paul's Cathedral', *Archaeologia* 43, 165–200.

Simpson, W S (ed.), 1873, *Registrum statutorum et consuetudinum Ecclesiae Cathedralis Sancti Pauli Londiniensis*. London.

Skinner, D, 2001, *The New Grove Dictionary of Music and Musicians*. London, 2nd edn.

Smith, D (ed.), 1986, *English Episcopal Acta IV. Lincoln 1186–1206*. London.

Smith, L T (ed.), 1964, *The Itinerary of John Leland in or about the years 1535–1543*, 5 vols. Carbondale Illinois.

Southern, R W, 1995, *Scholastic Humanism and the Unification of Europe, Volume 1: Foundations*. Oxford.

Southern, R W, 1995, *Scholastic Humanism and the Unification of Europe, Volume 2: The Heroic Age*. Oxford.

Sparrow Simpson, W (ed.), 1873, *Registrum Statutorum Sancti Pauli*. London.

Speed, J, 1616, *Theatrum Imperii Magne Britanniae ....* London.

Srawley, J H, 1965, *The Origin and Growth of Cathedral Foundations as Illustrated by the Cathedral Church of Lincoln*. Lincoln.

Srawley, J H (ed.), 1966, *The Book of John de Schalby ....* Lincoln.

Steer, F W, 1958, *The Vicars' Hall, Chichester and its undercroft*, The Chichester Papers 12. Chichester.

Stell, P M and Hampson L (eds.), nd [1999], *Probate Inventories of the York diocese, 1350–1500*. York.

Stenton, F M, 1967, 'The founding of Southwell Minster', *Transactions of the Thoroton Society* 71, 13–17

Stocker, D A, 1999, *The College of the Vicars Choral of York Minster at Bedern: Architectural Fragments*, The Archaeology of York 10/4. York.

Stocker, D A, 2001, 'Architectural Description [of Bedern Hall]' and 'Bedern Chapel' *The Vicars Choral of York Minster: the College at Bedern*, The Archaeology of York 10/5 (ed. J Richards 2001). York, 541–58, 583–98.

Summers, N, 1974, *A Prospect of Southwell*. Chichester.

Tatton-Brown, T, 1991, 'The Vicars' Close and Canon Gate', *The Chichester Cathedral Journal 1991*, 14–24.

Tatton-Brown, T, 1992, 'The cloisters at Chichester Cathedral', *The Chichester Cathedral Journal 1992*, 12–19.

Tatton-Brown, T, 1994, 'The buildings of the bishop's palace and the Close', *Chichester Cathedral, an historical survey* (ed. M Hobbs). Chichester, 225–247.

Thompson, A H, 1925, *The Cathedral Churches of England*. London.

Thompson, A H, 1947, *The English Clergy and their Organization in the Later Middle Ages*. Oxford.

Thorpe, B (ed.), 1848–9, *Florentii Wigorniensis Monarchi Chronicon ex Chronicis...*, Publications of the English Historical Society. Abingdon.

Tillott, P M (ed.), 1961, *The Victoria History of the Counties of England. A History of Yorkshire. The City of York*. London.

Tracy, C, 1986, 'Medieval Choir stalls in Chichester: a reassessment', *Sussex Archaeological Collections* 124, 141–155.

Tringham, N J, 1984, 'Two Seventeenth-Century Surveys of Lichfield Cathedral Close', *Transactions South Staffordshire Archaeology and History Society* 25, 35–49.

Tringham, N J, 1990, 'The Cathedral Close', *Victoria History of the Counties of England. Staffordshire Volume XIV, The City of Lichfield* (ed. MW Greenslade). London, 47–67.

Tringham, N J (ed.), 1993, *Charters of the Vicars Choral of York Minster: City of York and its Suburbs to 1546*, Yorkshire Archaeological Society, Record Series 148. Leeds.

Tringham, N J, 2001, 'Spitelcroft: an example of land-use in late medieval York', *York Historian* 18, 2–6.

Tringham, N J (ed.), 2002, *Charters of the Vicars Choral of York Minster: County of Yorkshire and Appropriated Churches to 1538*, Yorkshire Archaeological Society, Record Series 156. Leeds and Woodbridge.

Tweddle, D, Biddle, M, and Kjølbye-Biddle, B, 1995, *Corpus of Ango-Saxon Stone Sculpture, IV: South-east England*. Oxford.

Tyack, G, 1998, *Oxford. An Architectural Guide*. Oxford.

Tyson, R, 2000, *Medieval glass vessels found in England c. AD 1200–1500*. Council for British Archaeology Research Report 121. York.

Urseau, C (ed.), 1908, *Cartulaire noir de la Cathédrale d'Angers*. Paris and Angers.

[Venables, E], Precentor of Lincoln, 1883–4, 'The Vicars'

Court, Lincoln, with the Architectural History of the College, and an account of the existing buildings', *Associated Architectural Societies Reports and Papers* 17, 235–250.

Watkin, A (ed.), 1941, *Dean Cosyn and Wells Cathedral Miscellanea*, Publications of the Somerset Record Society 56.

Weaver, F W (ed.), 1903, *Somerset Medieval Wills*, Publications of the Somerset Record Society 19.

Webb, J, 1873, *Military Memoir of Colonel John Birch* (ed. T W Webb). London.

Wharton, H, 1691, *Anglia Sacra* 1. London.

Whatley, E G (ed.), 1989, *The Saint of London: the life and miracles of St Erkenwald*. London.

White, A J, 1979, 'Lincoln, Vicars' Court', *Lincolnshire History and Archaeology* 14, 73.

Whitehead, D, 1982, 'The Historical Background to the city defences', *Hereford City Excavations Volume 2, Excavations on and close to the defences*, Council for British Archaeology Research Report 46 (ed. R Shoesmith). London, 13–24.

Whitehead, D (ed.), 1995, *Hereford, Medieval Art, Architecture and Archaeology*, British Archaeological Association Conference Transactions 15. London.

Wiegand, W (ed.), 1879, *Urkundenbuch der Stadt Strassburg, I, Urkunden und Stadtrechte bis zum Jahr 1266*. Strassburg.

Williamson, D M, 1956, *Lincoln Muniments*. Lincoln.

Wilmans, R (ed.), 1859–68, *Westfälisches Urkundenbuch, III, Die Urkunden des Bisthums Münster 1201–1300*. Münster.

Wilmans, R (ed.), 1874–94, *Westfälisches Urkundenbuch, IV, Die Urkunden des Bistums Paderborn 1201–1300*. Münster.

Winnington, T (ed.), 1867, *Dingley's History from Marble*. Publications of the Camden Society.

Wood, M E, 1951, 'Lincoln – 3 Vicar's Court', *The Lincolnshire Historian* 1/7, 281–6.

Wood, M E, 1965, *The English Medieval House*. London.

Wright, C, 1989, *Music and Ceremony at Notre Dame of Paris, 500–1500*. Cambridge.

Ziegler, P, 1970, *The Black Death*. Harmondsworth.

Index